JUSTICE AND THE HOLY

Scholars Press
Homage Series

Israelite Wisdom: Theological and Literary Essays in Honor of Samuel Terrien
John G. Gammie, editor

Selected Papers of Lionel Pearson
Donald Lateiner and Susan A. Stephens, editors

Mnemai: Classical Studies in Memory of Karl K. Hulley
Harold D. Evjen, editor

Classical Texts and Their Traditions: Studies in Honor of C. R. Trahman
David F. Bright and Edwin S. Ramage, editors

Hearing and Speaking the Word: Selections from the Works of James Muilenburg
Thomas F. Best, editor

Greek Poetry and Philosophy: Studies in Honour of Leonard Woodbury
Douglas E. Gerber, editor

Nourished with Peace: Studies in Hellenistic Judaism in Memory of Samuel Sandmel
Frederick E. Greenspahn, Earle Hilgert, and Burton L. Mack, editors

Early Jewish and Christian Exegesis: Studies in Memory of William Hugh Brownlee
Craig A. Evans and William F. Stinespring, editors

Language and the Tragic Hero: Essays on Greek Tragedy in Honor of Gordon M. Kirkwood
Pietro Pucci, editor

Justice and the Holy: Essays in Honor of Walter Harrelson
Douglas A. Knight and Peter J. Paris, editors

JUSTICE AND THE HOLY
ESSAYS IN HONOR OF WALTER HARRELSON

edited by
Douglas A. Knight and Peter J. Paris

Scholars Press
Atlanta, Georgia

JUSTICE AND THE HOLY

Essays in Honor of Walter Harrelson

edited by

Douglas A. Knight and Peter J. Paris

© 1989

Scholars Press

Library of Congress Cataloging in Publication Data

Justice and the holy : essays in honor of Walter Harrelson / edited by
    Douglas A. Knight and Peter J. Paris.
    p.   cm. -- (Homage series)
    ISBN 1-55540-290-9 (alk. paper); ISBN 1-55540-393-X (pbk. alk. paper)
    1. Bible--Criticism, interpretation, etc. 2. Justice. 3. Holy,
The. 4. Harrelson, Walter J. I. Harrelson, Walter J. II. Knight,
Douglas A. III. Paris, Peter J. 1933-   . IV. Series.
BS540.J87   1989
220.6--dc19   89-6092
                                                        CIP

Printed in the United States of America
on acid-free paper

TABLE OF CONTENTS

Part One: PERSPECTIVES ON THE HEBREW BIBLE

Walter Harrelson

PREFACE

It is a singular tribute to Walter Harrelson that a volume of essays dedicated to him should have contributions from a diverse group of religious scholars. Walter's life work is itself a coat of many colors. Trained as a scholar of the Hebrew Bible, he has developed special interests in law, the prophets, the cult, the postexilic literature, and more recently the manuscriptal sources long hidden in Ethiopian monasteries. Yet since early in his career he has also rendered leadership in contexts extending far beyond these specific fields of intellectual inquiry.

One level of this is his innumerable responsibilities on behalf of professional societies and humanities organizations. Another is his steering roles in theological education, above all through a total of thirteen years as dean first of The University of Chicago Divinity School and later of Vanderbilt University Divinity School. A third can be seen in his efforts to advance ecumenical research and interfaith dialogue. A fourth, which in fact is woven through all the others and accounts also for the nature of his biblical scholarship, lies in his commitment to justice; no one who knows him can have missed his resolute call, often reminiscent of the ancient Hebrew prophets, for the disbanding of oppressive structures of whatever kind. In all of these areas he has repeatedly involved himself in raising financial support for various projects and institutions, just as he has regularly given counsel and assistance to students and colleagues alike.

Two themes prominent to Walter's work comprise the focus of this volume: justice and the holy. The contributors were invited to address some aspect of these subjects, either singly or intertwined, in their respective fields of research. The resulting collection of essays, which are grouped into three sections according to the historical reference points of the disciplines, displays well the multifaceted character of these themes so important to our honored colleague.

In the preparation of this volume, Thomas Craig of Vanderbilt University offered substantial assistance, not the least of which is represented in the compilation of Walter's extensive bibliography. We also express our thanks to Judy Matthews-Taylor at Vanderbilt for typing the entire manuscript. In other ways also this Festschrift has benefited directly by support from our two institutions, Vanderbilt Divinity School and Princeton Theological Seminary. For this as for the eager cooperation from all contributors we gladly acknowledge our deep appreciation.

Douglas A. Knight
Peter J. Paris

LIST OF CONTRIBUTORS

Bernhard W. Anderson, Professor of Old Testament, *Emeritus*, Princeton Theological Seminary; Adjunct Professor of Old Testament, Boston University

James Barr, Regius Professor of Hebrew, The University of Oxford

David B. Burrell, C.S.C., Professor of Philosophy and Theology, University of Notre Dame

James Tunstead Burtchaell, C.S.C., Professor of Theology, University of Notre Dame

James F. Childress, Edwin B. Kyle Professor of Christian Studies and Professor of Medical Education, University of Virginia

Toni Craven, Associate Professor of Old Testament, Brite Divinity School, Texas Christian University

James L. Crenshaw, Professor of Old Testament, Duke University

John R. Donahue, S.J., Professor of New Testament, The Jesuit School of Theology at Berkeley and Graduate Theological Union

Edward Farley, Drucilla Moore Buffington Professor of Theology, Vanderbilt University

H. Jackson Forstman, Charles G. Finney Professor of Theology and Dean of The Divinity School, Vanderbilt University

Moshe Greenberg, Professor of Bible, The Hebrew University of Jerusalem

Leander E. Keck, Winkley Professor of Biblical Theology and Dean of The Divinity School, Yale University

Douglas A. Knight, Professor of Hebrew Bible, Vanderbilt University

Charles H. Long, Jeannette K. Watson Professor of History of Religions, Syracuse University

Gerd Luedemann, Professor of New Testament, Georg-August-Universität, Göttingen

Thomas W. Ogletree, Professor of Theological Ethics and Dean of The Theological School, Drew University

Harry M. Orlinsky, Professor of Bible, *Emeritus*, Hebrew Union College–Jewish Institute of Religion, New York

Peter J. Paris, Elmer G. Homrighausen Professor of Christian Social Ethics, Princeton Theological Seminary

Lou H. Silberman, Hillel Professor of Jewish Literature and Thought, *Emeritus*, Vanderbilt University; Adjunct Professor, Oriental Studies, The University of Arizona

Phyllis Trible, Baldwin Professor of Sacred Literature, Union Theological Seminary, New York

WALTER HARRELSON
CURRICULUM VITAE

Born 28 November 1919, Winnabow, North Carolina

Studied at Mars Hill College, 1940-41

U.S. Navy, 1941-45

Married Idella Aydlett Harrelson, 20 September 1942 Children: Marianne McIver, 14 July 1943; David, 24 August 1947; and Robert, 1 January 1956

Phi Beta Kappa, 1946

A.B. (with honors in Philosophy), University of North Carolina, 1947

Instructor in Philosophy, University of North Carolina, 1947

Member, Society of Biblical Literature and Exegesis, 1948–

B.D., Union Theological Seminary, 1949

Ordination, Southport Baptist Association, North Carolina, 31 August 1949

Traveling Fellowship, Union Theological Seminary, 1949

Member, Society for Values in Higher Education, 1949–

Instructor in Old Testament, Union Theological Seminary, 1950

Turner Fellowship, Andover Newton Theological School, 1950-51

Senior Fellowship, American Council of Learned Societies, 1950-51

Studied at the University of Basel, Switzerland, 1950-51

Studied at Harvard University, 1951-53

Ordination recognized by the American Baptist Convention, 1951

Instructor—Professor of Old Testament, Andover Newton Theological School, 1951-55

Member, American Schools of Oriental Research, 1951–

Member, National Association of Biblical Instructors (after 1963: American Academy of Religion), 1951–

Th.D., Union Theological Seminary, 1953

Chairman of Organizing Committee, American Society for the Study of Religion, 1955-56

Member, Biblical Colloquium, 1955–

Associate Professor and Dean of the Divinity School, The University of Chicago, 1955-60

Initial member, Executive Council, American Society for the Study of Religion, 1956

Member, Committee on the History of Religions, American Council of Learned Societies, 1956-62; Chair, 1960-62

American Association of Theological Schools, member, Commission on Faculty Fellowships, 1958-62; member, Commission on Accrediting, 1960-64

Cole Lectures, Vanderbilt University, 1960

Professor of Old Testament, The Divinity School, Vanderbilt University, 1960-75

Chairman, Department of Religion, Graduate School, Vanderbilt University, 1961-62; 1964-67

Fulbright Research Scholar and American Association of Theological Schools faculty fellow, Rome, 1962-63

Chair, Planning Study for Vanderbilt Divinity School, 1964

Editor, "Newsletter," American Society for the Study of Religion, 1964-67

Member, Executive Committee, American Association of Theological Schools, 1964-70

Haskell Lectures, Oberlin College, 1965

Director, Study of the Teaching of the Biblical Languages (conducted for the American Association of Theological Schools), 1965-67

Executive Secretary, Society of Biblical Literature, 1967

Dean, The Divinity School, Vanderbilt University, 1967-75

Green Lectures, Andover Newton Theological School, 1968

Chairman, Biblical Studies Section of the American Academy of Religion, 1968-69

Chairman, Resources Planning Commission, American Association of Theological Schools, 1968-70

Chairman, Central Committee, Society for Values in Higher Education, 1969-70

Ordination, Christian Church (Disciples of Christ), 1970

National Endowment for the Humanities grant and American Council of Learned Societies Research Grant (August–December) for work in

Old Testament Pseudepigrapha, in Rome, Greece, and Ethiopia, 1970-71

President, Society of Biblical Literature, 1972

Chairman, Board of Directors, Society for Values in Higher Education, 1971-74

Chairman, Ethiopian Manuscript Microfilm Library, 1971-84

Chairman, Task Force on Faculty Tenure, The Association of Theological Schools in the United States and Canada, 1973-76

Beattie Lectures, The University of the South, 1974

D.D. (hon.), The University of the South, 1974

Chair, Vanderbilt University Press Committee, 1974-75

Editorial Chair, *Religious Studies Review*, 1974-80

Cole Lectures, Vanderbilt University, 1975

Distinguished Professor of Old Testament, The Divinity School, Vanderbilt University, 1975–

Member, Vice-Chairman, Metropolitan Nashville Commission on Human Relations, 1975-77

Member (Secretary, 1976-77), Tennessee Committee for the Humanities, 1975-77

Co-editor (with Edwin S. Gaustad), The Bible in American Culture Series, Society of Biblical Literature and Fortress Press, 1975-85

Phi Beta Kappa Lecturer, Vanderbilt University, 1976

Chairman, Board of Directors, "Probation and Reality," Nashville, 1976-77

Chairman, Research and Publication Committee, Council on the Study of Religion, 1976-80; Chair of the Council, 1982-85

Member, Revised Standard Version Translation Committee, 1976–; Vice Chairman, 1979–

Robinson Lectures, Wake Forest University, 1977

Litt.D. (hon.), Mars Hill College, 1977

Harvie Branscomb Distinguished Professor, Vanderbilt University, 1977-78

Rector, The Ecumenical Institute for Advanced Theological Studies, Tantur, Jerusalem, 1977-78, Spring 1979; Member, Advisory Council, 1980-84

Armstrong Lectures, Kalamazoo College, 1978

Chairman, Committee on Awards, Society of Biblical Literature, 1979-80

Vice-chairman, American Society for the Study of Religion, 1979-81

May Lectureship, Oberlin College, 1980

Chair, Faculty/Student Advisory Committee to the Chancellor Search Committee of the Board of Trust, Vanderbilt University, 1981-82

Chair, Faculty Senate, Vanderbilt University, 1981-82

Senior Fellow, National Endowment for the Humanities, 1983-84

Member, Council on Theological Scholarship and Research, The Association of Theological Schools in the United States and Canada, 1983–

Consultant, Ford Foundation grant to continue microfilming of Ethiopian manuscripts, 1984, 1986

King Lectures, Washburn University, 1985

Thomas Jefferson Award, Vanderbilt University, 1985

Chair, Senate Committee on the Future of the Library, Vanderbilt University, 1985-86

Chairman, Interfaith Association of Nashville, 1985-86

Chair, Committee on the Status of Women and Minorities, Vanderbilt University, 1986-87

Staley Lectures, Pembroke State University, 1986

Associate Editor, *Mercer Dictionary of the Bible*, 1986–

Beavan Lectures, Kentucky Wesleyan University, 1987

Bible Jubilee Lecture, Union Theological Seminary, New York, 1987

Alexander Heard Distinguished Service Professor, Vanderbilt University, 1987-88

Member, Advisory Board, FOCUS, Nashville, 1987–

Stiles Lectures, Memphis Theological Seminary, 1988

Member, Advisory Board, United Nations Association, Nashville, 1987–

Director, Ethiopian Bible Project (to produce a new edition of the Ge'ez [Old Ethiopic] Bible, with English translation), supported by the Ford Foundation, 1988-89

BIBLIOGRAPHY OF THE WRITINGS
OF WALTER HARRELSON

Compiled by
THOMAS D. CRAIG[1]
Vanderbilt University

1950   "Research in the Old Testament." *Journal of Bible and Religion* 18: 115-18.

1951   "The Idea of Agape in the New Testament." *Journal of Religion* 31: 169-82.

1952   "The Word of Life in Living Language." *Andover Newton Bulletin* 45 (October): 3-12.

1953   "The Book of Ecclesiastes—A Pilgrimage of Faith." *Kindergarten Teacher's Guide* (July-September): 4-5.

    Review of *The Dead Sea Scrolls: A Preliminary Survey* by A. Dupont-Sommer. *Journal of Bible and Religion* 21: 137-38.

1954   "A Comment on 'Concerning a Theology of Education' (by Howard B. Jefferson)." *The Christian Scholar* 37 (March): 60-62.

1955   "The Biblical Basis of the Gospel." *Baptist Leader* 17 (September): 18-21.

---

[1] I am most grateful to William Hook and Anne Womack of the Vanderbilt Divinity Library for their help in locating several references.

"Biblical Faith and Rural Life." *Town and Country Church* (January): 1-2.

"Guide to the Old Testament." *Advance* 147 (18 May): 10.

"Kierkegaard and Abraham." *Andover Newton Bulletin* 48 (February): 12-16.

Review of *Die Bücher Genesis-Exodus: Eine rhythmische Untersuchung* and *Jesaja: Eine rhythmische und textkritische Untersuchung* by Arvid Bruno. *Journal of Biblical Literature* 74: 286-87.

Review of *Gottesdienst in Israel: Studien zur Geschichte des Laubhüttenfestes* by Hans-Joachim Kraus. *Journal of Biblical Literature* 74: 131-33.

Review of *Das Wort ʿōlām im Alten Testament* by Ernst Jenni. *Journal of Biblical Literature* 74: 289-90.

1956   "Creation." *The Christian Scholar* 39 (March): 45-49.

"Fact and Implication in the Dead Sea Scrolls." *Christianity and Crisis* 16/7: 52-54.

"The Human Side of the Dead Sea Scrolls." *Advance* (27 June): 4-6.

"Manuscripts and Peoples of the Judean Desert." *Religion in Life* 25: 386-97.

Review of *Discovering Buried Worlds, The Flood and Noah's Ark,* and *The Tower of Babel* by André Parrot. *The Chicago Theological Seminary Register* 46/2: 78.

Review of *From Faith to Faith: Essays on Old Testament Literature* by B. Davie Napier. *The Chicago Theological Seminary Register* 46/2: 78.

Review of *The Jewish Sect of Qumran and the Essenes* by A. Dupont-Sommer; and *The Scrolls from the Dead Sea* by Edmond Wilson. *Westminster Bookman* 15/2: 13-14.

Review of *Nineveh and the Old Testament* by André Parrot; and *St. Paul's Journeys in the Ancient Orient* by Henri Metzger. *The Chicago Theological Seminary Register* 46/6: 15.

Review of *The Old Testament Since the Reformation* by Emil G. Kraeling. *The Christian Century* 63: 423.

Review of *Shechem: A Traditio-Historical Investigation* by Eduard Nielsen. *Journal of Biblical Literature* 75: 332-35.

1957   *I Met a Man Named Jesus*. Boston: Pilgrim Press.

"The Biblical Outlook on Life." *Advance* 149/22: 13-14.

"Shechem in Extra-Biblical References." *Biblical Archaeologist* 20: 2-10. [Reprinted in 1964 and 1975.]

"Worship Suggestions." *Baptist Leader* (June): 53-54, 87.

Review of *Atlas of the Bible* by L. H. Grollenberg; and *Rand McNally Bible Atlas* by Emil G. Kraeling. *Westminster Bookman* 16/2: 7-9.

Review of *Biblical Archaeology* by G. Ernest Wright; *The Geography of the Bible* by Denis Baly; *Everyday Life in Old Testament Times* by E. W. Heaton; *A Naturalist in Palestine* by Victor Howells; *Plants of the Bible* by A. W. Anderson; and *The Temple of Jerusalem* by André Parrot. *The Chicago Theological Seminary Register* 47/8: 16-17.

Review of *Exposition of Zechariah* by H. C. Leupold. *The Christian Century* 63: 561.

Review of *He That Cometh* by Sigmund Mowinckel. *Union Theological Seminary Quarterly Review* 12: 93-97.

Review of *Prophecy and Religion in Ancient China and Israel* by H. H. Rowley. *The Chicago Theological Seminary Register* 47/5: 17.

1958   *The Family Studies the Old Testament.* Boston: Pilgrim Press.

"The Biblical Basis of the Gospel." In *Great Themes in Theology*, ed. Lynn Leavenworth, 21-53. Philadelphia: Judson Press.

"Dead Sea Scrolls." *Britannica Book of the Year 1958*, 200-2. Chicago/Toronto/London: Encyclopædia Britannica, Inc.

Lenten Devotionals. *The Christian Century* 75/10: 267; /11: 299; /12: 331; /13: 363; /14: 395.

"Our Approach to the Bible." In *The Bible in Our Home*, ed. Ruth Sprague, 6-10. Boston: Pilgrim Press.

"Some Major Terms for the Church in the New Testament." *Foundations* 1/2: 4-17.

"Temptation and the Faithfulness of God." *The Divinity School News* 25/3: 1-8.

"Worship in Early Israel." *Biblical Research* 3: 1-14.

Review of *The Scrolls and the New Testament*, ed. Krister Stendahl; and *The Essenes and Christianity* by Duncan Howlett. *Religion in Life*: 305-6.

1959   *Jeremiah: Prophet to the Nations.* Philadelphia: Judson Press.

"Guidance in the Wilderness: The Theology of Numbers." *Interpretation* 13: 24-36.

Review of *Job: Poet of Existence* by Samuel Terrien. *Union Seminary Quarterly Review* 14: 51-53.

Review of *The Monuments and the Old Testament* by Ira M. Price, Ovid R. Sellers, and E. Leslie Carlson. *Foundations* 2/4: 376-77.

1960   "The Biblical Concept of the Free Man." *Review and Expositor* 57: 263-80.

"Elisha" (10: 244-45); "Ezekiel" (10: 685-87); "Ezekiel, Book of" (10: 687). *The Encyclopedia Americana.* New York/Chicago/Washington, D.C.: Americana Corporation.

"Freedom and Order in the American Baptist Convention." *Foundations* 3: 134-43.

"God's Sovereignty and Man's Dominion." *The Pulpit* 31/2: 4-5, 21-22.

"Koehler's *Old Testament Theology.*" *The Chicago Theological Seminary Register* 50/1: 14-15.

"National Purpose and Ancient Vision." *The Christian Century* 77: 770-73.

Review of *Luther the Expositor* by Jaroslav Pelikan. *The Chicago Theological Seminary Register* 50/1: 3-5.

Review of *More Light on the Dead Sea Scrolls: New Scrolls and New Interpretations* by Millar Burrows. *Archaeology* 13: 223-24.

Review of *Samaria* and *Babylon and the Old Testament* by André Parrot. *The Chicago Theological Seminary Register* 50.

1961   "The Prophets and God's Coming Rule." *The Outlook* 11 (October): 1-11.

1962   *Israel's Prophetic Heritage: Essays in Honor of James Muilenburg,* ed. with Bernhard W. Anderson. New York: Harper and Row.

"Blessings and Cursings" (1:446-48); "Calf, Golden" (1:488-89); "Council, the Council, Council House, Counsel" (1:710); "Court of Law" (1:713); "Covenant, Book of the" (1:723); "Decree" (1:812); "Honor" (2:639-40); "Law in the Old Testament" (3:77-89); "Obeisance" (3:581); "Poison" (3:838-39); "Ten Commandments" (4:569-73); "Testimony" (4:579); "Vengeance" (4:748); "Walls" (4:796). *The Interpreter's Dictionary of the Bible*, ed. Keith Crim. Nashville: Abingdon Press.

"Non-Royal Motifs in the Royal Eschatology." In *Israel's Prophetic Heritage*, 147-65. New York: Harper and Row.

"Salvation in Christian Faith." *Foundations* 5: 293-311.

Review of *Exodus: A Commentary* by Martin Noth. *Westminster Bookman* 21 (June).

Review of *Lex Tua Veritas: Festschrift für Herbert Junker*, ed. Heinrich Gross and Franz Mussner. *Journal of Biblical Literature* 81: 406-8.

Review of *Obadiah, Nahum, Habakkuk, and Zephaniah: Introduction and Commentary* by J. H. Eaton. *Journal of Biblical Literature* 81: 428-29.

Review of *The Religion of Israel: From its Beginnings to the Babylonian Exile* by Yehezkel Kaufmann. *Interpretation* 16: 457-60.

Review of *Theology of the Old Testament*, Vol. 1, by Walther Eichrodt; and *A Thousand Years and a Day* by Claus Westermann. *Student World* 4: 512-14.

Review of *Worship in Ancient Israel* by A. S. Herbert. *Journal of Biblical Literature* 81: 212.

1963   "Ark" (53), "Holiness" (387-88), "Images" (413), "Molech, Moloch" (669), "Queen of Heaven" (827), "Stranger" (940-41), "Worship" (1043-45). *Dictionary of the Bible*, ed. James

Hastings, rev. by Frederick C. Grant and H. H. Rowley. New York: Charles Scribner's Sons; Edinburgh: T. & T. Clark.

"The Biblical Understanding of Spirituality." *Ecumenical Review* 15: 252-63.

"Bonhoeffer and the Bible." In *The Place of Bonhoeffer*, ed. Martin E. Marty, 113-42. New York: Association Press.

"Children in the Church." *Foundations* 6: 136-45.

"God's Purpose for the Church." *Religion in Life* 32: 179-90.

"The Religion of Israel." In *A Companion to the Bible*, orig. ed. T. W. Manson, 2d ed. by H. H. Rowley, 335-80. Edinburgh: T. & T. Clark.

Review of *Michée, Sophonie, Joël, Nahoum, Habaqqouq* by Jean Steinmann and Abbé Hanon. *Journal of Biblical Literature* 82: 117-18.

Review of *Zacharie IX-XIV: Structure littéraire et messianism* by Paul Lamarche. *Journal of Biblical Literature* 82: 116-17.

1964   *Interpreting the Old Testament.* New York: Holt, Rinehart and Winston, Inc.

"Prophecy and Syncretism." *Andover Newton Quarterly* 4/4: 6-19.

"Shechem in Extra-Biblical References." In *The Biblical Archaeologist Reader*, vol. 2, ed. Edward F. Campbell, Jr., and David Noel Freedman, 258-65. Anchor Books, A250b. Garden City, NY: Doubleday Anchor Books. [Reprinted from 1957; see also 1975.]

Review of *Criterion for the Church: The Apostolic Witness Today* by J. Robert Nelson. *Religion in Life* 33: 478.

Review of *Essays on Old Testament Hermeneutics*, ed. Claus Westermann, translated by James Luther Mays. *Interpretation* 18: 482-85.

Review of *Four Prophets—Amos, Hosea, Isaiah, Micah: A Modern Translation from the Hebrew* by J. B. Phillips. *Journal of Biblical Literature* 83: 210.

Review of *Studien über Deuterosacharja* by Benedikt Otzen. *Journal of Biblical Literature* 83: 325-26.

1965   Introduction and annotations to the First Book of Esdras. *The Oxford Annotated Apocrypha*, ed. Bruce M. Metzger, 1-22. New York: Oxford University Press.

"The Work of the Deuteronomist" (24-25); "A Message of Renewal" (26-27); "The Acts of God in History" (28-29); "The Covenant of Faith and Love" (30-31). *Adult Teacher* 18/7.

Review of *La Sainte Bible, Vol. VIII, 1, Les Petits Prophètes, II (Michée–Malachie)*, ed. A. Deissler and M. Delcor. *Journal of Biblical Literature* 84: 449-50.

Review of *Der Sonntag: Geschichte des Ruhe- und Gottesdiensttages im Ältesten Christentum* by Willy Rordorf. *Scottish Journal of Theology* 18: 225-28.

Review of *Theological Dictionary of the New Testament*, vol. 1, ed. Gerhard Kittel, translated by Geoffrey W. Bromiley. *Foundations* 8/1: 78-80.

1966   "The Kingdoms of Israel and Judah." *Adult Student* 25/8: 28-33; 25/9: 21-33; 25/10: 23-33.

"Reader's Guide for Daniel." *Bible Reader's Service Guide.* O.T. 26.

"Wisdom and Pastoral Theology." *Andover Newton Quarterly* (September): 6-14.

Review of *Jeremiah: Introduction, Translation, and Notes* by John Bright. *Journal of Bible and Religion* 34: 52-53.

Review of *Die Zehn Gebote* by Eduard Nielsen. *Journal of Biblical Literature* 85: 502-3.

1967 *Teaching the Biblical Languages,* co-authored with Eugene V. N. Goetchius and George M. Landes. Dayton: American Association of Theological Schools.

"Social Science and Biblical Perspectives on Man." In *America and the Future of Theology,* edited by William A. Beardslee, 158-64. Adventures in Faith series. Philadelphia: Fortress Press.

Review of *Introduction to the Psalms* by Christoph Barth. *Union Seminary Quarterly Review* 22: 289-91.

Review of *Israelite Religion* by Helmer Ringgren. *Interpretation* 21: 104-5.

1968 "Abimelech" (1: 38-39); "Joshua, Book of" (13: 90-92); "Shailer Mathews" (14: 1110); "Prophet: Prophecy in World Religion" (with R. J. Zwi Werblowsky, 18: 633-39); "Wars of Yahweh, Book of the" (23: 230). *Encyclopædia Britannica.* 14th ed. Chicago: Encyclopædia Britannica, Inc.

"The Celebration of the Feast of Booths According to Zechariah XIV:16-21." In *Religions in Antiquity: Essays in Memory of Erwin Ramsdell Goodenough,* ed. Jacob Neusner, 88-96. Leiden: E. J. Brill.

"Guilt and Rites of Purification Related to the Fall of Jerusalem in 587 B.C." *Numen* 15: 218-21. Abstracted in *Proceedings of the XIth International Congress of the International Association for the History of Religions,* Vol. 2: *Guilt or Pollution and Rites of Purification,* 73-74. Leiden: E. J. Brill.

"Revelation and the Prophets." *The Voice* 60 (January): 4-6, 17.

1969   *From Fertility Cult to Worship*. Garden City, NY: Double-
            day & Company. [Reprinted in 1970 and 1980.]

1970   *From Fertility Cult to Worship*. Anchor Books edition, A713.
            Garden City, NY: Doubleday & Company. [Reissue of 1969.]

            "About to be Born." *Andover Newton Quarterly* 11/2
            (November): 56-60.

            "Secularization and the Bible." In *Essays for Educational
            Evasions*, ed. Gordon John Freer, 17-24. Toronto: Board of
            Christian Education, United Church of Canada.

            "The Significance of Cosmology in the Ancient Near East."
            In *Translating & Understanding the Old Testament: Essays
            in Honor of Herbert Gordon May*, ed. Harry Thomas Frank
            and William L. Reed, 237-52. Nashville: Abingdon Press.

            Review of *Die Wurzel sh-l-m im Alten Testament* by Walter
            Eisenbeis. *Journal of the American Academy of Religion* 39:
            200-1.

1972   Review of *The Interpreter's One-Volume Commentary on the
            Bible*, ed. Charles M. Laymon. *Adult Leader* 5/2: 27.

1973   "Resisting and Welcoming the New." In *To God Be the
            Glory: Sermons in Honor of George Arthur Buttrick*, ed. T. A.
            Gill, 116-22. Nashville: Abingdon Press.

            "A Theological View of History and Change." *Foundations*
            16/2: 132-42.

1974   "The Christian Congregation and the Bicentennial." *St.
            Luke's Journal of Theology* 18/1: 6-20.

            "Faith and Courage." *St. Luke's Journal of Theology* 17/4: 44-
            50.

            "The Significance of 'Last Words' for Intertestamental
            Ethics." In *Essays in Old Testament Ethics (J. Philip Hyatt,*

In Memoriam), ed. James L. Crenshaw and John T. Willis, 203-13. New York: KTAV Publishing House.

"Worship." *The New Encyclopædia Britannica: Macropædia*. 15th ed. Chicago: Encyclopædia Britannica, Inc. 19: 1014-18.

1975   "On God's Care for the Earth—Psalm 104." *Currents in Theology and Mission* 2: 19-22.

"On God's Knowledge of the Self—Psalm 139." *Currents in Theology and Mission* 2: 261-65.

"Patient Love in the Testament of Joseph." In *Studies on the Testament of Joseph*, ed. George W. E. Nickelsburg, Jr., 29-35. Society of Biblical Literature Septuagint and Cognate Studies, 5. Missoula, MT: Scholars Press.

"Shechem in Extra-Biblical References." In *The Biblical Archaeologist Reader*, vol. 2, ed. Edward F. Campbell, Jr., and David Noel Freedman, 258-65. Missoula, MT: American Schools of Oriental Research and Scholars Press. [Reprint of 1957 and 1964.]

Review of *Resurrection, Immortality, and Eternal Life in Intertestamental Judaism* by George W. E. Nickelsburg, Jr. *Journal of Biblical Literature* 94: 124-25.

1976   "Famine in the Perspective of Biblical Judgments and Promises." *Soundings* 59: 84-99. Reprinted in *Lifeboat Ethics: The Moral Dilemmas of World Hunger*, ed. George R. Lucas, Jr., and Thomas W. Ogletree, 84-99. New York: Harper & Row.

"Humanists and Public Policy." In *People and Issues: A 3 Year Report*. Tennessee Committee for the Humanities.

"Karl Barth on the Decalogue." *Studies in Religion* 6 (1976-77): 229-40.

"Knowledge of God in the Church." *Interpretation* 30: 12-17.

"Report of the Task Force on Academic Freedom and Faculty Tenure," W. Harrelson, et al. In *Theological Education* 12/2 (*Academic Freedom and Faculty Tenure*): 85-105.

"Response to the 'Boston Affirmations.'" *Andover Newton Quarterly* 16: 255-56.

Review of *Essai biblique sur les fêtes d'Israël* by Robert Martin-Achard. *Journal of Biblical Literature* 95: 136.

Review of *Yesterday, Today, and Tomorrow* by Simon J. De Vries. *Religion in Life* 45: 506-7.

1977   "Life, Faith, and the Emergence of Tradition." In *Tradition and Theology in the Old Testament*, ed. Douglas A. Knight, 11-30. Philadelphia: Fortress Press; London: SPCK. [French translation in 1982.]

"A Meditation on the Wrath of God: Psalm 90." In *Scripture in History and Theology: Essays in Honor of J. Coert Rylaarsdam*, ed. Arthur L. Merrill and Thomas W. Overholt, 181-91. Pittsburgh: Pickwick Press.

"Patient Love in the Testament of Joseph." *Perspectives in Religious Studies* 4: 4-13.

1978   Review of *The Old Testament as the Book of Christ: An Appraisal of Bonhoeffer's Interpretation* by Martin Kuske. *Interpretation* 32: 210, 212.

1979   *Aspects of Interfaith Dialogue*, ed. with Walter Wegner. Yearbook of the Ecumenical Institute for Advanced Theological Studies, 1975-1976. Jerusalem: Franciscan Press.

Concepts of Salvation in Living Faiths, ed. with Walter Wegner. Yearbook of the Ecumenical Institute for Advanced Theological Studies, 1976-1977. Jerusalem: Franciscan Press.

"Creative Spirit in the Old Testament: A Study of the Last Words of David (2 Samuel 23: 1-7)." In *Sin, Salvation, and the Spirit*, ed. Daniel Duirken, O.S.B., 127-33. Collegeville, MN: The Liturgical Press.

"The New American Bible." *The Duke Divinity School Review* 44: 124-36. [Reprinted in 1982.]

"Traditions and the Tradition: The Origin and Authority of 'Core' Traditions." *Perspectives in Religious Studies* 6: 184-89.

1980   *From Fertility Cult to Worship*. Missoula, MT: Scholars Press. [Reprint of 1969 and 1970.]

Kuyark Soungsoh Eui Eaebae, trans. Ill Sun Chang. Seoul: Korea Christian Publishing House, 1980. [Korean translation of *From Fertility Cult to Worship*, 1969.]

Prayer and the Mystery of Salvation, editor. Yearbook of the Ecumenical Institute for Advanced Theological Studies, 1977-1978. Jerusalem: Franciscan Press.

The Ten Commandments and Human Rights. Overtures to Biblical Theology, 8. Philadelphia: Fortress Press.

"Developments in Old Testament Research, 1970-1980." *St. Luke's Journal of Theology* 23: 169-76.

"Ezra Among the Wicked in 2 Esdras 3-10." In *The Divine Helmsman: Studies on God's Control of Human Events, Presented to Lou H. Silberman*, ed. James L. Crenshaw and Samuel Sandmel, 21-40. New York: KTAV Publishing Co.

"God's Covenant: Bond of Love." *Adult Leader* 13/1: 4-5.

Review of *Apocalyptic, Ancient and Modern* by D. S. Russell. *Theology Today* 37: 242-43.

Review of *Dynamic Transcendence* by Paul D. Hanson. *Interpretation* 35: 304-5.

1981   *Sacred Acts and Seasons* [booklet plus 24 slides]. Evanston: Religion and Ethics Institute.

"Foreword" to *Christianity in the Holy Land*, ed. D. M. Jaegar. Jerusalem: Ecumenical Institute for Theological Research.

Review of *Introduction to the Old Testament as Scripture* by Brevard S. Childs. *Journal of Biblical Literature* 100: 99-103.

Review of *When Prophecy Failed: Cognitive Dissonance in the Prophetic Traditions of the Old Testament* by Robert P. Carroll. *Zygon* 16: 383-84.

Review of *The Psalms: Structure, Content, and Message* by Claus Westermann. *Religious Studies Review* 7: 67.

1982   "Christian Misreadings of Basic Themes in the Hebrew Scriptures." *Quarterly Review* 2/2: 58-66. [Reprinted in 1987.]

"Ecumenism in Jerusalem." In *Testimonia Oecumenica: In honorem Oscar Cullmann octogenarii, die XXV Februarii A.D. MCMLXXXII*, ed. Karlfried Froehlich, 67-68. Tübingen: Hans Vogler.

"The New American Bible." In *The Word of God: A Guide to English Versions of the Bible*, ed. Lloyd R. Bailey, 139-51. Atlanta: John Knox Press. [Reprint of 1979.]

"The Trial of the High Priest Joshua: Zechariah 3." *Eretz-Israel* 16 [Harry M. Orlinsky Volume]: 116*-24*.

"La vie, la foi et la naissance de la tradition." In *Tradition et théologie dans l'Ancien Testament*, ed. Douglas A. Knight, trans. Jean Prignaud, 21-40. Lectio divina, 108. Paris: Cerf/Desclée. [French translation of "Life, Faith, and the Emergence of Tradition," 1977.]

Review of *Scriptures, Sects, and Visions: A Profile of Judaism from Ezra to the Jewish Revolts* by Michael E. Stone. *Journal of the American Academy of Religion* 50: 114.

1983   *The Messianic Hope in Judaism* [booklet plus 24 slides]. Evanston: Religion and Ethics Institute.

"Prophetic Eschatological Visions and the Kingdom of God." In *The Quest for the Kingdom of God: Studies in Honor of George E. Mendenhall,* ed. H. B. Huffmon, F. A. Spina, and A. R. W. Green, 117-26. Winona Lake, IN: Eisenbrauns.

Review of *The Bible in Its Literary Milieu,* ed. Vincent L. Tollers and John R. Maier. *St. Luke's Journal of Theology* 26: 252-53.

Review of *From Chaos to Covenant: Prophecy in the Book of Jeremiah* by Robert P. Carroll. *Journal of the American Academy of Religion* 51: 495-96.

1984   "The Limited Task of Old Testament Theology." *Horizons in Biblical Theology* 6: 59-64.

"The Religion of Ancient Israel." *Listening* (Winter): 19-29.

"Theological Education." *Encyclopedia of Religion in the South,* ed. Samuel S. Hill, 769-74. Macon, GA: Mercer University Press.

"Thoughts on Ecumenism." *Occasional Papers of the Institute for Ecumenical and Cultural Research* (April): 1-4. Collegeville, MN.

1985   "The CSR in Retrospect and Prospect." *The Council on the Study of Religion Bulletin* 16: 37-39.

"The Hebrew Bible and Modern Culture." In *The Hebrew Bible and Its Modern Interpreters,* ed. Douglas A. Knight and Gene M. Tucker, 489-505. The Bible and Its Modern Interpreters, 1. Philadelphia: Fortress Press; Chico, CA: Scholars Press.

Review of *Growth in Agreement: Reports and Agreed Statements of Ecumenical Conversations on a World Level*, Ecumenical Documents II, ed. Harding Meyer and Lukas Vischer, Faith and Order Paper 108. *Journal of Ecumenical Studies* 22: 799-800.

Review of *The Iconoclastic Deity: Biblical Images of God* by Clyde A. Holbrook. *The Christian Century* 102: 426.

Review of *The New Catholic Study Bible*. *Tennessee Register* (23 September): 5, 10.

1986   "Decalogue" (146-47); "Mosaic Law" (405-7); "Prophetic Ethics" (508-12); and "Wisdom Literature, Ethics in" (662-63). *Westminster Dictionary of Christian Ethics*, ed. James F. Childress and John Macquarrie. Philadelphia: Westminster Press.

"A Protestant Looks at Catholic Biblical Scholarship." In *The Biblical Heritage in Modern Catholic Scholarship* (Bruce Vawter Festschrift), ed. John J. Collins and John Dominic Crossan, 234-55. Wilmington, DE: Michael Glazier.

"What is a Good Bible Dictionary?" *Biblical Archaeology Review* 12/6: 54-61.

Review of *The Hebrew Bible: A Socio-Literary Introduction* by Norman K. Gottwald. *Union Seminary Quarterly Review* 41: 65-67.

Review of *The Prophets: The Babylonian and Persian Periods* by Klaus Koch. *St. Luke's Journal of Theology* 30: 74-75.

Review of *Theologians Under Hitler: Gerhard Kittel, Paul Althaus, and Emmanuel Hirsch* by Robert P. Ericksen. *Theology Today* 43: 142, 144.

1987   *Os Dez Mandamentos e os Direitos Humanos*, trans. Carlos S. Mesquitella, rev. Antônio Lúcio S. Lima and Nilo Luza. São Paulo: Paulinas. [Portuguese translation of *The Ten Commandments and Human Rights*, 1980.]

"Christian Misreadings of Basic Themes in the Hebrew Scriptures." *New Conversations* 9/3: 31-35. [Reprint of 1982.]

"The Creation That the Bible Insists Upon." *Touchstone: The Magazine of the Tennessee Humanities Council* 10: 10-11.

"Myth and Ritual School" (10: 282-85); "Ten Commandments" (14: 395-96); "Tithes" (14: 537-38). *The Encyclopedia of Religion*, ed. Mircea Eliade. New York: Macmillan Publishing Company; London: Collier Macmillan Publishers.

Review of *Illustrated Dictionary and Concordance of the Bible*, ed. Geoffrey Wigoder, Shalom M. Paul, Benedict T. Vivano, O.P., and Ephraim Stern. *Biblical Archaeology Review* 13/6: 10.

1988   *The Ten Commandments*. Growing Christians Series. Nashville: Graded Press.

"Eschatology and Ethics in the Hebrew Bible." *Union Theological Seminary Quarterly Review* 42: 43-48.

"Messianic Expectations at the Time of Jesus." *St. Luke's Journal of Theology* 32/1: 28-42.

"Reflections on the Value for Biblical Scholars of the New Encyclopedia of Religion." *Bulletin of the Council of Societies for the Study of Religion* 17/2: 29, 31.

Forthcoming

"Baruch"; "Baruch, Second"; "Hardening of the Heart"; "Kenaz, Kenizzites"; "Land"; "Oral Tradition"; "Ruth, The Book of"; "Song of Songs"; "Ten Commandments"; "Testaments, Apocryphal." In *Mercer Dictionary of the Bible*, ed. Watson E. Mills, assoc. ed. Joel Drinkard, Walter Harrelson, Edgar McKnight, and David M. Scholer. Macon, GA: Mercer University.

"Biblical Authority"; "Creation"; "Providence." In *Harper's Dictionary of Religious Education*, ed. Iris V. and Kendig B. Culley. San Francisco: Harper & Row.

"Introduction to the Old Testament," in *The Books of the Bible*, ed. Bernhard W. Anderson. New York: Macmillan.

"A Plea to God and a Promise of Salvation—Isaiah 63:7–65:25." *Cumberland Seminarian*.

"Ten Commandments." In *Dictionary of Pastoral Care and Counseling*, ed. Rodney Hunter, Newton Malony, Liston Mills, and John Patton. Nashville: Abingdon Press.

"Ten Commandments." In *The Oxford Companion to the Bible*, ed. Bruce M. Metzger. New York: Oxford University.

ABBREVIATIONS

AB	Anchor Bible
AJSR	*Association for Jewish Studies Review*
AnBib	Analecta biblica
b.	Babylonian Talmud
BA	*Biblical Archeologist*
BASOR	*Bulletin of the American Schools of Oriental Research*
BBET	Beiträge zur biblischen Exegese und Theologie
BDB	F. Brown, S. R. Driver, and C. A. Briggs, *A Hebrew and English Lexicon of the Old Testament*
Bib	*Biblica*
BibK	Biblische Konfrontationen
BibOr	Biblica et orientalia
BJRL	*Bulletin of the John Rylands University Library of Manchester*
BJS	Brown Judaic Series
BKAT	Biblischer Kommentar: Altes Testament
BLS	Bible and Literature Series
BMI	Society of Biblical Literature, The Bible and Its Modern Interpreters
BS	The Biblical Seminar
BSac	*Bibliotheca Sacra*
BT	*The Bible Translator*
CAD	*The Assyrian Dictionary of the Oriental Institute of the University of Chicago*
CBQ	*Catholic Biblical Quarterly*
CBQMS	Catholic Biblical Quarterly Monograph Series
CurTM	*Currents in Theology and Mission*
EHPR	Etudes d'histoire et de philosophie religieuses
EncJud	*Encyclopaedia Judaica* (1971)
EvT	*Evangelische Theologie*
ExpTim	*Expository Times*

FRLANT	Forschungen zur Religion und Literatur des Alten und Neuen Testaments
GTA	Göttinger theologische Arbeiten
HAR	*Hebrew Annual Review*
HTR	*Harvard Theological Review*
HUCA	*Hebrew Union College Annual*
IDB	G. A. Buttrick (ed.), *The Interpreter's Dictionary of the Bible*
Int	*Interpretation*
IRT	Issues in Religion and Theology
JBC	R. E. Brown et al. (eds.), *The Jerome Biblical Commentary*
JBL	*Journal of Biblical Literature*
JES	*Journal of Ecumenical Studies*
JNES	*Journal of Near Eastern Studies*
JQR	*Jewish Quarterly Review*
JRT	*Journal of Religious Thought*
JSNT	*Journal for the Study of the New Testament*
JSOT	*Journal for the Study of the Old Testament*
JSOTSup	Journal for the Study of the Old Testament, Supplement Series
JSS	*Journal of Semitic Studies*
m.	Mishna
MT	Massoretic Text
NCB	New Century Bible
NJB	*The New Jerusalem Bible*
NTS	*New Testament Studies*
OBO	Orbis biblicus et orientalis
OBT	Overtures to Biblical Theology
OTL	Old Testament Library
OTS	*Oudtestamentische Studien*
p.	Palestinian (Jerusalem) Talmud
PAAJR	*Proceedings of the American Academy for Jewish Research*
RSV	*Revised Standard Version*
SBLBSNA	Society of Biblical Literature, Biblical Scholarship in North America
SBLDS	Society of Biblical Literature Dissertation Series
SBLSCS	Society of Biblical Literature Septuagint and Cognate Studies
SBLSP	Society of Biblical Literature Seminar Papers

SBS	Stuttgarter Bibelstudien
SBT	Studies in Biblical Theology
SNTSMS	Society for New Testament Studies Monograph Series
SNTU	Studien zum Neuen Testament und seiner Umwelt
SPHS	Scholars Press Homage Series
StudOr	Studia orientalia
t.	Tosepta
TBl	*Theologische Blätter*
TDOT	G. J. Botterweck and H. Ringgren (eds.), *Theological Dictionary of the Old Testament*
THWAT	E. Jenni and C. Westermann (eds.), *Theologisches Handwörterbuch zum Alten Testament*
TWAT	G. J. Botterweck and H. Ringgren (eds.), *Theologisches Wörterbuch zum Alten Testament*
USQR	*Union Seminary Quarterly Review*
Vid	*Vidyajyoti*
VTSup	Vetus Testamentum, Supplements
WMANT	Wissenschaftliche Monographien zum Alten und Neuen Testament
WUS	J. Aistleitner, *Wörterbuch der ugaritischen Sprache*
ZAW	*Zeitschrift für die alttestamentliche Wissenschaft*

Part One:
Perspectives on the Hebrew Bible

THE HOLY ONE OF ISRAEL

BERNHARD W. ANDERSON
Emeritus, Princeton Theological Seminary

A striking feature of the book of Isaiah is the repeated reference to Yahweh as *qĕdôš yiśrā'ēl*, "the Holy One of Israel." The statistical evidence is impressive. The epithet occurs some twenty-six times in the book of Isaiah alone; and of this number eight are found in the prophecy of Isaiah of Jerusalem (1:4; 5:19, 24; 10:17; 30:11, 12, 15; 31:1), thirteen in Second Isaiah (41:14, 16, 20; 43:3, 14, 15; 45:11; 47:4; 48:17; 49:7 [2x]; 54:5; 55:6), and five in Third Isaiah (60:9, 14) and apocalyptic "in that day" passages (12:6; 17:7; 29:19). In addition, there is one occurrence in the historical narrative (Isa 37:23 = 2 Kgs 19:22). In the rest of the Hebrew Bible the epithet occurs only nine times.[1]

It is highly unlikely that this expression was first coined by Isaiah of Jerusalem in the eighth century and later was picked up in cultic (e.g., Ps 71:22, a lament), prophetic (Jer 50:29; 51:5; Ezek 39:7), and wisdom circles (Job 6:10). Apparently this is a much older epithet, one that was especially at home in the Jerusalem cult, to judge from occurrences in two psalms based on royal covenant theology (Pss 78:41; 89:18; cf. 71:22) as well as in the psalm of Habakkuk (Hab 3:3) in which the Divine Warrior is extolled for going forth to rescue "your people" and "your Anointed" (3:13). Isaiah inherited this old epithet along with others, such as "Yahweh of Hosts" (6:5, associated with the Ark, 1 Sam 4:4; 6:2), the title "the Lord" (*'ādôn*, 1:24; 3:1), "the Mighty One of Israel" (1:24), and "the God of Jacob" (2:3) which presumably go back to the time of the Israelite confederacy. In any case, Isaiah, who was profoundly influenced by the Jerusalem cult, gave this epithet special prominence and theological shading. Later interpreters, preeminently so-called Second Isaiah, nuanced the epithet somewhat differently as

---

[1] Jer 50:29; 51:5; Ezek 39:7; Hos 11:9; Hab 3:3; Pss 71:22; 78:41; 89:18; Job 6:10.

they transmitted and reinterpreted Isaiah's message. Since, however, it is found at all levels of Isaianic tradition, from the seminal message of the eighth-century prophet to the final apocalyptic re-reading of the whole,[2] a study of this leitmotiv provides an opportunity to consider from this angle the dynamic and unity of the Isaiah tradition.[3]

It is a pleasure to dedicate this essay to Walter Harrelson, a friend and colleague whose teaching and writing have enabled us to appreciate the character of the Israelite cult, and particularly the holiness of the God to whom Israel bears witness.

I

To begin with, it is noteworthy that the epithet, *qĕdôš yiśrā'ēl*, is invariably associated with the personal divine name, Yahweh. The epithet does not refer in a broad and general sense to numinous divine reality—the *mysterium tremendum* that excites fascination and dread, to recall the classical study of Rudolf Otto.[4] Rather, it refers to the God who has personal identity, who is bound in an I-Thou relationship with a people, and whose redemptive concern and sovereign demand are celebrated in worship—in short, the God whose cultic name is Yahweh and whose presence is confessed by telling and retelling the sacred story that centers in Exodus and Sinai. Accordingly, the epithet provides another way of invoking the sacred name, as indicated by the poetic parallelism:[5]

> They have rejected Yahweh,
>   have disdained the Holy One of Israel. (Isa 1:4b)

---

[2] See my essay, "The Apocalyptic Rendering of the Isaiah Tradition," in *The Social World of Formative Christianity and Judaism: Essays in Tribute to Howard Clark Kee* (ed. Jacob Neusner, Peder Borgen, Ernest S. Frerichs, and Richard Horsley; Philadelphia: Fortress, 1988) 17-38.

[3] A good number of years ago Helmer Ringgren observed that this epithet "is characteristical of the whole book of Isaiah"—"a fact that may also be of a certain significance to the question of the 'unity' of the book." *The Prophetical Conception of Holiness* (Uppsala and Leipzig: Uppsala Universitets Årsskrift, 1948) 24.

[4] Rudolf Otto, *The Idea of the Holy* (2d ed.; London: Oxford University, 1950).

[5] See also Isa 5:9; 30:11; 43:3, 14, 15; 45:11, etc. The parallelism is especially clear in 60:9.

> You shall rejoice in Yahweh,
>   in the Holy One of Israel you shall glory. (41:16b)

Moreover, the epithet is closely associated with Israel, the ʿam YHWH (Judg 5:11, 13), as indicated by the Hebrew construct relation, qĕdôš yiśrāʾēl. This formulation signifies close relationship between God and people, but not the kind of relationship that is, from the human standpoint, intimate or possessive, as is sometimes connoted in popular religion by the genitive formulation, "My God," or "Our God." The emphasis falls, rather, upon God's *involvement* in Israel's history, God's *initiative* toward the people. This is the case, for instance, in divine self-presentations such as:

> "I am Yahweh your [sg.] God,
>   the Holy One of Israel, your Deliverer." (43:3a)

or:

> "I am Yahweh, your [pl.] Holy One,
>   the Creator of Israel, your King." (43:15)

In these, and other cases (e.g., 49:7, referring to the Servant), the personal pronoun indicates the object of God's action: "your Deliverer" means "the One who has delivered you;" "your Maker" means "the One who made you" (54:5; cf. 45:11); and, accordingly, "your Holy One" means "the One who has manifested holiness to you" or "in your midst."

The theological meaning of the epithet is illuminated by the exquisite portrayal of the divine pathos in Hosea 11, which reaches a climax in the announcement that God's mercy preponderates over God's wrath:

> For a deity I am, and not a human being,
>   the Holy One [qādôš] in your midst,
>   and I will not come to consume [?]. (Hos 11:9b)

Notice that here qādôš stands by itself, not in construct relation with Israel, although the Holy One is perceived to be bĕqirbĕkā, "in the middle of" the people. Israel must learn what it means to live in the presence of the Holy God: it is to be the recipient of divine love which, on the analogy of a parent's love for its child, includes both judgment and mercy. In this sense, Yahweh is "with you" (cf. Amos 5:14b), "in your midst" (Isa 12:6b).

This epithet, which contains pregnantly the message of Isaiah and its subsequent reverberations in Isaianic tradition, introduces us to a profound theological issue: the relation between God's universal sway over all history and creation and God's disclosure in the historical particular, in this case Zion which symbolizes the people of God.[6] It would seem that the proper place to begin is with the universal, for holiness is that dimension of divine Reality which transcends the particularity of Israel's historical experience and Israel's cultic center. The holiness of God is fundamentally the power of God—power that is literally "out of this world" even though it may intrude surprisingly, as in the case of Jacob's dream at Bethel (Gen 28:17) or of Moses at the burning bush (Exod 3:5). In human experience divine holiness evokes a sense of awe and mystery precisely because it eludes understanding in human categories and defies control by human means. According to some interpreters, then, the proper place to begin is with religion in general, and thus with "God-in-general." The sense of the holy, it is held, is the fundamental awareness at the root of all religions; this basic religious sense finds only one illustration in the religion of Israel, where it acquired a peculiar "intensity" and ethical content.[7]

This is not the place to debate the huge question of the relation between the history of religions and Old Testament theology. Suffice it to say that in the book of Isaiah the epithet "the Holy One of Israel" suggests a movement in the opposite direction: from the particular to the universal. It is Yahweh, whose name is holy, who is God of creation and history. Yahweh, the Holy One "in the midst of Israel," is the inescapable God who "has a day that is against" all human pride (2:12-19). Yahweh of Hosts, who is enthroned upon the cherubim of the Ark (cf. Ps 99:1) and who is praised in the Jerusalem temple with the liturgical refrain "holy, holy, holy," is the God whose glory fills the whole earth (6:3).[8] In short, the book of Isaiah brings us before one of the "dialectical contradictions" inherent in the Israelite witness:

---

[6] For a discussion of the universal rule of "the great King" in the citadel of Zion, see Bennie C. Ollenburger, *Zion, the City of the Great King: A Theological Investigation of Zion Symbolism in the Tradition of the Jerusalem Cult* (Ann Arbor: University Microfilms, 1982).

[7] See J. Hänel, *Die Religion der Heiligkeit* (Gütersloh: Bertelsmann, 1931) Section I, 1-59; and especially Gerhard von Rad, *Old Testament Theology* (New York: Harper & Brothers, 1962) 1:204-12, who calls attention to a "quite different intensity, a vehemence even" in comparison with other religions (206).

[8] Notice that Psalm 99, cited in this connection, is structured by a thrice-repeated "holy is He" (v. 5), "Yahweh our God is holy" (v. 9).

"universality is implicit *in* the particular."[9] It is significant that the first major section of the book of Isaiah (chaps. 2-12) opens with the portrayal of an eschatological pilgrimage of all nations to the Center, Zion, where they will find peace by walking in the ways of the God of Israel (2:1-4).

The paradox that the universal God is manifest in the historical particular pervades all levels of Isaianic tradition. Yahweh of Hosts, the cosmic King, "dwells" on Mount Zion (8:8; cf. 18:7; 24:3). The "Light of Israel," whose "strange work" of judgment purges the dross from Jerusalem, will become "a fire," "a flame" that consumes an arrogant Assyrian empire (10:17). Yahweh, the Creator of the ends of the earth, who calls the stars by name (40:25-26, 28), is the Maker of Israel and its King (43:15; 45:11). Indeed, the God who "sits enthroned above the circle of the earth," "who stretches out the heavens like a curtain," and "who makes the rulers of the earth as nothing" (40:22-23), is involved redemptively in Israel's history and, through it, with the histories of all peoples.

> For your Maker is your husband,
> Yahweh of Hosts is his name;
> and your Redeemer is the Holy One of Israel,
> the God of the whole earth he is called. (Isa 54:5)

II

Our task, then, is to turn to the historical particular—to *this* people symbolized by Zion or "the City of God" (1:26)—and consider in this context the meaning of the holy, specifically "the Holy One" who is "great in your [Israel's] midst" (Isa 12:6). What does it mean to live in the presence of Yahweh, the Holy God, according to the book of Isaiah?

One way to deal with Yahweh's holiness is to start with Isaiah's experience in the temple of Jerusalem: his seeing the cosmic King "high and lifted up," his hearing of a trisagion that echoed from heaven to earth, and his cry of dereliction, "Woe is me. . ." This is essentially the approach of J. Hänel in his phenomenological study, *Die Religion der Heiligkeit*. Hänel maintains that Isaiah's temple experience provides a paradigm of the religion of the Old Testament which, he avers, is

---

[9] See Emil L. Fackenheim, *God's Presence in History: Jewish Affirmations and Philosophical Reflections* (New York: Harper Torchbooks, 1970) 17.

fundamentally a sense of the radical otherness of God refracted in its
various aspects in the history of Israelite religion: unapproachable-
ness, sublimity, jealousy/zealousy, perfection, and transcendence.[10] It is
doubtful, however, whether the story of the call of Isaiah provides a
proper starting point; for, as suggested above, Isaiah seems to have derived the epithet "Holy One of Israel" from older Israelite tradition
that was meditated through the Jerusalem cult.

A proper starting point is given in one of the most ancient hymns of
Israel, "The Song of the Sea" (Exod 15:1-18), in which Yahweh is ac-
claimed as the incomparable God.

> Who is like you, O Yahweh, among the gods?
> Who is like you, glorious in holiness,
> awesome in deeds, performing wonders? (Exod 15:11)

There was nothing unusual about this hymnic language in the ancient
world. Devotees in Canaan, Babylonia, or elsewhere could readily acclaim a high god or goddess as incomparably greater, more powerful,
and more wonderful than any member of the Heavenly Council. In the
Torah, however, the holiness of Yahweh is associated primarily with
"root experiences" that constituted Israel as a people—"the saving experience" and the "commanding experience" as Emil Fackenheim puts
it,[11] that is, Exodus and Sinai. It is with Israel's sacred story, enshrined
in the Mosaic tradition from its remote beginnings to its final canonical
completion, that a phenomenological study of Israel's experience of the
holy should begin. With this as a starting point, it is necessary to move
beyond reflection upon subjective response to the holy, as presented in
psychological or existential interpretations of Isaiah's experience in
the temple (lostness, unworthiness, guilt), and consider the holy as
divine *power*, which has its source outside the human world (von Rad:
"the great stranger in the human world"), but is manifest energetically
and even vehemently within it.[12] Israel's experience of the holy carries

---

[10] Hänel, *Die Religion der Heiligkeit*, Section II, 60-312. He maintains un-
convincingly that each of these five types of holiness is typical of a particular
stage of the history of Israelite religion: *Unnahbarkeitsheiligkeit* (pre-patriar-
chal period) *Hoheitsheiligkeit* (patriarchal period), *Eiferheiligkeit* (religion of
Moses), *Vollkommenheitsheiligkeit* (classical period of prophecy), and
Jenseitsheiligkeit (postexilic Judaism).

[11] Fackenheim, *God's Presence in History*, 8-16.

[12] Von Rad rightly observes (*Old Testament Theology*, 1:205-6) that the
limitation of Rudolf Otto's classical work is that "the holy is related much too

over "archaic" views of divine power that excites dread, precisely because it does not belong to the familiar world and thus threatens it. The holy as "otherworldly" power is magnificently portrayed in the story of the Sinai theophany in the old Epic tradition (Exodus 19). The people tremble in fear as the mountain is convulsed with seismic activity. They are told to stand back and not even touch it, as though it were charged with high voltage electricity. They are warned not "to break through to Yahweh and gaze," lest they perish. It is significant that the basic metaphors for describing the presence of God in the world are not derived from the serene side of nature (cf. Walt Whitman's "Leaves of Grass") but from the powerful, unruly, and even death-dealing aspects of the natural world: earthquake that shakes the foundations, storm with winds of violence, fire that strikes with destructive lightning force.

In Israelite tradition, however, the sense of the holy is qualified and even transformed by the basic "root experiences" in which Yahweh, the Holy One, is manifest. The holy is not just naked divine power that is incalculable, mysterious, and ineffable; rather, holiness has, so to speak, a favorable "face" (pānîm), a benign aspect. The holy is divine power manifest to an oppressed people as redemptive concern—as liberation from bondage and the opening of a future; and it is also manifest as ethical and cultic demand—as the call to a people, grateful for their liberation, to be obedient. In short, the holy is associated exclusively with the Holy One who has chosen to become involved in the life of this people, who has risked giving the personal name Yahweh for them to use in prayer and worship, and who in the freedom of grace is committed to them in ḥesed, covenant loyalty as shown in the great liturgical summary of Exod 34:5-8. Yahweh alone is holy, and things and people become holy by being drawn into relationship with the Holy One. Indeed, Yahweh's name is qannāʾ ("jealous/zealous") which means that Yahweh vehemently claims the exclusive devotion of the people (Exod 34:14).[13]

III

Oddly enough, Isaiah of Jerusalem slights the Exodus-Sinai tradition in favor of a royal covenant theology in which holiness is associ-

---

onesidedly to man and his soul," and does not consider sufficiently the holy "experienced as power, not something in repose."

[13] On the first commandment as the expression of Yahweh's holy zeal, see von Rad, *Old Testament Theology*, 1:207-12.

ated with the temple on mount Zion and in which the divine presence is mediated through the Davidic king, "the Anointed One" (messiah). Gerhard von Rad has gone so far as to question whether Isaiah even knew the classical Mosaic tradition and has maintained that the Davidic-Zion covenant theology, the platform of Isaiah's preaching, represented a completely independent election tradition.[14] The two covenant traditions, however, cannot be compartmentalized so neatly. Closer examination, initiated by Walther Eichrodt, has disclosed that Isaiah's message shows evidence of having been influenced by the Sinai covenant;[15] furthermore, the Sinai and Zion traditions interacted with one another, as Jon D. Levenson has shown.[16]

The recession of the Exodus-Sinai tradition is understandable when one considers the heavy emphasis that Isaiah put upon the Davidic-Zion theological perspective. The message of Isaiah, based on the conviction that Yahweh is the cosmic King of creation and the Ruler of the nations, is oriented primarily in the vertical plane of the relation between the cosmic and mundane spheres, heaven and earth. The decree announced in the Heavenly Council, overheard by the prophet in the Jerusalem temple, is to be executed in the mundane sphere so that God's kingdom may come and God's will be done on earth as it is in the celestial realm. This theological view does not negate the significance of Exodus or Sinai—or, stated in other terms, the horizontal plane of promise and fulfillment, of historical promise and realization or historical destiny; but it does allow Israel's history with Yahweh to be seen in a universal and cosmic perspective.[17] The theme that Yahweh

---

[14] Von Rad (*Old Testament Theology*, 1:73) remarks: "As far as we can see this tradition [the old confederate covenant tradition] is completely non-Judean. Isaiah nowhere mentions it and since he took his stand exclusively in the David and Zion tradition, it is questionable whether he even knew it." This view is elaborated in Part II, "The Theology of Israel's Historical Traditions" (105-305) and "Israel's Anointed" (306-54).

[15] Walther Eichrodt, "Prophet and Covenant: Observations on the Exegesis of Isaiah," in *Proclamations and Presence: Festschrift for G. H. Davies* (ed. John I. Durham and J. Roy Porter; Richmond: John Knox, 1970) 167-88.

[16] Jon R. Levenson, *Sinai and Zion: An Entry into the Jewish Bible* (New York: Winston, 1985), especially Part 3, 187-217. He challenges the frequently held view that the Sinaitic traditions were kept alive in North Israel (Ephraim) and were superseded in South Israel (Judah) by the Davidic-Zion tradition.

[17] For an excellent treatment of the relation between the two covenant perspectives, the Mosaic and the Davidic-Zion, see J. C. Rylaarsdam, "Jewish-Christian Relationship: The Two Covenants and the Dilemmas of Christology,"

is King, celebrated in an ancient Israelite poem redolent of Canaanite mythology (Exod 15:1-18), is now freed from its historical limitations to land and people, and is seen in the spacious vista of God's creation and God's rule over all nations.

The message of Isaiah of Jerusalem can best be understood by turning to the hymns that proclaim Yahweh's enthronement as cosmic Ruler and King in Zion (Psalms 47; 93-99).[18] Here we can leave aside the whole question of whether these psalms reflect the celebration of a New Year's festival in Jerusalem, comparable to festivals of divine kingship elsewhere in the ancient world. Suffice it to say that the theological perspective of these hymns is not only akin to the poetry of so-called Second Isaiah, as various scholars have recognized, but also is consonant with the message of Isaiah of Jerusalem.

In these hymns the classical Israelite story of Exodus and Sinai is pushed into the background but is not forgotten. Yahweh, the cosmic King and ruler of the nations, "chose our heritage" (47:4), guides the people as a shepherd leads the flock to pasture (95:7), and displays covenant loyalty (ḥesed) to "the house of Israel" (98:3). Moreover, the psalmists recall the tradition of murmuring in the wilderness (95:8-9) and the intercessory role of Moses and Aaron as priests and of Samuel as a prophet (99:6). Primarily, however, these psalms celebrate the supratemporal character of Yahweh's eternal kingship. To Yahweh is ascribed the title of the high God of the Heavenly Council: ʿelyôn, "Most High over all the earth," "exalted far above all gods" (97:9). All of the tenses of time are required to describe the eternal Kingship of the One who was, who is, and is to come: Yahweh's throne was "established from ancient time" (mēʾāz, 93:2), the ascension to Yahweh's throne is a present event (Ps 47:5, 8), and in the future Yahweh "comes to judge the earth with righteousness and the peoples with his truth" (96:13; 98:9). Furthermore, Yahweh is portrayed as enthroned

---

JES 9 (1972) 249-70; reprinted in *Grace upon Grace: Essays in Honor of L. J. Kuyper* (ed. James I. Cook; Grand Rapids: Eerdmans Publishing Co., 1975) 70-84.

[18] To these should be added other festival psalms such as Psalms 24, 78, 89, 132 and Songs of Zion such as Psalms 46, 48, 76, 84, 87. In this connection, see Ollenburger, *Zion, the City of the Great King*, especially chap. 2, "Yahweh as King in Zion."

cosmically over the powers of chaos, symbolized by the mythical "floods" or "Sea," which menace the creation (Ps 93:3-4; cf. 29:3-4).[19]

Yet the poetic vision of these psalms, which reaches into a universal dimension and sweeps from *Urzeit* to *Endzeit*, from Alpha to Omega, never loses contact with the Center: the holy mountain of Zion.

> Exalt Yahweh, our God,
> and worship at his holy mountain,
>   for Yahweh our God is holy. (Ps 99:9)

And specifically holiness attaches to the temple:

> Your decrees are very enduring,
> holiness befits your temple,
>   O Yahweh for all times! (Ps 93:5)

The reference to Yahweh's "decrees" or "testimonies" (*ʿedôt*) shows that the Sinai tradition is not absent from Zion theology. "By the 'testimony' of God," observes Artur Weiser, "is probably meant the tradition of the *Heilsgeschichte* which was recited in the covenant cult."[20] It is noteworthy, however, that if we limit our attention to these psalms, the divine law is not rooted in the "commanding experience" of Sinai but rather is grounded transcendentally in the cosmic order of creation. Accordingly, in the context of a universal theophany that lightens the whole world and causes the earth to tremble, it is said that "righteousness and justice are the foundation" of Yahweh's cosmic throne (Ps 97:2; cf. 89:15; Prov 16:12; 20:28). Here, perhaps on the analogy of Egyptian *Maʿat*,[21] righteousness is a cosmic reality belonging to the created order which gives security to the temple of Zion and the dynasty of David (cf. Ps 89:14).[22] Indeed, in the ancient Near East "legal order belongs to the order of creation."[23]

---

[19] I discuss this more broadly in *Creation Versus Chaos: The Reinterpretation of Mythical Symbolism in the Bible* (New York: Association Press, 1967; republished, Philadelphia: Fortress, 1987), chap. 3, "Creation and Worship."

[20] Artur Weiser, *The Psalms* (OTL; Philadelphia: Westminster, 1962) 620.

[21] "*Maʿat*," writes John A. Wilson, "was the cosmic force of harmony, order, stability, and security, coming down from the first creation as the organizing quality of created phenomena and reaffirmed at the accession of each god-king of Egypt." *The Burden of Egypt* (Chicago: University of Chicago, 1951) 48.

[22] See H. Brunner, "Gerechtigkeit als Fundament des Thrones," *VT* 8 (1958) 426-28. Commenting on Ps 89:15, H.-J. Kraus gives other ancient Near

Isaiah's message accords in many ways with these hymns of praise. For the eighth-century prophet, Yahweh of Hosts is *the* King par excellence (Isa 6:1, 5), enthroned in cosmic majesty, whose holy presence is known in the temple of Zion and who presides over the destiny of Israel and the nations. In a key passage, which serves as a kind of hymnic coda in its literary context,[24] it is affirmed that Yahweh's holiness, before which everything human and mortal has only relative and passing value, is manifest in transcendent righteousness.

> Humanity must bow down,
>> Mortal beings be abased,
>> the eyes of the proud humbled;
> But Yahweh of Hosts is exalted in justice,
>> the holy God proves holy in righteousness.
>
> (Isa 5:15-16)

In Isaiah's message the conflict between the cosmic order and the mundane sphere, which evokes the judgment of God, is basically the clash between the righteousness that belongs to the cosmic realm and the gross injustice that prevails in human society. That glaring discrepancy will be overcome in that Day when Yahweh comes to judge the earth (Isa 2:6-22; cf. Pss 96:13; 98:9), beginning first with the "strange work" of divine judgment on Mount Zion (Isa 28:21) and ultimately extending to all the nations, which at times are portrayed in mythical terms as powers of chaos arrayed against God's purpose (17:12-14). No human being can hide from the inescapable God whose holiness is a fire that consumes everything impure so that a just social order may be established. Divine judgment, however, is for the purpose of salvation with the result that, in the case of Zion, "afterward you shall be called the city of righteousness, the faithful city" (1:26). The

---

Eastern parallels; *Psalmen* (BKAT 15; Neukirchen: Neukirchener Verlag, 1960) 621.

[23] This point is made somewhat onesidedly by H. H. Schmid, "Creation, Righteousness, and Salvation: Creation Theology as the Broad Horizon of Biblical Theology," abbreviated translation in *Creation in the Old Testament* (ed. B. W. Anderson; IRT 6; Philadelphia: Fortress, 1984) 102-17.

[24] On the literary structure and theological context of this passage see my essay, "'God With Us'—in Judgment and in Mercy: The Editorial Structure of Isaiah 5-10 (11)," in *Canon, Theology, and Old Testament Interpretation: Essays in Honor of Brevard S. Childs* (ed. Gene M. Tucker, David L. Petersen, and Robert R. Wilson; Philadelphia: Fortress, 1988) 230-45.

saving intention of Yahweh's display of holiness, always implicit in Isaiah's message of judgment, is beautifully expressed in a passage from later Isaianic tradition (so-called Third Isaiah), where the motif of the "way" in the wilderness is picked up (cf. Isa 40:3-5):

> For thus says the high and holy One,
>> who inhabits eternity,
>> whose name is holy:
> I dwell in the high and holy place,
>> and also with those of a humble and contrite spirit,
>> reviving the spirits of the lowly,
>> quickening the hearts of the contrite. (Isa 57:15)

IV

Finally, let us return to a consideration of the way the expression qĕdôš yiśrā'ēl functions in the book of Isaiah. The question is whether the usage of this epithet in the various levels of the Isaianic tradition helps us to understand the overall unity and theological dynamic of the book of Isaiah.

On examination of the various occurrences of the epithet in the three major parts of the book of Isaiah, differences of theological accent become evident. In so-called First Isaiah qĕdôš yiśrā'ēl invariably functions in contexts of divine judgment, where the people are rebuked for offending the divine majesty: for disdaining Yahweh (1:4), despising Yahweh's word (5:24), or challenging Yahweh's purpose (5:19; 31:1). This is the case, for example, in 30:8-14. The prophet denounces "a rebellious people" who refuse to hear the torah of Yahweh and who demand that prophets stop speaking of "the Holy One of Israel." This diagnosis is the basis for the ensuing sentence of judgment: "Therefore, thus says the Holy One of Israel. . ." Divine judgment is even the tenor of a passage that is often quoted out of context with a positive ring:

> For thus says Lord Yahweh, the Holy One of Israel:
>> In returning and rest you shall be saved;
>> In quietness and trust will be your strength. (Isa 30:25)

The passage ends gloomily, however, by saying that the people refused this word, insisting rather on following a military policy of anxiety, with the result that disaster would overtake them.

On the other hand, when one turns to the second part of the book of Isaiah the situation is quite different. In so-called Second Isaiah the epithet invariably functions in contexts of salvation and often is specifically defined by terms such as "your Redeemer," "your Savior."

> For I am Yahweh, your God,
>   the Holy One of Israel, your Savior (Isa 43:3).

The same holds true when one turns to so-called Third Isaiah (e.g., 60:9) or to passages introduced with the apocalyptic cliché "in that day" (e.g., 29:9). In all these instances qĕdôš yiśrā'ēl is used to emphasize that Yahweh is Israel's redeemer.

Brevard Childs, whose canonical approach to Scripture has reopened the question of the unity of the book of Isaiah, maintains that the book in its final form has been organized around the themes of judgment and promise: chapters 1-39 from the Assyrian period deal with God's judgment and chapters 40-66 from the Persian period treat God's promise that supervenes on the judgment.[25] This broad generalization is a helpful start in tackling the question, but it hardly does justice to the redactional structure of the book as a whole.[26] From my point of view, the main weakness is that it fails to consider the final apocalyptic rendering of the Isaiah tradition which is evident in 1) the final part known as Third Isaiah, 2) in the strategically located apocalypses: the "Isaiah Apocalypse" (chaps. 24-27) and the "Little Apocalypse" (chaps. 34-35), and 3) even in the first part (chaps. 1-32 [33]) which contain intermittent "in that day" passages with an apocalyptic flavor. The usage of the epithet "the Holy One of Israel" in all major parts of the book of Isaiah provides another evidence that this book has undergone a dynamic movement from prophecy to apocalyptic.[27]

---

[25] Brevard S. Childs, *Introduction to the Old Testament as Scripture* (Philadelphia: Fortress, 1979), especially pp. 311-41. On this matter he agrees with Ronald E. Clements, "The Unity of the Book of Isaiah," *Int* 36 (1982) 117-29.

[26] In his illuminating essay, "Unity and Dynamic in the Isaiah Tradition" (*JSOT* 29 [1984] 89-107), Walter Brueggemann adheres to the view that the book has been redacted around the theme of judgment and redemption, but he expresses uncertainty about this paradigm which, as he says, provides "the present shape of the argument" (90).

[27] See further my previously mentioned essay, "The Apocalyptic Rendering of the Isaiah Tradition," where I explore the major themes of the

Here we cannot go into the question of which portions of Isaiah 1-39 can be assigned with a reasonable degree of confidence to the eighth-century prophet.[28] There is clear evidence, however, that Isaiah's message was in line with the social criticism offered by other preexilic prophets, particularly Amos. Isaiah insisted that the presence of the holy God "in your midst" or "God with you" (Amos 5:24), far from being a comforting opiate or a guarantee of favoritism, exposed the people to the consuming fire of divine holiness (cf. Amos 7:4-6). Even though Isaiah was profoundly influenced by the theology of the "everlasting covenant," with its twin convictions of the choice of Zion as God's abode and the election of the Davidic king as God's Anointed, he turned against the Zion theology insofar as it was an ideology to justify an oppressive social system.[29] No prophet could outdo him in his scathing criticism of temple worship (1:12-17), of the use of political power to devour the poor (3:13-15; 5:8-10), of a lifestyle based on the inversion of values (5:18-23), or of the reckless pursuit of a militaristic foreign policy (31:1-2). Isaiah's message was addressed to a people who were in open "rebellion" against Yahweh (1:2-3) and who therefore must suffer the consequences of their sin. The "fire of Yahweh" is in Zion, "the furnace of Yahweh" is in Jerusalem (31:9b); and while this means that Assyrian power cannot run wildly out of divine control, it also means that Zion cannot escape purging judgment. A late prophetic liturgy, modeled after antiphons used when approaching the temple (Pss 15; 24:3-6), echoes this Isaianic note:

> The sinners in Zion are afraid;
>> trembling has seized the godless:
> "Who among us can dwell with the devouring fire?
>> who among us can dwell with everlasting burnings?"
>> (Isa 33:14, *RSV*)

---

apocalyptic rendering: The Cosmic King of Zion, The Mystery of God's Kingdom, The Triumph of the Divine Warrior, and Waiting for God.

[28] For recent judgments on the relative dating of passages, see Ronald E. Clements *Isaiah 1-39* (NCB; Grand Rapids: Eerdmans, 1981); and Joseph Jensen, *Isaiah 1-39* (Old Testament Message, 8; Wilmington: Michael Glazier, 1984).

[29] Walter Brueggemann has an especially fine treatment of Isaiah's exposé of the dominant royal ideology which he labels "Israel's fraudulently constructed social reality"; see "Unity and Dynamic," 92-94.

By the time of Second Isaiah, however, the whole social situation has changed. The destruction of Jerusalem and the exile of many of the people are interpreted to mean that Israel has suffered the consequences of her sin and now divine forgiveness makes possible a new beginning. Evil is understood in larger dimensions than sin and lack of knowledge of God (1:2-3), which once evoked Isaiah's call for repentance and social change (1:18-20). Israel is now the victim of powerful forces in history, concentrated in, and symbolized by, the oppressive empire of Babylon. In such a situation, comparable to the time when the people were once slaves in Egypt, the prophet proclaims comforting good news that Yahweh, the Holy One of Israel, will deliver Israel from her enemies and open up a way into the future.

> Thus says Yahweh,
>   your Redeemer, the Holy One of Israel:
> For your sake I will send to Babylon
>   and break down all the bars,
> and the shouting of the Chaldeans
>   will be turned to lamentations.
> I am Yahweh, your Holy One,
>   the Creator of Israel, your King. (Isa 43:14-15)

In the ensuing verses the poet resorts to exodus typology to portray the "new thing" that Yahweh is on the verge of doing (43:16-21).[30]

As we have seen, Israel's *Heilsgeschichte* was pushed into the background in the message of Isaiah of Jerusalem, and dimensions of royal covenant theology were highlighted. The situation of the Exile, however, provided an occasion to reaffirm what was experienced at the sources of the Israelite tradition: that the holy is power manifest in redemptive concern as well as in sovereign demand. Thus the "saving experience" of the Exodus was made accessible in the present by an inspired poet who combined the Exodus-Conquest story with dimensions

---

[30] For discussions of this motif, which is echoed in Third Isaiah (62:10-12) and the "Little Apocalypse" (35:8-10), see my "Exodus Typology in Second Isaiah," in *Israel's Prophetic Heritage: Essays in Honor of James Muilenburg* (ed. Bernhard W. Anderson and Walter J. Harrelson; New York: Harper & Row, 1967) 172-95; also Walther Zimmerli, "Der 'neue Exodus' in der Verkündigung der beiden grossen Exilspropheten," *Gottes Offenbarung* (Munich: Chr. Kaiser, 1963) 192-204; Carroll Stuhlmueller, *Creative Redemption in Deutero-Isaiah* (Rome: Biblical Institute, 1970) 59-98, 272.

of royal covenant theology.[31] It is striking that the poetry of Second Isaiah elaborates the mythic pattern of the ancient Song of the Sea (Exod 15:1-18): the opening of a way through the wilderness (Isa 40:3-5), the divine *Chaoskampf* that recreates a people (55:9-10), and the jubilant march of liberated people to the sacred mountain where they acclaim the Divine Warrior as king (52:7-10; cf. Exod 1:18).

The final apocalyptic rendering of the Isaianic tradition, undertaken during the period of the restoration when the Jewish community was a small enclave in an increasingly hostile world, brings out the universal sway of Yahweh, the Holy One of Israel, which was implicit in the historical particular from the first. No longer can suffering be understood as deserved punishment for sin, as with Isaiah of Jerusalem; rather, humanity itself, along with Israel, is in the grip of massive evil forces which crush and oppress. In the oracles against the nations, Babylon (as in 13:1-11) is not just a political regime but a symbol of tyrannical power that in *hybris* seeks to usurp the sovereignty of God (14:3-23), and in doing so victimizes the weak and the helpless.[32] According to a passage in the Isaiah Apocalypse that echoes the Canaanite myth of the Divine Warrior's victory over the chaos monster, "the dragon that is in the sea" (Isa 24:1), ultimately Yahweh will win the victory over the forces of evil at work in human history. Beyond the suffering of the present age God will usher in a new day, indeed a new creation (65:17-19), when Israel and the poor of the earth will be liberated from oppression and the fear of death (25:6).

In the final apocalyptic interpretation the message of Isaiah is a "vision" (note the superscription in 1:1)—"like the words of a book that is sealed" (29:11-12). Those to whom it is given to know the "mystery" of God's kingdom realize that divine victory is on the way, indeed it is

---

[31] I have pursued this further in my essay, "Exodus and Covenant in Second Isaiah and Prophetic Tradition," in *Magnalia Dei, The Mighty Acts of God: Essays on the Bible and Archaeology in Memory of G. Ernest Wright* (ed. Frank Moore Cross, Werner E. Lemke, and Patrick D. Miller, Jr.; Garden City: Doubleday and Co., 1976) 339-60.

[32] Brevard Childs observes that from the perspective of the final redaction of the book the oracles against the nations (chaps. 13-23) receive their meaning from the ensuing oracles in chaps. 24-27 and that "the redactional connection between chs. 13 and 24 points to Babylon's representative role among the nations" (*Introduction*, 332). Since chaps. 24-27 constitute "the Isaiah Apocalypse," this redactional connection in my judgment indicates an apocalyptic interpretation of oracles which come from various periods.

coming soon. The eschatological victory of Yahweh, the Holy One, will prompt Israel to burst out in hymnic singing, as we hear in "in that day passages" (12:1-6) which provide the doxological conclusion to chaps. 2-12:

> Exult and shout with joy, O inhabitant of Zion,
>   for great in your midst is the Holy One of Israel!
>   (Isa 12:6)

However, the vindication of Zion will have universal significance for the poor and oppressed of the earth, for the Holy One of Israel is the sole power, the Creator and Redeemer.

> In that day the deaf will hear the words of a book,
>   the eyes of the blind will see in pitch darkness.
> The meek will increase joy in Yahweh,
>   and the poor of humanity exult in the
>   Holy One of Israel. (Isa 29:18-19)

* * *

In summary, the movement from prophecy to apocalyptic, traceable in the various stages of the Isaiah tradition, rings the changes on the motif that Yahweh is the Holy One of Israel. Living in the presence of the holy God means to be exposed to God's judgment from which there is no escape, but more than that: to be embraced by divine concern and purpose. Indeed, it is not divine judgment first and divine mercy beyond, rather God's saving purpose is operative through the judgment, in order that there may appear a new Jerusalem, a new humanity, a new creation. The final apocalyptic shaping of the book of Isaiah elicits the universal meaning of what was given in the historical particular and thus invites all peoples to join in praising Yahweh, the Holy One of Israel.

ANCIENT BIBLICAL LAWS
AND MODERN HUMAN RIGHTS

JAMES BARR
The University of Oxford

It was characteristic of the spirit of Walter Harrelson, and of the genius of his scholarship, that he should devote a book to the relationship between the Ten Commandments and human rights.[1] We see in this a combination of two excellences: on the one hand a warm devotion to the biblical text as the Word of God and the source of guidance to his will; and on the other side a personal commitment to the achievement of justice, equity, and understanding, especially for the weak, the deprived, and the minorities in our modern society. For Harrelson the "relevance" of the Hebrew Bible is not something that has to be painfully searched for or ingeniously deciphered, but something that is present and immediate, waiting only to be stated. And in just this respect he represents what the best of modern biblical scholarship has been, both in the attitudes with which it has approached scripture and in the kind of results that it has drawn from it.

Equally, however, Harrelson has been aware of an ambiguity or (his own word) an "irony" in the relation between the Bible and the modern quest for human rights, or for a morality based upon these rights. The same biblical material that has inspired the quest for social justice has been appealed to and used as an instrument for rejecting that quest.[2] "Every breakthrough toward human liberation in Western society has been both *affirmed* and *denounced* on the basis of

---

[1] *The Ten Commandments and Human Rights* (OBT 8; Philadelphia: Fortress, 1980).

[2] W. Harrelson, "The Hebrew Bible and Modern Culture," in *The Hebrew Bible and Its Modern Interpreters* (ed. D. A. Knight and G. M. Tucker; BMI 1; Philadelphia: Fortress; and Chico: Scholars Press, 1985) 489-505, esp. pp. 495f.

appeals to biblical religion, biblical thought, and biblical practice."[3] If "the crucial case was slavery, which positive law commonly recognized but natural law condemned,"[4] the biblical material, or most of it, must certainly stand alongside other systems of positive law in recognizing it. It is sometimes said that the Bible, though it did not strive to abolish slavery, at least did something to *regulate* it; but this argument cannot be pushed very far because the degree of regulation or limitation applied was in fact very slight, was applicable only to one limited class of slaves (probably to be understood as free Israelites who had become temporary slaves through debt: Exod 21:2-6 is the primary passage), is coupled with a provision through which the temporary slave may become a permanent slave and thus envisages an extension of his slavery, and in any case is closely parallel with comparable provisions of Mesopotamian law (on this, more below). Thus, if slavery is the fundamental test for the idea of human rights, it is no wonder that history has used the Bible in ways that engender that same ambiguity and irony that Harrelson remarked. The line from the Bible to human rights is not a straight or an easy one.

In addition we have the problem of *universality*. The idea of human rights seems to be predicated upon universality: the rights apply to all human beings as human beings. But quite a lot of the law of the Hebrew Bible refers to institutions that seem to be peculiar to ancient Israel. The prominence of the Ten Commandments derives in considerable measure from the fact that they have been generally perceived as possessing a higher degree of universality and being less confined to the culture of Israel in particular. Even in the Decalogue, however, the commandment not to work on the seventh day is largely peculiar to Israel. If one can argue from the seventh-day commandment to the beneficial character of a weekly day of rest for the sake of leisure and reflection, then one might also argue, in the opposite direction, that, since the commandment sanctioned the Israelite cultural custom of the avoidance of work on this day, it would equally well sanction the practice of arranged marriages, common in other Oriental societies but implicitly or expressly disapproved of by most ideas of human rights. The argument would be: the Ten Commandments sanction something that is a peculiar and local Jewish custom or institution, and appear to give it universality. But other peoples than the Jews have

---

[3] Harrelson, "The Hebrew Bible and Modern Culture," 496.

[4] Article "Human Rights," in *The Oxford Companion to Law* (ed. D. M. Walker; Oxford: Oxford University, 1980) 591.

customs and institutions to which they are equally attached. Arranged marriages are such a custom or institution in many parts of the world. Why then should it be supposed that the Jewish institution of the Sabbath has a positive connection with universal human rights, but that universal human rights contradict our dearly loved practice of the arranged marriage?

There are in fact a considerable number of unclarities and difficulties in the linkage between biblical materials and ideas of human rights, and the foregoing are only examples among others. Even if we grant that *historically* much was both attempted and achieved for the advancement of human rights by groups, both Jewish and Christian, who were enthusiasts for Hebrew law and who greatly emphasized the Ten Commandments,[5] this historical reality does not in itself demonstrate that the connections between biblical materials and ideas of human rights, as discerned by these groups, were logically or exegetically sound. Similarly, arguments that turned out to be ethically salutary some hundreds of years ago will not necessarily have the same positive value today.

These, then, are some of the problem areas in the relation between the biblical commandments and the modern conception of human rights; but the one that comes even more to the fore in the writer's mind is another. Even where a clear relation in terms of act, practice, or content can be discerned, there seems, at least at first sight, to be a striking difference in terms of approach and expression. In the one case there is a command from God; in the other there is a right that attaches intrinsically to a human person. In the former the command comes from God, and its impact falls, it would seem, upon the human actor or potential actor: "thou shalt not kill" is addressed to the person who might conceivably kill. Human rights, by contrast, appear to be invested in the human person who suffers wrong or may suffer wrong: you have a right not to be killed, a right to life, just as you have a right to a fair trial, a right not to be made a slave, a right not to have your property arbitrarily taken away from you, and so on. These two attitudes appear, at least on the face of it, to be very different. To be commanded not to kill is a very different thing from saying that you have a right not to be

---

[5] From within a vast mass of literature, I would mention Dietrich Ritschl, "Der Beitrag des Calvinismus fur die Entwicklung des Menschenrechtsgedankens in Europa und Nordamerika," in *EvT* 40 (1980) 333-45; for a representative Jewish view, focusing on the pro-Hebraic attitudes of the American Puritans, cf. Abraham I. Katsh, *The Biblical Heritage of American Democracy* (New York: KTAV, 1977), especially chaps. 5 and 6.

killed. And, as is obvious, the effectiveness of the command as a moral guide depends on belief in the existence and the moral authority of this particular deity who thus commands, while human rights by their nature attach to the human person and are independent of the religious attitudes of that person (or absence of any such attitudes). This point is correctly realized by Harrelson,[6] who expresses it by saying that the traditional affirmations which ground purpose in God belong "within the circle of faith," while the import of the same for the public world "is found in its actual *content*": that is to say, the traditional expression "thou shalt not kill," grounding purpose in God and his will, remains effective and authoritative within the circle of faith, but the public import lies in the content, i.e., the affirmation that it is wrong to kill and, conversely, that all human beings have the right to live and not to be killed.

The difference here adumbrated may be one that underlies the very different attitudes found in the use of the Bible in the discussion of any moral question today. Harrelson has shown great sensitivity to this issue also: "The Bible and Political Conservatism" is the title of one of the sections in his essay of 1985.[7] Among religious people and believers in biblical authority there is some resistance to the increasing emphasis upon human rights; and although those concerned seldom have the wit to work it out in these terms, much of that resistance may come from what has just been mentioned, namely, that they want their ethical guidance to be expressed in the biblical style of command and (especially) prohibition, preferably accompanied with divine vengeance, direct or indirect, against the wrongdoer, rather than in the more humanistic form of statement of a right which persons in themselves possess. Moreover, given the complexities of the modern world, they may feel that rights fail to protect the innocent while they enable the guilty to escape justice: your right to live does not prevent the burglar from shooting you, while his rights may make it more difficult for him to be convicted. Realism requires that we follow Harrelson in observing the seriousness of such reactions against the ethic of human rights and the influence which, at least as people perceive it, the biblical form of ethical expression by command and prohibition has upon it. Any attempt to validate the conception of human rights through appeal to the biblical laws has to seek to build a bridge over

---

[6] Harrelson, "The Hebrew Bible and Modern Culture," 499.
[7] Ibid., 490.

the difference between personal commands of God and human rights which are intrinsically invested in the human person.

Or, to put the same point in another way, the biblical commandment seems to be theonomous, while human rights are anthroponomous. Human rights appear to be largely predicated upon the value of *freedom*; the person has the right to freedom in general, including freedom of movement, freedom of thought, conscience and religion, freedom of association; and the person cannot rightly be coerced by the state or any other institution in these respects. Within this framework, given freedom as a supreme value, certain moral imperatives have to be expressed as *limitations of freedom*, limitations to be justified because anyone who used freedom beyond the limits would be infringing upon the freedom of another person. Thus, for example (a case which will be familiar to many readers of this essay), one might wish to kill another theologian, and one might feel that one's own freedom pointed naturally to the carrying out of the action; but it would be wrong because that other theologian, however unpleasant as a person, continued to have the right to live, a freedom which one would be infringing if one were to terminate that person's life. As against all this type of calculation of freedom and its limits, some will feel that it would be better to work by an ethic of direct divine command under which killing is simply prohibited. Once again this formulation expresses something very real in the modern uncertainty about the place of the Bible in relation to moral decision.

The contrast, however, is not as complete as it may appear to the casual reader of the Bible, for there is certain evidence that a concept similar to that of "rights" does exist and is visible even on the surface of the Hebrew Bible text. One thinks most naturally of certain departments within the manifold meanings of that many-sided word *mišpāṭ* The most relevant cases are those that talk of the *mišpāṭ*, the "right" or "rights," *of* someone, that to which he or she has a right, which belongs to him or her.[8] It is not always easy to distinguish this usage from others that border closely upon it, but certain rather obvious cases may be mentioned. Perhaps the most obvious is at Deut 21:17: a man has two wives, of whom he loves one and dislikes the other, but his firstborn is the son of the disliked wife. When this is so he cannot transfer the firstborn status to the son of the loved wife, but must allot

---

[8] Cf. G. Liedke in *THWAT*, 2:1005, who uses the terms "das, was den Armen usw. 'gehört'" and "das, was einem zukommt"; cf. also G. Liedke, *Gestalt und Bezeichnung alttestamentlicher Rechtssätze* (WMANT 39; Neukirchen-Vluyn: Neukirchener Verlag, 1971).

the normal double portion to the true firstborn, even if his mother is disfavored: because he is the first, the right of firstbornship is his (*lô mišpaṭ ha-běkōrâ*).This is his right; it belongs to him and cannot be taken away from him. Similarly, in the family of Jeremiah, in a discussion about the ownership of land, one tells another, "you have the right of redemption" (*mišpaṭ ha-gě'ullâ*) or likewise "the right of inheritance" (Jer 32:7,8). A prominent passage in Deuteronomy is introduced by saying "this will be the right (*mišpāṭ*) of the priests," namely that they will receive certain portions of the sacrifices (Deut 18:3). Such cases are certainly "rights," but they are not general rights belonging to persons as human beings, but rights attached to family position or distinctive class and function. Cases of the *mišpāṭ* of the king or of the kingdom (e.g., 1 Sam 8:9,11; 10:25) are less certain, for they may well be considered to belong to a different department of the semantics of this word: in other words, if so, they refer not to the "rights" which the king or the kingdom will have, but to the "ways" or "pattern" or "style" under which the kingship will be exercised. On the other hand the cases which refer to the *mišpāṭ* of the poor, the orphan, the *gēr* or dependent foreigner (e.g., Exod 23:6; Deut 24:17) seem clearly to refer to rights which these persons, because of their social weakness, will be unable to defend by their own action: their defense depends, therefore, on one side on God's action to protect them, on the other side on his prohibition against any taking advantage of the weakness of these persons.

This mention of the "right" or "rights" of the widow, the orphan, the poor, and the resident foreigner brings us particularly close to the idea of "human" rights. For, unlike some cases mentioned just above, this is not a matter of innate family position or special function. Any child could become an orphan, any woman a widow, any wealthy man a poor one. If the orphan, the widow, the poor man had a *mišpāṭ* which had to be protected, it implies that this was a "right" which Israelite persons "naturally" possessed and which, if it is rather seldom mentioned or even hinted at, must nevertheless be assumed to have underlain much of what is expressly said in the Hebrew Bible. If it extended to the *gēr*, that only strengthens the case: the *gēr* was a foreigner, but within the land of Israel it was to be recognized that such a person too had certain rights; outside that territory, naturally, Israelite law could not legislate. Thus the biblical and Hebraic foundation for something like human rights is not as thin as might appear; or, to put it in another way, the strongly theonomous approach of the biblical commandments deserves to be balanced with the observation of the existence of "rights" in ancient Israel which were assumed by the commandments rather than positively asserted by them.

The New Testament also seems to present a mixed picture. Not much is expressly said about people's "rights" within it. The high value set on martyrdom, on giving up one's life for the kingdom of God, suggests that, even if one may have a "right to life," the more important thing is to give up that right when required, so much so that the mere existence of any such right hardly calls for mention. If one is to give up one's coat to anyone who asks for it, it is not very important whether one has a "right" to that piece of property or not. "Rights" seem to appear more in the parables, as part of illustrations from contemporary life, than in actual moral instruction. Caesar of course has a "right" to exact taxes from the subject peoples, but little or nothing is said about rights that the subject peoples have against him. All this might suggest that the idea of "rights" counted for little. Against this, however, we have one powerful piece of counter-evidence: St. Paul's insistence, repeated more than once in Acts, that as a Roman citizen he had the right to a proper trial under due legal process, and his appeal to Caesar. Should he not just have accepted beatings and imprisonment—of which he seems to have suffered plenty in any case—independently of his rights as a Roman, considering that these citizen's rights must have been infinitely unattainable for most other Christians of his time, and similarly for Jews? Yet Acts clearly regards Paul's invocation of his rights as a Roman citizen as a fine act and a highlight of his story, as well as part of the machinery that will eventually bring Paul to Rome and into reach of the imperial presence. Rights, then, within early Christianity seem not to be always without importance.

The points here made lead us on to formulate another insight that is significant for our general theme. Dietrich Ritschl, to whom I owe some of the main insights expressed in this article, can speak of the current concept of human rights as "the best of all systems to protect men and women and sustain the world"—high praise, for numerous serious criticisms of this concept as culturally conditioned and as unrealistically idealistic could be thought of.[9] But, he goes on, the declarations on human rights that have thus far been formulated "reflect an optimistic picture of humanity and the world which makes it the duty of all human beings to insist on their own rights and those of others." Quite so. There is such a thing as a zealotic legalism of insistence upon

[9] D. Ritschl, *The Logic of Theology* (London: SCM, 1986) 215ff.—unfortunately a very short statement of the issues. German original, *Die Logik der Theologie* (Munich: Chr. Kaiser, 1984) 261ff.

one's rights, an idea that the insistence upon one's rights is, and should be, the normal mode of interrelation between human persons, that cannot be other than a source of friction, misunderstanding, and eventual rupture in human relations. Ritschl singles out the difference between concern for the rights of others and standing on one's own rights; and, he says, he learned this insight from the black Christians among those who joined in the struggle of the American civil rights movement, who "kept making it clear that Christians should not demand their own rights—at any rate not in the name of the gospel—but should insist on new rights only as the committed representatives of others." Such an insight is closely parallel to the interest of Walter Harrelson in the black church and the way in which he has learned from its experience. But it does mean—quoting Ritschl once more—that we are mistaken if we expect to find or form an *identity* between any concept of human rights and the perspective of the Bible itself. Relations between biblical materials and the legal concept of human rights must be expected to be *oblique*: and that, as we have seen, is what they are.

It is time, however, to return to the Old Testament. As we have seen, the usage of a word like *mišpāṭ* suggests that "rights" of some kind were much more fully recognized than a first impression of the material would suggest, and formed a much wider basis for moral judgments than the surface dominance of direct divine commandment might suggest. To this can be added a further argument. A considerable amount of the material which is presented in the biblical text as outright divine commandment must in fact have been accepted law or folk-custom. In many features—not necessarily in all, but in many—the legislation represented as "Mosaic" must have been in large measure a restatement of customary law that was already ancient. Such material is of course *presented* in the Bible *as if* it were revelatory and novel, but a little thought quickly shows that this presentation cannot be accepted as final. For if revelation only revealed to us something slightly different from what was already standard and accepted morality, to insist on its revelatory quality is only to trivialize the concept of revelation. The key to this problem lies in one's awareness or otherwise of moral traditions that lie outside the Bible. The Bible was not unique in disapproving of murder, theft, and adultery, for example. From the way in which some people talk about the Bible, one would imagine that the law of extra-biblical civilizations permitted or even encouraged murder, theft, and adultery as desirable practices. This was not at all the case. In disapproving of such actions and forbidding them, the Bible was only acting in accordance with the general consensus of other and often "pagan" societies. Penalties exacted for such offenses were severe and often horrendous, at least in theory; and any theoretical character attaching to them does not differentiate them from the biblical laws in principle, for the biblical laws also had a theoretical character and may seldom have been carried out literally in the form in which they are set out. The severity of penalties for these offenses was well known to scholars of the Reformation and succeeding periods because they were well trained in the classical sources; this fact was a force which led them arbitrarily toward a recognition of "natural law" even when they also regarded the biblical commandments as belonging to an exceptional class of absolute authority.[10] Modern scholars know something of the same sort from ancient Near Eastern sources. In between the two there lies, however, a stratum of people who, unaware of the moral standards of extra-biblical civilizations, think of the biblical commandments as if they were quite unique expressions of moral requirements such as had never before been heard of in the world.

The force of this argument was greatly strengthened through the ancient Near Eastern sources, which have just been mentioned in passing. On certain of the biblical laws, such as the law of the Hebrew slave (Exod 21:2ff.) or the law of the goring ox (Exod 21:28f.), the Mesopotamian parallels bring about a decisive transformation of our thinking.[11] The Mesopotamian laws are not identical with the biblical, but the general structure is very similar. It is impossible to suppose that the Hebrew law is an expression of divine revelation that produces a moral discourse of totally different order from the Mesopotamian. Far from such legal materials having come into existence long after Moses' time, they probably existed, and were familiar, long before Moses could have been born. Far from their being in the Bible because they are a totally new revelation just come from God, they are there because they were already common practice and generally known and accepted from ancient times.

---

[10] For example, cf. the way in which those who favored the death penalty for adultery by the Act of 1650 in Puritan England were aware of the practice of Greek and Roman, Egyptian and other, antiquity for violent punishment—if anything *exceeding* the strictness of the Mosaic law; see Keith Thomas, "The Puritans and Adultery: The Act of 1650 Reconsidered," in *Puritans and Revolutionaries* (ed. D. Pennington and K. Thomas; Oxford: Clarendon, 1978) 268ff.

[11] I have developed this argument already in my *Beyond Fundamentalism* (Philadelphia: Westminster, 1984) 91-95, and repeat only a thin portion of what was there said.

And the same is true of the *lex talionis*, "an eye for an eye and a tooth for a tooth": the principle of strict and exact retribution, insofar as it applies in biblical law (the three main places, in Exodus, Leviticus, and Deuteronomy, attach it to different kinds of actual application), is not something given to Israel by unique divine command but is something that at least as a general principle is shared with some parts of the Oriental environment. Retribution in this sense is not a unique biblical insight; it is, on the contrary, there in the Bible because Israel inherited it from and shared it with some of her "heathen" neighbors.

Naturally I do not for a moment seek to show that this is true of *all* the Hebrew legal material: all I argue is that there is enough material of this kind for it to have a significant effect on our general assessment of the nature of ancient Hebrew law. And when it comes to the Ten Commandments as the most central case, we may be inclined to discern something of a mixture: some of the elements may well be peculiar to Israel (no other god but one, no graven image, the sabbath day), but others were certainly expressions of an ethic that would have been widely approved (honoring of parents, prohibition of murder, adultery, theft, false witness). And even of some of the cases that appear to be peculiar to Israel we may well ask whether these were received in Israel as pure and external commandments from on high. Some of these principles, like the monotheism, the forbidding of graven images, the keeping of the seventh day, were not "natural law" in the sense that all peoples and nations acknowledged something of the kind. But *within Israel* they may have been "natural" in the sense that they were already accepted custom, in some form, long before they came to be "commanded" in the form in which we have them now. For are we to believe that Israel simply had no institution of a sabbath, a day of rest, a prohibition of certain kinds of work, at all, and that then suddenly, on the basis of a command transmitted by Moses, the keeping of the sabbath came full-fledged into being like Athena emerging from the head of Zeus?

What we are saying, then, is that the commandments, in some cases, perhaps in many, represent the taking up into the realm of divine will of ethical norms that were already known and accepted in society, or in some traditions of society more than in others. The importance of the commandment form, in such cases, is not that the commandment conveys a norm that was previously unknown, but that it is God, the God of Israel, who places his name and his authority behind that norm. This is how the commandments still function: people know already that theft is wrong, one can learn that from many sources, and the commandment not to steal is powerful and influential because it is *God* and no less who is placing himself behind this ethical perception and insisting upon it in a most solemn and serious way. And this perception does something to bridge the apparent gap between an ethic of divine command and ideas such as natural law which in turn lead us toward a concept of human rights.

There remains, in conclusion, one other body of material from the Hebrew scriptures that may well be relevant: I refer to those psalms which are particularly devoted to *torah*, in particular Psalms 1, 19, and 119. These poems celebrate *torah*, which in this case we may translate as "instruction," as the center of piety and the basis of morality. As is well known, the terms for statutes, ordinances, and the like occur frequently in them. Yet, as Jon Levenson has pointed out in a recent and very striking article,[12] these terms are by no means clearly predicated upon the extant books of Moses which are commonly called "the Torah" or "the Pentateuch." Moses is not mentioned; the word "book," so central to Deuteronomic theology, does not occur; the exodus, the promised land, and even the people Israel are left unnoticed.[13] Moreover, in spite of the emphasis upon the commandments, statutes, and ordinances, no specific detail is provided—a striking fact when one considers the great length of Psalm 119 in particular: there is no mention of keeping the sabbath, for instance, so that from these poems, if we had no other information, it would be very hard to know the actual content of the norms referred to.[14] But all this means that, although it is *possible* to read these poems as referring to the Pentateuchal legislation, their own textual fiber leads us to think of the *torah* here venerated as something both vaguer and wider, closer (as Levenson argues) to the "instruction" of the Wisdom literature. But such instruction, although the psalms celebrate it as coming from God, will certainly include much that is, from another point of view, traditional moral wisdom. It will also very probably include an emphasis on creation and the conception that God's Word or Wisdom is built into the created order (cf. Ps 119:89-91).[15]

---

[12] Jon D. Levenson, "The Sources of Torah: Psalm 119 and the Modes of Revelation in Second Temple Judaism," in *Ancient Israelite Religion: Essays in Honor of Frank Moore Cross* (ed. P. D. Miller, Jr., P. D. Hanson, and S. D. McBride; Philadelphia: Fortress, 1987) 559-74.

[13] Ibid., 564.

[14] Ibid., 566.

[15] Ibid., 570.

This, if right, will have important repercussions on the understanding of Psalm 19. To take it as a single poem, in the correct canonical
style, only emphasizes the more the parallelism between the
universality of the heavens and the sun on one hand and the perfections
of *torah* on the other. *Torah* here is certainly divinely given and commanded, but it is, or at least it may very likely be, a total body of
divinely given truth, not to be taken as identical with or limited to a
particular book or set of books. *This* kind of *torah* is universal in its
scope and effect, like the circuit of the sun from end to end of the world,
and nothing is hidden from its effect.[16]

If this is correct, it means that the relation between divine commandment and humanly known and accepted moral norms, as we have
sketched it, does not by any means depend solely on "critical" opera-
tions, on getting "behind" the text to some reconstructed prehistory of it,
or on insights from comparative study of the environment: on the contrary, there are biblical text units which in their textual form, as they
stand, point most naturally in this direction. This insight may therefore be another means by which we can hope to see a connection across

---

[16] Incidentally, these observations render vain certain arguments of Karl
Barth about the understanding of Psalm 19: see *Die Kirchliche Dogmatik* II/1
(2d ed.; Zollikon-Zürich: Evangelischer Verlag, 1946) 112 and 118-19 (E.T., pp.
101, 107-8). Barth is here talking about natural theology, which is not exactly the
same subject as our present one, but as reflections on exegetical principle his
thought is significant for us. He argues that, whatever the case with Psalm 19,
the message of the Psalter as such and as a whole derives from the exodus, the
mission of Moses, the temple, and so on. Perhaps so: perhaps no one, in a
sense, ever doubted this (although Barth greatly distorts the *degree* to which
these various elements of the history of salvation are important for the Psalter).
But a poem like Psalm 19 is not just a "part" of the Psalter: it is a unity of its
own, and the fact that this unity does *not* deem it necessary to *include* all these
elements is highly significant for it. And this point about the 19th Psalm is enor-
mously strengthened by what we have said about Psalm 119: no Barthian
Psalmist would ever have written this long and methodical poem without *mentioning* (as distinct from merely presupposing, even if he did presuppose) all
these elements of historical revelation. And the same is true of Psalm 19. Barth
rails against scholars who on literary-critical grounds have divided this into two
separate poems, Psalms 19a and 19b: he implies that the citation of the psalm
as support for natural theology derives force from the neglect of the second
part of it. Actually, the reverse is true, as we have suggested above: the taking of
the poem as one unit has the effect of universalizing the *torah* therein celebrated: it thus brings it closer to "natural theology" or to universalized morality.

the space that appears to separate direct divine commandment from human morality and human rights. These thoughts are offered in the hope that, if they slightly modify, they will at the same time confirm and support the directions of thought which Walter Harrelson has so finely set out before us.

WOMEN WHO LIED FOR THE FAITH

TONI CRAVEN
Texas Christian University

Nowhere does the Decalogue say, "Thou shalt not lie". The ninth commandment, "Thou shalt not answer thy neighbor as a false witness" (Exod 20:16; Deut 5:20), is a prohibition against perverting the truth in legal testimony.

> This commandment has in view the public testimony of individuals before the judges, in social and commercial dealings, and in gatherings for public worship where evildoers were publicly accused and where false accusation could be devastating.[1]

Law required that a person's public testimony have constancy and reliability. The law prohibited a person from witnessing falsely against another, obliged a witness to come forward (Lev 5:1), and prescribed severe punishment for one who gave malicious testimony (Deut 19:19). In light of Lev 19:11, "You shall not steal, nor deal falsely, nor lie to one another," it is too extreme to claim as Ludwig Koehler did that the Bible contains "no clear and simple statement" which explicitly prohibits lying.[2] This text in Leviticus does prohibit "any form of lying or deception."[3] Nonetheless, Koehler was right that biblical injunctions against forms of lying which might be called "private" lying—as distinguished from "public" lying in legal

---

[1] Walter Harrelson, *The Ten Commandments and Human Rights* (OBT 8; Philadelphia: Fortress, 1980) 143.

[2] Ludwig Koehler, *Old Testament Theology* (London: Lutterworth, 1957) 251 n. 155.

[3] Roland J. Faley, "Leviticus," in *JBC* (1968) 79.

testimony—are not as dominant nor as explicit as modern ethical sensibilities might prefer.

Ps 15:2 encourages a person to "speak truth from the heart," and Prov 6:17 lists "a lying tongue" as one of the seven characteristics which God hates (cf. Prov 12:22). Yet negative statements about lying are overshadowed by positive results effected by lying. In discussing the Hebrew Scriptures' endorsement of "necessary deception," Karl Burger expresses an opinion others may share: "Perhaps such deception is justifiable where a human life is at stake, or where a lie seems necessary to the accomplishment of some higher good; but even then it should be possible to surmount the difficulty without lying."[4]

The fact is that in many biblical stories lies are told for the preservation of the community. The covenant and maintenance of tradition—not a legal prescription—are the moral standards against which "truthfulness" is measured.[5] In stories about "effective lies,"[6] truth is not a fixed standard; it is personal and relational.[7] Truth is not "fact," rather it is "process."[8] It happens more often than might be expected in the Hebrew Scriptures that lying is a tool for the maintenance of personal and relational truth. In what follows, we will critically reflect on seven stories about women who lied to preserve the covenant community.[9] We will look at how and to whom they lied; on

---

[4] Samuel Macauley Jackson and Lefferts A. Loetscher, eds., *The New Schaff-Herzog Encyclopedia of Religious Knowledge* (Grand Rapids, MI: Baker Book House, 1967), s.v. "Lie," by Karl Burger.

[5] For helpful observations about different uses of the word "truth," see James A. Rimbach, "Truth: A Biblical Word Study," *CurTM* 7 (1980) 171-75.

[6] F. D. McConnell, "Effective Lies," *Soundings* 53 (1970) 282, borrows the term "effective lie" from Thomas Mann and defines it as a "factualistic" betrayal that is not a deceit but rather a processive and self-critical fiction.

[7] See M. E. Andrew, "Falsehood and Truth," *Int* 17 (1963) 434.

[8] McConnell ("Effective Lies," 281-84) makes the further case that cross-disciplinary studies of language have disclosed "binary germs of 'fact'" as well as "effective lies" that illustrate the hard lesson of "conditional, processive 'truth'" learned by our age which "needs desperately to find within that process an order and a sense which can be both acceptable and humanizing."

[9] I had originally planned to examine ten stories in honor of Walter Harrelson. Length restrictions for this Festschrift have dictated the exclusion of three, indeed four, important stories: (1) the two daughters of Lot who purposely made their father drunk so that they could have intercourse with him and thus preserve offspring (Gen 19:30-38); (2) Ruth who obediently promised, "All that you say I will do," and then independently proposed to Boaz on the threshing floor (Ruth 3); (3) Michal who lied to her father that

what authority they lied; and the effect of their lie. In the end, we will ask why they lied.

Genesis 27-28

Rebekah is first in the canonical company of women who lied for the sake of the faith. She lied to Isaac, her husband, twice. Through the direction of a ruse, she tricked Isaac into giving their younger son, Jacob, the patriarchal death-bed blessing (Gen 27:1-45). Through a verbal pretense, she insured Jacob's escape from his brother's sworn revenge: "If Jacob marries one of the Hittite women such as these, one of the women of the land, what good will my life be to me?" (Gen 27:46). Isaac responded as she desired and charged Jacob to go to Paddanaram to seek a wife from among the daughters of Rebekah's brother, Laban.

Both of Rebekah's lies to her husband worked. Jacob was blessed, and his life was preserved. Rebekah's motive in engineering preference for their younger son is not specified in Genesis 27-28. In the context of the larger narrative about Rebekah (Genesis 24-28), her actions are justified by God's prior revelation that, "Two nations are in your womb, and two peoples, born of you, shall be divided; the one shall be stronger than the other, the elder shall serve the younger" (Gen 25:23). Her lies made true God's private disclosure to her. The effect of her lies changed the course of the ancestral history. On her account the younger twin assumed dominance. As Claudia Camp has said, "Rebekah steals for the next generation."[10]

Genesis 38

Tamar is another who "steals for the next generation." In fact, she stole the next generation by her lie to Judah, her father-in-law. By pretending to be a harlot at Timnah, she tricked him into impregnating her. Three months later when the pregnancy had become public and Tamar was being brought before Judah, she sent him word saying, "By the man to whom these belong, I am with child. Mark, I pray you,

---

David was sick when in fact she had helped him escape Saul's messengers (1 Sam 19:11-17); and (4) Esther who lied about wanting nothing but the opportunity to prepare a second dinner for the king and Haman in order to time most advantageously her request for accomplishing the deliverance of her people and the demise of their enemy (Esther 5).

[10] Claudia Camp, interview by author, 29 June 1987, Texas Christian University, Fort Worth, TX.

whose these are, the signet and the cord and the staff" (Gen 38:25). Before Judah realized that he himself had impregnated her, he rendered the judgment: "Take her out, and let her be burned" (Gen 38:24).

Tamar had put herself in grave danger. A misfit because she had no offspring and no spouse, she had risked losing her life to become pregnant.[11] She had broken the law[12] in order to fulfill the societal convention that married women bear children. Whether her actions were motivated by self-concern or concern for the continuance of her dead husband's name, the narrative does not say. It does document that God dealt harshly with evil, contemptible behavior. God had slain Judah's first-born, Tamar's first husband, Er, because he was "evil in the sight of the Lord" (Gen 38:7). God had also slain Onan, Judah's son who spilt his semen on the ground rather than give Tamar an offspring for his brother, because "what he did was evil" in God's sight (Gen 38:10-11).

Since Tamar was not slain by God as a consequence for her deed, the story implies that her deceit was not contemptible in God's sight. Acknowledging ownership of the signet, cord, and staff, Judah retracted his judgment that she should be burned, saying, "She is more righteous than I, inasmuch as I did not give her to my son Shelah" (Gen 38:26).

As Gerhard von Rad has indicated, "Tamar, in spite of her action which borders on a crime, is the one justified in the end."[13] She bore twin sons by a breach birth. Perez, though first to emerge fully from her womb, was rivaled by Zerah who had stuck out an arm which a midwife had marked with a scarlet thread (Gen 38:27-30). Tamar's self-authorized lie resulted in two sons from whom descended most of the tribe which became the state of Judah in the time of David. Perez (whose descendants included Boaz, Obed, Jesse, and David [see Ruth

---

[11] Susan Niditch points out that in most tribal, patriarchal societies young women were allowed only two proper roles: unmarried virgin in her father's home or faithful, child-producing wife in her husband's or husband's family's home; "The Wronged Woman Righted: An Analysis of Genesis 38," *HTR* 72 (1979) 143-49.

[12] The incest law in Lev 20:12 prescribed death for a man and a daughter-in-law who had intercourse. Gen 38:26 makes it clear that Judah did not lie with Tamar again.

[13] Gerhard von Rad, *Genesis* (OTL; rev. ed.; Philadelphia: Westminster, 1972) 362.

4:12, 18-22])[14] and Zerah were ancestors of two of the three chief families of the tribe of Judah (Num 26:19-21).

Susan Niditch reports that in *m. Megilla* 4:10 the Rabbis judged Genesis 38 a story worthy to be read and translated in the synagogue. By contrast the stories of Reuben's intercourse with his father's concubine Bilhah (Gen 35:22) and David's adultery with Bathsheba (2 Sam 11:2-17) were to be read but not translated. Amnon's rape of his sister Tamar (2 Samuel 13) was not to be read aloud at all. "The Rabbis wish to set the tale of Tamar apart from the other three incidents and thereby acknowledge its sociologically constructive message."[15] Making a similar judgment, Franz Delitzsch claimed that Tamar is "a saint according to the Old Testament standard."[16]

Exodus 1-2

The opening chapters of Exodus record a series of lies told by women which had positive national and personal consequences. The two midwives, Shiphrah and Puah, lied to the king of Egypt about why they had not killed the Hebrew males at birth: "Because the Hebrew women are not like the Egyptian women; for they are vigorous and are delivered before the midwife comes to them" (Exod 1:19). The midwives feared God (Exod 1:17, 21),[17] not the king of Egypt. Two consequences resulted from their faithful deception: the people multiplied and grew very strong; the midwives were blessed by God and granted families (Exod 1:20-21).[18]

---

[14] According to the genealogy in Matt 1:3, Perez was an ancestor of Jesus.

[15] Niditch, "The Wronged Woman Righted," 149.

[16] Franz Delitzsch, *A New Commentary on Genesis* (Edinburgh: T. & T. Clark, 1894) 2:276.

[17] Rita J. Burns' discussion of the midwives' "fear of God" includes the following: "In Israel's wisdom tradition the expression 'fear of God' bears strong ethical connotations (see Prov 2:1-22; 8:13; 14:2; 15:33; 16:6). Persons who feared God were those who acted according to a moral imperative or standard. This standard was learned through examination both of human experience (Prov 19:6-7; 20:4, 14, 19, 25; 23:1-3, 29-35; 24:30-34) and of the process of nature (Prov 6:6-7; 26:20-22; 27:18; 28:3)"; *Exodus, Leviticus, Numbers* (Old Testament Message, 3; Wilmington, DE: Michael Glazier, 1983) 30.

[18] Reading with *RSV*. Verse 21 in MT reads, "Because the midwives feared God, he made them (masc. pl.) houses." LXX corrects, "they made for themselves houses." J. Cheryl Exum's analysis of this text includes the following three points of information: (1) "House," progeny, is a blessing

Two family members, mother and daughter,[19] also lied to preserve the life of a "goodly child" (Exod 2:2). Refusing to cooperate with the royal order that newborn males be cast into the Nile, the mother hid her child for three months, then put him in a basket at the river's edge. The daughter "stood at a distance, to know what would be done to him" (Exod 2:3-4). When the daughter of Pharaoh showed pity toward the baby, Moses' sister unhesitatingly proposed, "Shall I call for you a nurse from the Hebrews to nurse this child for you?" (Exod 2:7).[20]

Like her mother who had put the child in the Nile on her own authority for her own purpose, so next the daughter acted. Feigning interest in the daughter of the Pharaoh, the sister of Moses volunteered to find a Hebrew nurse. Mother and daughter accomplished a deceit that insured the preservation of the child's life. Their lies were effective and perhaps even lucrative. The princess unknowingly offered to pay the child's mother to nurse her own child.[21]

Further securing the life and rights of the child, the princess participated in the most outrageous lie of all. She claimed him as her own son and named him Moses (Exod 2:10). The fact was she knew him to be a Hebrew child. She ought not have brought him home, but she did. Since she is not mentioned again in the story, the personal consequence of her action is not recorded. Nonetheless, the havoc Moses caused in the land and royal household allows us to surmise that her father cannot have been pleased.

Two midwives, a mother and a daughter, and the royal princess herself circumvented a Pharaoh's decree. These women shaped the nation's history and their own personal lives by lies that found ways

---

traditionally reserved for men (Exod 1:1; 20:17; 1 Sam 25:28; 2 Sam 7:11; 1 Kgs 2:24; Rachel and Leah are credited with building up the house of Israel, Ruth 4:11). (2) Most interpreters understand the reference as God's reward to the midwives. (3) "In spite of the difficulty of the pronouns, it is clear that the growth of the Hebrew people has been made possible by the midwives." "'You Shall Let Every Daughter Live': A Study of Exodus 1:8–2:10," *Semeia* 28 (1983) 74.

[19] Mother and daughter, unnamed in the opening chapters of Exodus, are identified elsewhere as Jochebed (Exod 6:20; Num 26:59) and Miriam (first so named as prophet and sister of Aaron in Exod 15:20).

[20] For discussion of the rhetorical patterns in this text, see Exum, "'You Shall Let Every Daughter Live,'" 77.

[21] Ibid., 78, for information on this act as an expression of the right of possession.

around and through political oppression. Each in her own way supported life even though under order to destroy it.

Joshua 2

Rahab is a foreigner who lied to preserve the lives of Joshua's spies. She lied to the king of Jericho saying she did not know the whereabouts of the spies when she knew full well they were hidden on the roof of her house (Josh 2:4-5). Before she allowed the spies to escape by a rope through her window,[22] she made them swear by YHWH that when Jericho was taken they would protect her father, mother, brothers, and sisters and all who belonged to them (Josh 2:13). The spies swore that a scarlet cord bound in her window would protect all who were in her house. When Jericho was burned, Joshua was true to the spies' promise. Rahab and her immediate family were spared (Josh 6:22).

A woman of intelligence, courage, and decisive action, Rahab knew that Jericho's end was coming. She lied boldly to the king, bargained shrewdly with the spies, helped them escape from her house, and suggested the strategy that the spies hide three days in the hills to the west to elude their pursuers who would have headed east in the direction of Joshua's camp. She betrayed her own community to deliver Israel. Faith in the God YHWH, born of "hearing" (Josh 2:10, 11) about God's mighty deeds, motivated her actions. Following the note that "she dwelt in Israel to this day" (Josh 6:25), Rahab, an unmarried harlot,[23] is never mentioned again in the Hebrew Scriptures.[24]

---

[22] Rahab owned a house in the wall of the city, which may reflect her lowly social status not her poverty; so Athalya Brenner, *The Israelite Woman: Social Role and Literary Type in Biblical Narrative* (BS 2; Sheffield: JSOT, 1985) 80. For a brief but illuminating discussion of Rahab, see Brenner, 79-81.

[23] Only once does the episode of the hiding of the spies state that Rahab was a harlot (Josh 2:1); three times in the story of the fall of Jericho she is so designated (Josh 6:17, 22, 25). Her help was not shunned because of her occupation. And other than the fact that men could come and go easily from her house (Josh 2:4-5), the accounts disclose little about harlotry. Her actions in Joshua 2 develop a life-portrait of female wisdom and courage, not of prostitution; the references in Joshua 6 are non-judgmental identifications. On the issue of harlotry, see two articles conveniently reprinted in *The Bible and Liberation: Political and Social Hermeneutics* (ed. Norman K. Gottwald; rev. ed.; Maryknoll, NY: Orbis, 1983): Phyllis A. Bird, "Images of Women in the Old Testament," 272 (first published in *Religion and Sexism: Images of Women in*

Judges 4-5

Jael, a Kenite, lied in order to smash the skull of the enemy. This foreign woman lied to Sisera, general of king Jabin of Hazor's army, by inviting him to accept the hospitality of her tent: "Turn aside, my lord, turn aside to me, have no fear!" (Judg 4:18). She covered him; she gave him to drink. He trusted her to protect him (Judg 4:20). While Sisera rested, Jael the wife of Heber took a tent peg and a hammer and drove a peg through his head (Judg 4:21).[25] Then she went out to meet Barak who pursued Sisera and said, "Come, and I will show you the man whom you are seeking" (Judg 4:22). And so the text records, "On that day God subdued Jabin the king of Canaan before the people of Israel" (Judg 4:23).

God—not Jael—is credited with subduing the enemy. Only in the poetic account of Deborah's song in the next chapter is Jael praised: "Most blessed of women be Jael, the wife of Heber the Kenite, of tent-dwelling women most blessed" (Judg 5:24).

Personally Jael gained nothing for her act. By her hand YHWH subdued Israel's enemy, not the Kenites'. She violated the law of hospitality for a general who was entitled to seek refuge with her because there were "friendly relations" between Jabin and the Kenites (Judg 4:17).[26] Indeed, her act is "sinister."[27] Yet it is God's purpose for Israel that she accomplished.

---

the Jewish and Christian Traditions [ed. Rosemary Radford Ruether; New York: Simon and Schuster, 1974] 41-88); and Carol L. Meyers, "The Roots of Restriction: Women in Early Israel," 300 (reprint from *BA* 41 [1978] 91-103).

[24] Elsewhere Rahab is remembered well. The genealogy in Matthew memorializes Rahab as part of a company of three heroic women—all of whom it may be said lied for the faith—by identifying her as the mother of Boaz (Matt 1:5), between references to Tamar and Ruth. J. F. Ross notes that according to the rabbinic tradition Rahab, one of the four most beautiful women in the world, was an ancestor of eight male prophets (including Jeremiah) and a female prophet (Huldah); "Rahab," *IDB* 4:6.

[25] J. Alberto Soggin notes that it is still a Bedouin woman's task to put up the tent; *Judges* (OTL; Philadelphia: Westminster, 1981) 67.

[26] To account for Jael's act, F. Charles Fensham in "Did a Treaty between the Israelites and the Kenites Exist?", *BASOR* 175 (1964) 51-54, has argued for the existence of a Kenite-Israelite alliance. "As a result of the treaty between her people, the Kenites, and the Israelites, she felt herself obliged to kill the enemy of the other party of the treaty" (53). The text does not document an alliance with Israel, while it does say there was *šālôm* between Jabin and the Kenites (Judg 4:17).

A clue to what is happening in this text may be found in P. C. Craigie's assessment that the Song of Deborah "is sung not merely to recount events, but to celebrate them and impart to them religious significance" in ways which may be remarkably subtle.[28] He argues that Deborah's role in the war is like that of the Canaanite goddess, Anat, so that "poetically speaking, similar power could be seen in a human Hebrew woman, though that strength was not her own, but was rooted in her commitment to Yahweh."[29] Documenting a similar linkage, J. Glen Taylor has argued that Jael's role in the war is like that of the Canaanite goddess, Athtart (Astarte).[30] Could it be that the poetic glorification of Jael (Judg 5:24) was a subtle glorification of YHWH who controlled the destiny of a foreign woman whose strength was like that of a goddess? In other words, a poetic recognition that YHWH—no earthly motive—caused Jael to act. If so, then this perhaps oldest of biblical texts testifies to God's responsibility for and sanction of a woman's lie. As Deborah prophetically foretold, "YHWH will sell Sisera into the hand of a woman" (Judg 4:9), so it happened. God, the all-powerful divine warrior, accomplished the deliverance of Israel through the act of the foreign woman Jael.[31]

---

[27] So Soggin, who also argues incorrectly, I believe, that Jael, "incapable because of her own weakness of preventing the fugitive general from entering her tent, pretended to accede to his request, only at a later stage to act in accordance with what she considered to be her real duty" (*Judges*, 78). Judg 4:18 claims that Jael came out to meet Sisera. She invited him into her tent.

[28] P. C. Craigie, "Deborah and Anat: A Study of Poetic Imagery (Judges 5)," *ZAW* 90 (1978) 374.

[29] Ibid., 381.

[30] J. Glen Taylor, "The Song of Deborah and Two Canaanite Goddesses," *JSOT* 23 (1982) 99-108.

[31] Barnabas Lindars's assemblage of information about Judges 4-5 in "Deborah's Song: Women in the Old Testament," *BJRL* 65 (1983) 158-75, is very informative. Some of his conclusions, however, do not reflect the nuance of the narrative. Since God is credited with subduing Jabin (Josh 4:23), it seems inadequate to say Jael "acts entirely on her own initiative" (173). While Jael is a model for the story of Judith, and the details of how the Judith story influenced the telling of the Jael story in Pseudo-Philo are fascinating (174), I take issue with Lindars's statement that in later works it is "simply assumed that, if a woman is the heroine, she is bound to owe her success to her beauty and her sex appeal, which puts the strong male opponent off his guard" (174). The enemy may assume this, but some of the women know otherwise. Judith, for example, expressly acknowledges *God* as the one who delivers or destroys the faithful.

2 Samuel 14

The woman of Tekoa, in the guise of a widow, lied to David by telling him of an imaginary tragedy about to befall her.[32] Claiming that her relatives were seeking the death of her only living son because he had murdered his brother, she enlisted David's sympathy and favorable legal judgment. At her insistence, twice David promised protection (2 Sam 14:8, 10). Finally she convinced him to invoke God's protection of her son (2 Sam 14:11). When David had so sworn, the woman indicted him saying, "In giving this decision the king convicts himself, inasmuch as the king does not bring his banished one home again" (2 Sam 14:13).

It had been at Joab's instruction (2 Sam 14:1-3) that the woman had pled "her" case, which was really a case for the preservation of the life of Absalom. When David inquired about Joab's part in the affair, she explained that Joab had told her what to say to "change the course of affairs" in the kingdom (2 Sam 14:19-20). The plan was Joab's, but the action was her own. She had knowingly given false testimony, breaking the prescription of the Decalogue (Exod 20:16; Deut 5:20) in order to charge David himself. As a consequence of her effective lie, the king instructed Joab to bring Absalom back to Jerusalem, though he ruled that Absalom was not to come into his presence.

On account of the Tekoite woman's actions, Joab, Absalom, and David each benefited. Joab knew he had "found favor" in David's sight (2 Sam 14:22); David and Absalom took first steps toward reconciliation. No consequence, positive or negative, is recorded for the woman of Tekoa. She was already known as a "wise woman" at the opening of the episode (2 Sam 14:2).[33] At its close she had proven herself skillful and had gained the king's cooperation. She had influenced the course of personal and political disputes which

---

[32] Uriel Simon, "The Poor Man's Ewe-Lamb: An Example of a Juridical Parable," *Bib* 48 (1967) 207-42, defines this genre as a juridical parable, a "realistic story about a violation of the law, related to someone who had committed a similar offense with the purpose of leading the unsuspecting hearer to pass judgement on himself" (220).

[33] On the societal implications of this function, see Claudia Camp, "The Wise Women of 2 Samuel: A Role Model for Women in Early Israel?", *CBQ* 43 (1981) 14-29.

threatened the fabric of the nation.[34] For others, she had done what was hers to do.[35]

Judith 8-16

Judith, a widow of Israel, lied in order to free her people from fear and to destroy their Assyrian enemy. She alone of all biblical women asked God to make her a good liar: "By the guile of my lips, smite slave with prince and prince with his servant. Break into pieces their high estate by the hand of a female" (Jdt 9:10). During a suspenseful three-day stay in the enemy camp and an evening in the enemy general's tent, she systematically set about deceiving the Assyrians.[36] On the fourth night, she beheaded the drunken general of the enemy forces, Holofernes, with his sword while he slept on his bed (Jdt 13:6-8). Upon her return to her own people, she credited God for destroying their enemies by her hand (Jdt 13:14).

Greatly astonished, the Israelites bowed down and worshiped God (Jdt 13:17). Secondarily, Uzziah, a leader of the people of her town, praised Judith as "blessed by the Most High God above all women on earth" (Jdt 13:18). Her deed was further celebrated by Achior, a foreigner who believed firmly in God on her account and joined the house of Israel the very night of her return to Bethulia (Jdt 14:6-10). In the enemy camp, the terror-stricken eunuch Bagoas shouted, "One Hebrew woman has brought disgrace upon the house of King Nebuchadnezzar! Look, here is Holofernes lying on the ground, and his head is not on him!" (Jdt 14:18). From Jerusalem, Joakim the high priest and the senate came and testified, "You are the exaltation of Jerusalem, you are the great glory of Israel, you are the great pride of our nation! You have done all this singlehanded; you have done great good to Israel, and God is well pleased with it. May the Almighty Lord bless you forever!" (Jdt 15:10).

---

[34] So Brenner, *The Israelite Woman*, 35.

[35] For discussion of the "authority" with which the woman of Tekoa acted, see Camp, "The Wise Women of 2 Samuel," 17-21.

[36] Her works in Jdt 10:11–13:10a are sometimes true in a factual sense (cf. 11:10), sometimes true in the sense of having double meanings (cf. 11:6), and sometimes outright lies (cf. 11:8). For elaboration, see Toni Craven, *Artistry and Faith in the Book of Judith* (SBLDS 70; Chico: Scholars Press, 1983) 94-100.

What her community praised and even her enemy acknowledged, critics have found more troublesome.[37] Wayne Shumaker has "compunctions about her methodology. If she had said only what was misleading instead of what was downright false then my response would have been different. I can grant a heroine in that kind of situation the right to be deceptive but to be false raises other kinds of problems."[38] W. O. E. Oesterley finds certain passages in the story "distinctly revolting."[39] Solomon Zeitlin summarizes: "Many writers condemn Judith. While she was devoted to God and to her people, they say, she was most frivolous, unscrupulous, and a liar; and used feminine guile and seductiveness to achieve her noble end by ignoble means."[40]

Not only did Judith lie in order to destroy all enemies of her community, she also chose to remain a childless widow all her days. For herself, she did not seem to care about upholding the societal convention dictating that she ought to be a child-bearing wife. Though "many desired to marry her" (Jdt 16:22), she simply remained on her estate, more honored and more famous, a widow until her death at one hundred five years of age (Jdt 16:23). Her work, by her own definition, had been to undo all that terrorized her people, their internal fears and their external military foes. At this she succeeded greatly.

Conclusion

Convention breakers all, the women whose stories we have examined each lied to men, inside or outside the family of faith, for the sake of shaping their own and the next generation in ways they judged appropriate.

---

[37] Carey A. Moore suggests that comments about Judith's character and conduct tell as much about the scholars "themselves and their times as about Judith." See his full discussion in *Judith* (AB 40; New York: Doubleday & Company, 1985) 64-66.

[38] Wayne Shumaker, "Minutes of the Colloquy of March 11, 1974," *Protocol Series of Colloquies of the Center for Hermeneutical Studies in Hellenistic and Modern Culture* (ed. W. Wuellner) 11 (1974) 50.

[39] W. O. E. Oesterley, *The Books of the Apocrypha* (New York: Macmillan, 1935) 176.

[40] Morton S. Enslin and Solomon Zeitlin, *The Book of Judith* (Leiden: E. J. Brill, 1972) 14. Zeitlin concludes that, "These accusations against Judith are not justified."

	Status	To whom she lied	On whose behalf
Rebekah	wife	husband	Jacob
Tamar	widow	father-in-law	?self or dead spouse
Exod	midwife	King of Egypt	male Israelites
	wife	King of Egypt	Moses
	daughter	Princess of Egypt	Moses
	princess	King of Egypt	Moses
Rahab	harlot	King of Jericho	Joshua's spies family females/males
Jael	wife	Hazorite General	Israel
Tekoite	"widow"	King of Israel	David, Absalom, Joab
Judith	widow	Assyrian General	Israel

With the exception of Miriam who lied to the princess—a lie which would have been unnecessary had the king of Egypt not ruled that male babies must die—all the other women lied to men, primarily for the sake of men.[41] Their actions unquestionably preserved the societal structures of patriarchy. Esther Fuchs is surely correct that "female deception of men stems from women's subordinate social status and from the fact that patriarchy debars them from direct action."[42] But more needs to be said.

Claudia Camp points out that "indirect action or trickery . . . may be used by any person or group that is out of power at a given moment."[43] In referring to women whose deeds were for the good of the community,

---

[41] Rahab, of course, expressed concern for the protection of the females as well as the males of her family (Josh 2:13). Esther Fuchs, "The Literary Characterization of Mothers and Sexual Politics in the Hebrew Bible," in *Feminist Perspectives on Biblical Scholarship* (ed. Adela Yarbro Collins; SBLBSNA 10; Chico: Scholars Press, 1985) 134, points out that biblical women's roles, which are largely restricted to reproductive and protective functions, never model active maternal interference on behalf of a daughter.

[42] Esther Fuchs, "Who is Hiding the Truth? Deceptive Women and Biblical Androcentrism," in *Feminist Perspectives on Biblical Scholarship*, 144.

[43] Claudia Camp, *Wisdom and the Feminine in the Book of Proverbs* (BLS 11; Sheffield: Almond, 1985) 124. For her references to men who deceive, see 310 n. 43. For an additional listing of stories about male deception, see John H. Otwell, *And Sarah Laughed* (Philadelphia: Westminster, 1977) 108.

Camp says that when the women's actions served the deity's purpose there was a *"disruption* of the established hierarchies of society which inhibit human life and Yahweh's action and the *creation* of a new order of life and freedom for both people and God."[44]

For women as well as for men, this disruption and creation are possible, I submit, because truth is not absolute. Truth is a personal and relational process disclosed in the "doing" of covenant. Deception is justifiable when it is congruent with the active maintenance of the essentials of tradition, namely the individual and corporate faith, hope, and trust that God is with the covenant community, that God sees those things which bind the community, and that God holds out to the community a future of hope.[45]

Dangerous as it may seem, the women in these seven stories were entitled to lie because of the process of tradition-making, not because of the stasis of patriarchy. Socially transmitted behavior patterns shut these women out from the hierarchy of power, but participation in the process of shaping tradition—even in their patriarchal world—allowed them to accomplish remarkable deeds. No standard except the covenant with God was absolute. Quite simply, these women lied because by right of God's created order it was theirs to do.

These stories about women who told effective lies in order to preserve the covenant community are not prescriptive—surely not all are called to lie. They are, however, exemplary stories of radical faithfulness that finds ways of overcoming oppression. These stories model congruence between self-understanding, understanding of God, and action. Though these shocking stories yield no behavioral prescriptions, they do raise difficult questions about proper limits and appropriate boundaries. A partial answer comes from another context. When speaking of the "risk" involved in challenging structure-legitimation, Walter Brueggemann comments, "One never knows, until the bold act is done, whether one has gone too far."[46]

By the example of successful bold lies these women teach that truth is not to be measured against law of societal conventions, but rather against responsible doing of covenant and shaping of tradition. Truth is

---

[44] Camp, *Wisdom*, 124-25.

[45] For elaboration on the "core tradition" and its process of maintenance, see Walter Harrelson, "Life, Faith, and the Emergence of Tradition," in *Tradition and Theology in the Old Testament* (ed. Douglas A. Knight; Philadelphia: Fortress, 1977) 11-30.

[46] Walter Brueggemann, "A Shape for Old Testament Theology, II: Embrace of Pain," *CBQ* 74 (1985) 404.

personal, relational, and revealed in process. As Walter Harrelson has maintained that continuity and change are the hallmarks of tradition which "does not remain fixed; it grows,"[47] so now I suggest that truth is not fixed but grows in a personal and relational process involving choice of direction and movement toward divine-human congruence. For some makers of tradition—like the women whose stories we have examined—it is wholly appropriate to lie for the faith.

---

[47] Harrelson, "Life, Faith, and the Emergence of Tradition," 23.

CLANGING SYMBOLS

JAMES L. CRENSHAW
Duke University

Skillful writers weave a pattern of expectation and consequence, introducing just enough ambiguity to alert readers to the possibility of unexpected surprises. Context, shifts in grammar, slight alterations of vocabulary, and so forth attach unaccustomed meaning to familiar phrases. When expressions lead readers along well-traveled paths of thought and then veer off in an entirely different direction, they produce a collision of anticipation and result. I call this phenomenon clanging symbols, a formulation that itself illustrates the shift in language from an expected "clanging cymbals."[1]

Edwin M. Good's analysis of the initial poem in Eccl 1:2-11 closely approximates the approach I have in mind, although Good did not focus on unexpected consequences.[2] Preferring an analogy from music, he replaced the usual mode of viewing a text—which resembles the way one looks at a painting—with a linear view of the process by which the composition came into being. Good noted that a work "sets up in the reader a tendency to respond, arouses the expectation of a consequent, then inhibits the tendency, and finally brings the (or an) expected

---

[1] The allusion to 1 Cor 13:1 presupposes a familiarity on the part of readers; in the same way, my approach to literary analysis assumes considerable sophistication on the part of authors and interpreters in the ancient world. Literary conventions, formulas, topoi, metaphors, vocabulary, and an intellectual tradition in general weave an intricate tapestry that is capable of multiple designs. The task of modern interpreters is to imagine the several possibilities and to recognize the reasons for the final shape of a given text.

[2] "The Unfilled Sea: Style and Meaning in Ecclesiastes 1:2-11," *Israelite Wisdom: Theological and Literary Essays in Honor of Samuel Terrien* (ed. John Gammie et al.; SPHS; Missoula: Scholars Press, 1978) 59-73.

consequent."[3] An attentive reader distinguishes between the expected consequents and actual ones. In the process, hypothetical meanings yield evident meaning which in turn yields determinate meaning. In Good's view, three stylistic techniques delay the expected consequent: using the interrogative; holding off the key word for some time; and interposing something unexpected. His last point deserves further articulation than the study of Eccl 1:2-11 prompted.

I believe this particular approach illuminates many biblical texts in ways not possible when interpreters used more conventional modes of interpretation.[4] I intend, therefore, to apply my version of this manner of reading the Bible to the sayings of Agur in Prov 30:1-14.[5] The debate over these aphorisms so far has failed to generate anything resembling consensus.[6] In all probability, that disparity in opinions will continue regardless of the approach taken, but the very inability to clarify its meaning invites a different perspective. I shall concentrate on the surprises that punctuate the text, hoping by that means to understand the present form of the brief section attributed to Agur.

The opening word, *dibrê*, offers an ambiguous clue with regard to the realm of discourse into which readers are drawn. By far the dominant use of this superscription occurs in prophecy (Jer 1:1; Amos 1:1; in the singular form, Hos 1:1; Joel 1:1; Mic 1:1; Zeph 1:1). Nevertheless, since this expression also introduces the book of Ecclesiastes (*dibrê qōhelet*), the expectation that a prophetic utterance follows must allow for the remote possibility that sapiential instruction issues forth. When the

---

[3] Good, "The Unfilled Sea," 62.

[4] The recent burst of activity in literary criticism of the Bible continues unabated. Two recent publications bring that research into focus for the general reader: Alex Preminger and Edward L. Greenstein, eds., *The Hebrew Bible in Literary Criticism* (New York: Ungar, 1986); and Robert Alter and Frank Kermode, eds., *The Literary Guide to the Bible* (Cambridge, MA: The Belknap Press of Harvard University, 1987).

[5] In the Septuagint, Prov 30:1-14 was believed to constitute a unity, for it follows the section in Prov 22:17—24:22 in which several sayings from the Egyptian Instruction of Amenemopet appear. The ensuing verses in Hebrew (30:15-33) do not follow immediately in the Septuagint, but are separated from 30:1-14 by 24:23b-33.

[6] For a penetrating study, see the article by my former student, Paul Franklyn, "The Sayings of Agur in Proverbs 30: Piety or Scepticism?" *ZAW* 95 (1983) 238-52. Otto Plöger, *Sprüche Salomos (Proverbia)* (BKAT 17; Neukirchen-Vluyn: Neukirchener Verlag, 1984) 351-62, gives a helpful analysis of the many difficulties in understanding this section.

opening word is prophetic, it is normally governed by a divine appellation, usually the Tetragrammaton, or by a proper name. Appearance of the divine name would therefore resolve the issue, whereas a proper name would not indicate whether the word is prophetic or sapiential.

In this instance the proper name, Agur, appears. Elsewhere it does not occur in known Hebrew literature, although the name does show up in northwest Semitic. Precedent from sapiential literature leads one to look for an acronym, a pen name, or a title.[7] The grammatical form of the name suggests something gathered, unless one drops the initial ʾālep and derives the word from the verb "to sojourn." The passive participle seems to rule out a title (contrast Qoheleth, the one who assembles). In addition, no clue survives that gives weight to the hypothesis that Agur stands for something else. Therefore, we understand it as a name of a foreigner, either prophet or sage.

We expect further identification of Agur, and we are not disappointed. The appositional phrase bin-yāqeh supplies the name of Agur's father, an otherwise unknown Jaqeh. These three consonants have tickled the imagination of one scholar, who thinks they conceal an acronymn, YHWH qādôš hûʾ ("the Lord is holy").[8] Thus understood, Jaqeh designates Israel's God, and Agur stands for the nation as embodied in the sojourner, Jacob. More probably, the reference is to Agur's father.[9] But we still await some information about this unknown Agur, presumably a description of his place of origin or his actual activity. This datum does not follow; instead, we encounter technical vocabulary from prophecy, hammaśśāʾ ("the oracle, burden"). The initial impression that prophetic discourse follows seems to be confirmed at this point, unless we point the word as a gentilic (hammaśśāʾî, "the Massaite") or, less likely, add a prefix in the place of the initial hē, yielding "from Massa." This reading accords with the foreign proper name, Agur, and parallels the geographical designation in Prov 31:1.

---

[7] See my discussion of this issue with regard to the name Qoheleth in Ecclesiastes (OTL; Philadelphia: Westminster, 1987) 32-34.

[8] Patrick W. Skehan, Studies in Israelite Poetry and Wisdom (CBQMS 1; Washington: Catholic Biblical Association, 1971) 42-43.

[9] Bin-yāqeh could be translated "son of piety," that is, the devout one. The pointing of bin is rare regardless of its meaning.

The words *nĕʾum haggeber* ("whisper or prophetic utterance of the man") return to the realm of prophetic discourse, albeit with an astonishing twist. Technical vocabulary for a divine oracle appears as a human possession. One expects *nĕʾum YHWH, nĕʾum YHWH ṣĕbaʾôt,* or something comparable. In no case does one anticipate a human source for an oracle. A more striking juxtaposition of words can scarcely be imagined. They do appear, nevertheless, in two other places (Ps 36:2 is textually uncertain). The first, Num 24:3, resembles Agur's remarks so closely that we suspect conscious interplay (v. 3, *nĕʾum haggeber, bĕnô, bĕʿōr, wayyiśśāʾ mĕšālô*[10]; v. 16, *nĕʾum šōmēaʿ ʾimrê-ʾēl, wĕyōdēaʿ daʿat ʿelyôn*). The other place, 2 Sam 23:1, refers to an oracle of David the son of Jesse (*nĕʾum dāwid ben-yišay ûnĕʾum haggeber*). Both passages supply additional information about the men whose utterance follows, ultimately clarifying the divine origin of the oracles.

The absence of the divine name in connection with a prophetic oracle arouses suspicion of blasphemy, which may find confirmation in the contents itself (*lĕʾîtîʾēl lĕʾîtîʾēl wĕʾukāl*): "There is no god, there is no god, and I am powerless." Or the message is garbled: "To Ithiel, to Ithiel, and Ukal." The first translation requires the assumption that the foreigner speaks his native tongue, Aramaic. Because Hebrew and Aramaic intermingle elsewhere in the Bible, this possibility gains plausibility here. The second translation takes the initial *lāmed* as a sign of dedication; in this case the oracle is dedicated to two persons, the first of whom is mentioned twice. The name Ithiel appears in Neh 11:7, and although Ukal does not, the form is appropriate and therefore does not undercut this supposition. On this reading, Agur's utterance resembles a Delphic oracle, a mysterious garbling of sounds that remain meaningless until interpreted by an expert.

Repetition of the first name renders this second option improbable, whereas the reiteration of a solemn declaration heightens the poignancy and reinforces the soundness of this interpretation. The same phenomenon surfaces in Isa 24:16 (*rāzî-lî rāzî-lî ʾôy lî,* "I languish, I languish! Woe on me!"). Similar rhetoric may lie behind Agur's utterance; if one abandons the assumption of blasphemy, an emended text yields the translation: "I am weary, God, I am weary, God, and exhausted."[11]

---

[10] The Septuagint has Agur lift up his *māšāl* (proverb, analogy). The association of an oracle (*maśśāʾ*) and the verb *nāśāʾ* occurs in Isa 14:4; Mic 2:4; Hab 2:6, each time with *māšāl.*

[11] The resemblance to Jer 20:9 has not escaped detection: "Then I said, 'I shall not remember him nor speak any longer in his name,' but it became in my heart like a raging fire shut up in my bones; and I was weary [from] re-

Along similar lines, but in accord with the supposition that Agur's utterance deviates from pious norms, the text has been read, "I am not God, I am not God, and I lack power."[12] Such articulation of the obvious seems highly bland and unlikely as a theological statement.

The second verse offers a rationale for the assertion, thus ruling out the understanding of the utterance as proper names, unless the particle *kî* is emphatic ("surely").[13] The nature of the rationale, a confession of ignorance, reinforces the emphatic understanding of the particle. Otherwise, one expects Agur to set forth powerful credentials for such expressions of atheism and ennui. This is why many interpreters read Agur's remarks as irony or sarcasm *(kî ba'ar 'ānōkî mē'îš wĕlō'-bînat 'ādām lî*, "For I am stupid beyond human [norms], and I lack ordinary knowledge"). Agur claims that his ignorance removes him from the social realm, linking him with the animal kingdom. Where we expected heavenly wisdom, we must be content with insight from the kingdom of beasts. The sapiential fondness for this image as an indication of ignorance yields another possibility, for at least one psalmist who became aware of brutish reasoning hastened to the holy place and proceeded to purify such thoughts (Ps 73:22, "As for me, I was stupid and ignorant" [*wa'ănî-ba'ar wĕlō' 'ēdā'*], "I was animalistic toward you" [*bĕhēmôt hayîtî 'immāk*). Dare we entertain similar hopes for Agur? No, for he has not finished expressing inadequacy in intellectual circles (*wĕlō'-bînat 'ādām lî*, "nor do I have ordinary human understanding"). The genitive relationship, subjective rather than objective, implies that the understanding extends beyond psychology and human nature to embrace knowledge of all kinds, not just information about humankind. The latter point would require an objective genitive (understanding about people).

The sages often join together several intellectual categories in stereometric fashion,[14] each image conveying a different aspect of the scholarly repertoire. The three favorite terms, *bînâ, ḥokmâ,* and *da'at*

---

straining it, and could not" (*wĕnil'êtî kalkēl wĕlō' 'ûkāl*). Plöger, *Sprüche Salomos (Proverbia)*, 351, translates Prov 30:1b: "Ich habe mich abgemüht, Gott, auf daß ich es fassen könnte." The previous phrase he understands similarly: "der sich um Gott abmühte."

[12] C. C. Torrey, "Proverbs Chapter 30," *JBL* 73 (1954) 95-96.

[13] James Muilenburg, "The Linguistic and Rhetorical Usages of the Particle *kî* in the Old Testament," *HUCA* 32 (1961) 135-60; and Antoon Schoors, "The Particle *kî*," *OTS* 21 (1981) 243-45.

[14] Gerhard von Rad, *Wisdom in Israel* (Nashville: Abingdon, 1972) 13 and 27, uses this language.

occur here in this order. One is tempted to relate the first to anthropology, the second to mythic speculation, and the third to theology. The Septuagint introduces the notion of divine instruction (*theos dedidachen me*, "God has taught me"), in this instance, wisdom. On this reading, the allusion to knowledge of the Holy One (*wĕdaʿat qĕdōšîm*[15] *ʾēdāʿ*) becomes a possession granted Agur, whereas the Hebrew text implies a continuation of the negative, although it is missing ("nor do I have knowledge of the Holy One").

An alternative translation of the Hebrew is syntactically possible, inasmuch as the conjunction can be adversative ("but I do possess knowledge of the Holy One"). Curiously, Agur uses the ambiguous *qĕdōšîm* as an oblique reference to God. The three terms for wisdom, understanding, and knowledge appear together in an instructive proverb (9:10, *tĕḥillat ḥokmâ yirʾat YHWH / wĕdaʿat qĕdōšîm bînâ*, "the fear of the Lord is the beginning of wisdom / and the knowledge of the Holy One is understanding").

The first defense of Agur's radical skepticism restricts itself to the intellectual sphere, even if the words *bînâ*, *ḥokmâ*, and *daʿat* specify distinct cognitive disciplines. The second rationale for his sharp sarcasm derives from a strong awareness of finitude. The vastness of the universe, like the mysteries of knowledge, lies beyond human access. One can neither comprehend the enigmas of human existence nor control the forces of the universe. In both realms we stand helpless before the unknown and the impossible, wisdom's celebrated claim to enable persons to cope notwithstanding. Four questions using the interrogative particle *mî* ("who") employ hymnic language in an effort to widen the chasm between creator and creature.[16]

The four questions probe divine sovereignty, specifically the coronation of the universe's ruler, the taming of violent winds, the restricting of the chaotic waters, and the establishing of earth's limits. The first hymnic snippet (*mî ʿālâ šāmayim wayyēred*, "who has gone up to heaven and assumed dominion?") requires a slight change in vocalization.[17] This reading appears vastly superior, inasmuch as the remain-

---

[15] Although increasing evidence points to polytheism in Israel's popular culture, the parallel with Prov 9:10 makes it probable that Agur refers to a single deity. On polytheistic images, see Bernhard Lang, *Wisdom and the Book of Proverbs* (New York: Pilgrim, 1986).

[16] For a recent analysis of hymns in Job, see Sharon Hels Waddle, "Dubious Praise: The Form and Context of the Participial Hymns in Job 4-14" (Ph.D. Dissertation, Vanderbilt University, 1987).

[17] *wayyāred* for *wayyĕrad*.

ing interrogatives specify three acts by which the deity exercised sovereignty. Mastery of the powerful winds (mî ʾāsap-rûaḥ bĕḥopnāyw)[18] for useful purposes facilitated the victory over recalcitrant flood waters (mî ṣārar-mayim baśśimlâ,) here imagined as clothing Baby Chaos in a diaper, and eventuated in the delimitation of the earth from heaven (mî hēqîm kol-ʾapsê-ʾāreṣ). Mythical images from Enuma elish, mediated through the book of Job, seem to lie behind these questions, however attenuated the symbolism.[19] The divine speeches in the book of Job mock human defiance with such questions designed to crush every delusion of grandeur seething within Job's exalted self-image.

On the basis of similar hymnody in the rest of the Bible one expects a concluding refrain that identifies the one who actually achieved these extraordinary feats. No such conclusion occurs, neither YHWH šĕmô[20] ("The Lord is his name") nor the longer variants (YHWH ṣĕbāʾôt šĕmô, YHWH ʾĕlōhê ṣĕbāʾôt šĕmô). Perhaps in their universalism the sages saw no need for combatting different cultic appearances of idolatry.[21] In Ezekiel's fertile imagination (48:35) the formula YHWH šĕmô produced the majestic shout YHWH šāmmâ ("The Lord will be there") as the supreme blessing in the restored eschatological community. The mood in Prov 30:4 approaches ridicule, not celebration (mah-šĕmô ûmah-šem-bĕnô kî tēdāʿ). The rhetorical question, "What is his name and what is his son's name? Surely you know!," concludes with a stinging putdown derived from Job 38:5. Rendering the final kî tēdāʿ differently ("if you know") changes its meaning only slightly, if at all. The semantic range of bĕnô may extend beyond the actual family to the relationship between a teacher and student.[22] The implication then is that anyone who achieves such extraordinary accomplishments would

---

[18] The Septuagint implies that God catches the wind in the bosom or fold of a garment, a possible meaning of ḥōpen; K. J. Cathcart, "Proverbs 30,4 and Ugaritic ḤPN, 'Garment,'" CBQ 32 (1970) 418-20.

[19] Othmar Keel's various publications have greatly clarified our knowledge of ancient symbols.

[20] I have examined this refrain in great detail in Hymnic Affirmation of Divine Justice (SBLDS 24; Missoula: Scholars Press, 1975).

[21] How different the situation became in later Judaism, particularly in the Wisdom of Solomon. See Maurice Gilbert, La critique des dieux dans le Livre de la Sagesse (Rome: Biblical Institute, 1973).

[22] The Septuagint took that step, rendering children (tois teknois autou) just as it had earlier translated verse 1 by "my son, reverence my words and receive them, and repent."

obviously attract a student entrusted with transmitting the master's insights to later generations.

The fifth verse serves notice that such nonsense contradicts the community's sacred testimony. Private sentiment must submit to collective judgment: kol-ʾimrat ʾĕlôah ṣĕrûpâ / māgēn hûʾ laḥōsîm bô, "Every word of Eloah is reliable; He is a shield for those who trust in him." Scripture bears witness against such blasphemy as Agur expresses it. Here a new speaker takes a sacred scroll and beats Agur over the head with it. Indeed, this advocate of conventional piety may have uttered the kî tēdāʿ in effect ridiculing Agur's ignorance. The scriptural allusions echo the language of Ps 18:31 and 2 Sam 22:31 (cf. Ps 119:140). The minimal differences shift the emphasis from an all-embracing protectorship to a total reliability of divine words and from exclusive allegiance to Israel's deity to the broader terminology for God employed by foreigners in the book of Job. Expectations explode in this instance, possibly as an accommodation to foreign speech. This explanation will not suffice for the use of an image derived from metallurgy (ṣĕrûpâ, "refined") rather than theological categories like ʾĕmûnâ and ʾĕmet ("faithfulness," "reliable").

Have we taken a false path from the very beginning? Does Agur cite dubious speculation to discredit practical atheism?[23] If this is true, an unknown atheist's confession of ignorance evokes hymnic questions and positive testimony from sacred tradition. Three questions introduced by the interrogatives mî and mah combine with an expression of totality, kol, to place the unknown thinker in the dunce's chair. In this view, Agur proceeds to warn the uninformed person in the same way ancient teachers harshly rebuked students: ʾal-tôsēp ʿal-dĕbārāyw / pen-yôkîaḥ bĕkā wĕnikzābtā, "do not add to his words / lest he rebuke you and constitute you a liar." Once again the language echoes similar sentiment in Deut 4:2 and 13:1 (EV, 12:32), where adding to and taking from the divine decree are mentioned. In many other cases which employ a quotation of questionable ideas to introduce a rejection of such forms of reasoning, the polemicist carefully labels the thinkers fools and charlatans. Lacking some such disclaimer, the actual sayings of Agur probably begin in verse one. They end with the fourth verse, after which confessional theology offers a ringing contrast. Two competing claims collide, the personal testimonies of skeptic and religious devotee. The religious individual appears to assume that putative scripture

---

[23] Franklyn, "The Sayings of Agur in Proverbs 30," defends this hypothesis.

validates itself, for no rationale reinforces the assertions that divine utterance and deity will stand the test like refined metal.[24]

Agur's feigned humility conceals the dogmatism residing in his denial of Transcendence, whereas his detractor's narrow-mindedness is fully exposed. In this respect, the two thinkers share a fundamental likeness. Absolute statements of both kinds represent a universalization of private experience which ignores the limitations imposed on human knowledge. Both claims require confirmation from the experience of others. Agur's faulty logic failed to distinguish between penetrable and impenetrable mystery. Confronting the former, he denied the reality of the latter. His critic also did not take sufficient account of mystery, for this believer presumed too much. This overly optimistic removal of the gulf between the phenomenal and the noumenal realms makes a mockery of realists. The resulting babble estranges as certainly as the confusion of language at the mythical tower of Babel.

What happens then? It appears that the pious critic withdraws from conversation with Agur, despairing of fruitful exchange of ideas. At the very least, we expect some defense of the absolute claims concerning divine revelation, particularly in the light of contradictory experience. This expectation seems imperative after Agur's conscious allusions to Job's struggle to make sense of reality when religious conviction about reward and retribution ebbed away under the impact of harsh circumstances. To one whose integrity hung in the balances, assurances by Job's friends that the old verities retained their power sounded hollow.[25] Perhaps the fragility of their argument did not escape Agur's opponent, who dared to soften the punishment for adding to God's words.[26]

---

[24] Literature of dissent in Israel and Mesopotamia cast doubt on assertions of this kind in such a way that traditionalists could no longer assume that divine justice was universally acknowledged.

[25] See the series of articles in the December, 1987, issue of The World and I (Washington: The Washington Times Corporation), 344-97, focusing on the book of Job. They are Stephen Mitchell, "The Book of Job," 346-67; Edwin M. Good, "Stephen Mitchell's Job: A Critique," 368-74; James L. Crenshaw, "The High Cost of Preserving God's Honor," 375-82; Lonnie D. Kliever, "The Two Voices of Job," 383-93; and Lionel Abel, "The Book of Job: Its Place in Literature," 394-97. In addition, William Blake's twenty-one illustrations for the Book of Job have been reproduced in their original order.

[26] The earlier promise entailed life and death; here the emphasis falls on rebuke.

Having given up on Agur, the detractor turns to converse with the one whose existence Agur has denied. The shift from earthly to heavenly audience does not come easily, as we can see from the curious opening words (*šĕttayim šā'altî mē'ittāk*). Normally, the first word implies a numerical saying,[27] either "two things ... yea three" or "one thing ... indeed two." Behind this form of the request may lie Job's plea that the divine enemy do two things so that the afflicted one could present his case before a higher tribunal (13:20). The anticipated number, whether one or two, does not appear in this imitation of Job's speech. Instead, we get a strange intensified petition that seems not to have been thought through carefully, given its cumbersome language (*'al-timna' mimmennî bĕṭerem 'āmût*, "do not withhold them from me before I die"). A proper petition would have emphasized the present moment rather than delaying the gifts until some unforeseen hour of death. This anomaly has prompted one interpreter to connect the petition with a dying Agur.[28]

So far nothing in the request requires the hypothesis of a shift into vertical discourse. One human being could ask another to grant a couple of requests, although we lack any clue about the sociological context. Indeed, the specific requests, which add up to two only by juggling the figures, do not absolutely demand an interpretation that we have entered the realm of prayer. "Empty, lying words keep far from me" (*šāwe' ûdĕbar-kāzāb harḥēq mimmennî*) is, however, the sort of petition one directs to deity. The same is true of the other request, which has two facets and for which a powerful rationale follows: *rē'š wā'ōšer 'al-titten-lî / haṭĕrîpēnî leḥem ḥuqqî* ("give me neither poverty nor riches / tear off [for me] my allotted bread"). Parents, teachers, even kings could evoke such requests.[29] Do the explanations for the particular petitions settle the matter of addressee?

Not really, although they probably narrow the possibilities to parents or teachers, if this is not a prayer.[30] The first reason for

---

[27] Georg Sauer, *Die Sprüche Agurs* (Stuttgart: W. Kohlhammer, 1963), emphasizes the numerical sayings in Proverbs 30 and postulates a Canaanite background.

[28] Franklyn, "The Sayings of Agur in Proverbs 30," 249.

[29] Moshe Greenberg, "On the Refinement of the Conception of Prayer in Hebrew Scripture," *AJSR* 1 (1976) 57-92, especially 59-65.

[30] Defining prayer in the Bible has not been easy, but recent studies have made considerable progress. See especially Greenberg, "On the Refinement of the Conception of Prayer in Hebrew Scripture," and *Biblical Prose Prayer as a Window to the Popular Religion of Ancient Israel* (Berkeley/Los Angeles/

requesting neither extreme, riches or poverty, addresses the dangers accompanying vast wealth: "lest I be full and lie / and say, 'Who is the Lord?'" (pen ʾeśbaʿ wĕkiḥaštî /wĕʾāmartî mî YHWH).[31] The second rationale for the specific petition recognizes the danger arising from hunger: "lest I be destitute and steal / and I sully the name of my God" (ûpen-ʾiwwārēš wĕgānabtî / wĕtāpaśtî šēm ʾĕlōhāy).[32] Surprises abound in this rationale for the two requests. Why does the concept of lying follow the verb for satiety, when one anticipates a reference to godless thought, idolatry, for instance? The Septuagint translator perceived this problem, rendering "who sees me?" for "who is the Lord?" (me horą, which in Hebrew, mî yeḥĕzeh, is not orthographically distant from mî YHWH). In some contexts, the rhetorical question "who sees me?" functioned as an emphatic denial that anyone observed villainy, hence constituted a lie. Another unexpected verb may have the connotation of taking hold of and grasping something precious without recognizing its sanctity.[33] The anticipated allusion to profaning the sacred name does not occur here, despite the surprising personal pronoun ("my God").

On any understanding of this petition, problems remain. Still, the evidence seems to point toward its interpretation as prayer. Why the coolness? One expects a vocative, "O Lord," and direct address instead of indirect reference to "the name of God." Although some biblical prayers uttered by persons who believed themselves in disfavor with the deity lack the vocative,[34] the present context may suggest another explanation for its absence in the unit being discussed. Does the prayer for a comfortable existence at neither end of the social scale conceal a stinging attack on Agur, who represents the sapiential privileged class? The request to be spared blasphemous inanities gains poignancy when juxtaposed alongside Agur's opening declaration. If the prayer lingers on the threshold of discourse between humans and communion

London: University of California, 1983); Jeffrey H. Tigay, "On Some Aspects of Prayer in the Bible," AJSR 1 (1976), 363-79; Ronald E. Clements, In Spirit and in Truth: Insights from Biblical Prayers (Atlanta: John Knox, 1985); and Samuel E. Balentine, "Prayer in the Wilderness Traditions: In Pursuit of Divine Justice," HAR 10 (1986) 53-74.

[31] This negative attitude toward wealth represents a decided shift from the dominant sapiential understandings of rewards that accrued for moral persons.

[32] Prov 6:30 implies that society does not condone theft even if its purpose is to avoid starvation.

[33] William McKane, Proverbs (OTL; Philadelphia: Westminster, 1970) 650, is drawn to an emendation (tāpaštî) yielding "I besmirch."

[34] Greenberg, Biblical Prose Prayer, 23.

with the deity,[35] its coolness and distancing from the flame of devotion make sense. Nevertheless, the speaker is drawn closer to the fire, ultimately uttering profound insight: destitute conditions force persons to adopt criminal behavior, and living in luxury's lap tempts individuals to imagine self-sufficiency. The first response sullies the divine name; the second response blinds one to the possibility of Transcendence.[36]

No "Amen" concludes the prayer. An admonition returns to the other side of the threshold: ʾal-talšēn ʿebed ʾel-ʾădōnāw / pen-yĕqallelkā wĕʾāšāmĕtā ("do not belittle a servant to his master / lest he curse you and do you harm"). If Agur's critic has just slandered him before his heavenly master, one begins to see the utility of this verse as a transition from prayer to human discourse once more. The double meanings of slave and master make the shift possible. This understanding of the verse implies that Agur's integrity has borne fruit, for an unknown individual rushes to his defense and rebukes the defender of traditional spirituality. Astonishingly, Agur's detractor has failed to produce progeny.

The final four verses continue the idea of progeny, each time beginning with the Hebrew word dôr ("generation, group, or class").[37] One expects a particle of existence, yēš, if the series of statements merely observe facts of life without pressing a moral judgment. Because of the earlier negative particles in Agur's opening declaration, contrasting particles at the end would accomplish a fitting closure, especially if doubling also takes place to emphasize a positive viewpoint. The conclusion may not be so encouraging; in that case, something like hôy ("alas, woe to") or tôʿebat YHWH ("an abomination to the Lord") would alert readers to what follows. As the text stands, we have no initial clue about the nature of what follows.

Dôr ʾābîw yĕqallēl / wĕʾet-ʾimmô lōʾ yĕbārēk ("a class of people makes light of its father and does not bless its mother"). The first two words arouse expectations wholly at odds with what comes next. We await

---

[35] Ibid. Greenberg insists that prayer followed the patterns of social discourse; hence, imaginative or fictive prayers in the Bible actually use authentic language of prayer in Israel's daily life.

[36] "It is rather the deepest form of prayer which instead of seeking 'answers to prayer' in the accustomed way, is concerned to discover 'the Answering One'" (Clements, In Spirit and in Truth, 141).

[37] Peter R. Ackroyd, "The Meaning of Hebrew dôr Considered," JSS 13 (1968) 3-10; G. Johannes Botterweck, David Noel Freedman, and J. Lundbom, "dôr," TDOT 3 (1978) 169-81, especially 180 ("a bad generation").

the verb for honoring, obeying, or listening attentively to one's father. Nothing has prepared us for a term of disrespect with reference to the father or for the negative before the verb "bless" associated with mother. Nothing, that is, unless the verse also functions as transition by alluding to the profaning of the heavenly Father's name, a reprehensible act comparable to failure to honor mother and father.

The next verse opens on a promissory note as well (*dôr ṭāhôr*, "a class of people is pure"), but it hastens to disabuse anyone of such optimism (*bĕ'ênāyw*, "in its own estimation" [literally eyes], *ûmiṣṣō'ātô lō' ruḥāṣ*, "and is not cleansed of its filth"). Now that two negative observations have disturbed our thoughts, perhaps we shall encounter offsetting realities. This hope quickly fades (*dôr mâ-rāmû 'ênāyw | wĕ'ap'appāyw yinnāśē'û* "a class, how exalted its eyes [self-importance] and its eyebrows are raised high"). The last verse abandons altogether the initial deception, moving directly into condemnation (*dôr ḥărābôt šinnāyw | ûma'ăkālôt mĕtallĕ'ōtāyw*, "a class, sharp its teeth and knives its grinders"). Or does it? The answer depends on the sequel, which identifies the victims of such vicious mastication (*le'ĕkōl 'ănîyyîm mē'ereṣ | wĕ'ebyônîm mē'ădāmâ*, "to devour the poor of the earth and the needy of the land"). The last word in the Masoretic Text reads *mē'ādām*, which may be a conscious allusion to the earlier ironic comment about ignorance separating one from the human race, although *mē'îš* occurs there along with *'ādām*. What links this list of inveterate sinners to the foregoing discussion? One conceivable answer is that true brutish conduct extends beyond intellectual poverty to embrace villainy of a far more destructive kind, one that deprives the poor of their humanity.[38]

The sayings of Agur and his detractor seem to end at verse 14. They present readers with an assemblage of clanging symbols. Frustrated expectations and surprises confront us again and again. The different genres—prophetic oracle, hymnic affirmation, debate form, prayer, admonition, and list—join together to form a choir in which singers compete with one another rather than strive for harmony. Nevertheless, nobler instincts strain to introduce a melody that persists ever so faintly despite the cacophony. The words of this melody are barely audible: "In God's sight persons who claim to possess knowledge of the Holy One but lack respect for parents, behave hypocritically, think too highly of themselves, and oppress the defenseless are in fact

---

[38] See the illuminating discussion in Gustavo Gutiérrez, *On Job: God Talk and the Suffering of the Innocent* (Maryknoll, NY: Orbis, 1987).

the real atheists of society; for they dissociate justice and the Holy." If this summary accurately characterizes Agur's tune, I for one shall raise my voice in song along with him. I firmly believe a third voice will reinforce our faint melody; the fervent strains of my former teacher, colleague, and friend, Walter Harrelson, will not be silenced.

THE ETHICS OF HUMAN LIFE IN THE HEBREW BIBLE[1]

DOUGLAS A. KNIGHT
Vanderbilt University

Morality in Israel was heavily oriented toward relationships among people, indeed toward the creation of a moral society in which all persons would act in a manner conducive to the well-being of others. Yahwistic theology envisioned God as a just, compassionate, demanding deity, and this provided the model for the people's moral ideals and social contract. To be sure, divergent perceptions of the nature of God—as a force tied intimately to nature, as a violent deity, as a whimsical power—persisted among many of the inhabitants of ancient Palestine and left their mark on both the social structure and the biblical literature. Yet whatever the character of their religious beliefs, the people assumed a relationship between moral standards for the human sphere on the one hand and the nature of God on the other.

While Israelite morality was more geared toward the social, economic, and political sphere than to private benefit (as can be the case in, e.g., a religio-moral system that aims to secure a person's salvation for an after-life), it was founded on a personal morality in which the actions of the individual were of key significance. Yet what precisely constituted the individual, both alone and in relation to others, according to viewpoints prevalent at the time is not a self-evident matter. This question, basic to the analysis of personal morality, is of all the more importance for the modern task of historical ethics because, as can be shown, the ancients' conception of the human being varied markedly

---

[1] This essay was written in Tübingen during my 1987-88 sabbatical leave supported by grants from the National Endowment for the Humanities and from the Vanderbilt University Research Council. To both I wish to express my grateful appreciation.

from our own. For one thing, they would have held little sympathy for the privatism and individualism characterizing much of modern Western thought. For another, they did not—except in some late, apocalyptic circles—subordinate the value of life in this world to an other-worldly, after-life home reachable through satisfying specific religious and moral requirements. For a third, they did not have the benefit of modern biological, psychological, sociological, and other research into the nature of human life and existence, and some of their perceptions can now seem curious, quaint, and even patently wrong. Yet at the same time they envisioned the individual to be integrated in body, mind, and affect, to have an identity inclusive of the larger context of relationships and possessions, to be responsible for all conduct by oneself as well as by others in the group, and to deserve enjoyment of life in this world in consort with others. In order to appreciate their positions on the range of moral issues they faced, it is incumbent on us to understand their ways of thinking about life. To be sure, Israel did not develop an abstract, systematic doctrine of human nature, and in many respects their literary remains divulge more about their conception of the human community than about their understanding of the individual. Yet in stories, laws, proverbs, and songs they repeatedly engaged the nature and meaning of life and associated with it certain moral problems requiring specific forms of conduct and attitude.

The following analysis will, as a part of the study of both personal and social morality in ancient Israel, focus on only one specific question: the nature and value of human life. We should note in advance that two related subjects will necessarily be excluded from the scope of this discussion: first, the general conception of humanity, particularly its purpose, destiny, possibilities, and limitations;[2] and second, specific

---

[2] For more general treatments, most of which attend especially to theological issues, see Hans Walter Wolff, *Anthropology of the Old Testament* (Philadelphia: Fortress, 1974; German original, 1973); Ludwig Köhler, *Hebrew Man* (Nashville: Abingdon, 1956; German original, 1953); Werner Schmidt, "Anthropologische Begriffe im Alten Testament: Anmerkungen zum hebräischen Denken," *EvT* 24 (1964) 374-88; A. R. Johnson, *The Vitality of the Individual in the Thought of Ancient Israel* (Cardiff: University of Wales, 1949); Kurt Galling, *Das Bild vom Menschen in biblischer Sicht* (Mainzer Universitäts-Reden, 3; Mainz: Florian Kupferberg, 1947); Walther Eichrodt, *Man in the Old Testament* (SBT 4; London: SCM, 1951; German original, 1947); H. H. Rowley, *The Faith of Israel: Aspects of Old Testament Thought* (London: SCM, 1956), especially 74-176; Georges Pidoux, *L'homme dans l'Ancien Testament* (Cahiers Théologiques, 32; Neuchâtel/Paris: Delachaux & Niestlé,

aspects bearing on the individual's capacity for moral action and development of moral character.[3] Instead, we will attempt to determine what the Israelites thought human life to be and what implications this had for their morality. While some variation on these issues is evident in the biblical texts, at the same time a remarkable unanimity existed on substantial points. Certainly this evaluation of life was a matter of considerable importance inasmuch as it affected other moral values and choices.

Pervasive Vitality

To identify the Israelite understanding of the nature of life itself is no slight undertaking. The people of antiquity did not make a practice—neither for themselves nor for the benefit of others—of clarifying their perspectives on such a basic matter. Furthermore, the terms employed in their literature frequently bear diverse meanings as one moves from context to context. Yet the indications concerning aspects of this understanding are sufficient for us to draw certain conclusions about their import for the world of morality.

The ancient Israelites included under the category of life a range of aspects and perspectives that would normally not be incorporated within the modern Western understanding. In observing this, however, we must be cautious not to attribute it facilely to the "dynamistic thinking" and "primitive mentality" identified by some early anthropologists, above all Lucien Lévy-Bruhl, in a number of non-Western societies.[4] Not only is our knowledge of Israel too incomplete to allow us

---

1953); and, focusing on other ancient Near Eastern materials, Giovanni Pettinato, *Das altorientalische Menschenbild und die sumerischen und akkadischen Schöpfungsmythen* (Abhandlungen der Heidelberger Akademie der Wissenschaften, Philosophisch-historische Klasse, 1971/1; Heidelberg: Carl Winter Universitätsverlag, 1971).

[3] For a discussion of moral agency according to one portion of the Hebrew Bible, see my "Jeremiah and the Dimensions of the Moral Life," in *The Divine Helmsman: Studies on God's Control of Human Events, Presented to Lou H. Silberman* (ed. James L. Crenshaw and Samuel Sandmel; New York: Ktav, 1980) 87-105.

[4] Lucien Lévy-Bruhl, *Les fonctions mentales dans les sociétés inférieures* (Paris: Félix Alcan, 1910) = *How Natives Think* (London: G. Allen & Unwin, 1926); idem, *La mentalité primitive* (Paris: Félix Alcan, 1922) = *Primitive Mentality* (London: G. Allen & Unwin, 1923); see also G. van der Leeuw, *La structure de la mentalité primitive* (Strasbourg: Imprimerie Alsacienne, 1928).

to profile their way of thinking in much detail, but also it is method-
ologically problematic to reason from contemporary non-industrialized
cultures with "prelogical" thought processes back to putative parallels
in the ancient Near East. Nonetheless, Israel was clearly a prescien-
tific people, and it belongs to the fundamental principles of biblical research that we must always reckon with at least the potential for substantial differences between their perspectives and ours. At the moment
our concern is only their immediate view of life, about which their literary heritage and social customs give more indication than they do
about their formal thought processes more generally.

For the Israelites, life imbued and integrated the entirety of the
body. Negatively, this means that they did not consider the living
human being to be a dichotomy (body/soul) much less a trichotomy
(body/soul/spirit), notions current in later Greek thought[5] and subse-

---

This notion, which long enjoyed notable influence among biblical scholars, has
fallen under heavy criticism by more recent anthropologists and others; see,
e.g., E. E. Evans-Pritchard, *Theories of Primitive Religion* (Oxford: Clarendon,
1965), especially 78-99; idem, *A History of Anthropological Thought* (ed. André
Singer; London/Boston: Faber and Faber, 1981) 119-31; and the various articles
in *Modes of Thought: Essays on Thinking in Western and Non-Western Societies* (ed. Robin Horton and Ruth Finnegan; London: Faber & Faber, 1973). Johannes Pedersen incorporated the theories of Lévy-Bruhl into his work on Israelite psychology and impacted decades of scholarship specifically on this
subject of Israel's view of life and the "soul"; Pedersen, *Israel: Its Life and Culture* (vols. I-II and III-IV; London: Oxford University; Copenhagen: Povl Bran-
ner, 1926 and 1940; Danish original, 1920 and 1934). For criticism of Pedersen,
see especially Gustav Hölscher, "Johannes Pedersen, 'Israel,'" *Theologische
Studien und Kritiken* 108 (1937-38) 234-62; James Barr, *The Semantics of Biblical Language* (London: Oxford University, 1961) passim; J. W. Rogerson, *Anthropology and the Old Testament* (Oxford: Basil Blackwell, 1978) 46-65, 108-9,
117; and J. R. Porter, "Biblical Classics III. Johs. Pedersen: 'Israel,'" *ExpTim* 90
(1978) 36-40.

[5] It is important to note, however, that in pre-Platonic Greek the word *psychē* did not carry this dualistic sense of a personal soul contrasting with the
body. It was generally used either for biological features (breath, throat, life, in
connection with blood) or psychological aspects (sensitivities, feelings, desires,
will, thinking, religious and moral expression, personal identity, soul in an
abstract sense), as well as for the human being altogether. The LXX, in
selecting *psychē* as the usual translation for *nepeš*, was therefore remarkably
closer to the Hebrew notion than has normally been thought. See Nikolaus
Pan. Bratsiotis, "*Nepheš—Psychē*: Ein Beitrag zur Erforschung der Sprache und
der Theologie der Septuaginta," *Volume du Congrès Genève*, VTSup 15 (1966)

quent Jewish and Christian traditions. An individual was perceived as a unity—with multiple parts, to be sure, but each contributing to and sharing in the nature of the whole. In part, this integration found expression through attributing to a given component a variety of intertwining capacities. Thus physical organs and limbs served not only their respective bodily roles but could also represent emotional and intellectual functions: the heart—reason, will, desires, and feelings; the kidneys—conscience, affections; the hand—power; the flesh—frailty; the ear—receptivity.[6] In literature of all types but especially in poetry, these and other organs occurred repeatedly in a manner which pointed to the whole person. What the hand did, or the mouth said, or the heart willed implicated the entirety of the individual, for the internal and external, the tangible and intangible, belonged together as one piece. This understanding undergirded also the Israelite system of moral and legal accountability. The human being was characterized not by a composite of detached organs or divided impulses but by a dynamic solidarity of life.

The most fundamental and most frequently used term in the Hebrew Bible for the individual human being casts considerable light on this understanding as well as on its moral implications: *nepeš*, the word often translated misleadingly as "soul" in versions of the Bible. The 754 occurrences of the noun form display a broad semantic field ranging from "throat," "neck," and "breath" to "life" and "self."[7] Like some of the

---

58-89; and Daniel Lys, "The Israelite Soul According to the LXX," *VT* 16 (1966) 181-228.

[6] Among the best overviews of the metaphorical meanings attached to various parts of the body, comparing Hebrew with Akkadian and Assyrian texts, is still the study by Edouard Dhorme, *L'emploi métaphorique des noms de parties du corps en Hébreu et en Akkadien* (1923; reprinted, Paris: Paul Geuthner, 1963).

[7] For discussion and additional literature, see especially A. Murtonen, *The Living Soul: A Study of the Meaning of the Word næfæš in the Old Testament Hebrew Language* (StudOr 23/1; Helsinki: Suomalaisen Kirjallisuuden Kirjapaino Oy, 1958); Daniel Lys, *Nèphèsh: Histoire de l'âme dans la révélation d'Israël au sein des religions proche-orientales* (EHPR 50; Paris: Presses universitaires de France, 1959); Josef Scharbert, *Fleisch, Geist und Seele im Pentateuch: Ein Beitrag zur Anthropologie der Pentateuchquellen* (SBS 19; 2d ed.; Stuttgart: Katholisches Bibelwerk, 1967), especially helpful in demonstrating differences among Pentateuchal sources; Wolff, *Anthropology*, 10-25; C. Westermann, "*næfæš* Seele," *THWAT* 1:71-96; and H. Seebass, *næpæš*," *TWAT* 5:531-55. These provide more discussion of etymology, the range of meanings, and occurrences in biblical and other ancient Near Eastern texts. Much of this

words for organs, it also could incorporate a plethora of functions that we would tend to separate among physical, mental, and emotional categories—e.g., hunger, intentionality, greed, depression, love.

The use of *nepeš* to designate desires and yearnings can serve as a suitable example of its compelling role in a person's life, particularly its impact on moral decision-making. While the term could refer to simple desires without an explicitly moral overtone (e.g., desire, as opposed to urgent need, for kinds of food—Deut 12:15; 14:26; 1 Sam 2:16; Micah 7:1; for homeland—Jer 22:27; 44:14; for YHWH—Isa 26:8-9; Ps 143:8), it expressed in many other instances a unity of purpose that approached a craving or striving for some object with a determination so consuming as to affect one's moral life. Thus kings sought power and control (1 Sam 23:20; 2 Sam 3:21; 1 Kgs 11:37), the wicked were obsessed with greed and doing evil (Ps 10:3; Prov 21:10; Micah 7:3), an unrestrained appetite (*nepeš*) could yield deleterious results (Prov 23:2; 13:25; Ps 78:18; Qoh 6:7; Deut 23:24 [Hebrew 25]), treacherous persons exhibited a lust for violence (Prov 13:2), and even God could not be diverted from a firm desire to make Job's life miserable (Job 23:13). On the other hand, this powerful yearning could also be appropriate. Hired laborers wanted and needed to receive their wages daily because they were poor (Deut 24:15); and a captive woman made wife had a right, if she was no longer wanted as a wife, to leave freely according to her will (*nepeš*) and not to be sold as a slave (Deut 21:14; Jer 34:16). Somewhat related were the instances in which the *nepeš* expressed not only desires but feelings as well: those of the stranger, which the Israelites should have been able to understand in light of their own sojourn in Egypt (Exod 23:9); and the passions or attitudes of bitterness,[8]

---

is not of direct relevance to the moral issues of human life, which is our primary concern here.

[8] The root *mrr* "to be bitter" appears fifteen times in the Hebrew Bible in conjunction with *nepeš* see Westermann, "*næfæš* Seele," 79-80. While this often conveys a sense of distress not directly related to moral conduct (e.g., 1 Sam 1:10; Isa 38:15; Ezek 27:31), there are three specific usages carrying special significance for moral analysis: In Prov 31:4-7 is a wisdom instruction advising kings not to drink wine because it might impede their beneficence, whereas alcoholic drink should properly be given to the impoverished and distressed (*mārê nāpeš*, v. 6) as an opiate against their misery. Second, for Job (3:20; 7:11; 10:1) the anguish was of such an extent as to make him weary of life. Third, in three instances *mar/mārê nepeš* occurs together with *ʾîš /ʾănāšîm* "person/s" and seems to classify those individuals whose "bitterness," whatever its cause, had made of them angry discontents to be feared by others: the Danites, in Judg

impatience (Num 21:4), distress (Gen 42:21), despair (Ps 44:25 [Hebrew 26]; Lam 3:20), love (Cant 1:7; 3:1-4), hate (2 Sam 5:8 [Qere]), and more. Other body parts such as the heart, the spirit (rûaḥ), and the liver were similarly thought to be seats of the emotions and desires, but in all the texts just cited the word nepeš was the word of choice to designate a person's affective core. The individual was thought to be motivated or even compelled—not externally but by means of a deep urge from within—to act in whatever moral or immoral manner. Not merely incidental, superficial, or easily controllable emotions, such desires and motives were for the Israelites part of an individual's very character or nature, and therefore one could be held legally, morally, and religiously liable for the conduct issuing from these passions. The nepeš constituted this purposive, intentional force within a person and left little grounds for pleading inculpability.

In an even more fundamental sense, nepeš could designate the principle or force of life itself, both in humans as well as in animals.[9] A living being was considered a vibrant entity with the vigor of life pervading all parts. As will be discussed below, the Israelites did not conceive of this vitality as a constant, static, or absolute property, for it could ebb and flow depending on the individual's health and well-being. In fact, it was not a property at all in the sense of something a person possessed; a living being is a nepeš—not has a nepeš.[10] Thus it did not refer to some element in a person—a "soul"—thought to be distinct from all else, such as an immortal essence or identity which would survive

---

18:25; and the warriors gathered around David, in 1 Sam 22:2 and 2 Sam 17:8. In the Proverbs and Job texts and perhaps also in 1 Sam 22:2 the bitterness resulted presumably from mistreatment or misfortune of a socioeconomic nature, while for the other two texts the causes for the anger are not specified. All of these instances, however, describe a type of embittered feeling that could so overcome persons as to render them virtually beyond help, hope, or control. To be sure, the advice in Prov 31:6-7 to anesthetize the poor against their misery might well have been a rhetorical overstatement to make the point that kings needed to tend without lapse to their role as protector of the disadvantaged.

[9] The Akkadian cognate napištu also carried this meaning of life and vitality—but not soul—in addition to a range of usages roughly parallel to Hebrew (CAD, s.v.). Ugaritic npš bore a somewhat comparable flexibility (WUS 1826), although it appears fewer times in the more limited corpus of literature.

[10] Ludwig Köhler, Theologie des Alten Testaments (4th ed.; Tübingen: J. C. B. Mohr [Paul Siebeck], 1966) 129: "Der Mensch ist eine lebende Seele. . . . Die Seele ist des Menschen Wesen, nicht sein Besitz."

death.[11] No such division was possible in their understanding of the unity of a living being. Interestingly, *nepeš* and the other general term *ḥyh* "to live" were used only of humans and animals and never of plants, which Israelites apparently did not consider alive in the same sense;[12] the implications of this for their ecological morality remain to be explored.

Consistent with this notion of unity, *nepeš* occurred frequently to denote the entire person, even functioning in place of a personal pronoun. Consider the following examples of this widespread usage: "so that I [my *nepeš*] may bless you before I die" (Gen 27:4b); "I too could speak as do you, if you [your *nepeš*] were in my [my *nepeš's*] place" (Job 16:4a); "they [their *nepeš*] go into captivity" (Isa 46:2b). In such instances the *nepeš* was clearly not a part but the whole of the individual in question, all of whom was infused by the vital force. It was not a collective term, as was *ʾādām* "humanity"; its focus fell instead on the person qua individual. And unlike *ʾîš* which was restricted to men, *nepeš* included both male and female, hence "a human being." For instance, to refer to an individual many casuistic laws[13] employed the formula *nepeš kî*, "if any person" (e.g., Lev 4:2; 5:1), or *nepeš ʾăšer*, "any person who" (e.g., Lev 5:2; 17:15); the person to be punished for violating the laws was also often called by this word (e.g., Exod 31:14 — "that person [*nepeš*] should be cut off from among one's people"). Consequently, this term of individuation constitutes a key point of entrée to ancient Israel's personal ethics, the study of the moral nature and responsibilities of persons viewed more as individuals than as a collective group.

The Seat of Life

Even with life permeating the entire being, could more be said about where the vital force especially resided? Were any moral im-

---

[11] Westermann ("*næfæš*" 77-82, 84) suggests that certain contemporary meanings attached to the German word "Seele" might correspond approximately to *nepeš* when used for feelings such as depression, distress, happiness, and greed. Cf., however, Seebass, "*næpæš*," 543-45.

[12] G. Gerleman, "*ḥjh* leben," *THWAT* 1:551-53.

[13] Interestingly, however, this was not the case in the older laws of the Covenant Code. There, instead of *nepeš*, the word regularly used to name the person being enjoined is *ʾîš* "a man." The extent to which these laws, as also many other directives and injunctions, intended nonetheless to control the actions of women in ancient Israel requires more attention than can be included here.

plications associated with this? While modern science tests for human life by clinically examining the heart or the brain or indeed the molecular level, for the Israelites the breath and the blood served primarily as the seat of life.

The original concrete meaning of *nepeš* was probably "throat" or "neck," and very early if not even from the outset *nepeš* must also have designated the breath which goes through this passageway. At points the biblical literature employs this term to refer to life-sustaining breath; in other instances the more specialized word *nĕšāmâ* occurs. In the Yahwistic creation account, the form crafted out of dirt became a "living being" (*nepeš ḥayyâ*) only after YHWH infused into it "the breath of life" (*nišmat ḥayyîm*) (Gen 2:7; cf. also 7:22; Isa 57:16). Since respiration is common to humans and animals alike, Hebrew could use the phrase "all that breathe" as an idiom to embrace all living creatures (e.g., Deut 20:16; Josh 10:40; 11:11,14; perhaps Ps 150:6 also carries the sense of all created beings). Elijah's miracle of bringing the *nepeš* back into the widow's son and thus reviving him probably referred to the breath (1 Kgs 17:21-22). The reverse of this—depriving someone of breath and thus of life—was the culminating item in Job's asseveration of innocence:

> If I have eaten [the land's] produce without payment
> and caused the *nepeš* to go out of its owners,
> let thornbushes grow instead of wheat
> and rye-grass instead of barley. (Job 31:39-40a)

According to the Hebrew notion, as we will discuss further below, the vitality of a person was a relative matter, such that a person's *nepeš* could be diminished without resulting in death, and this could be expressed as breathing out, sighing, or exhaling the life force: the gasp of the bereaved mother (Jer 15:9) or the loss of hope by the wicked (Job 11:20); perhaps even Job 31:39, just interpreted in terms of the death of the landowners, is to be understood more in this sense of suffering affliction. That this breath (*nĕšāmâ*), and with it life itself, was believed to have stemmed from God (Job 33:4; 34:14) conveyed the sense of its essential character, and thereby also its priority position for morality as a place where life was especially concentrated.

An alternative—and not necessarily contradictory—answer to the question of the locus of life in the human body is mentioned at several other points in the Hebrew Bible. According to this view, blood was identified with the vital power and was therefore to be revered in moral and religious practices.[14] The tie between *nepeš* and blood (*dām*) existed for all living creatures, human and animal alike (although never mentioned for fish), and in fact represented one of the primary points of connection among them—and of their difference from the world of flora. Concerning animals, the Hebrew Bible forbade the people to consume blood or meat with blood in it (Gen 9:4; Lev 7:26-27; 17:10-14; 19:26a MT; Deut 12:16, 23-24; 15:23; 1 Sam 14:32-34). The reason was provided explicitly in the motive clause: "for the *nepeš* of all flesh is its blood" (Lev 17:14bα),[15] or again "for the blood is the *nepeš*" (Deut 12:23). It is impossible to reconstruct the explicit origins for blood taboos, which in fact were widespread in the ancient Near East and beyond; the religious motivations (redemption and sacrifice) evident in especially Leviticus 17 represent theological developments of the custom.

Concerning humans, on the other hand, blood required treatment of a quite different sort. Human blood—in direct contrast to animal blood (Deut 12:16, 24)—must not be spilled on the ground, i.e., shed in an act of killing. This, as also the prohibition against eating flesh with blood in it, was one of the Noachide laws, emphasized by later Jewish interpreters to be applicable to all of humanity, not just to the people of Israel.

> I will surely requite your own blood. I will exact it from every beast,
> and from every human being I will exact the life of a person.
>   Whoever sheds human blood,
>   by a human shall that person's blood be shed.
>   For in the image of God
>   did God make humans. (Gen 9:5-6)

---

[14] See, in addition to publications cited in notes 2 and 6 above, J. Bergman and B. Kedar-Kopfstein, *"dām," TWAT* 2:248-66 = *TDOT* 3:234-50; and G. Gerleman, *"dām* Blut," *THWAT* 1:448-51.

[15] The first phrase in the same verse (Lev 17:14aα) is identical except for reading *dāmô bĕnapšô hû*ʾ in place of *dāmô hîʾ* [Ketib with *wāw*]. This first sentence would then be: "For the *nepeš* of all flesh is its blood; it [masc.: the blood] is its *nepeš*" (reading with *bêt*-essentiae, rather than "the blood is in its *nepeš*"). While this phrase, just as the whole verse, is repetitive, the tradition was intent on drawing an identity between blood and *nepeš*. The LXX and Syriac (cf. Vulgate.."in sanguine") omitted *bĕnapšô* in order to simplify the text. Similarly, 17:11aα should probably also read with *bêt*-essentiae (and LXX): "For the *nepeš* of the flesh is its blood."

On the juridical principle of equal retribution, the *lex talionis* pre-scribed death for anyone guilty of taking another's life (Exod 21:23; Lev 24:17-21; Deut 19:21); unlike these other statements of the law, only Gen 9:5-6 referred to blood in expressing this life-for-life punishment. Notably, the talion of blood applied to animals as well as humans: an animal guilty of killing a person was to be slain (Gen 9:5; Exod 21:28-32), while anyone who caused the death of another's animal had to pay restitution (Lev 24:18,21). A human life was of considerably more worth than an animal's, but taking the life of either was treated as a tort requiring commensuration. The practice of blood-vengeance or blood-feuds, common throughout the ancient Near East,[16] reflected this notion that accounts could be settled only by exacting payment in kind. Indeed, innocent blood shed would itself, in their thinking, bring about its disastrous effect on the guilty.[17] In cases of intentional homicide, the court could deliver the murderer over to the avenger of blood (*gōʾēl haddām*, literally "the redeemer of the blood") for retaliation (Num 35:16-21; Deut 19:11-12). Deuteronomic law included a case especially helpful in demonstrating this importance of expiating shed blood: If a murder occurred in the open field and the slayer could not be found, then the elders and judges were to measure the distances to the nearby cities to ascertain which was the closest, and that city was then obliged to carry out a ritual killing of a heifer in order to "remove the innocent blood from your midst" (Deut 21:1-9).[18] As we will note later, the issue in all of this was not the taking of human life per se, for killing in re-sponse to acknowledged capital offenses as also slaying enemies in

---

[16] See, e.g., Godfrey Rolles Driver and John C. Miles, *The Assyrian Laws* (Oxford: Clarendon, 1935; reprinted, Aalen: Scientia, 1975) 33-36, 344-45; idem, *The Babylonian Laws* (2 vols.; Oxford: Clarendon, 1952 and 1955) 1:314-17, 497-98.

[17] Klaus Koch, "Der Spruch 'Sein Blut bleibe auf seinem Haupt' und die israelitische Auffassung vom vergossenen Blut" (1962), *Um das Prinzip der Vergeltung in Religion and Recht des Alten Testaments* (ed. Klaus Koch; Wege der Forschung, 125; Darmstadt: Wissenschaftliche Buchgesellschaft, 1972) 432-56.

[18] In the Ugaritic Legend of Aqhat (19.151-69) a similar principle of communal responsibility for murder accounted for Daniel's cursing the three towns nearest the place where his son Aqhat was killed. See also 2 Sam 1:21, David's malediction against Mt. Gilboa where Saul and Jonathan fell in battle against the Philistines. For other ancient Near Eastern examples, consult Driver and Miles, *Babylonian Laws*, 1:110-11.

battle[19] was condoned. But with these exceptions, human blood, as a seat of life, could be expected to "cry out" for vindication if it was deliberately shed, as did Abel's when spilled by his brother Cain (Gen 4:10-11). This last example, incidentally, demonstrates yet another point of difference from modern usage, in which blood serves as an image of kinship relations; for Israel blood denoted not ancestry[20] but life, and on that basis Cain's crime was in itself heinous, yet also more pointedly problematic because it was his own brother's life he took.[21]

The significance attached to blood might well have been due to a mystery surrounding its very nature or the weakening effect resulting from substantial loss of it. Since it was associated with the vigor of life, it could take on a dangerous aspect as well. Especially threatening religiously was menstrual blood, considered by priestly law as a pollutant which contaminated both the woman and any man or object coming in contact with her during her menstruation and for seven days thereafter (Lev 15:19-24; 18:19; cf. also Gen 31:35). The uncleanness

---

[19] According to the Chronicler, however, David's considerable bloodshed in war constituted the reason for his not being permitted by God to build the temple (1 Chr 22:8; 28:3). This later theological interpretation, offered by the Chronicler to account for why the great temple was not raised by his idealized figure of David, ignored the belief that David's wars were sanctioned by God. Its basis was apparently 1 Kgs 5:3 [Hebrew 5:17], according to which the battles kept him from temple construction only in the sense that they did not leave him enough peace time to accomplish it. The heavily Deuteronomistic passage in 2 Samuel 7 (see also 1 Kgs 8:17-19), on the other hand, ascribed the decision to God's will, not to David's career. It is also possible that the Chronicler drew inventively on the tradition in which Shimei cursed David as a "man of blood" (2 Sam 16:5-13) and was pardoned by David (19:16-23), who later on his death bed nonetheless instructed Solomon to seek vengeance for him (2 Kgs 2:8-9, probably Deuteronomistic).

[20] In Akkadian, however, "blood" could designate kinship relationships; *CAD* s.v. *damu*. In Hebrew *bāśār* "flesh" (e.g., Gen 37:27; Lev 25:49) or "my bone and my flesh" (e.g., Gen 29:14) expressed this kinship; see Dhorme, *L'emploi métaphorique*, 9-11; and Wolff, *Anthropology*, 29.

[21] Drawing on ethnographic evidence from African kinship groups, Isaac Schapera argues that this as well as other instances of fratricide in the Hebrew Bible posed a direct conflict for Israelite values and customs since the family members could not very well both seek vengeance on and at the same time give protection to a murderer who was their kin; consequently, expulsion from the group would be a compromise solution. See Isaac Schapera, "The Sin of Cain" (1955), in *Anthropological Approaches to the Old Testament* (ed. Bernhard Lang; IRT 8; Philadelphia: Fortress; London: SPCK, 1985) 26-42.

associated with this extended beyond temporary exclusion from the cult; a man and woman who had sexual relations during her menstrual period were to be "cut off from the people," which apparently meant either banishment or actual punishment with death (Lev 20:18). Negative attitudes involving risks from menstruation are widely known among cultures, although not all primitive peoples have regarded menstrual blood as lethal.[22] Any number of factors might have played a role in Israel's customs: apprehension over bodily emissions of any kind (note that Leviticus laws also specified that discharge from infection, seminal emission, and child birth caused uncleanness), misogyny within the patriarchal society, fear or fascination over the women's role in childbirth, or reaction against foreign cultic practices. At one level, these priestly laws betray a distinctly ominous valence, indicative of the anti-female bias which found expression in so many of the Israelite social and religious restrictions. Yet beyond this may be another level as well: In Hebrew the plural form of certain nouns could designate the unnatural condition of natural products;[23] hence, blood outside the body, no longer coursing through a living being, was typically rendered in the plural. While this usually referred to blood shed in killing, in Lev 20:18 it was menstruation[24] and in Lev 12:4, 5, and 7 post partum bleeding. The ancient people understood the biological processes of reproduction as little as they did the actual physiology of life, and for them a woman's bleeding—though normal enough to be called "the way of women" (derek nāšîm, Gen 31:35)—obviously counted as a precarious phenomenon. In this as in a slaying, the blood possessed powers capable of infecting others in the community.

The theological basis for such high value placed on the breath and blood, symbols for life itself, was YHWH's immediate association

---

[22] For a recent survey see Erich Püschel, *Die Menstruation und ihre Tabus: Ethnologie und kulturelle Bedeutung: Eine ethnomedizin-geschichtliche Übersicht* (Stuttgart/New York: Schattauer, 1988).

[23] For example, the word for tree (*ʿēṣ*) occurred usually in the plural when it designated pieces of wood, i.e., a tree hewn for fire or building and thus no longer in its natural, living state. See Gesenius § 124 m for further examples.

[24] The singular of *dām* was used in Lev 15:19 for menstrual bleeding and in 15:25 for bleeding at other times. This chapter contains laws dealing with types of discharge (*zôb*) from the genitals of either man or woman, and the singular *dām* occurs in both instances as a genitive identifying the type of issue. The purpose of the priestly laws in Leviticus 11-15 was to enumerate the causes of uncleanness and to specify rituals for purification.

with both. The Yahwist described the first creation as a breathing of life into the human being (Gen 2:7), and the sage confessed:

> The spirit (*rûaḥ*) of God has made me,
>   and the breath (*nišmâ*) of Shaddai has brought me to life.
>   (Job 33:4)

Similarly, shed blood was interpreted as an assault on "the image of God" (Gen 9:6, probably a later priestly addition to the law preceding), and this life fluid figured centrally in sacrificial and juridical practices according to Pentateuchal law. Of special moral concern was "the blood of the innocent" (Deut 27:25; 1 Sam 19:5; Jer 7:6; Pss 94:21; 106:38; Prov 6:17) spilled through violence and producing blood guilt. YHWH, according to Isa 1:15, finds it abhorrent to look down on worshipers who in praying betray their blood-besmirched hands. Such beliefs gave expression to the high value placed on life in this world and emphasized that it could not be destroyed or diminished with impunity.

Vital Needs and the Diminishment of Life

What is essential to maintain life? Privation, suffering, and early death were no strangers to the Israelites. For all their affirmation of life in this world, they displayed a realism about the risks and fragility of existence. Times of prosperity could raise the expectations of those powerful enough to secure comfort and abundance, but the vast majority of the population was not so fortunate as to escape the daily struggle to survive. For the most part, life was shared with relatives and friends, and together people sought to meet their common needs, especially in the face of the all-too-common exploitation, taxation, and war. Close relationships with others surely made possible the happiness and well-being (*šālôm*) associated with the full life.

The Hebrew Bible does not contain much explicit discussion of vital human needs as such, at least not in a continuous discourse. Primarily in comments dispersed throughout the biblical literature, above all in contexts where a person's very existence was threatened, the Israelites conveyed some sense of what was needed to support life. Beyond such statements there is no listing of fundamentals, such as food, clothing, and shelter, nor of other significant ingredients which we would associate with the quality of life. Perhaps this was due to the fact that such necessities were self-evident; certainly their unitary view of life did not encourage their making a distinction between essentials for sheer survival and options for enrichment. Life was of one fabric, ideally whole and attractive.

A very important aspect of their view of life, which may seem at first quite foreign yet perhaps also understandable to us, figured prominently in their identification of basic needs. For Israel, a person's vitality counted not as an absolute but a relative characteristic, capable of being diminished in degree by sickness, deprivation, emotional distress, and finally death.[25] As if there were a continuum stretching from full life on the one end to death on the other, a person's *nepeš* could seemingly take position at any point along this scale. The Israelites, of course, did not use a quantified image such as this, yet a good number of their expressions would suggest that full life and final death constituted two poles between which there could be distinct fluctuation. Vital needs, therefore, included also those ingredients that contributed to a full life, not simply to mere animation of the body.

As described above, the *nepeš*, through its concrete association with "throat" and "neck," could carry the meaning of "breath" or "hunger." Regarding the former, the fundamental importance of respiration was so obvious to the people that they viewed breath itself to be one of the seats of life. Their notion of a nuanced vitality, however, introduced a further dimension as well. The breath of life was thought to be capable of diminishment through weariness or stress, and this perhaps accounted for the recognition that everyone—the free population, slaves, aliens, and animals alike—needed a weekly day for rest and refreshing. The ancient humanitarian law in Exod 23:12 used the verbal form (*Niphʿal*) of *nepeš*, connoting "taking a breath" or "catching one's breath" (see also 2 Sam 16:14), to urge this weekly pause for all living beings to reinvigorate themselves.[26] This, just as the fallow year law for the land, counted not as a luxury but as a requisite for the full life.

Hunger and thirst were likewise identified with the *nepeš*, and not only as an essential for life itself to continue. When the supply of food and drink did not suffice, the *nepeš* could be said to "wither" (Num

---

[25] For further discussion and additional texts beyond the examples offered here, see Johnson, *Vitality*, 13-26; and Wolff, *Anthropology*, 36-37, 143-48.

[26] This motivation for a weekly rest contrasted with the later sabbath ordinances, which identified explicitly religious goals: to model on God's creation day of rest (Gen 2:3 and Exod 20:11); or to signify the covenant relationship with God (Exod 31:13-17; *npš* as a verb in the sense of refreshing occurs only here in v. 17 among these more cultic ordinances); or to commemorate the exodus (Deut 5:15). However, even with these other considerations, the people's rest remained a purpose as well.

11:6), "faint" (Ps 107:5), be "weary" (Prov 25:25) or "empty" (Isa 29:8), or "drain away" (Lam 2:12). This represented a debilitated state—less than full vitality yet not to the point of death. Access to the necessary nourishment could allow the *nepeš* to revive or, in the Hebrew idiom, to "return" (*šûb*).

> All her people groan
>   while searching for bread;
> they give their treasures (Qere) for food
>   in order to revive their *nepeš.* (Lam 1:11)

The need for food spurred the laborer to work (Prov 16:26; 19:15) and preoccupied the dreams of the destitute (Isa 29:8). Animals also have need of food and other basic comforts, and one must show proper concern (*ydᶜ*) for their *nepeš* (Prov 12:10). It was accordingly imperative to satisfy these essentials for all living beings and reprehensible to refuse such help:

> For the disgraceful brute speaks foolishly,
>   and his mind works wickedly—
> to practice godlessness,
>   to utter perversion concerning YHWH,
> to leave unfed the *nepeš* of the hungry
>   and to deprive the thirsty of drink. (Isa 32:6)

Nourishment, just as breath, was an obvious sine qua non for the very life of every individual, and no one must be blocked from such minima by the economic or social practices of others. While YHWH could meet the elemental needs (Ps 107:9; Prov 10:3), it was the responsibility of the community to ensure that no one suffered a lack of these essential means for ongoing life.

Sickness and injury, though normally not expressed in terms of the *nepeš*, constituted a similar sapping of a person's vitality. The word commonly used to describe illness, *ḥlh*, connoted such a weakening. Recovery could be described with the verb *ḥyh* "to live," referring not to a static condition but a progressive process, "to come back to life"—from sickness (Num 21:8-9; Josh 5:8; 2 Kgs 1:2; 8:8-14; 20:7), from severe thirst (Judg 15:19), as also from death (1 Kgs 17:22; 2 Kgs 13:21; Ezekiel 37 passim; Job 14:14). Uncleanness also rendered a person unfit to participate in normal communal activities, especially cultic, until the prescribed waiting periods and purifying rituals had been fulfilled.

Emotional states of distress, bitterness, despair, and the like had effects comparable to physical decline: the *nepeš* could "languish" (because of dread, Deut 28:65), "pine away" (because of terror and sickness, Lev 26:16), "melt" (with failing courage, Ps 107:26), or "pour itself out" (due to terror and affliction, Job 30:16); the Israelites in Egyptian bondage were said to have had "shortness of spirit," i.e., a broken spirit (*qōṣer rûaḥ*, Exod 6:9). For life to be replenished, someone must remove the causes of such depletion ("He will become for you a restorer of *nepeš*," Ruth 4:15; "far away from me is a comforter, someone to restore my *nepeš*," Lam 1:16).

There are other references to basic needs beyond these. For instance, two which reveal special sensitivity for the poor occurred in the course of regulating credit practices. According to Deut 24:6 lenders were forbidden to take the household mill or the upper millstone as collateral for a loan since that "would be taking a *nepeš* as security" inasmuch as the grinding of grain was so basic to the everyday survival of the family. Similarly, a poor person's cloak should not be held by the creditor overnight since it might be the only means for warmth (Exod 22:26-27; Deut 24:12-13; cf. Amos 2:8).

In all of these instances we can see at work an understandable notion that, in order to be fully alive, an individual needs sustenance, health, and emotional stability. Anything short of these would be enervating and devitalizing. So viewed, the nature of human life carried with it moral claims on those elements which contributed to well-being. For anyone to deprive others of the basics necessary for a happy existence constituted immoral conduct. When the cause for distress seemed to lie outside human control, complaint could be brought against God. Life in this world was too precious to relinquish and too promising to accept anything less than the ideal.

The Worth of Life

In the narrative prologue which sets the scene for testing the limits of Job's faith and endurance, the Adversary responds to YHWH with cynical realism: "One would give all one's possessions to save one's own life (*nepeš*) (2:4). After YHWH permits everything but life itself to be taken away, Job displays first acquiescence in the narrative framework but then, in the dialogues that comprise the bulk of the book, heated protest and even a preference to die. The extraordinary poem with which the first round of dialogues concludes (14:1-22) constitutes a classic description of the transitory, confined, solitary, and hopeless life which humans are compelled to endure. It is a confession of frustration, an accusation of injustice. Even life itself under the terms given to him can offer no solace.

For Job as for the virtual entirety of the Hebrew Bible, life was a this-worldly phenomenon. Until the eventual rise of apocalyptic thought in early Judaism and primitive Christianity, Israelites did not believe in an after-life or resurrection and could not thereby mitigate their sufferings and fears in the face of death.[27] Life was to be experienced on this earth and in this age alone, and for that reason it became especially urgent for each individual to live as long and comfortably as possible. If accounts could not be settled here, if undeserved suffering prevailed, if the wicked thrived while the good anguished, Job and all those not too pious or naïve to face the world candidly knew that they had been deprived of the only happiness they would be able to enjoy. Life itself ranked as one of the greatest of all values for the ancient Israelites, and preserving and enhancing it comprised a moral—both personal and social—imperative of the first order.

This central importance found its theological warrant in the picture of YHWH as the giver of life (Deut 30:19; Job 33:4), the fountain of life (Ps 36:9 [Hebrew 10]) and of living waters (Jer 2:13; 17:13), the preserver of life (Ps 64:1 [Hebrew 2]), to whom the troubled worshiper could appeal for deliverance.[28] While "the living God" was invoked in oaths and in polemics, the Hebrew literature portrayed life not as an abstract attribute of God but primarily as a property conveyed by YHWH to humanity and animals;[29] this emphasized again the this-worldly character of life. Life, though from God, was not considered holy by orthodox Yahwism, at least not in the fashion in which neighboring

---

[27] Christoph Barth, *Diesseits und Jenseits im Glauben des späten Israel* (SBS 72; Stuttgart: KBW, 1974), describes the development of the other-worldly orientation during the period from the Maccabees to Bar Kochba and indicates that traditio-historical ties extend back into the Israelite period. He also argues that a this-world/other-world model is of modern origin and presents some difficulties when imposed on ancient ways of thinking.

[28] Christoph Barth, *Die Errettung vom Tode in den individuellen Klage- und Dankliedern des Alten Testamentes* (Zollikon: Evangelischer Verlag, 1947); and Erhard S. Gerstenberger, *Der bittende Mensch* (Neukirchen-Vluyn: Neukirchener Verlag, 1980).

[29] Gerleman, "*ḥjh* leben," 554-55. In this respect the belief preserved in the Hebrew Bible varied considerably from those of others in the ancient Near East, where gods were often described as being alive, even as being the deification or hypostatization of life powers; Barth, *Errettung*, 36-44.

cultures deified the life force. Yet its divine authorship legitimated its high valuation as well as all appropriate efforts by the people, both individually and collectively, to keep alive, especially through direct petition to God. Thus Hezekiah, sick to the point of death, pled with YHWH to heal him and then in the thanksgiving psalm ascribed to him praised God for granting him fifteen more years of life (Isaiah 38; 2 Kgs 20:1-11). Or again, employing an intriguing image occurring thus only once in the Hebrew Bible, Abigail wished for David that his "nepeš be bound up in the bundle of the living (ṣĕrôr haḥayyîm)" (1 Sam 25:29). Presumably this meant that God was to preserve him carefully together with other living beings, just as one would keep silver pieces (Gen 42:35; Hag 1:6; Prov 7:20) or myrrh (Cant 1:13) in a pouch.[30] A more common image, probably later, was that of a book in which were recorded the names of those whom God designated for safe-keeping (Exod 32:32; Isa 4:3; Mal 3:16; Ps 69:28 [Hebrew 29]; Dan 12:1).

What did life in this world signify? As indicated above, at the minimum it meant that the seat of physical life, identified variously as the breath and the blood, must be performing properly within the body. More than that, it connoted a life undiminished by sickness, injury, handicap, oppression, distress, hunger, thirst, or impurity. By no means did it include a notion of life after death, a shade-like existence in She'ol, lent a somewhat congenial valence when interpreted as joining one's ancestors (frequently in the ancestral stories and elsewhere in the historical literature) but usually feared and resisted as the termination of life among one's present family and community.[31]

Yet the mere continuation of physical life was not sufficient to satisfy the longing for this world. Job's death wish (Job 3) showed forcefully that he sought more than sheer survival. For the Israelites life was to be pregnant, consisting of a wide range of pleasures and relationships: children, marriage and sex, relatives, tribe and nation, friend-

---

[30] Otto Eissfeldt, *Der Beutel der Lebendigen: Alttestamentliche Erzählungs- und Dichtungsmotive im Lichte neuer Nuzi-Texte* (Berichte über die Verhandlungen der Sächsischen Akademie der Wissenschaften zu Leipzig, Philologisch-historische Klasse, 105/6; Berlin: Akademie-Verlag, 1960).

[31] For further discussion, see especially Nicholas J. Tromp, M.S.C., *Primitive Conceptions of Death and the Nether World in the Old Testament* (BibOr 21; Rome: Pontifical Biblical Institute, 1969); Lou H. Silberman, "Death in the Hebrew Bible and Apocalyptic Literature," in *Perspectives on Death* (ed. Liston O. Mills; Nashville: Abingdon, 1969) 13-32; Lloyd R. Bailey, Sr., *Biblical Perspectives on Death* (OBT 5; Philadelphia: Fortress, 1979); and Otto Kaiser and Eduard Lohse, *Death and Life* (Nashville: Abingdon, 1981) 11-91.

ships, peace, property, possessions, work, strength, reputation, beauty, wisdom, nature. The confluence of these comprised the state of well-being, *šālôm*, which should characterize the ideal life in this world. It is a catalog of the other values that found expression in Israel's morality, and all were connected in some way with YHWH and the divine will for humanity.[32] The world was thereby affirmed as the proper arena for life; the priestly account of creation (Gen 1:1–2:4a), in which each new product of God's activity was adjudged "good," served as a paradigmatic evaluation.[33] Order and structure were posited by both orthodox and popular circles—paralleled by his friends and Job himself—although the evil done by humans as mythically portrayed in Genesis 3 and the repeated afflictions introduced by nature and circumstance posed problems threatening to subvert this belief. The Israelites longed for *šālôm*, even if they might seldom have experienced it because of fragility of health, oppression by the strong, and hostilities with neighboring peoples.

Some expressions for longevity reflect this desire for a lengthy life of peace and comfort. Of Abraham (Gen 15:15, JE; and 25:8, P), Gideon (Judg 8:32), and David (1 Chr 29:28) it was said that they reached "a good old age" (*śêbâ ṭôbâ*). Alternatively, a person at death could be described as being "satisfied" or "filled" (*śb'*), as in the phrase "old and full of days" (literally, "sated with days"): Abraham (Gen 25:8), Isaac (Gen 35:29), David (1 Chr 23:1; 29:28), the chief priest Jehoiada (2 Chr 24:15), and Job (Job 42:17).[34] Such was the ideal, and the tragedy was early death. The Hebrew Bible normally reports the age at which a prominent or legendary individual died, coupling this often with an evaluation of that person's life. A correspondence should exist between length of life and moral, religious rectitude. Symbolically this found expression in Genesis with age decreasing as evil and sin in the world increased: individuals often living many centuries until the ancestral

---

[32] Lorenz Dürr, "Die Wertung des Lebens im Alten Testament und im antiken Orient," *Verzeichnis der Vorlesungen an der Staatl. Akademie zu Braunsberg im Winter 1926/27* (Kirchhain N.-L.: Buchdruckerei für fremde Sprachen Max Schmersow, 1926) 1-43.

[33] See my "Cosmogony and Order in the Hebrew Tradition," in *Cosmogony and Ethical Order: New Studies in Comparative Ethics* (ed. Robin W. Lovin and Frank E. Reynolds; Chicago: University of Chicago, 1985), especially 144-45.

[34] Job's complaint in 14:1 represented a direct reversal of this idiom: "A person born of woman is short on days and full of turmoil" (*qĕṣar yāmîm ûśĕba'-rôgez*).

and Mosaic period, when ages approximated the life span of 120 years set by YHWH in the time of the Nephilim (Gen 6:3). After Moses the only ones reputed to have lived extraordinarily long were Joshua (110 years, Josh 24:29), Job (140, Job 42:16), and Jehoiada (130, 2 Chr 24:15). Later the psalmist observed:

> Our years are seventy
> > or, because of strength, eighty;
> yet their pride is but toil and trouble;
> > they vanish quickly, and we fly away. (Ps 90:10)

Certainly even reaching such an age must have been an extreme rarity in a culture lacking modern medicine, and "toil and trouble" were abundant in any case. The average age reported for fourteen Davidic kings of Judah after Solomon was only 44; evidence gathered from more recent comparable cultures would suggest a life expectancy for the general population of less than 40.[35] Infant mortality rates might well have been upwards of 50%. Considering such factors, the high value Israel placed on life and longevity becomes all the more comprehensible to us.

Another side to this, however, can appear all too perplexing, if not even repugnant, to modern readers of the biblical literature. If life itself was valued so highly, how can one explain the apparent readiness to execute persons for crimes and sacrilege, to wage bloody war against other people, to reduce individuals to slavery, to marginalize women, children, and foreigners in the only life they would live? There are aspects to these issues that need further scrutiny beyond what is here possible, but one cannot help at this point wondering whether the life of certain persons in that ancient society—as perhaps in modern cultures as well—was held to be worth more than the life of others of their contemporaries. Surely the king and his family received better care than the peasant, and the rich and powerful would likewise have expected to enjoy benefits not available to the common citizen. The Hebrew Bible exhibits some concern for fairness and equality of rights—e.g., that the reputation or money of a wealthy person should not affect the outcome of a trial—but does not reflect comparably on the more basic issue of relative valuation of lives. Even the prohibition against murder, both

---

[35] See Wolff, *Anthropology*, 119.

a Noachide and a Mosaic law, was not a prohibition against all killing; indeed, taking the lives of certain persons was required.[36]

Our above conclusions about the nature and value of human life can throw some light on what might appear to us today as a relative "cheapness" of life prevailing in ancient Israel. Their readiness to eliminate certain criminals and enemies arose out of a desire to eradicate what was held to be severe threats to the very existence of all other Israelites. The Deuteronomic expression "purge the evil (or blood guilt) from your midst" suggests a symbolic or magical view of evil requiring apotropaic rites for exterminating it from the community, such as the ritual in Deut 21:1-9 discussed above. Notably, in nearly all instances it was not evil in principle but a specific person, scil. the evildoer, who was exterminated; 2 Sam 4:11, in fact, makes the murderers themselves the explicit object of the same verb "purge" (b'r, in Pi'el). Deuteronomic provisions for the Holy War reflected similar intents. When any cities within the land of Israel were defeated, the people were to "let live nothing that breathes," whereas for cities further removed only the males were to be killed; the purpose was to eradicate any potential undermining influences (Deut 20:10-18). Such laws, used by the later Deuteronomists to the special end of convincing the exilic generation of Israel's long history of wrong-doing, were compatible with the popular attitudes about threatening forces able to undo the people collectively and individually. The imperative to live was not to be subverted by any others, whether from within or without, who might take the life of Israelites.

The valuation of all who were not free adult males—particularly women, children, the poor, slaves, and foreigners—lends itself less easily to clarification. Certainly, as we have already seen, their life was considered to be similar to that of free men, for identical terms applied to the life principle, vital needs, and diminishing influences for all individuals. The inferior status assigned to these groups was not argued on the grounds that they were "less alive" than males, nor that their lives were in principle worth any less, nor that their nature was essen-

---

[36] Walter Harrelson, *The Ten Commandments and Human Rights* (OBT 8; Philadelphia: Fortress, 1980), 107-22, indicates that, while the sixth commandment in its present form can be understood as forbidding killing in any and all forms, ancient Israel certainly did not intend to prohibit justified capital punishment and war. Nonetheless, he argues, this commandment with its comprehensive wording did achieve an effective affirmation of the fundamental value of human life.

tially different[37]—as Aristotle, for one, sought to show, thereby influencing centuries of subsequent generations.[38] At least the available Hebrew texts from the Israelite period do not explicitly report such views, even though these notions might well have circulated among the people and prompted the various structures of oppression. The functional result of the inferior status, however, was a devaluation of these persons individually and as classes. As the growing body of studies of these groups indicates, the immediate explanation for this subordinate status rests elsewhere, especially in the historical development of traditional roles within the familial, social, and economic contexts.

In light of the high value placed on life, we can see all the more clearly why the Israelites—as so many others in history—would seek means to improve and prolong it. In their case, while death might come through natural disaster, accident, or illness for no ostensible reason, length of life was as a rule linked to the system of reward and punishment on the basis of one's own and others' moral and religious practices. The translations of Enoch (Gen 5:22-24) and Elijah (2 Kgs 2:11) symbolized this connection between avoiding death and leading a life approved by God. Israel's response to the natural perplexity about the ending of life was thus to lay its cause at the feet of the people themselves. In the Yahwistic creation story, the tree of life represented not life itself but immortality, and this chance to live forever like the heavenly beings was removed only because of the rebellious act of humans (Gen 2:9; 3:22).[39] With it gone, the sapiential tradition later retrieved the same image of the tree in arguing that Lady Wisdom was the key means available to persons who hoped for longevity:

> Length of days is in her right hand;
>   in her left hand are riches and honor.
> Her ways are pleasant lanes,

---

[37] To interpret—as some do—the word "impure" in Job 14:4 as referring to "woman" in 14:1 is unwarranted and "gratuitous" (Norman C. Habel, *The Book of Job: A Commentary* [OTL; Philadelphia: Westminster, 1985] 240).

[38] Gerda Lerner, *The Creation of Patriarchy* (New York/Oxford: Oxford University, 1986) 205-10.

[39] Comparable motifs elsewhere in the ancient Near East, such as the plant of life sought by Gilgamesh in the classic Babylonian "Epic of Gilgamesh" (Tablet XI), represented also the desire for divine-like longevity. In this story of a persistent striving for longevity, the hero lost his prize not through disobedience but through inattention: as he bathed, a serpent made off with the plant.

and all her paths are well-being (šālôm).
She is a tree of life to those who grasp her,
and those who hold her are made happy. (Prov 3:16-18)

Similarly, Solomon, because of his prayer for understanding and discernment, was rewarded also with riches, honor, and long life (1 Kgs 3:3-14). Both the Deuteronomists and the wisdom circle elevated this ethic to preeminent position, although skepticism about its accuracy circulated among the sages to an equal extent. Certainly prophets and priests were also persuaded that living the obedient and moral life was necessary if the people as a whole hoped to survive.

Life in this world, therefore, ranked among the highest moral values in Israel. Ensuring it was so crucial that the community sought to eliminate any potential threats and risks, including dangerous persons, that could jeopardize the survival of others. The demands and expectations they placed on each other corresponded to the requirements they felt from God. An individual's mere physical continuation was not sufficient, for what was at stake was a full, vigorous life spent in the context of one's people and possessions. The optimum, not the minimum, stood as the standard in this ethic. The Edenic ideal beckoned as God's will, and through their conduct the Israelites hoped to reach it and enjoy its abundance.

THE FORENSIC CHARACTER
OF THE HEBREW BIBLE

HARRY M. ORLINSKY
Emeritus, Hebrew Union College–Jewish Institute of Religion,
New York

An important area of biblical thought that has been insufficiently studied is the basic character of the Bible as a lawbook and the way in which more terms than is generally realized, even ordinary terms, are used forensically. All too often, even when scholars have drawn attention to the technical character of a term, translators of the Bible have continued with the traditional, bland renderings, denying their readers, as well as the text itself, the meaning that the original authors intended to convey.

Thus, for example, one of the most common words in the Bible is *nātan* (2,007 occurrences according to B[rown]DB), with the general meaning "give, put, set," or the like. But the use of its direct counterpart in Aramaic, *yhb*, in inheritance and property documents of Jewish origin, more or less contemporaneous with the biblical passages involved, indicates clearly that *ntn* in biblical passages of like character should be comprehended as denoting, and therefore to be rendered, not simply "give" but "assign, transfer, deed," or the like.[1] There are numerous instances, for example, where God on the one hand and Abraham or Isaac or Jacob or the Israelite people on the other enter voluntarily into a contract according to which God agrees (sometimes by a

---

[1] See, e.g., the references to Y. Muffs and to H. Z. Szubin and B. Porten in n. 5 of H. M. Orlinsky, "The Biblical Concept of the Land of Israel: Cornerstone of the Covenant Between God and Israel," *Eretz-Israel* 18 (1985, the Nahman Avigad Volume) 43*-55*; reproduced on pp. 31-33, with additional data, in *The Land of Israel: Jewish Perspectives* (ed. L. A. Hoffman; Notre Dame: University of Notre Dame, 1986) 27-64.

vow or by accepting the sacrifice that seals the agreement) that the land of Canaan become their property and that of their heirs forever; Gen 12:1-7 constitutes a typical statement to this effect:

> The Lord said to Abram: Go forth from your native land
> and from your father's house to the land that I will show you.
>> (2) I will make you a great nation,
>> And I will bless you. . . .
>> (3) I will bless those who bless you,
>> And curse those who curse you. . . .
> (4) And Abram went forth as the Lord had spoken to him. . . .
> (5) . . . When they arrived in the land of Canaan. . . . (7) The Lord appeared to Abram and said, "I will assign (ʾettēn) this land to your offspring (lĕzarʿăkā). And he built an altar there to the Lord. . . .

Thus Abraham agreed to God's proposition; he went to the land of Canaan, and there they entered into a contract with one another.

Yet such modern translations as the first edition of the New Jewish Version of *The Torah* (NJV; 1962), the Jerusalem Bible (JB; 1966—following the Bible de Jérusalem, 1956) and the New Jerusalem Bible (NJB; 1985), New English Bible (NEB; 1970), and the New American Bible (NAB; 1970), rendered ʾettēn in v. 7 by "give." The new edition of NJV (*TANAKH*; 1985) has rendered the term correctly: "I will assign (this land to your offspring)."[2]

A second passage of this sort may be found in Gen 35:9-15:

> (9) God appeared again to Jacob, on his arrival from
> Paddan-aram, and He blessed him. (10) God said to him:
>> You whose name is Jacob,
>> You shall not be called Jacob any more;

---

[2] Alas, the term "offspring" does not do justice for zeraʿ in this context since Ishmael too is an offspring. The rendering should be "(rightful, major) heir"; for though Ishmael was the firstborn and legally the major heir, it was Isaac who became legally the primary inheritor, and Ishmael had to leave the land of Canaan and enjoy elsewhere, in another land, the blessings of God. The land of Canaan was assigned by God to the patriarchs and their heirs forever, this clause constituting the central element of His covenant with them.

It is not easy to indicate in acceptable English the emphasis on "your heirs" ("It is to your heirs. . . ."); the Hebrew achieves it by placing the indirect object lĕzarʿăkā before the verb ʾettēn.

But Israel shall be your name. . . .
(12) The land that I assigned
to Abraham and Isaac,
To you I herewith assign it;
And to your heirs to come
I assign the land.[3]

And so Jacob too entered into the covenant with God, a contract sealed by the erection of a sacred stele accompanied by a libation offering:

(14) And Jacob set up . . . a pillar of stone, and he offered a libation on it and poured oil on it.

Other terms in this category are, for example, zeraᶜ and ʾāhab; the former denotes not merely "seed, offspring, descendants" generally, but also "heir" specifically, so that while both Ishmael and Isaac are descendants of Abraham, Isaac is the major heir. As for ʾāhab, in addition to "love" it also denotes to "favor" forensically in the matter of inheritance; thus whereas Abraham loved his firstborn Ishamel and Isaac loved his firstborn Esau, in the matter of inheritance Abraham favored Isaac,[4] and Isaac, even if unknowingly, favored Jacob.

The uses to which the Bible has been put since it became canonized, essentially by the end of the first century,[5] have created even among scholars the view that it is a collection of individual books that contain or deal with, among other things, history, saga, prayers, wisdom, literature, ritual, (auto)biographies, moral exhortations, individual laws and collections of laws, and ethical pronouncements. What has

---

[3] As in the case of the emphasis indicated by the syntax lĕzarᶜăkă . . . ʾettēn in 12:7 (see preceding note), so here in 35:12 the syntax wĕʾet-hăʾăreṣ . . . lĕkă ʾettĕnennă and immediately following ûlĕzarᶜăkă . . . ʾettēn presents the same problem to translators. It should be noted that whether it be J, or (J)E, D, or P, the argument of nătan, zeraᶜ, etc., remains secure; the Genesis 12 passage happens to be the product of J, the Genesis 35 passage of P. See n. 3 in the articles cited in n. 1 above.

[4] "God put Abraham to the test. He said, 'Take your son, your only one, ʾăšer-ʾăhabtă, Isaac, and go to the region of Moriah . . .'" (Gen 22:1-2), where ʾăhabtă denotes "(whom) you favor," the one designated as sole or major heir; see Orlinsky, in The Land of Israel, 33.

[5] Cf. "The Canonization of the Hebrew Bible and the Exclusion of the Apocrypha," in Orlinsky, Essays in Biblical Culture and Bible Translation (New York: KTAV, 1974) 257-86.

been overlooked is the basic fact that the Bible is a lawbook, a compilation which in its totality derives from (even if sometimes in adjusted form) and constitutes the expression and concept of law.

The law, without which there would be no Bible, is the contract that God and Israel entered into, voluntarily and as equals, according to which each of the two parties agreed to remain loyal to one another to the exclusion of all other parties: Israel would worship no other god, and God would protect and prosper no other people. Following legal procedure, both parties "sign" the contract, usually by a vow or a sacrifice.[6]

This legal contract and mutual contractual obligation, in action, is what the Bible is all about. For from beginning to end, the Bible presents only the careers of God and Israel on earth, in their covenanted relationship to one another, the acting out of their contract in the most concrete form possible. The careers of everything and everyone else—Gentile nations, heavenly bodies, natural phenomena, animal life—all are but incidental in the biblical comprehension of the universe.[7]

It should come, then, as no surprise that numerous words and phrases in the Bible possess forensic nuance hitherto overlooked. Thus attention was drawn recently[8] to the probability that the term šālaṭ (e.g., in Ezek 16:30 and Gen 42:6) has the force of "be in control/charge of, have the authority over/to," just as it has in legal (Jewish) Aramaic documents from Elephantine, so that Joseph, as šallîṭ, was Pharaoh's deputy, manager, controller, "he had the authority to dispose of the produce/wealth of the land." Similarly, it may well be that the root gāraš, in addition to the general meaning "cast/drive out, banish, evict, expel," is used as a technical term, "to disinherit," for example, in Gen 21:10 (Hagar's son Ishmael, vis-à-vis Sarah's son Isaac) and Judg 11:2-7 (where his half-brothers act to disinherit Jephthah).[9] Noteworthy in

---

[6] On the writer's skeptical attitude from the outset toward this covenant as being essentially but a reflection or variation of the Mesopotamian concept of the suzerain treaty—and the increasing diminution of scholarly enthusiasm for it generally—see Orlinsky, in *The Land of Israel*, 16-17 n. 4.

[7] On the proper way to comprehend the biblical material in relation to the Gentile cultures about them, especially the Canaanite, see the excellent discussion by D. R. Hillers, "Analyzing the Abominable: Our Understanding of Canaanite Religion," *JQR* 75 (1984-85) 253-69.

[8] J. C. Greenfield, "Two Biblical Passages in the Light of Their Near Eastern Background—Ezekiel 16:30 and Malachi 3:17" (Hebrew), *Eretz-Israel* 16 (1982, the Harry M. Orlinsky Volume) 56-61 (English summary, p. 253).

[9] See Orlinsky, in *The Land of Israel*, 57-58 n. 5.

this connection is the fact that, whereas such technical terms as *gāraš* and *yāraš* are used for the nations that God was evicting—in this case, disinheriting (*hôrîs*)—from the land of Canaan/the Amorites in fulfillment of His covenant with Israel, these terms are not used for God's punishment of Israel for transgressing that covenant; Israel may be exiled (*gālâ*) or banished (*nidḥê yiśrāʾēl*), but never disinherited!

An excellent case in point is the root *ṣdq* in its various forms, chiefly the nouns *ṣedeq* and *ṣĕdāqâ* (respectively 121 and 157 occurrences; BDB 842-43), the verbal forms (40 occurrences: 21 in the qal—14 of them in Job; 12 in the hiphil), and the adjective *ṣaddîq* (206 times, frequently used as a noun).[10] As for the meanings given to these various forms in various contexts, BDB (841b-842a) offers "rightness, righteousness" for *ṣedeq*, with a host of variations and other meanings for specific contexts, such as "*what is right, just, normal; rightness, justness*, of weights and measures . . . *right paths . . . offerings . . . righteousness*, in government . . . of law . . . of Davidic king, Messiah . . . of Jerusalem . . . of God's attributes as sovereign . . . *righteousness, justice* . . . God (*šāpṭēnî YHWH kĕṣidqî* Ps 7:9) *judges according to righteousness . . . righteousness*, as ethically right . . . *victory, prosperity.* . . ." For *ṣĕdāqâ*, BDB (842ab) offers one major meaning, "righteousness," with other meanings similar to those given for *ṣedeq*, including "as ethically right."

It is hardly worthwhile going into any detail in dealing with BDB; the analysis of *ṣdq* set forth by Briggs is confused, burdened with ad hoc opinions and explanations. If the picture is less confusing in the versions of the Bible, be they in the Tyndale–King James–Revised–American Standard–Jewish Publication Society (1917)–Revised Standard tradition, or in the more recent versions generally, it is only because it is overwhelmingly the terms "righteous, righteousness" that are employed for forms of *ṣdq*, with "just, justice," or a similar term used far less frequently, and such other terms as "vindication, salvation, victory, prosperity" drawing up in the rear.[11]

---

[10] In his article on "'Righteousness'—Some Issues in Old Testament Translation into English," *BT* 38 (1987) 307-15—following on his detailed and useful dissertation on *"Righteousness" in the Septuagint of Isaiah: A Contextual Study* (SBLSCS 8; Chico: Scholars Press, 1979)—J. W. Olley (p. 308 n. 4) has broken down the occurrences of the nouns *ṣedeq/ṣĕdāqâ* and the adjective *ṣaddîq* in the book of Isaiah, as given by K. Koch, "*ṣdq* gemeinschaftstreu/heilvoll sein," *THWAT* 2:507-30.

[11] A note on "prosperity" (and in favor of BDB): The RSV may well be the first official version to render *ṣĕdāqâ* in Prov 8:18 by "prosperity" (as against traditional "righteousness"), both because of the context (*ʿōšer-wĕkābôd . . . hôn*

What needs to be considered and kept in mind, constantly, is the biblical framework in which words such as ṣedeq, ṣĕdāqâ, ṣādaq, and ṣaddîq are used. Since the Bible is the preserved account of God and His convenanted partner Israel in constant action—a contractual relationship that explicitly and repeatedly bars the entry of any third party, be it a deity or a people—then that concrete relationship can be comprehended properly only in legal terms: if the two parties involved carry out their binding obligations to one another, then the stipulated rewards ensue; but if Israel worships any other deity, or if it fails to execute justice within its community, disobeying the commandments of God as imparted by His spokespersons, then God punishes His people.[12]

Basically, concepts such as morality, ethics, fairness, and righteousness have no meaning in the Bible outside the legal framework; indeed, there is no term in the Bible for these concepts. Put differently, what the Bible originally conceived as concepts and expressions of law came to be regarded in postbiblical times, especially in consequence of the rise and nature of Christianity and its understanding of biblical thought and terminology, as non-legal exhortations to lead a moral life, to conduct oneself ethically; no longer being legally binding, immoral and unethical acts are not punishable in a court of justice—unless a secular agency established by an independent community is given that authority. God and His covenant and His laws and commandments are no longer directly involved; and terms such as "righteous, righteousness," not being legal terms—and so not to be found, for example, in Black's *Law Dictionary* (5th ed., 1979)—should be avoided by translators.[13]

ʿātēq) and in accord with Abraham ibn Ezra's comment (. . . kĕtaʿam haṣlaḥâ); see "Teaching Bible in a Rabbinical School," in Orlinsky, *Essays in Biblical Culture and Bible Translation*, 1-4. It is not known generally that BDB (1906) offers this rendering.

[12] Of course it is unthinkable that God, whose qualities are known to us only from what the Bible tells us about Him, would fail to carry out His part of the contract with Israel. Amos in the eighth century put it one way (e.g., 2:7-16), Second Isaiah in the sixth century in several other ways—every part of the Bible expressing this concept or taking it for granted.

[13] A case in point is offered at Exod 21:1. The first printings of the New Jewish Version of *The Torah* (1962) rendered [wĕʾēlleh ham]mišpāṭîm by "norms," a reading adopted after considerable discussion. Later printings, however, in recognition of the fact that, in contrast to mišpāṭ, "norm" is not a legal term (and is therefore not to be found in Black's *Law Dictionary*), "rules" replaced "norms"—such better terms as "statutes" and "laws" having been preempted

A word of explanation and caution. Probably the most striking and best known passage in the Bible in this connection is Deut 16:20, ṣedeq ṣedeq tirdōp, universally translated by a legal term: "That which is altogether just shalt thou follow" (KJ, RV, ASV; Douai: "Thou shalt follow justly after that which is just"), "Justice, only justice shalt thou pursue" (Leeser), "Justice, and only justice, you shall follow" (RSV), "Strict justice must be your ideal" (JB–NJB), "Justice and justice alone shall be your aim" (Confraternity–NAB; NEB: "you shall pursue"; Moffatt: "Justice, justice you must aim at").[14] However, it is this forensic element that translators fail to carry over into many scores of passages elsewhere in the Bible, because of their failure to keep it in mind as the leitmotiv that it constitutes in the Bible.[15]

Another term that has been generally deprived of its forensic essence is ḥesed, usually translated "loving-kindness, kindness, mercy," or the like; but however "loving-kindness" is to be understood— "affection or tenderness stemming from sincere love for someone" is the definition given in The American Heritage Dictionary—scholarship, especially since Nelson Glueck's dissertation on this word appeared,[16] has come to recognize in the term the basic element of "loyalty, faithfulness, devotion" that derives from a legally recognized, contractual relationship, one that is inherent in the relationship between the head of a household and its members and among these members, between a

---

for ḥuqqîm and tôrâ see Orlinsky, ed., Notes on the New Translation of the Torah (Philadelphia: Jewish Publication Society of America, 5710/1969) 177 ad loc.

[14] One has but to read the section in which this phrase occurs to appreciate the completely forensic element involved, especially the accompanying use of the legal term šāpaṭ ("judge, arbitrate"): "(18) You shall appoint magistrates and officials for your tribes . . . and they shall render decision (wĕšāpĕṭû) for the people with due justice (mišpaṭ-ṣedeq). (19) You shall not pervert justice. . . ." Equally pertinent is the famous statement in Mic 6:8: ". . . and what the Lord requires of you: Only to do justice and to love faithfulness (ḥesed). . . ."

[15] For the forensic character of the book of Job from beginning to end, see L. H. Thal's Master's-Ordination thesis, "The Legal Terminology and Context of the Book of Job" (Hebrew Union College–Jewish Institute of Religion, New York, 1973); parts (pp. 16-18) of my Horace Kallen Lecture (New York, 1976), The Bible as Law: God and Israel under Contract (New York: Horace M. Kallen Center for Jewish Studies, 1978), derive from this meritorious thesis.

[16] Das Wort ḥesed im alttestamentlichen Sprachgebrauche als menschliche und göttliche gemeinschaftgemäße Verhaltungsweise (Jena 1927), reprinted 1961, and subsequently published in an English translation by A. Gottschalk, Ḥesed in the Bible (Cincinnati: Hebrew Union College, 1967).

master and a slave, between God and Israel. Translators have begun to indicate this concept by deleting the first half of the awkward word and using only "kindness," or by dropping the second half of the word and turning the first half into "steadfast love," though many continue to use "mercy." To appreciate the forensic character of ḥesed, one has but to note how it is used in association with such other legal terms as mišpāṭ (e.g., Mic 6:8), ṣĕdāqâ, and ʾĕmet, and with the same kind of verbs (e.g., ʿāśâ) and contexts (e.g., Psalm 136—kî lĕʿôlām ḥasdô).

In retrospect, it is the Bible as a lawbook, the divine origin of the Law, Moses as a lawgiver, the seventy-two Jewish translators of the Septuagint as experts in the Law, and the like, that come through in the so-called Letter of Aristeas. It is not that Hellenistic wisdom is downgraded—not at all; the translators were themselves also learned in Greek culture. But the Torah as a lawbook takes precedence, and it is to it that what is worthwhile in Greek wisdom is adjusted. And the same is true of Ben Sira's widely read work, his book of wisdom that came to be called Ecclesiasticus; he too appreciated the wisdom of the Hellenistic society about him, but the true and highest form of wisdom can be comprehended only in God's Law. And, finally, law as the essence of the Bible was naturally, and correctly, understood by the rabbis, so that it is the halakah of the Mishnah and the Gemara that dominates the extension and application of the Bible after it is canonized and begins another kind of career in the Diaspora, without benefit of a sovereign Jewish state.

This postbiblical career of the Bible may be described here, if only briefly, because it reflects the essence of the career of the honoree of this volume. Even if the authors of the Bible, the prophets more eloquently than the others, addressed themselves only to their fellow Israelites and saw justice only in terms of their covenant with their God, their ringing words have carried from age to age their belief that justice was for the weak as well as for the strong, that its fulfillment was as much a matter of the spirit as the letter of the law, that one could not serve God at the same time while mistreating a fellow person, that to love God was to love justice, and that the love of justice placed within the conscience of each human being the ultimate inescapable obligation to denounce evil wherever it appeared, to defy a ruler who commanded one to break the covenant, and to live in the law and the love of God no matter what the cost.[17]

---

[17] Cf. the last paragraph of chap. 7, "The Hebraic Spirit: The Prophetic Movement and Social Justice," in Orlinsky, *Ancient Israel* (Ithaca: Cornell University, 1954; numerous printings and editions); or *Understanding the Bible through History and Archaeology* (New York: KTAV, 1972).

SUBVERSIVE JUSTICE:
TRACING THE MIRIAMIC TRADITIONS

PHYLLIS TRIBLE
Union Theological Seminary, New York

This essay practices subversive exegesis for the sake of justice. Both the adjectival description and the purposive noun characterize the prophetic faith to which the career of Walter Harrelson bears witness. What differs here is that the call for justice undermines a triumphal voice in Scripture by heeding a defeated one.[1] It listens to Miriam rather than Moses. Though her story survives in bits and pieces, even a sketch of it challenges interpretations old and new.[2]

In the Beginning

Miriam enters Scripture obliquely. No lineage, birth announcement, or naming ritual proclaims her advent. Instead, she is the unnamed sister in a story of unnamed women who defy Pharaoh's decree to kill Hebrew sons (Exod 2:1-10). In the first half of the account (Exod 2:1-6), nar-

---

[1] Cf. Walter Harrelson, "The Hebrew Bible and Modern Culture," in *The Hebrew Bible and Its Modern Interpreters* (ed. Douglas A. Knight and Gene M. Tucker; BMI 1; Philadelphia: Fortress; and Chico: Scholars Press, 1985) 494-95.

[2] This essay is taken from a larger study, with full documentation, to be published subsequently. For a comprehensive investigation of the Miriamic traditions (excluding Exod 2:1-10), see Rita J. Burns, *Has the Lord Indeed Spoken Only Through Moses? A Study of the Biblical Portrait of Miriam* (SBLDS 84; Atlanta: Scholars Press, 1987). For a wide-ranging structuralist reading, see Edmund Leach, "Why did Moses Have a Sister?" in *Structuralist Interpretations of Biblical Myth* (Cambridge: Cambridge University, 1983) 33-67. My sustained conversation with these and other analyses awaits the larger study.

rative discourse introduces these females. A host of active verbs secures the presence of the daughter of Levi. She conceived and bore a son; she saw how good he was; she hid him until she could hide him no longer; she took for him a basket, sealed it, put him in it, and placed it at the river's bank. Opposing the daughter of Levi, in artistic symmetry, is the daughter of Pharaoh. A multitude of active verbs also establishes her presence. She came to bathe at the river, saw the basket, sent her maid to fetch it, opened it, saw the foreign child, had compassion on him, and hailed his identity: "This is one of the Hebrews' children!" she said.[3]

In the middle of this unit, narrative structure locates the sister of the baby just as content makes her the mediator. Between the placing and discovering of the new born child "his sister stood at a distance to know what would be done to him" (Exod 2:4). The designation "sister" is odd, however, because a preface has already implied that the son is the first-born. It reports a marriage. "A man from the house of Levi went and took to wife a daughter of Levi" (Exod 2:1). Immediately follows a birth announcement: "The woman conceived and bore a son" (Exod 2:2). Yet despite the preface, nothing in the narrative requires that the son be the first-born. To the contrary, his sister's appearance shows that he is not. Moreover, the absence of the father, "the man from the house of Levi," in the story proper arouses further suspicion about the preface. Perhaps a redactor's contribution, it effects the elevation of Moses at the expense of his sister.[4] And so the siblings begin their lives together in narrative tension.

In the second half of the story (Exod 2:7-10), the unnamed sister moves closer into view. She speaks to Pharaoh's daughter: "Shall I go and call for you (lāk) a woman nursing from the Hebrews so that she nurses for you (lāk) the child" (Exod 2:7)? By putting the phrase "for you" directly after both the verbs *call* and *nurse*, the sister expresses solicitude and offers servitude. She also shapes the future by defining the need of Pharaoh's daughter to obtain a Hebrew nurse. So the royal command, "Go," is but the desired reply to the sister's question. To re-

---

[3] Unless specified otherwise, biblical translations come from the *Revised Standard Version*. An asterisk after a scriptural reference indicates my alteration of the *RSV*.

[4] For differing views on the presence, role, and namelessness of the sister, see the commentaries: e.g., Martin Noth, *Exodus* (OTL; Philadelphia: Westminster, 1962) 24-27, 122-23; U. Cassuto, *A Commentary on the Book of Exodus* (Jerusalem: Magnes, 1967) 17-21; Brevard S. Childs, *The Book of Exodus* (OTL; Philadelphia: Westminster, 1974) 18-19.

port her action, the storyteller plays with vocabulary. Though the crucial verbs *go* and *call* are repeated, their subject is a new noun: "the young woman" rather than "his sister." An independent description replaces a derivative identity. Further, the object of the verb is a new noun: "the mother of the baby" rather than "the daughter of Levi" (cf. Exod 2:1). "The young woman went and called the mother of the baby" (Exod 2:8b*). The maternal noun makes explicit the beautiful irony of her proposal. "A woman nursing from the Hebrews" *is* the child's own mother. Thus the story comes swiftly to a climax. Princess and slave meet to work out a plan. Nursed by his natural mother, the child grows to become the adopted son of Pharaoh's daughter and receive from her the name Moses.[5]

Central to this happy solution is the unnamed Miriam. Her first appearance is from afar; she stands "at a distance." With speech, she moves closer to unite two daughters for the sake of a male child. Model of discretion and timing, the sister astutely negotiates, mediates, and leads. Having succeeded, she disappears from the narrative.

Attention shifts to the adult Moses who, assisted by his brother Aaron, dominates the struggle against Pharaoh. Their triumphal feat signals another beginning for Miriam. This time she has her name, and also a title, "the prophet," but she is in danger of losing her voice.[6] The regnant tradition attributes her song to Moses. He, along with the sons of Israel, sings a lengthy poem to celebrate YHWH's victory at the sea (Exod 15:1-18).[7]

---

[5] Most recently, Nahum M. Sarna has attempted to account historically for the details of this story: *Exploring Exodus: The Heritage of Biblical Israel* (New York: Schocken, 1986) 28-33. My literary reading moves in a different direction. Cf. Robert B. Lawton, S.J., "Irony in Early Exodus," *ZAW* 97 (1985) 414; J. Cheryl Exum, "'You Shall Let Every Daughter Live': A Study of Exodus 1:8–2:10," *Semeia* 28: *The Bible and Feminist Hermeneutics* (ed. Mary Ann Tolbert; Chico, CA: Scholars Press, 1983) 74-81.

[6] Contra Burns, *Has the Lord Indeed Spoken Only Through Moses?*, 41-79, I do not regard the title "the prophet" an anachronism. Cf. Joseph Blenkinsopp, *A History of Prophecy in Israel* (Philadelphia: Westminster, 1983) 63-64; Urs Winter, *Frau und Göttin: Exegetische und ikonographische Studien zum weiblichen Gottesbild im Alten Israel und in dessen Umwelt* (OBO 53; Freiburg, Schweiz: Universitätsverlag, 1983) 51-57.

[7] Bibliography on the so-called Song of the Sea is enormous. Cf. Childs, *Exodus*, 240-53. For a recent discussion, see Carola Kloos, *Yhwh's Combat with the Sea: A Canaanite Tradition in the Religion of Ancient Israel* (Leiden: E. J. Brill, 1986) 127-57.

Immediately there follows a brief recapitulation of the event
(Exod 15:19-21). It culminates with Miriam and the women of Israel:

> Then Miriam the prophet, the sister of Aaron,
>   took timbrel in her hand. And all the women
>   went out after her, with timbrels and dancing.
> And Miriam answered them:
>   Sing to YHWH
>   Most glorious deity!
>   Horse and rider
>   God has hurled into the sea! (Exod 15:20-21*)

Miriam's song repeats with variations the first stanza of the long
poem attributed to Moses. At first glance, the repetition suggests that
her contribution is derivative and his original. Further, though he can
sing an entire song, she can remember, and then not perfectly, only the
first stanza. By comparison, her performance seems deficient as does
this entire small unit which awkwardly follows the grand Mosaic ending. A second closure, it is anti-climactic, no more than an afterthought,
a token of the female presence.

Divergent in length, content, and emphasis, the two endings work in
tension, not in tandem. The Mosaic conclusion overpowers the Miriamic
to raise the question of why the latter ever survived. Surely, retention
argues for its antiquity and authority. So tenacious was the tradition
about Miriam that redactors could not eliminate it, no matter how much
they tried. Once upon an early time, before editors got jobs, the entire
Song, not just the first stanza, was ascribed to Miriam and the women of
Israel. Later, redactors intent upon elevating Moses took the text right
out of her mouth and gave it to him in company with the sons of Israel
(Exod 15:1-18). Thus they constructed an ending for the Exodus story
that contradicted the older tradition. Unable to squelch that tradition
altogether, they appended it in truncated form to their preferred version (Exod 15:20-21). To separate the two endings as well as to introduce
the Miriamic appendage, they inserted a summary of the victory at the
sea (Exod 15:19).[8] By such a procedure redactors both preserved and de-

---

[8] Though the development of this view is my own, it resonates with earlier
scholarly proposals; see the commentaries. See in particular the designation of
Exodus 15 as "The Song of Miriam" by Frank M. Cross, Jr., and David Noel
Freedman, "The Song of Miriam," *JNES* 14 (1955) 237-50. Cf. Maria-Sybilla
Heister, *Frauen in der biblischen Glaubensgeschichte* (Göttingen: Vanden-
hoeck & Ruprecht, 1984) 49-50.

stroyed the women's story. They kept Miriam but diminished her importance. While the latter act heightens the apotheosis of Moses, the former subtly undermines it. Within and behind the text, then, conflict mounts. The female voice struggles to be heard; a Miriamic presence counters a Mosaic bias. What began as a cloud the size of a baby's hand rising out of the river Nile and grew into a man's hand stretched over the sea (Exod 14:21) will in time burst forth in a storm of controversy about authority.

From Water to Wilderness

If water locates the beginning of Miriam's story, wilderness contains the center. Symbol of complaint, confusion, and conflict, wilderness denotes places of sojourn and connotes modes of being. Moving from site to site, the people of Israel murmur, indeed rebel. Their deity replies with ambivalence. Kindled anger and gracious acts mingle. Nothing happens orderly or narrates smoothly. Entangled in the wilderness, multiple layers of tradition defy source analysis and internal coherence to become the chaos they report.[9] The task of the interpreter is to discern Miriam's story amid the muddle.

Her portrait lodges in controversies about authority and prophecy. Moses is overwhelmed. Caught between the demands of the people and the blazing anger of YHWH, he seeks a new kind of leadership, a shared responsibility. But efforts in this direction fail (Num 11:10-30). As the people journey to a new site, the power struggle rages.[10] Miriam enters the fray, and for the first time she lacks the company of women. Supported by Aaron, she speaks against Moses.

A confused text (Numbers 12) makes difficult the hearing of her word. Priestly and prophetic issues emerge in jumbled fashion.[11] Narrated discourse reports the first challenge. "And Miriam spoke, and Aaron, against Moses because of the Cushite woman whom he married,

---

[9] On the theme of rebellion and the difficulties of source analysis, see George W. Coats, *Rebellion in the Wilderness* (Nashville: Abingdon, 1968).

[10] On the wilderness controversies, cf. Murray Newman, *The People of the Covenant* (New York: Abingdon, 1962) 72-101.

[11] George W. Coats argues that the received text focuses on Moses: "Humility and Honor: A Moses Legend in Numbers 12," in *Art and Meaning: Rhetoric in Biblical Literature* (ed. David J. A. Clines, David M. Gunn, and Alan J. Hauser; JSOTSup 19; Sheffield: JSOT, 1982) 97-107. Robert R. Wilson argues that prophecy was the original focus: *Prophecy and Society in Ancient Israel* (Philadelphia: Fortress, 1980) 155-56.

for he had married a Cushite woman" (Num 12:1*). The information and charge appear *in medias res*. The matter is not explained, but the accusation appears to entail cultic dimensions. Cited only once, the problem of the Cushite (black) wife yields quickly to a prophetic issue.[12] If the cultic purity of Moses can be criticized, then his supreme authority can be disputed. Unlike the first, this second challenge occurs in direct discourse. Miriam and Aaron ask:

> Has the Lord indeed spoken only through Moses?
> Has the Lord not spoken through us also? (Num 12:2a*)

For Miriam the prophetic task centers not upon a single male but embraces diverse voices, female and male. Her questions seem to harmonize with Moses's own wish that "all the Lord's people were prophets" (Num 11:29). But Miriam makes clear what Moses did not: that "all the Lord's people" includes women. After all, as "the prophet" she has already spoken for YHWH at the sea, even though the Mosaic bias would drown her voice there. So now in the wilderness she seeks an equal sharing of prophetic leadership. Hers is a commanding word, and the "Lord hears it" (Num 12:2b).

Alas, the price of speaking out is severe. Breaking ominous silence, YHWH summons Moses, Aaron, and Miriam to come forth. Addressed to her and Aaron, the divine explanation comes with the power of poetry and the exclusivity of grammatical gender. It attends to the prophetic but not the priestly issue.[13]

> Hear now my words;
> If there be a prophet among you,
> In a vision to him I make myself known;
> In a dream I speak with him.
> Not so (with) my servant Moses;
> In all my household he (alone) is faithful.
> Mouth to mouth I speak with him.
> In clarity and not in riddles;
> The form of YHWH he beholds. (Num 12:6-8a*)

---

[12] Cf. Burns, *Has the Lord Indeed Spoken Only Through Moses?*, 48-79.

[13] The translation comes from Frank Moore Cross, *Canaanite Myth and Hebrew Epic* (Cambridge, MA: Harvard University, 1973) 203-4.

The divine speech requires little commentary. It proclaims a hierarchy of prophecy with Moses peerless at the top. While not denying a role to Miriam, it undercuts her in gender and point of view. Ironically, it also undermines Moses's wish for egalitarian prophecy. Pursuing the point, the deity rebuffs Aaron and Miriam: "Why were you not afraid to speak against my servant Moses?" (Num 12:8b). Though Moses may attack God, even accuse the deity of oppression unto death (Num 11:11-15), God decrees that no one may attack Moses. With this intimidating question, YHWH speaks to Miriam for the first and only time. She has no opportunity to reply. Instead, to the crushing power of the divine words the narrator adds a seething conclusion: "And the nostril of YHWH burned against them, and God left" (Num 12:9*). While the mouth of the Lord glorifies Moses, the nose attacks Aaron and Miriam. This divinity is made of stern stuff.

Yet the kindled anger of the divine does not treat its targets equally, for Miriam alone emerges the culprit. Behold (*hinnēh*), she is stricken with scales like snow. Red-hot anger becomes a cold-white disease; a searing emotion yields a scarred body. The form of the punishment may relate to the priestly issue of the Cushite wife. She who opposed Moses because of his marriage to the black woman stands condemned in scaled white. If the Cushite woman be outside a system of ritual purity, Miriam is there also. She has become leprous, not with the raw flesh of uncleanliness but with dead flesh, aftermath of the all-consuming disease.[14] Divine anger has run its course.

Turning toward Miriam, Aaron beseeches Moses, rather than the Lord, not to "hold against us the sin that we have done foolishly and have sinned" (Num 12:11*). In spite of efforts to disassociate this priest from the woman, he pleads on her behalf:[15]

> Let her not be as one dead, of whom the flesh is half
> consumed when it comes out of its mother's womb.
> (Num 12:12*)

Aaron seeks a miracle: the restoration of Miriam to her pre-leprous condition. After all, such a miracle was once visited upon the hand of

---

[14] See David Jobling, "A Structural Analysis of Numbers 11-12," *The Sense of Biblical Narrative* (JSOTSup 7; Sheffield: JSOT, 1978) 32-33; cf. 2d ed. (1986), 37-38.

[15] Cf. Aelred Cody, *A History of the Old Testament Priesthood* (AnBib 35; Rome: Pontifical Biblical Institute, 1969) 150-51, who argues against a priestly identification of Aaron in Numbers 12.

Moses (Exod 4:6-7), though in a different context. By appealing now to
Moses, Aaron acknowledges supremacy in the hierarchy. Moses com-
plies: "Heal her, O God, I beseech thee" (Num 12:13)! Whatever tensions exist between Miriamic and Mosaic points of view, they have not
destroyed sibling affection. Having been saved at birth through his sister, Moses petitions here to have her saved from living death. In a
cryptic reply YHWH confines her outside the camp for seven days.
That period of time verifies her cleanliness but does not restore her to
wholeness. Miriam remains a marked woman, indeed, a warning for
generations to come: "Remember what the Lord your God did to Miriam
on the way as you came forth out of Egypt" (Deut 24:9).[16]

The vendetta continues unto her death. By silences and juxtaposi-
tions the tale unfolds. From her punishment on, Miriam never speaks
nor is she spoken to. For a while she even vanishes from the wilderness
narrative. Then, just preceding her obituary, comes a lengthy section of
ritual prescriptions (Num 19:1-22).[17] Its content as well as placement in-
dicts Miriam. The first prescription involves a special water for impurity. To the burning of a cow the priest adds cedarwood, hyssop, and
scarlet yarn. Though this text fails to specify the meaning of the three
ingredients, Lev 14:4 indicates their use in the cleansing of a leper—
truly a reminder of Miriam's punishment. At the appropriate moment,
running water is added to the mixture. Its function awaits a second prescription about those who become unclean through contact with the
dead. The water for impurity is thrown upon the unclean. Purification
requires seven days, the same time needed for the cleansing of a leper.

Immediately after these prescriptions, the one alluding to leprosy
and the other emphasizing the uncleanliness of the dead, comes the announcement of Miriam's death:

> And the people of Israel, the whole congregation, came
> into the wilderness of Zin in the first month, and the
> people stayed in Kadesh; and Miriam died there, and
> was buried there. (Num 20:1)

No ordinary obituary is this but rather the culmination of the priestly
vendetta against Miriam. If reasons for the attack are difficult to dis-

---

[16] Cf. Calum M. Carmichael, *Law and Narrative in the Bible* (Ithaca: Cornell University, 1985) 263-64.

[17] See Noth, *Numbers* (OTL; Philadelphia: Westminster, 1968) 138-43.

cern,[18] the threat that she represented to the cultic establishment is abundantly evident. And that threat testifies to her prominence, power, and prestige in early Israel. So important was this woman that detractors tabooed her to death, seeking to bury her forever in disgrace.

Until the Consummation

But detractors do not have the final word. Fragments within Scripture subvert the dominant stance to yield a different version. It appears first among the people whom Miriam served. At the end of the leprosy account a certain poignancy characterizes their behavior: "The people did not set out on the march till Miriam was brought in again" (Num 12:15). No matter that YHWH has decreed the supreme leadership of Moses; no matter that the divine anger has already shown its power against the will of the people; no matter that the white-scaled Miriam stands before them as proof of indictment and intimidation; no matter. The people remain steadfast in loyalty to her.

The symbol of water also supports Miriam. First seen at a distance, she soon moves to the river's bank. In a triumphal appearance she sings at the shore of the sea. No life-giving waters emerge, however, when in the wilderness authorities conspire to punish her. Leprous flesh bespeaks arid land. In the ritual prescriptions preceding her obituary, the symbol recurs with ambivalence. "The water for impurity" mediates between cleanliness and uncleanliness. Miriam dies, becoming thereby unclean. Yet at her death no water for impurity is invoked. Instead, the wells in the desert dry up. In Kadesh "Miriam died and was buried there. Now there was no water for the congregation" (Num 20:1-2). Nature mourns her demise. Like the people of Israel, it honors Miriam.

After her burial, the lack of water introduces a long narrative critical of Moses and Aaron (Num 20:3-29).[19] In structure, it balances the ritual prescriptions preceding her obituary. In effect, it counters the vendetta against her. If the prescriptions implicitly demean Miriam, the subsequent account explicitly debases Moses and Aaron. Once again

---

[18] For a helpful analysis of the priestly ascription of ritual purity to the deity, with its concomitant rejection of women, see Nancy Joy, "Throughout Your Generation Forever: A Sociology of Blood Sacrifice" (unpublished dissertation, Waltham, MA: Department of Sociology, Brandeis University, 1981).

[19] See Katharine Doob Sakenfeld, "Theological and Redactional Problems in Numbers 20.2-13," in *Understanding the Word: Essays in Honour of Bernhard W. Anderson* (ed. James T. Butler, Edgar W. Conrad, and Ben C. Ollenburger; JSOTSup 37; Sheffield: JSOT, 1985) 133-54.

the people attack their leaders because of overwhelming miseries. The two men appeal to God who instructs them to secure water from a rock. Though they are successful, the deity is so displeased that God decrees neither man shall lead the people into the land.[20] Miriam's death has initiated their demise. And soon thereafter, when the congregation has journeyed from Kadesh to Mount Hor, Aaron dies. In time, Moses will follow. If Miriam never reached the promised land, neither did her brothers. Indeed, efforts to discredit her have backfired in the censure of them. Juxtaposition of texts dramatizes the point. After the death of Miriam, the wells in the desert dry up, the people rebel again, God censures Moses and Aaron, Aaron dies, and the days of Moses are numbered. However much the detractors of Miriam have tried, they do not control the story.

Beyond the Exodus and wilderness accounts, fragments of a pro-Miriamic tradition continue to surface. If the priesthood has repudiated Miriam forever, prophecy reclaims her. It states boldly what others worked hard to deny: that in early Israel Miriam belonged to a trinity of leadership. She was the equal of Moses and Aaron. Thus the prophetic deity speaks in Micah:

> For I brought you up from the land of Egypt,
>   and redeemed you from the house of bondage;
> and I sent before you Moses, Aaron, and Miriam. (Mic 6:4)

Here prophecy acknowledges the full legitimacy of Miriam, its own ancestor, who was designated "the prophet" even before Moses.

Another prophetic reference to Miriam may be tucked away in Jeremiah.[21] Envisioning the restoration of defeated Israel, Jeremiah evokes the vocabulary of the Exodus to portray an era of grace and joy. The deity addresses the people as female:

---

[20] See Jacob Milgrom, "Magic, Monotheism and the Sin of Moses," in *The Quest for the Kingdom of God: Studies in Honor of George E. Mendenhall* (ed. H. B. Huffmon, F. A. Spina, and A. R. W. Green; Winona Lake, IN: Eisenbrauns, 1983) 251-65; M. Margoliot, "The Transgression of Moses and Aaron—Num 20:1-13," *JQR* 74 (1983) 196-228.

[21] See Bernhard W. Anderson, "The Song of Miriam Poetically and Theologically Considered," in *Directions in Biblical Hebrew Poetry* (ed. Elaine R. Follis; JSOTSup 40; Sheffield: JSOT, 1987) 285-96.

> Again I will build you, and you shall be built,
>   O virgin Israel!
> Again you shall adorn yourself with timbrels,
>   and shall go forth in the dance of the merrymakers.
>   (Jer 31:4)

This imagery may be read in two directions. It recalls Miriam at the sea, and it forecasts her restoration. Returned to her rightful place, she along with other women will again lead with timbrels and dancing. She participates in the eschatological vision of Hebrew prophecy.

Miriam also animates the musical life of Israel. If Jubal be its mythical father (Gen 4:21), she is its historical mother. With timbrel in hand, she inaugurates a procession of women who move throughout Scripture, singing and dancing in sorrow and joy.[22] The daughter of Jephthah (Judg 11:34), the virgin daughters of Shiloh (Judg 21:21), and women of the monarchy (1 Sam 18:6-7) are her heirs.[23] From narrative texts her legacy passes into liturgical traditions. Rejected by the priesthood, Miriam nevertheless resounds in the cultic experience of the people. A psalm describes a parade entering the temple with

> the singers in front, the minstrels last,
>   between them maidens playing timbrels.
>   (Ps 68:25; cf. Pss 81:2; 149:3-4)

And in the grand finale of the Psalter, where everything that breathes is called upon to praise God, the woman Miriam breathes in the line:

> Praise the Lord with timbrel and dance! (Ps 150:4)

The people, nature, textual juxtaposition, prophecy, and hymnody all honor Miriam, a female whom the triumphal male voice of Scripture would discredit. To recover her story from bits and pieces scattered here and there is to practice subversive exegesis. Though the job remains unfinished, Professor Harrelson can know that justice is being served.

---

[22] Cf. Winter, *Frau und Göttin*, 32-35.

[23] See Eunice Blanchard Poethig, "The Victory Song Tradition of the Women in Israel" (unpublished dissertation, New York: Union Theological Seminary, 1985).

Part Two:
Perspectives on Early Christianity and Judaism

IS THE TORAH OBSOLETE FOR CHRISTIANS ?

JAMES TUNSTEAD BURTCHAELL, C.S.C.
University of Notre Dame

"The Christian community of those who are witnesses to the Resurrection is a community marked by a new perception of the possibilities of human life and human community. Human beings need no longer live under compulsions and restraints that long have bound and sometimes enslaved them. . . . Is there," asks Walter Harrelson, "any place for the Ten Commandments in such a community of the Resurrection?"[1]

What obedience, if any, should the Ten Words, or the entire Torah, or indeed the full extent of Israel's moral injunctions, exact from those who identify themselves as a New Israel?

The question has had a keen bite for the communities of the Reformation. The same founders who revived so learned a reverence for the Bible had made Romans and Galatians the rate of exchange for the whole of Scripture. All that was authentically Christian was seen as innovative, and as a breakaway from its Jewish antecedents. On this view of the gospel as a revolt, it was difficult not to follow Marcion's example and regard the code of Israel as utterly obsolete: inspired but archaic, like the leather-bound family Bible reverently displayed in the living room, but reverently unread.

The evangelical and fundamentalist traditions have had an especially vexed relationship with Old Testament law. Convinced that all divine teaching is to be found in the Bible (not in germ alone, but in full fruit and flower), and convinced as well that this revelation has conveyed a moral doctrine to be received attentively, Christians of this persuasion have had to go to the Hebrew Scriptures to find much of their ethical program. Since it is not really there, they have had to

---

[1] Walter Harrelson, *The Ten Commandments and Human Rights* (OBT 8; Philadelphia: Fortress, 1980) 6.

ignore some commands that are there in full sight, and impose a sense of their own on others. Thus the Christians who confess most dependence upon the closely read biblical text have sometimes hearkened least to its original imperatives.

A more scholarly tradition has sought other ways to evaluate the ancient laws. Reinhold Niebuhr has portrayed the older ethic, unlike the newer, as one that is possible of fulfillment. "The social justice which Amos demanded represented a possible ideal for society. Jesus' conception of pure love . . . transcends the possible and historical."[2] Jesus' command to forgive the aggressor, for example, which forbids prudent self-defense and ignores natural impulses and social consequences, can have only a transcendent meaning for us, not a normative instruction. "Surely this is not an ethic which can give us specific guidance in the detailed problems of social morality where the relative claims of family, community, class, and nation must be constantly weighed. One is almost inclined to agree with Karl Barth [something Niebuhr never did eagerly] that this ethic 'is not applicable to the problems of contemporary society nor yet to any conceivable society.'"[3]

But Niebuhr's erstwhile student at Union, Dietrich Bonhoeffer, brought a starkly different interpretation to the same text: "You have heard how it was said: Eye for eye and tooth for tooth. But I say this to you: offer no resistance to the wicked" (Matt 5:38-39 NJB):

> In the Old Testament personal rights are protected by a divinely established system of retribution. Every evil must be requited. The aim of retribution is to establish a proper community, to convict and overcome evil and eradicate it from the body politic of the people of God. . . . The Church is not to be a national community like the old Israel, but a community of believers without political or national ties. The old Israel had been both—the chosen people of God *and* a national community, and it was therefore his will that they should meet force with force. But with the Church it is different: it has abandoned political and national status, and therefore it must patiently endure aggression. Otherwise evil will be heaped upon evil.[4]

---

[2] Reinhold Niebuhr, *An Interpretation of Christian Ethics* (New York: Harper & Brothers, 1935) 31.

[3] Ibid., 51.

[4] Dietrich Bonhoeffer, *The Cost of Discipleship* (trans. R. H. Fuller & Irmgard Booth; rev. ed.; New York: Macmillan, 1963) 157.

Unlike Niebuhr, Bonhoeffer thinks non-resistance should be practiced in public life, but he admits that only a Christian living forthrightly under faith in the Cross will be empowered to do so.

Despite their differing applications of Scripture, both master and pupil were in agreement that an authentic Christian ethic was to be found only in the documents of the new covenant, not in the old.

Walter Harrelson, standing about as far from them as Alexandria stands from Antioch, argues that the absolute prohibitions of the Ten Commandments can indeed yield divine guidance to the Christian, provided that they are taken as guidelines, not as explicit norms.

> The Ten Commandments are much more akin to statements about the character of life in community than they are to cases of violation of the law of the community and what punishment is to be dealt out when violations occur. Put in constitutional terms, the Ten Commandments are much more like the Bill of Rights and its amendments than the United States Code.[5]

Combining exegetical precision with pastoral shrewdness, he sees the Commandments as suggestive first principles which, when put into Christian service, become the outline of a moral guide for life. My concern about this proceeding, which Harrelson pursues as eloquently and persuasively as any I have read, is that in the end it seems to rescue the Old Testament from obsolescence by bleaching out of it the original concerns of the authors, which were very explicit, normative, particular, and grounded on suppositions far more primitive than we could accept. My counter-proposal is to accept not only the entire Old Testament in its original sense as obsolete for Christians, but the New Testament as well.

* * *

In the final scenes of both *The Merchant of Venice* and *The Comedy of Errors* the chaos of previously confused identities is handsomely resolved. Portia and Nerissa, and the two pairs—Antipholus and Dromio—of Ephesus and of Syracuse are discerned at last. What really happens in each finale is not simply that the characters disclose who

---

[5] Harrelson, *Ten Commandments*, 12-13. He goes on eloquently to argue that the Commandments foreshadow the 1948 Universal Declaration of Human Rights.

they are, but that they reconstrue what they all mean to each other. I want to suggest a way to reconstrue the continuous Jewish and Christian tradition of moral injunction, not by altering its content, stringency, or definition, but by proposing a more nearly correct understanding of what these ancient yet normative teachings, underwritten by God, can require of the Christian community in a much later day.

Christians are the heirs of a continuity in community and inquiry, both of which we trace back to Abraham and Sarah. Along that journey we have beckoned strangers into fellowship with us: companions in both our inquiry and our community. There were other times when some of our comrades broke away and walked with us no longer. The account of those mergers and those disengagements has left its geological record, so to speak, in our ancient documentation.

The construction of the canon has been a function of realignments among the biblical people. The tribal unity between the tribes had been sundered at the death of Solomon, when Judah went its own way from the other brothers. Eventually the Jews received the narratives and oracles of the prophets into their sacred collection, while the Samaritans would add nothing to the Torah. Evidence suggests that the later rifts between the Pharisees and the Sadducees, and between the houses of Hillel and Shammai, were reflected in differing lists of books "that defile the hands."[6] The separation of Christians from Jews entailed acceptance by the former and repudiation by the latter, not only of the new Christian writings but of earlier Jewish documents: books thought to have been written in Greek, and particularly essential to the Christian sense of continuity because of their testimony to the late-developing belief in resurrection and after-life for the just in the heavenly court. Gnostics later canonized many gospels and apocalypses which the Catholics repudiated, and this confirmed those two communities as going their separate ways. On every one of those occasions when the community drew itself closely together on matters of crucial identity, it determined at the same time which books it would hold sacred.

Canon-making is community-making. The selection of which writings are to be read aloud before the community in God's name is an act of self-definition by a family of faith. It is a primal loyalty test whereby a people identifies itself by its narrative and liturgical and moral and

---

[6] See Solomon Zeitlin, "An Historical Study of the Canonization of the Hebrew Scriptures," in *Studies in the Early History of Judaism* (New York: KTAV, 1974) 1:1-42; Roger Beckwith, *The Old Testament Canon of the New Testament Church and its Background in Early Judaism* (Grand Rapids: Eerdmans, 1985).

doctrinal antecedents. Yet the chosen corpus of sacred writings—selected at great cost of membership—is no testimony to uniformity. While the books were honored as the ground of the newly defined faith, they did not embody a homogeneous or synoptic view among themselves. The Christian Bible retains (wittingly or unwittingly) much diversity—and disagreement as well. Genesis, which retains long documents partisan to the northern kingdom and to Joseph, its dominant tribe, is revered alongside the Early Prophets, whose final loyalties were truculently for Judah. Joshua gives a different account of the conquest than that of Judges. Ruth and Jonah were written with an eye to contradicting the message of Ezra. Jesus' teaching about response to enemies is hardly that of the Psalmist. The attitudes toward civil authorities ascribed to Peter and to Paul are certainly more benign than those which scorch the Book of Revelation.

The canonical Scriptures, despite the tendentious process which led to their selection, do not provide the community with a creed. They are a mosaic, an amalgam of the early past that the community must always be unpuzzling in order to formulate its contemporary beliefs. The individual elements in Scripture each represent a viewpoint particular to its author, stress, and context. But the collection, as a selective composite of those elements, is enacted from the much later viewpoint of the canonical moment. Scripture, then, is a retrospective archive of the earliest remembered trajectory of the traditional faith. Like all archives, it is of little use and possibly even some misunderstanding to laypersons unless learned scholars versed in the ancient ways of thought help them unroll and expound the canonized books: both in their original sense, and in their contribution to the ongoing perspective.[7]

---

[7] Jacob Neusner comes at this same point from a slightly different direction, but his conclusion is harmonious with mine. "The system comes before the texts and defines the canon. No universally shared traits or characteristics, topical, logical, rhetorical, within the diverse texts can account by themselves for the selection of those texts for places in the canon. . . . The canon (so to speak) does not just happen after the fact, in the aftermath of the texts that make it up. *The canon is the event that creates of documents holy texts before the fact: the canon is the fact.* The documents do not (naturally, as a matter of fact) *coalesce* into a canon. They (supernaturally, as a gesture of faith) are *constructed* into a canon. . . . *The system does not recapitulate the canon. The canon recapitulates the system*" (emphasis his); *Canon and Connection: Intertextuality in Judaism* (New York: University Press of America, 1987) 157-59. See

Crises over the long past have provoked the community to isolate and disavow various equivocations, misunderstandings, and misjudgments. The community has nevertheless retained various inconsistencies and insufficiencies. They will either stymie the believing community, or somehow spur it on to play its own needful, contemporary part in drawing the tradition further along into restatement. To remain alive in faith the community must both hold fast to the conclusions of the past and reach new surmises and resolutions and insights of its own. The growing tip of the tradition must be alive with new growth for it to have a strong enough draw on its root system for nourishment.

The most honored records of the past show us that our contemporary conclusions will sometimes diverge from those of our forbears, but that need not mean we break faith with them. As present inquiry telescopes out of past understanding, the process requires a discerning initiative by the community. Beholden to the inspired meditations of the past, the present church believes that she too has the same Spirit that spoke through the prophets and apostles, and that she is a coactive party to the making of the never-closed creed.

Christians are therefore unable to say simply, "It says here . . .," because the church, who has already decided repeatedly which sayings count most, must continue to reflect actively upon her own past sayings and frame a sequel which is faithful to that foundation, not by mere repetition but by development. As I have already mentioned, it is those who imagine that the Spirit guides them to find in Scripture a library of one single perspective and doctrine that are in fact the most prone to subject the documents of revelation to their own perspective, fancy, and doctrine.

Since the canon represents early editions of the continuing faith, they have to be read first of all exactly as they were meant, in the sense and force of their original authorship. They need not be allegorized or spiritualized or forced to fit any more current edition of the faith. The same community, led by the same Spirit, is inspired by those earlier accounts of faith and then endeavors to do for its generation what those seers did for theirs. The Scriptures provide the inspiration, but not the text, of our creed.

Consulting the sacred writings is therefore an active undertaking. In the biblical sense, one hearkens in order to hear; one must be creative to be receptive.

also his *First Principles of Systemic Analysis: The Case of Judaism within the History of Religion* (New York: University Press of America, 1987) 131-53.

* * *

A common assumption among Christians is that the flash of brilliance marking the arrival of Jesus paled and darkened all that had gone before.

> When the moon shone, we did not see the candle.
> So doth the greater glory dim the less.[8]

All of Israel became preamble, archive, ancient history, obsolete. But I want to argue that it is obsolete in much the same way the Christian Scriptures are also obsolete.

Faith and scholarship have been at cross purposes in their estimate of the relative worth of what is older and what is later. Church doctrine has usually assumed that when comparing Jewish with Christian Scriptures it is the ancient that must be read in light of what followed. But when scholars examine individual passages, they usually value the more ancient over the more recent. In studying the New Testament documents, higher critics have tended to distrust the later developments in favor of the most primitive traces. A dogmatic *Ur*-fixation has turned every exegete into an archaeologist, shoveling away all the debris and clutter to get back to the pure faith closest to the source. This method may rest on a theological motive more than a scholarly one, however.

The presupposition, of course, has been that utterances of Jesus enjoy a higher clarity and credibility than utterances of his disciples. And among the discipleship, priority must go to the eyewitnesses, with a supposed cooling-off of charism the further one got from Galilee. The handicap in this theory is that we probably never do get to Jesus himself. All that we have is from the disciples. And there is abundant evidence in the New Testament to suggest that whatever they heard that was radical, explosive, and *bouleversant* fell on dull and unprepared ears. Faith came through hearing . . . but it came at a slow and plodding pace. The witnesses admitted that his teaching, his mission, and his character had all gone right past them. It was only after he had been tortured, slain, raised, and exalted that they began to reflect on what they had heard. And then it began to dawn on them. We have good reason to believe that it was a long dawn. But the disciples were getting better, not worse, at unpuzzling the drift of Jesus' teaching with

---

[8] *The Merchant of Venice*, V, 1.

the passage of time. Thus the later layers of literary evolution may not be all shards and debris. The documents may have gained in perspective. Some may also on occasion have regressed, but each editorial adaptation must be surveyed on its own to determine that.

If one accepts this view that the community of faith has generally, by divine assistance, looked back and gained an enhanced understanding, one then sees faith as following a trajectory, with a beginning but not yet an end. Though the Scriptures give us access to the founding times, our venture of understanding has never come to a standstill. The canonical books are normative, not by being the Last Word, but by being the First. They are annunciation and gestation to the faith, not myrrh and aloes. It derogates not a bit from our confession that the full face of the Father—or as much sight of it as we could bear—has shone upon us in Jesus, if we admit that it was more than the first disciples could make full sense of, and that we have been deciphering their ecstatic blurtings ever since.

The Christian Scriptures do represent an abrupt innovation in the tradition, but it was already a tradition in which abrupt innovations were conventional. Christians see in Jesus an apocalypse without precedent. But Israel was not unfamiliar with being yanked into disclosures that made all things new. When every token of divine predilection had been annihilated—royal house, holy city, promised land, and temple-home for the ark and the glory—and this devastation then gave birth to a young, new faith of even greater tenacity: it took their breath away. And when in their deepest disgrace they heard their prophets making mockery of all rival gods, and proclaiming that their Yahweh was the only god, the creator of the heavens and the earth and therefore—this was what really sent them gagging—he was also the fond father of the Assyrian and Babylonian slaughterers: this too took their breath away. And when in the very teeth of holocaust by the effete cosmopolites of Syria they first heard it whispered that God's great life-and-death promises were not all to be cramped and squeezed into Judah and into three-score-and-ten years, but that those who walked honorably before the Lord would laugh at their tormentors from the divine retinue in heaven: this seemed to leave them with no breath at all. No matter how strong our sense of innovation in Christ, the Jewish Scriptures prepare us for the unanticipable by establishing the expectation of the unimaginable. And the unimaginable came, repeatedly.

Dramatic permutations of faith were already traditional in Israel long before Jesus. And the New Testament in its turn discloses not one but several convulsive new disclosures. The acknowledgment of Jesus as Messiah was tumultuous, but it was followed a while later by the unthinkable admission of Gentiles to table-fellowship, and later still by recognition of Jesus as the Only Begotten. It is not the case that transfiguration of faith is peculiar to the Christian Scriptures; only that its tempo had picked up. There is then a continuing itinerary of development that wends its way through both Testaments.

The history of the people of Abraham numbers certain very privileged witnesses to more enlightened discoveries in faith. Those who accept the Bible as inspired should have no difficulty honoring some of the ancient seers as more intensely exposed to the Mystery than others—and Jesus as invested with its fullness. But the rate of absorption by which the believing community took in those insights, integrated them with all it knew from beforehand and otherwise, and then drew revised conclusions from them—the rate at which Israel, Old and New, metabolized those disclosures—was spiked by the surges of high charism in peak individuals, but overall it followed a more steady climb. And what we have in the Bible is more a residual account of what the community was absorbing than an account of what God had to disclose. Thus the textual community might take considerable time to digest and take the benefit of its greatest visionaries. The Bible exposes us to the greatest, most insightful prophetic leaders in those early ages. But the trajectory of understanding faith resolutely gained in perspective such that its steady, fitted curve absorbed those sometimes scattered points above and below. The elements of faith were being reconsidered, recast, and re-applied from Canaan to Corinth. From Genesis to Revelation (or, perhaps, from Exodus to the Pastorals) that faith was constantly developing . . . though not always in an upward vector, for there were times of regression and eddies of confusion. Jesus may be the flashpoint of God's revelation, but the faith neither then nor now reached its apogee. The revelation may be definitive but the faith is not. The community and the inquiry move on, and so too does the absorption of revelation into faith.

* * *

How might this bear on the applicability of Israel's ethics for Christianity? I would propose two different relationships which those ancient moral and legal codes bear to the faith in its contemporary moment. In one sense that ancient material is primitive and obsolete; in another, it is invaluable.

The New Testament does convey a radically new perspective on ethical obligation. Jesus, presented as our best glimpse of the Father, best displays his own character and that of the Father when he dies for those who kill him: Judaean establishment, Jerusalem populace, forsworn Peter, treacherous Judas, craven disciples, Pilate, Herod, Roman cohort. As Peter in Acts puts it more cosmically: it was done by those under the Law and those outside it. In a word, by everyone. Readers of the gospel are given to understand that they too would have had a hand in it had they been there. Jesus would fare as badly in Jacksonville, Jakarta, or Johannesburg as he did in Jerusalem. We are all standing there at Calvary with silver in our purses and hammers in our hands.

What Jesus reveals is a relentless love for those who relentlessly kill him. And he reveals a Father who loves sinners. His love is not like ours, we being so handicapped. He loves, not for the goodness he finds in us but for that which is in him. He cherishes us regardless of our behavior. There is no wrath in him. As Jesus dies stubbornly cherishing those who for every sort of expediency and malice shifted around aimlessly in their efforts to rid themselves of his compelling presence, he reveals a Father whose love is not a response but entirely initiative. His is an originating love, fastened upon us like that of the Prodigal Father, whether we serve or whether we renege. The Father of Jesus cannot be offended. Nor can he be pleased. He is disclosed to us as One whose attitude toward us is not governed by our characters but by his own. His attitude does not pivot on our performance. It is we who pivot. He cannot turn his back on us, but we are inveterate in turning our backs on him and on one another. Or, to put it in John's terse way, God is love.

If this be so, it quarrels with the notion of a God who will punish those who violate his law. This was put well enough by a Louisville foundry worker who, as a folk philosopher, was interviewed by a local journalist.

Crowe's view of the hereafter is beautiful. His God is a good guy who eats chicken, drinks beer, loves moonlight on the river and would even smoke a joint if you offered it to him. "I can't believe what churches and so-called religious people say," says Crowe. "I had eight or 10 people tell me that the tornado of '74 was God's warning. My God isn't in charge of tornadoes. He wouldn't throw one at you just for kicks. My God's waiting over there with a table laid for me. When I get there, he's going to say, 'I'm God, and I love you. Forget all the bull you heard on earth.'"[9]

His theology is anthropomorphic, but no more so than what biblical scholars should be comfortable with. What makes Crowe interesting is that he is criticizing Christians for behaving like they left the tradition sometime back.

The New Testament is every bit as concerned about right moral behavior as is the Old. But it is incompatible with the gospel's disclosure of the Father of Jesus for us to portray God as threatening with wrath and punishment those who disobey his law. Whatever the sense of the New Testament, it cannot imply that failure before the law will cause God to reject us. What we do see is that wrongful behavior will cause us to reject God.

The payoff in the teaching remains very much what it was before: that if we act in certain ways we shall surely die. But it will be at our hand, not at God's. By the way we live we can destroy ourselves morally, personally, spiritually. And we also know that by God's enablement there are other patterns of behavior that bring life, that vitalize our ability to go out unselfishly in love to serve others, and build up our strength and gumption.

What the believing community—and consequently its enlightened scriveners who have given scriptural expression to the community's past—had done was to sense the life-or-death importance of human behavior, but in doing so they projected onto God what is all too human: alienation. Sin does not incur divine wrath, but it does cause us to wither, to sicken, to be estranged, to die, to reject that wrathless love. Sin can be mortal, not because it will interdict God's love for me but because it will disable me from taking it in and responding with a like heart. Grace empowers me to recover and surmount my self-mutilating sin by emerging from selfishness into love: indeed, by assimilating myself to the Lord. By the Lord's empowerment I can come to cherish those who do not cherish me, in hope of being such a grace to them (as others are to me) that I might prevail over their egotism as God through Jesus wears down mine.

On this view of things, the Law of Israel must be rhetorically and ethically obsolete for the Christian. For one thing, it is grounded on the assumption that God will surely abominate those who violate it. But

---

[9] Paul Bryan Crowe, quoted by John Flynn, (Louisville) *Courier-Journal*, 21 January 1977, B1.

even if one reconstrues the ancient code as an inspired warning about what behavior leads humans to be alienated from one another and from their Lord, and what behavior enhances human ability to cleave to the Lord and one another, it is still obsolete, for it represents only a very early stage of reflection by the community. In this latter sense, the insights of the first Christians, memorialized in the Old Testament, are also obsolete, for the community's reflection has already moved forward from them.

It should be obvious that by "obsolete" I do not characterize the canonical texts as abrogated or extinct. They belong to another time, a privileged and classical time for the believing community. Their force consists in their anchoring and sustaining the tradition. They are not an account of the community's faith, for that must always be a contemporary composition. The Scriptures are of a different genre of discourse. They are ancient, even primitive; they represent the tradition as it was first being formed. They are "obsolete" as every past text of the tradition is now obsolete. But they are valuable beyond every other past text of the tradition because we must be in communion with them in order to be the heirs of the faith of the prophets and apostles. No single element of the canon is identical with the faith as it has thus far developed. Each belongs to its time and author. But assembled purposefully into a canonical collection all these components acquire a new clarity, for they resolve into a trajectory that points to where we believe, and beyond.

But that directs us to the aspect of incalculable value which the Commandments, though obsolete, have for the Christian believer. The Law expresses the first cumulative wisdom of the community of faith about what various behaviors do to those who avoid or perform them.

The church believes that it is an inspired community, endowed by a prophetic vision to help us see what we would otherwise have neither the mind nor the will to see. Its genre of ethical discourse is therefore highly experiential. The community has observed what gives life and what depletes it.

Thou shalt not steal. In Saudi Arabia the government may chop off your hand if you do. More enlightened governments like our own will imprison you if you are a poor robber, fine you if you are middle-class, and give you a suspended sentence if your stealing has been massive. But the cumulative lesson in Scripture is a warning that the thief is robbed by his own hand. By violating his neighbor to steal her goods, he has incapacitated his ability to be her neighbor, and also his ability to receive the clasp of the everlasting arms pulling him into embrace.

Thou shalt not bear false witness against thy neighbor. For the understanding reader this becomes not a warning of a vengeful God but an alert to the relentless lethal nature of lying. Those who lie lose the truth. They cannot look God in the eye because they can't look themselves or anyone else in the eye.

Do not commit adultery. You will be disenabled to cleave fast to anyone.

Do not pass up the refugee, the handicapped, the humiliated. You will be victimizing yourself. Your eternity is at stake in how you deal with others.

Obviously this was not the understanding of the original authors of the *miṣwôt*. Their prohibition against false witness, of course, forbade perjured testimony in a society where tort and crime were mostly settled on the word of reliable witnesses. In its original meaning it did not suggest a global command against all fraud. And the canonical author and primary audience believed that it was a divine imperative with a divine sanction.

For the believing reader who takes those as early expressions of a communal inquiry for which God has provided both the receptivity and the nourishment, those commands, exegeted in their original apodictic simplicity, convey the beginning convictions about how we are to wend our way to God. For the original addressees they were definitive on their author's terms. For us, the latter-day readership, they present us with the first prophetic insights in our tradition. The tradition continues on, and there is much in it which has enhanced our insight into stealing from the poor and truth-telling and life-giving. The fact that there are outright prohibitions in the Scriptures against sodomy or crustacea or unveiled women or murder does not conclude our search for moral truth in these matters. It grounds the search. It is not enough to locate the logia in the text; we must account to ourselves why our ancestors in faith saw those to be evil, and how that judgment was in partnership with their understanding of God, and the human community, and family, and neighborhood, and property, and child-bearing, and fidelity, and the rest. We cite the ancient command as a moral authority, not insofar as it lays down a certain course of action, but insofar as that imperative has been reconsidered, reiterated, and reinforced while the tradition was gaining momentum and resolve. If, on the other hand, the ancient command has been marginalized or repudiated or refined as the faith-community has clarified its vision, the commandment's authority is accordingly vacated.

* * *

The same pro-active kind of reverence for our faith-community's past obtains whether we are consulting the Old Testament, the New Testament, or normative documents from the tradition that came forth from them. Let one later example help illustrate this. There is but a single Torah text on abortion, Exod 21:22, permitting a husband or master to recover compensation from anyone who injures a woman and causes her to abort. The New Testament is silent on the subject. But the tradition immediately after the New Testament period bursts into a forthright condemnation of abortion (*Didache, Letter of Barnabas,* Minucius Felix, Athenagoras, Tertullian, Clement of Alexandria, Hippolytus). The language is aggressive: the character of this sin is no longer one of property damage but of merciless destruction of the most helpless.

Now one cannot erect a moral imperative merely by citing these texts. But when one examines the turn of mind characterizing the late first and early second centuries, one sees this prohibition as one element of a new moral program that is new but entirely in continuity with the tradition. The Christian community had inherited from its Jewish antecedents an emphatic priority of obligation to care for the widow, the pauper, the resident alien, and the orphan. The first Christian ethical treatises extend this concern to four other vulnerable categories. Beyond the widow was the wife (men are no longer free to divorce their wives); beyond the pauper was the slave (master and slave must be brothers, not owner and chattel); beyond the resident alien was the foreign enemy (who must now be loved, not hated); and beyond the orphan were the unborn and newborn, who must no longer be destroyable at the will of their father. Here is one of the most entrenched and resolute convictions in the Christian moral tradition, with no direct textual authorization in either Testament. But neither the mere absence of explicit biblical warrant nor the mere presence of explicit patristic warrants is decisive. The contemporary moralist must study the documents in context to see that a clutch of moral injunctions of mercy that arise with a clamor in the Jewish Scriptures, and are given a wider application in the Christian Scriptures, congruously give birth to a stringent prohibition that telescopes with utter authenticity out of its biblical antecedents, and was begotten by the biblical commitments to the helpless. To ratify this as binding today requires that one verify how rooted it is in those elements of our moral tradition which have been reinforced, not marginalized. The fact that this particular injunction is at odds with much modern social thought is but an echo of the invective it first encountered nineteen centuries ago.[10]

Walter Harrelson, *cujus festum colimus*, has argued that the commandment not to kill casts its wider concern over such matters as armed warfare, capital punishment, abortion, euthanasia, and the slaying of the very ill or disabled. "In my judgment, all these matters do relate to the intention of the sixth commandment, especially as that commandment is developed through the centuries in Judaism and Christianity."[11] It seems clear that these are matters repeatedly addressed by the moral wisdom of the believing community—indeed several are very actively debated today. The *miṣwâ* itself, I would say, took no notice of them, but its sharp note of command wrote an inaugural passage in the long fugue which both exceeds and ratifies its ancient ancestor, the law of Moses.

---

[10] See James Tunstead Burtchaell, C.S.C., with Daniel C. Maguire, "The Catholic Legacy & Abortion: A Debate," *Commonweal* 114/20 (1987) 662-80.

[11] Harrelson, *Ten Commandments*, 116.

Two Decades of Research on the Rich and the Poor in Luke–Acts

JOHN R. DONAHUE, S.J.
Jesuit School of Theology at Berkeley

In his study of the Decalogue Walter Harrelson notes that its final three commands deal with basic rights and social obligations that touch the goods and lives of the community.[1] After commenting that the prohibition of theft has been misused to protect accumulated wealth and power without concern for the common good, Harrelson locates this command in the context of the Hebrew Bible's pervasive concern for the marginal and as a warning against unjust accumulation of wealth.[2]

Within the New Testament, the Lukan writings show paramount concern for the danger of riches and the proper use of the goods of the world.[3] In the past two decades, under the influence of redaction criticism, an increasing number of studies have probed the background to Luke's teaching, what ethical posture Luke urges toward wealth and riches, and what kind of community was addressed by Luke-Acts.[4] Both the issue of rich and poor in the biblical tradition and Luke's distinctive perspectives achieve a new urgency in our age, when the gap

---

[1] Walter Harrelson, *The Ten Commandments and Human Rights* (OBT 8; Philadelphia: Fortress) 135.

[2] Ibid., 136-42.

[3] J. A. Fitzmyer, *The Gospel According to Luke I-IX* (AB 28; Garden City, NY: Doubleday, 1981) 247-51. For an overview of Luke's teaching on possessions see Johnson, *Sharing Possessions*, 11-25.

[4] See the general survey in F. Bovon, *Luke the Theologian: Thirty-three Years of Research (1950-83)* (Alison Park, PA: Pickwick Publications, 1987) 390-400. D. L. Meland (*Poverty and Expectation in the Gospels* [London: SPCK, 1980] 16-20) is one of the few scholars who claim that this aspect of Luke has been exaggerated.

between rich nations and poor nations and between the rich and poor in our own nation has become a concern for theology and church life, and not simply for economic analysis and social policy.[5] After a brief description of the material in Luke which evokes such concern (I), I will survey the major studies of wealth and poverty in Luke beginning with Hans-Joachim Degenhardt's study in 1965 and concluding with the work of Philip Esler published in 1987 (II), and I will conclude with summary comments on problems remaining and on directions for future research.

Bibliography: Degenhardt, H.-J., *Lukas—Evangelist der Armen: Besitz und Besitzverzicht in den Lukanischen Schriften* (Stuttgart: Katholisches Bibelwerk, 1965); Dupont, J. *Les béatitudes* (3 vols.; Paris: Gabalda, 1969, 1973), esp. 2:19-142; 3:41-64, 151-206, 389-471; "Community of Goods in the Early Church," in *The Salvation of the Gentiles: Studies in the Acts of the Apostles* (New York: Paulist, 1979) 85-102; "The Poor and Poverty in the Gospels and Acts," *Gospel Poverty* (ed. M. D. Guinan; Chicago: Franciscan Herald, 1977) 25-52; Esler, P. F., *Community and Gospel in Luke-Acts: The Social and Political Motivations of Lucan Theology* (SNTSMS 57; Cambridge: Cambridge University, 1987); Horn, F. W., *Glaube und Handeln in der Theologie des Lukas* (GTA 26; Göttingen: Vandenhoeck und Ruprecht, 1983); Karris, R. J.,

---

[5] Some important biblical studies are: A. Gelin, *The Poor of Yahweh* (Collegeville: Liturgical, 1964; French orig. 1953); A. George, "Poverty in the Old Testament," in *Gospel Poverty* (ed. M. Guinan; Chicago: Franciscan Herald, 1977) 3-24; D. Gowan, "Wealth and Poverty in the Old Testament: The Case of the Widow, the Orphan and the Sojourner," *Int* 41 (1987) 341-53; M. Hengel, *Property and Riches in the Early Church* (Philadelphia: Fortress, 1974); L. Hoppe, *Being Poor: A Biblical Study* (Wilmington, DL: Michael Glazier, 1987); N. Lohfink, *Option for the Poor: The Basic Principle of Liberation Theology in the Light of the Bible* (Berkeley, CA: Bibal Press, 1987); "Von der 'Anawim-Partei' zur 'Kirche der Armen'," *Bib* 67 (1986) 153-76 (with extensive bibliography). R. D. Paterson, "The Widow, the Orphan and the Poor in the Old Testament and Extrabiblical Literature," *BSac* 130 (1973) 223-234; M. Schwantes, *Das Recht der Armen* (BBET 4; Frankfurt: Lang, 1977); G. Soares-Prabhu, "Class in the Bible: The Biblical Poor a Social Class?" *Vid* 49 (1985) 322-46; W. Stegemann, *The Gospel and the Poor* (Philadelphia: Fortress, 1984). For an example of the concern of churches for this issue, see *Economic Justice for All: Pastoral Letter on Catholic Social Teaching and the U.S. Economy* (Washington, DC: National Conference of Catholic Bishops, 1986), esp. par. 30-55 (on Bible). For a bibliography and description of the activities of the World Council of Churches, see R. D. N. Dickinson, *Poor, Yet Making Rich* (Geneva: World Council of Churches, 1983).

"Poor and Rich: The Lukan *Sitz im Leben*" in *Perspectives on Luke-Acts* (ed. C. H. Talbert; Danville, VA: Association of Baptist Professors of Religion, 1978) 112-25; **Johnson**, L.T., *The Literary Function of Possessions in Luke-Acts* (SBLDS 39; Missoula, MT: Scholars, 1977); *Sharing Possessions: Mandate and Symbol of Faith* (Philadelphia: Fortress, 1981); **Pilgrim**, W. E., *Good News to the Poor: Wealth and Poverty in Luke-Acts* (Minneapolis: Augsburg, 1981); **Schmithals**, W., "Lukas— Evangelist der Armen," *Theologia Viatorum* 12 (1973-74) 153-67; **Seccombe**, D. P., *Possessions and the Poor in Luke-Acts* (SNTU B/6; Linz: SNTU, 1982); **Stegemann**, W., "The Following of Christ as Solidarity between Rich, Respected Christians and Poor, Despised Christians (Gospel of Luke)" in L. Schottroff and W. Stegemann, *Jesus and the Hope of the Poor* (Maryknoll, NY: Orbis, 1986) 67-120 (German orig. 1978).

I.

Luke-Acts' special concern for the rich and the poor has been discussed since the advent of historical criticism, manifest in the discussions throughout the past century on the "early communism" of Acts 2:42-47; 4:32-37, and the "Ebionite" strain of the Gospel.[6] Examination of places where Luke appropriates and edits Markan material on riches and poverty, incorporates related Q material, and especially introduces his significant special material (L) discloses abundant and varied perspectives on the poor, the rich, and the attitude toward possessions.

In his redaction of Mark, Luke "retains virtually all passages or sayings which reveal an antipathy for the rich and a sympathy for the poor."[7] In the calls of both the disciples (Luke 5:1-11; cf. Mark 1:16-20) and Levi (Luke 5:27-32; Mark 2:13-17), only in Luke (5:11, 28) do the disciples leave "everything" to follow Jesus. In the allegory of the seeds (Luke 8:11-15; Mark 4:13-20) Luke repeats the tendency of riches to choke the word (8:14; Mark 4:19), but adds the phrase "as they go on their way" to accentuate the danger of riches along the "way" of discipleship. Luke repeats Mark's instructions to the disciples to take minimal possessions on a journey, but denies them even a staff (Mark 6:6b-9 = Luke 9:1-3; cf. 10:4). He takes over the saying on gaining the world but

---

[6] H. J. Cadbury, *The Making of Luke-Acts* (New York: Macmillan, 1927) 260.

[7] Esler, *Community*, 165; Esler also calls attention to two "surprising" omissions of Markan material, Mark 7:11-12 and Mark 14:3-9, cf. Luke 7:36-50.

losing one's life (9:25; Mark 8:36), as well as the story of the rich young man (18:18-29; Mark 19:17-31), but in the latter makes significant alterations. The "man" is not young but "a ruler," and Luke highlights the danger of riches by calling him "very rich." Luke omits Mark's positive response of Jesus to his observance of the commandments (Mark 10:21), quotes Jesus as urging him to leave "*all* that you have" (Luke 18:22; cf. 5:11, 28), and has Jesus address directly to this ruler, rather than the disciples, the saying on the difficulty of the rich entering the kingdom of God (Luke 18:24; Mark 10:23).[8] Luke then repeats the saying on the rewards of leaving family to follow Jesus (Luke 18:28-30), but in a more radical sense since disciples must leave their spouses (18:29). He follows Mark in reporting the condemnation of the scribes who "devour widows' houses" (Luke 20:47; Mark 12:40), along with the "lament" about the widow who gives all she has to the temple treasury (21:1-4; Mark 12:41-44).[9]

Since there is no certainty as to whether Luke or Matthew preserves a given Q saying in its original form, comments about Luke's editing of Q are tentative. Nonetheless, when Luke's version of a Q saying reflects an emphasis in his redaction of Mark or in his special material, there is high probability that we are dealing with Lukan additions or editing of traditional material. In other cases Luke may preserve a more nearly original form of a Q saying because it fits in better with a particular theme of his Gospel. The principal examples are the following.

To the Q preaching of John (Luke 3:7-9; Matt 3:7-10) Luke adds an exhortation to share one's coat with the needy (Luke 3:11) and a warning to tax collectors and soldiers against acts of injustice associated with material goods (3:12-14). Whereas in Matt 4:4 Jesus responds to the first temptation by saying, "Man shall not live by bread alone, but by every word that proceeds from the mouth of God" (= Deut 8:3), Luke 4:4 reads "Man shall not live by bread alone."[10] In Luke's Beatitudes it is simply "the poor" (6:20; cf. Matt 5:3, "poor in spirit") who are blessed, and Luke adds a series of woes against the rich and the satis-

---

[8] Johnson, *Literary Function*, 145.

[9] Most commentators interpret the widow's action as a symbol of total dedication. However, A. Wright ("The Widow's Mites: Praise or Lament?—A Matter of Context," *CBQ* 44 [1982] 256-65) has argued from the context (Mark 12:38-40=Luke 21:46-47) that Jesus laments the widow's action as a consequence of the misuse of religion by the scribes; see similarly J. Fitzmyer, *The Gospel According to Luke X-XXIV* (AB 28a; Garden City, NY: Doubleday, 1985) 1320-21.

[10] Esler (*Community*, 168) and Fitzmyer (*Luke I-IX*, 515) both hold that Luke preserves a more nearly original form of the citation of Deut 8:3.

fied (6:24-26). Luke's teaching on non-retaliation reads, "Of him who takes away your goods, do not ask them again" (6:30; cf. Matt 5:42, "Do not refuse him who would borrow from you"), and his version of the saying on love of enemies is illustrated by a metaphor dealing with possessions ("do good and lend, expecting nothing in return, 6:35; cf. Matt 5:43-48). To the warning against judging (Luke 6:37; Matt 7:1-2), Luke adds "Give, and it will be given to you" (6:38). In Luke's version of the healing of the Centurion's son (Luke 7:1-10; Matt 8:5-13, the only Q miracle), the centurion is described as one who "built us our synagogue," providing an example of the proper use of possessions (cf. Acts 10:31). Luke's version of the contrast between John the Baptist and those who live in palaces heightens the wealth of the latter (7:25; cf. Matt 11:8), depicting them living in luxury like the condemned rich man of 16:19. Luke adds an exhortation to almsgiving to the criticism of the Pharisees (Luke 11:41; Matt 23:26), and to the warnings against anxiety (Luke 12:22-34; Matt 6:25-33) he adds the exhortation to sell one's possessions and give alms as an index of one's true treasure (12:33-34; cf. Matt 6:19-21).

Luke's distinctive concerns with the rich and the poor and with possessions emerge most strongly in material peculiar to his Gospel (L). The early chapters provide an overture to the whole Gospel. The infancy narratives show special concern for the ʿānāwîm, people without money and power.[11] In her Magnificat Mary praises a God who puts down the mighty from their thrones, fills the hungry with good things and sends the rich away empty (Luke 1:52-53). Mary and Joseph cannot find lodging in an inn, and the first proclamation of Jesus' birth is to people on the margin of society ("shepherds," 2:8-14).[12] The sacrifice offered at the presentation of Jesus in the temple is that determined by law for poor people (Luke 2:24 = Lev 5:11); Simeon and Anna (a widow) represent a faithful and just people (2:25-38). Luke begins Jesus' public ministry not with the proclamation of the imminence of the kingdom (cf. Mark 1:15; Matt 4:17), but with Jesus' citing Isa 61:1-2, "the good news to the poor" (Luke 4:17-19; cf. 7:22).

Most of such material occurs in the "travel narrative" where Jesus, on his way to Jerusalem, teaches extensively on the way of discipleship (Luke 9:51-19:27). Only Luke contains the parable of the Rich Fool

---

[11] R. E. Brown (*The Birth of the Messiah* [Garden City, NY: Doubleday, 1977] 350-55) argues that the infancy narratives derive from the ʿānāwîm, the poor of the Jerusalem Church.

[12] On "shepherds" as one of the "despised trades" see J. Jeremias, *Jerusalem in the Time of Jesus* (London: SCM, 1969) 306.

(12:13-21), introduced by a warning against covetousness (*pleonexia*, lit. "the love of more"), as well as the parables of the Unjust Steward (16:1-8) and the Rich Man and Lazarus (16:19-31).[13] Luke alone calls the Pharisees "lovers of money" (16:14). Only in Luke is the "great banquet" to be celebrated with "the poor, the maimed, the lame, and the blind" (14:31, 21). Luke contains the parable of a widow (mentioned frequently in the OT with the poor, e.g. Deut 14:28-15:11; 24:14-17; Job 22:7-9) who seeks justice from a callous judge (18:1-8). Luke alone recounts the story of Zacchaeus the "chief tax collector" (19:1-10) who, upon his conversion, is willing to give half his goods to the poor (19:8).

Though with different emphases, the Acts of the Apostles reflects a similar concern, depicting both negative and positive use of possessions. In Acts' version of the death of Judas (Acts 1:18-20), in contrast to Matt 27:3-10, Judas does not return the money but buys property ("a field") with the "payment of his injustice" (Acts 1:18, auth. trans.); he seems to die accidentally and the property is deserted (cursed).[14] The early community is one which holds "everything in common" and where there is no needy person (2:42-47; 4:32-37).[15] Ananias and Sapphira (Acts 5:1-11) by withholding the "proceeds of the land" are guilty of deceiving God. As in the Gospel, almsgiving is stressed (Acts 10:2, 4, 31; 24:17; cf. Luke 11:41; 12:33; 19:8). Simon (8:9-24) tries to use money (v. 18) to buy power. Lydia, "the seller of purple," who was a worshiper of God, offers Paul hospitality—an example of good use of resources (16:11-15, cf. 17:12). Upper-class men and women accept the Gospel (17:12). Concern for possessions motivates opposition to Paul. He and Silas are beaten for freeing a slave girl from venal owners (16:16-24), and in 19:23-41 silversmiths of Ephesus see their livelihood threatened by Paul's preaching. Paul concludes his final address to the Ephesians with comments about the proper use of goods and concern for the poor (20:32-35).

Other motifs and themes of Luke are allied to his concern for the rich and the poor. Throughout the Gospel Luke presents Jesus in the form of an OT prophet who takes the side of the widow (7:11-17; 18:1-

---

[13] For more detailed study of these parables in relation to the theme of the rich and poor, see J. R. Donahue, *The Gospel in Parable: Metaphor, Narrative and Theology in the Synoptic Gospels* (Philadelphia: Fortress, 1988) 162-80.

[14] Johnson, *Literary Function*, 178-82.

[15] Though these are the "classic" texts adduced for early Christian "communism based on love," virtually all recent scholars interpret "having all things in common" from its widespread usage in Hellenism to describe friendship. For a good list of pertinent texts see Seccombe, *Possessions*, 200.

8), the stranger in the land (10:25-37; 17:16), and those on the margin of society (15:1-2; 14:12-13, 21). Many of these parables, not directly concerned with possessions, use economic images for comparison, e.g., the payment of the innkeeper by the Samaritan (10:35), the misuse of resources by stewards (12:44-46; 19:11-27), the finding of a coin (15:8-10), and the "squandering of possessions" by the younger son along with his restoration by receiving the father's goods (15:11-32). The inaugural sermon of Jesus is couched in the language of the biblical Jubilee (with its remission of debts).[16]

While there is almost universal agreement on the importance of possessions, there is no consensus on major issues of interpretation, nor any consistent perspective within Luke-Acts. While the Gospel stresses complete dispossession as a condition for discipleship, it and, more strongly, Acts praise those who use (rather than abandon) their resources to aid the disciples. Dispossession of goods, common possession, and almsgiving are all praised. Though the Lukan Jesus proclaims "good news to the poor," the evil of the rich is mentioned far more frequently than the goodness of the poor, and especially in Acts it is those of some resources who further the spread of the good news.

There is also no consensus on the translation and interpretation of the term *ptōchos* (lit. "beggar"), used almost exclusively in Luke and the NT for the poor.[17] Does Luke have in mind the literal poor, the poor "as a class," or is "poverty" metaphorical of a religious attitude of one's need for God? Does Luke hand on the traditions about radical dispossession and sharing of goods only as something which belonged to the initial period of the church (Conzelmann) or as a utopian ideal of "primordial beginnings" (Johnson)?[18]

Although these questions, which are a healthy sign of both the importance and the urgency of the issue, merit extensive discussion, I will attempt no summary or evaluation of the solutions offered to particular issues. Rather, I will concentrate on one issue which has characterized the discussion from the beginning but which has emerged recently as the central topic: the audience of Luke's teaching and the makeup of

---

[16] S. Ringe, *Jesus, Liberation, and the Biblical Jubilee* (OBT 19; Philadelphia: Fortress, 1985), esp. 33-49.

[17] Stegemann (*The Gospel and the Poor*, 14) notes that of the other terms for the poor in Hellenistic literature, *penichros* appears only in Luke 21:2; *penēs* only in 2 Cor 9:9, *endeēs* in Acts 4:34, and *aporos* (used frequently in Josephus) not at all in the NT.

[18] H. Conzelmann, *The Theology of St. Luke* (New York: Harper and Row, 1960) 233; Johnson, *Sharing Possessions*, 128.

the community addressed. Is the community composed primarily of poor and marginal people or of those with some resources and status in the Hellenistic world? Does Luke address his two-volume work primarily to the poor in his community to encourage them that God is on their side and will punish the rich for their blindness, or is Luke's intention to warn the rich about the danger their wealth poses to salvation and exhort them to almsgiving and concern for the poor? Due to limits of space, as well as to the sheer volume of published material, my survey cannot do justice to the works treated. I propose an overview and an invitation to further engagement with the works themselves.

II.

Hans-Joachim Degenhardt argues that Luke tells the story of the past "with a concern for reform of the church of his own time."[19] Like many of his successors, he proceeds from the attempt to reconcile the demand for disciples to leave all to follow Jesus with the fact that in Acts (and in the Zacchaeus story) complete dispossession is not demanded of those who are offered salvation. His solution is that the disciples in Luke stand for "special office holders" in the community, perhaps missionaries or itinerant preachers, and Luke addresses the radical demands of Jesus only to them.[20] The majority of the community (composed mostly of Gentiles) was exhorted to almsgiving and beneficence (*Wohltätigkeit*) to the less fortunate, in a social environment where such behavior is not respected.[21]

Though foundational in focusing subsequent attention on the pertinent texts of Luke-Acts, Degenhardt's proposal for a "two-level" morality of possessions has been strongly rejected. "Disciple" in Luke-Acts is used not simply for a select group within the larger number of followers of Jesus (e.g., Luke 6:17; 14:12-26; Acts 6:1; 9:1).[22] Also, for many, Degenhardt's proposal is too resonant of the traditional Catholic distinction between the "evangelical counsels" to be observed only by those in the church called to religious life and "precepts" to be observed

---

[19] Degenhardt, *Evangelist der Armen*, 19.

[20] Ibid., 39, 215-22.

[21] Ibid., 221-222.

[22] Karris, "Poor and Rich," 114; Seccombe, *Possessions*, 14: "*Mathētai* in Luke denotes a wider group than the semi-professional band that followed Jesus" (see also 148-50).

by the majority of Christians.[23] A third response to Degenhardt was articulated by Walter Schmithals who argued strongly that the setting for Luke's teaching on possessions was persecution.[24] The Beatitudes suggest this context, and the community was to be prepared to lose family and possessions if they confessed Jesus. Only this "extreme situation" explains Luke's teaching; Luke offers no religious ideal of poverty or of communal possession.[25]

The extensive writings of Jacques Dupont provide the next major phase in the discussion.[26] Since the 1950s, French scholarship under the influence of Albert Gelin's work (above, n. 5) had been vigorously concerned with the poor in the Bible. Gelin argued that the "poor" were primarily the humble and faithful remnant of Zeph 1:2–2:3 and that the poor in the NT were primarily the humble and those open to God, rather than the economically poor.[27] Dupont disagrees strongly with those who define the poor principally in terms of a religious attitude, or who spiritualize the promises given to the poor.[28] His fundamental claim is that, in pronouncing the poor blessed, Jesus addressed people in real physical need who were blessed not because future happiness was to be the reward of their fidelity, but because God was concerned about them. The kingdom which Jesus proclaimed and enacted was to challenge and alter the conditions under which the poor lived.[29] Luke, according to Dupont, adapted Jesus' proclamation to his own community composed mainly of the poor, encouraging them with the blessings of the kingdom and disclosing to them God's judgment on the rich (who were mainly outsiders).

After the studies by Degenhardt and Dupont, the first full-scale study of possessions in Luke-Acts was by Luke Johnson (1977, see bibliography), who was less concerned with the ethics of possessions or with the community addressed by Luke than with the metaphorical meaning

---

[23] Bovon, *Luke the Theologian*, 390.

[24] Schmithals, "Lukas—Evangelist der Armen."

[25] Ibid., 164-65.

[26] Dupont's magisterial studies of the background, tradition history, and redaction of the Beatitudes are indispensible for study of biblical themes such as justice, the kingdom of God, and concern for the poor and marginal.

[27] See the discussion of Gelin, in Lohfink, *Option*, 59-63.

[28] Not only against Gelin, but against Bultmann, Jeremias, and T. W. Manson who present variations of this position, see *Les béatitudes*, 2:13-15.

[29] *Les béatitudes*, 2:151-81, summarized in "The Poor and Poverty in the Gospel and Acts," in *Gospel Poverty*, esp. 37-41.

of possessions within the larger literary pattern of Luke-Acts.[30] Johnson argues that Luke-Acts is structured by a dramatic pattern of the people's either accepting or rejecting Jesus, the prophet. Riches and poverty become metaphorical of reactions to the prophet Jesus: poverty, of openness to his message; riches, of blind self-interest which leads to rejection. Though aware of the need to describe the communities behind NT documents, neither in *The Literary Function of Possessions* nor in subsequent works has Johnson attempted to describe the community for which possessions functioned in such a powerfully symbolic manner.[31]

The 1980s have thus far witnessed four major studies of the theme of possessions in Luke. In 1981, in his *Good News to the Poor*, Walter Pilgrim subjected the pertinent material to a fresh analysis. After a rather rapid survey of the poor in the OT and Intertestamental literature, he devotes most of the work to the rich and poor in Luke.[32] He moves away from an overly spiritualized or religious understanding of the poor as the humble or pious and argues that they comprise those who lived a marginal economic existence as well as those who were socially marginal, e.g., tax collectors. These people are promised "a radical social reversal of their lot in the coming age."[33]

Pilgrim argues that Luke does not hand on the call to total surrender of possessions as a demand on all Christians of his time, but recalls it as an ideal from the life and teaching of Jesus to motivate his community to share their possessions with the needy. Luke's message, according to Pilgrim, addresses both the poor and the well-off in his community. The former are to recall that Jesus took the side of the poor and that he summoned his original disciples to live without resources. The well-off are exhorted to be like Zacchaeus—to express their conversion by putting their goods at the service of the less fortunate. Luke offers a vision of community "whose sense of oneness was evidenced by their readiness to provide for the economic needs of one another," and "in

---

[30] See also R. Tannehill, *The Narrative Unity of Luke-Acts: A Literary Introduction* (Vol. 1; Philadelphia: Fortress, 1986) 127-32.

[31] Johnson details his reservations about describing a community setting on the basis of a literary work in "On Finding the Lukan Community: A Cautious Cautionary Essay," SBLSP 17 (ed. P. J. Achtemeier; Missoula, MT: Scholars, 1979) 1:87-100.

[32] Pilgrim, *Good News*, 64-165. Of the works discussed, Pilgrim's is the best suited for non-specialists.

[33] Ibid., 83.

which possessions are placed radically at the service of those in need."[34]

In his 1982 study, David P. Seccombe examined the material on possessions with the purpose of reconciling the apparent contradiction alluded to above, the demand for renunciation and the picture of the well-to-do receiving favor from Jesus and assisting the spread of the Christian movement in Acts. In contrast to virtually every other author, he argues that "the poor" in the OT, especially the Psalms and Deutero-Isaiah, refers neither to the humble and pious, nor the economically disadvantaged, but to Israel as a whole nation in need of God's salvation. This meaning of "poor" is found in Jesus' inaugural sermon (Luke 4:18 = Isa 61:1-2) and is behind the reversal of the rich and the poor in the Magnificat and the Beatitudes. In contrast to the dominant contemporary trend, Seccombe writes, "There is nothing socio-economic or socio-religious about Luke's use of 'poor' terminology in these passages. . . . To seek to ground a liberation theology or an ethic of poverty upon these texts would be to misunderstand and misuse them."[35]

Seccombe interprets the calls for renunciation of property as a sign that "in the extreme situation it is revealed that discipleship has no limits."[36] In assessing those passages which deal with the challenge possessions pose to discipleship, Seccombe first argues that, although possessions "are about to become valueless with the approaching eschatological crisis" and "although even now they are seen to have infinitesimal worth compared to the true values of the Kingdom, they are nonetheless to be faithfully employed by the sons of light."[37] He concludes by arguing that Luke's purpose is "evangelistic," that is, "to convince the not yet convinced and to push the not yet committed, rather than to confirm and instruct the converted."[38] The community addressed by Luke was made up of "well-to-do hellenistic God-fearers who were attracted to the Christian movement," those with "a good knowledge and appreciation of Jewish ways of thinking, as well as some degree of sophistication in terms of classical hellenistic culture," but "hesitant as to whether such a newcomer on the scene could possibly

---

[34] Ibid., 150, 165.

[35] Seccombe, *Possessions*, 95. For critical reactions to Seccombe, see the reviews by D. Goldsmith, *JBL* 104 (1985) 148-50; and J. Topel, *Bib* 66 (1985) 274-77.

[36] Seccombe, *Possessions*, 133.

[37] Ibid., 171-72.

[38] Ibid., 228.

be authentic, and afraid what might be the cost to them socially and economically if they were to declare themselves publicly and unreservedly for Christ and his church."[39]

Two articles from the 1970s anticipate the major studies on the community of Luke in the 1980s by Horn and Esler (see bibliography). In dialogue primarily with the work of Degenhardt, Dupont and Schmithals, Robert Karris proposed that Luke's community was composed of rich and poor members, but that Luke was primarily taken up with "the rich members, their concerns, and the problems they pose for the community."[40] The stories of the rich young man (18:18-25) and Zacchaeus (19:1-10) are directed to their concerns—whether possessions prevent their becoming genuine Christians. The predominance of material dealing with the danger of possessions rather than praise of the poor supports this perspective.

In the same year, Wolfgang Stegemann arrived at virtually the same conclusion by combining literary and theological criticism with an explicit "sociohistorical" analysis. By pointing to similarities with the Cynic and Stoic criticism of wealth and praise of poverty, Stegemann argues that the simple life of the disciples in the Gospel functions as a criticism of the rich in Luke's community.[41] He stresses that Luke (alone among the evangelists) attributes the classic Hellenistic vices of greed (*pleonexia*, Luke 12:15) and avarice or love of money (*philargyria*, Luke 16:14) to the rich in his community, and directs other warnings and parables to them. The rich like Zacchaeus (Luke 19:1-10) are to be saved by repentance expressed in acts of justice and almsgiving.

Luke proposes a "concrete social utopia" directed at an independent community in a city of the Roman empire. It does not have members who belong to the upper class, but neither does it have the very destitute. The "social utopia" consists of a vision of solidarity where the more prosperous break down the barriers erected by status and possession by their acceptance of and concern for the less prosperous and less respected members in the community.[42]

The two most noteworthy studies of possessions in Luke-Acts in this decade are by Friedrich W. Horn and Philip F. Esler. From a careful tradition-history method, Horn reconstructs the situation of Luke's community. He follows Conzelmann in locating it in the third genera-

---

[39] Ibid., 228, 229.
[40] Karris, "Poor and Rich," 124.
[41] Stegemann, "The Following of Christ," 83-87.
[42] Ibid., 116-20.

tion (c. CE 100), but rejects the views of Schmithals and Karris that the community faces persecution.[43] He argues that Luke's shaping of traditional material is best seen in Acts 2:42-47, especially vv. 42 and 45, and 4:32-37, especially vv. 32-35, which do not portray "early communism" but a fellowship of love concerned for the needs of others, especially by almsgiving.[44] The calls for total dispossession of goods in following Jesus are part of the tradition Luke receives. He retains them not as a mark of Christian existence for the whole community or as a way of life for office holders, but as examples of distancing from possessions.[45] Luke adapts this tradition as well as the negative portrait of the rich to a community in danger of "worldliness" (*Weltlichkeit*). Christians are falling away from the faith into a pre-Christian ethos which no longer allows them to be distinguished outwardly from their non-Christian environment.[46] Horn, then, joins those other authors who see well-off Christians as the primary audience of Luke's parenesis.

The study of Philip Esler (completed in 1985) represents an important shift in the method of describing the community of Luke and locating it in its socio-economic environment.[47] Esler's goal is "to analyze the interrelationships between Luke's theology and the social and political pressures upon his community" by a method called "socio-redaction criticism."[48] It consists of careful attention to historical, economic and social factors in first-century Hellenistic culture (e.g., the need for food and shelter, the understanding of status and class), as well as the use of sociological models to describe Luke's community.

Following the majority opinion, he locates Luke between the mid-80s and mid-90s in a Hellenistic urban setting. From a study of the conversion stories in Acts, especially that of Cornelius (Acts 10), he argues that Luke's community is composed of Jews and Gentile "God-fearers" who had been "adherents of Yahweh and synagogue-attenders prior to their becoming Christians."[49] Esler notes: "There is not a single example in Acts of the conversion of a Gentile who had been an idolater previously."[50] Using sociological studies of sectarian communities, Esler

---

[43] Horn, *Glaube und Handeln*, 215-20.

[44] Ibid., 39-49.

[45] Ibid., 199-203.

[46] Ibid., 221.

[47] Esler, *Community*.

[48] Ibid., 24, 4-5 (on socio-redaction criticism).

[49] Ibid., 44.

[50] Ibid., 42.

describes Luke's two volumes as "an exercise in the legitimation of a sectarian movement, as a sophisticated attempt to explain and justify Christianity to the members of his community at a time when they were exposed to social and political pressures which were making their allegiance waver."[51]

His study of the poor and the rich is set in this larger context. He argues initially that "we must examine his [Luke's] message in light of what it was actually like to be rich or poor in the Hellenistic cities of the Roman East," and then describes social stratification and the experience of poverty in these cities.[52] He finds it possible that Luke's community included (like Corinth at the time of Paul) a few people of wealth or power (the *honestiores*), as well as many from the "urban poor," who needed basic necessities such as food and shelter. He then argues convincingly that the reversal of the fate of the rich and poor proposed in the Gospel is not simply an "otherworldly hope" but is "a vital constituent of Christianity in this world, here and now."[53]

The composition of Luke's community became the stimulus for his teaching on wealth and poverty. The social context of this teaching is that in Hellenistic cities the upper and lower classes had little contact and "the destitute got little if any help from the civic authorities, the *collegia* or from private benefactors.[54] Luke's two-volume work presents a challenge to the reigning ethos and values of the Hellenistic world and "imposes on the rich an indispensable requirement, quite at odds with the social values of their own society"—to aid the destitute and seek *koinōnia* with them.[55]

Conclusion

Three issues stand out from the survey. *First*, there is the meaning of poverty and the poor. These terms have a complex history and meaning in both the Bible and Luke-Acts. While their religious use in reference to the faithful remnant, the "righteous poor," and those who are open to God is still maintained, there is growing consensus that these terms

---

[51] Ibid., 222; see also 46-70. Elser's argument (203-19) that Luke legitimates Christianity to a Roman audience as an "ancestral religion" rather than as a *religio licita* or as politically harmless is an important contribution on the purpose of Luke-Acts.

[52] Ibid., 171-79.

[53] Ibid., 193.

[54] Ibid., 198.

[55] Ibid., esp. 187-97.

also describe real social conditions. Recent studies calling attention to fundamental differences between our world and culture and that of the first century in understanding "wealth" and "poverty" also caution against "anachronism" in interpreting rich and poor from our socio-economic background.[56] Yet there remain fundamental similarities between these two worlds, not only in large parts of the world where the social conditions are not unlike those addressed by Luke, but even in the urbanized West where the experience of powerlessness and marginalization, as well as the destruction of community brought about by poverty, is a challenge to the Gospel today, no less than in Luke's time.

Second, there is an emerging consensus that Luke retains the calls for radical dispossession not as a lifestyle to be imitated, either by the community at large or by particular groups, but as symbolically powerful narratives. To say that Luke's statements on dispossession are symbolic or have a literary function is not to deny their power to address the "real world." Through image and narrative Luke creates a "symbolic world" which, by giving a different vision of reality, has power to shape the "real world" of his audience. *Third*, there also seems to be a consensus that Luke is written primarily for the "rich" in the community described as either the socially more respected or the economically more prosperous.[57] Luke warns the well-off that their wealth and power can bring about greed, blindness, and ultimately loss of salvation, while he simultaneously summons them to conversion and offers them examples of the proper use of possessions, especially almsgiving. We should be cautious, however, about thinking of Luke's community as a homogeneous group. The varied postures toward possessions

---

[56] Especially P. Hollenbach, "Defining Rich and Poor Using Social Sciences," SBLSP 26 (ed. K. H. Richards; Atlanta, GA: Scholars, 1987) 50-63; B. J. Malina, *The New Testament World: Insights from Cultural Anthropology* (Atlanta: John Knox, 1981) 82-85; "Interpreting the Bible with Anthropology: The Case of the Rich and the Poor," *Listening* 21 (1986) 148-59; "Wealth and Poverty in the New Testament and its World," *Int* 41 (1987) 354-69.

[57] A certain caution is necessary here. Though people from the "ruling elite" are favorable to the Gospel, e.g. Joanna (Luke 8:3), Manaen (Acts 13:1), and Greek women of noble birth (Acts 17:2), and others use their resources favorably (Esler, *Community*, 184), Luke never uses "riches" in a positive sense or commends a "rich" person. This polemic against the rich is part of the tradition he inherits; see especially G. Nickelsburg, "Riches, the Rich, and God's Judgement in 1 Enoch 92-105 and the Gospel According to Luke," *NTS* 25 (1978-79) 324-44. See also, T. E. Schmidt, "Hostility to Wealth in Philo of Alexandria," *JSNT* 19 (1983) 85-97.

may simultaneously incorporate and address concerns of different groups within the community.

Despite the intense study of the rich and poor in Luke, certain questions need further research. Work on the community behind Luke will continue, but less along the lines of "mirror theology," which sees events of the community reflected in an almost allegorical fashion in the Gospel and Acts.[58] Esler's careful integration of social science method with detailed attention to the social *realia* of the first century marks a new (or renewed) direction in study of Luke's community.[59] Esler has also called attention to the need for more study of famines in antiquity and their effects on the urban poor.[60] There is also need for work on "alms" and "almsgiving," both as a religious practice and a social institution.[61] Equally necessary is reflection on the social context of contemporary interpreters. Esler argues that "the ingrained disregard among scholars for the social and economic setting of Luke-Acts, and their corresponding enthusiasm for its alleged spiritual and individualistic approach to salvation originate in a clear middle-class bias," and he urges that we allow Luke to speak through this layer of *embourgeoisment*.[62] The contributions of the past two decades offer insights and challenges rather than clear solutions in the quest for Luke's good news to the poor.

---

[58] See Johnson, "A Cautious, Cautionary Essay," 87; and R. J. Karris, "Windows and Mirrors: Literary Criticism and Luke's Sitz im Leben," SBLSP 17 (1979) 1:47-58.

[59] See also the forthcoming work by Halvor Moxnes, *The Economy of the Kingdom: Social Conflict and Economic Realities in Luke's Gospel* (OBT; Philadelphia: Fortress).

[60] Esler, *Community*, 177.

[61] See the older study, H. Bolkestein, *Wohltätigkeit und Armenpflege im vorchristlichen Altertum* (Utrecht: A. Oostehoeck, 1939); and the collection of texts in A. R. Hands, *Charities and Social Aid in Greece and Rome* (London: Thames and Hudson, 1968).

[62] Esler, *Community*, 170.

JEWISH CONCEPTIONS OF THE HUMAN FACTOR IN BIBLICAL PROPHECY

MOSHE GREENBERG
The Hebrew University of Jerusalem

Fellow-feeling with Walter Harrelson grew out of our meetings and conversations in Jerusalem, attendant upon his reconciling directorship of the Ecumenical Institute at Tantur. This essay in Jewish theology is offered to him in appreciation of his manifold contributions to biblical thought, hermeneutics, and interfaith understanding.

Modern critical study of Hebrew Scriptures by Jews has seldom been conducted in the light of any theological principle.[1] Its proponents have either ignored the tenets of traditional religion in philological-historical inquiries that avoid engagement with theology or existential issues, or have focused on different objects of inquiry, such as poetics, in which the historical factor is muted.[2] By orthodoxy, biblical

---

[1] For rare exceptions see the prefaces of S. D. Luzzatto to his commentaries to the Pentateuch (1829) and Isaiah (1855), available in S. D. Luzzatto, *Ketavim* [Selected Writings] (ed. M. E. Artom; Jerusalem: Bialik Institute, 1976) 2:97-134, 206-16. Also consult Franz Rosenzweig's letter to J. Rosenheim, in F. Rosenzweig and M. Buber, *Die Schrift und ihre Verdeutschung* (Berlin: Schocken, 1936) 46-54, disproportionately famous owing to the scarcity of theological deliberation by Jewish scholars with critical sophistication.

[2] Examples of the first category: Y. Kaufmann, H. L. Ginsberg, H. M. Orlinsky, E. A. Speiser; of the second, U. Cassuto, M. Weiss. For brief surveys of modern Jewish critical exegesis, see M. Waxman, *A History of Jewish Literature* (New York: Bloch, 1947) 4:633-70; *EncJud* (Jerusalem: Keter, 1971) 4:899-903.

criticism is generally regarded as incompatible with the foundations of Jewish belief.[3]

This situation differs from that obtaining in Christianity. Both the Protestant and Roman Catholic Churches have accommodated themselves to the practice and main findings of criticism: theological seminaries are today the academic berths of most biblical critics. This was not accomplished without overcoming opposition, but the battles fought in the Churches in the nineteenth and twentieth centuries and the conceptual refinement and clarification resulting therefrom have had no counterparts in the Synagogue.[4] It is in order to contribute to the assessment of the relation of critical principles to Judaism and to the practice of Jewish exegetes that this essay is undertaken. It focuses on one aspect of the critical stance: the supposition that in the formulation of prophetic writings (and most of Scripture is ascribed by Jews to prophets) a human factor was present to such an extent that no account of them can overlook the personal circumstances and particular situation of their human authors.[5]

---

[3] See S. Shaw, "Orthodox Reactions to the Challenge of Biblical Criticism," *Tradition* 10 (1969) 61-85 (with bibliography); Sh. Rosenberg, "Biblical Criticism in Modern Jewish Religious Thought" (in Hebrew), in *Ha-miqra va'anaḥnu* [We and the Bible] (ed. U. Simon; Tel Aviv: Dvir, 1979) 86-110 (extensive bibliographic survey). A good exposition of theological reactions to criticism is R. J. Z. Werblowski, "Biblical Criticism as a Religious Problem" (in Hebrew), *Molad* 18 (1960) 162-68.

[4] The distinctions certain Rabbis made between allowed and prohibited criticism (Hirschensohn) or the metaphysical accommodation of it to faith (Kook) described by Rosenberg (see previous note) remained private musings for all practical purposes. Decades later M. Kapustin ("Biblical Criticism: A Traditionalist View," *Tradition* 3 [1960] 25-33) could still crudely characterize and reject "Biblical criticism [for which] the Torah is not word for word and letter for letter direct divine revelation. Neither are the writings of the *Nevi'im* (Prophets) or the *Ketuvim* (Hagiographa) divinely inspired, products of the *ruach ha-kodesh* (holy spirit). For the critics [they are] the works of certain individual personalities representing the 'Hebraic genius.'" Contrast the position of S. R. Driver—an eminent British critic—adduced ahead in the body of this article.

[5] The question is this: when the prophet says, "Thus said YHWH," and proceeds to deliver a speech, what is the relation of his speech to what God said to him? I shall not deal with the question of how the prophet receives revelation or what form the divine communication to him takes, but only with the question of the immediate origin of the speech issuing from the prophet, and which he commonly prefaces by the formula, "Thus said YHWH" or the like. How precise is "thus"?

That this supposition is not in itself a denial of divine inspiration or revelation has been affirmed vigorously by modern Christian critics. Canon S. R. Driver stated in the Preface to the 8th edition of his *Introduction to the Literature of the Old Testament* (Edinburgh, 1909):

> It is not the case that critical conclusions, such as those expressed in the present volume, are in conflict either with the Christian creeds or with the articles of the Christian faith. Those conclusions affect not the *fact* of revelation, but only its *form*. . . . That both the religion of Israel itself, and the record of its history embodied in the Old Testament, are the work of men whose hearts have been touched and minds illumined, in different degree, by the Spirit of God, is manifest: but the recognition of this truth does not decide the question of the author by whom, or the date at which, particular parts of the Old Testament were committed to writing. . . . There is a human factor in the Bible, which, though quickened and sustained by the informing Spirit, is never wholly absorbed or neutralized by it; and the limits of its operation cannot be ascertained by an arbitrary *a priori* determination of the methods of inspiration; the only means by which they can be ascertained is by an assiduous and comprehensive study of the facts presented by the Old Testament itself.
> (pp. viii, ix, xi)

Such a latitudinarian approach to Scripture would seem to have no place in Judaism. Certainly Maimonides' formulation of the eighth of

---

The views presented in this essay are chiefly those arising from explication of scriptural data, whether by exegetes or others. They are not such as are primarily grounded in a theology, in which extra-scriptural (often extra-Jewish) systematic thinking is determinative. (Even the citation of the theologian Joseph Albo—see note 20—bases itself on scriptural phenomena.) I seek to document the acknowledgment of literary facts, particularly those that resist easy accommodation to dogma. It is notable that when Abarbanel writes as a philosophic critic his position is more doctrinaire than when he writes as an exegete; see note 21.

For the following selection of sources I have drawn heavily on the monumental collection of A. J. Heschel, *Torah min ha-shamayim be-aspaklaria shel ha-dorot* [Torah from Heaven in the perspective of the ages] (London: Soncino, 1965) 2:123-298; and on the treatise on "The order in which the Torah was written," in *Torah Shelemah* (ed. M. Kasher; New York: American Biblical Encyclopedia Co., 1959) 19:328-79. Selection, arrangement, and interpretation are my own.

his thirteen principles of faith (a byword among orthodox Jews) leaves little room for it:

> [The] Torah from Heaven. To wit: we believe that the whole of this Torah that we have today is the selfsame that was given to Moses; and all of it is from the Power [= God]; that is, it came to him, all of it did, from God—a coming called metaphorically speech, but whose manner is unknown to all but him (peace be to him) to whom it came; and that he was in the capacity [lit. degree] of a scribe to whom one dictates, and he wrote it all down—dates, stories, and commandments.[6]

This rigorous formulation is directed against Moslem attacks on the integrity of the Torah, and the charge or the suspicion that Moses, independently of God, invented it.[7] A glance at talmudic antecedents shows that Maimonides chose the language of the most uncompromising of several views found in that compendium of classical (and wellspring of all subsequent) Jewish thought.

It was a jealously guarded dogma of early Judaism that "[the] Torah was from Heaven," meaning that not a word of the Pentateuch

---

[6] Maimonides, Commentary to Mishnah Sanhedrin 10.1; *Mishnah ʿim Perush Rabbenu Moshe ben Maimon, Seder Neziqin* (ed. J. Kafaḥ; Jerusalem: Mossad Harav Kook, 1964) 214.

[7] See, for example, *Samauʾal al-Maghribī: Ifḥam al-Yahud* (Silencing the Jews), ed. M. Perlmann, *PAAJR* 32 (1964) 53-57.

K. P. Bland ("Moses and the Law According to Maimonides," in *Mystics, Philosophers, and Politicians* [ed. D. Swetschinski; Durham: Duke University, 1982] 49-66) argues that Maimonides "does not believe that Moses ever received the particulars of his law in revelation," but rather "considered Moses to have been the direct author of the Law" (63)—despite "the obvious efforts [in the thirteen principles] to find language that emphasizes the divine origin of the Law while minimizing the creative role of Moses in its promulgation" (65). Bland's argument has cogency for Maimonides' esoteric doctrine; however, no reading of the eighth principle will yield a "minimizing" of Moses' "creative role" but a forceful denial of it: Moses is figured as a scribe taking dictation. That is how believers through the ages have understood the principle, and Maimonides' choice of language and figure indicates that that is how he intended to be understood by the masses.

I am grateful to Alfred Ivri for calling my attention to Bland's stimulating article.

was—as charged by anti-Jewish writers of Hellenistic-Roman times[8]—an invention of Moses:

> And these have no portion in the world to come: Whoever says ... [the] Torah is not from Heaven.
>
> (m. Sanhedrin 10.1)

Another tannaitic dictum:

> "Because he has spurned the world of the Lord" (Numbers 15:31)—this refers to whomever says, "[the] Torah is not from Heaven"; and even if he said, "The whole Torah is from Heaven excepting a given verse, which the Holy One—blessed be He—did not utter, but Moses, on his own [lit. from his own mouth]," he is one who "has spurned the word of the Lord."
>
> (b. Sanhedrin 99a)

This dogma had to be adjusted to evidence contrary to several scriptural passages. For example, the final verses of the Pentateuch told of Moses' death and burial.

> "There died Moses, the servant of the Lord" (Deut 34:5): Is it possible that Moses wrote "There died Moses" while he was still alive? Rather, up to that verse Moses wrote, but from that verse onward Joshua wrote; so Rabbi Judah. Simon bar Yoḥai retorted: Is it possible that the Torah scroll [that Moses delivered into the custody of the levite-priests] was missing even a letter? Yet it is written, "Take this Torah scroll" (Deut 31:26, the account of the delivery)! Rather, up to that verse ["There died Moses"] the Holy One—blessed be He—was speaking and Moses was writing; from that verse on, the Holy One—blessed be He—was speaking and Moses was writing with tears, as it is written [of a similar procedure], "Baruch said to them, 'He [Jeremiah] recited aloud [lit. from his mouth] to me all these things while I wrote in a scroll with ink.'"
>
> (b. Menaḥot 30a)

---

[8] See M. Stern, *Greek and Latin Authors on Jews and Judaism*, III: Indexes (Jerusalem: Israel Academy of Sciences and Humanities, 1984) 137, s.v. Moses: legislator of Jews.

Other difficulties arise, perhaps the foremost being the style of
Deuteronomy in which Moses speaks in the first person and appears to
gloss freely, on his own, quotations of God's utterances (e.g., the insert,
"as the Lord your God commanded you," in the Sabbath commandment
of the Decalogue, 5:12). The Rabbis described the difference between
the curses at the end of Leviticus (26:14ff.) and the curses at the end of
Deuteronomy (28:15ff.) as follows:

> Those [of Leviticus] are couched in the plural and Moses said
> them from the mouth of the Power, while these [of
> Deuteronomy] are couched in the singular and Moses said them
> on his own [lit. from his own mouth].
>
> (b. Megillah 31b)[9]

This blatant contravention of the Sanhedrin passages troubled
commentators. The Tosaphists took the edge off the Megillah statement by qualifying "Moses said on his own" with the explanation "and
by the Holy Spirit [of prophecy]" which at least derives Moses' speech
from divine inspiration. Abarbanel made a distinction:

> Moses . . . said these things and expounded the commandments
> mentioned here to Israel under the necessity of his taking leave
> of them, and the Holy One wished that after he finished saying
> them . . . all should be written down in the Torah scroll just as
> Moses said it. . . . Hence, while the saying of these things to
> Israel was of Moses . . . the writing of it in the Torah scroll was
> not. . . for how could he write down anything on his own in God's
> Torah?. . . So this book is included among the divine books just
> like the others. Whoever says that Moses wrote down any given
> verse of them on his own—he is one who has "spurned the word
> of the Lord. . . ." That is why they said in Megillah, "The curses
> in Deuteronomy . . . Moses said them on his own"—said them, not
> wrote them. . . . Similarly Moses prayed on behalf of the people
> at the incident of the Golden calf on his own, for he was not
> commanded to do so by God—indeed to the contrary, He

---

[9] "'Moses said those [of Leviticus] from the mouth of the Power'—having
been commissioned by Him to say, . . . 'I shall set [such a curse], I shall visit [you
with such a bane], I shall let loose [such a scourge]'—He who has the ability to
do speaks so. But in Deuteronomy . . . Moses speaks on his own, 'He will visit
[you with such a bane]'" (Rashi). Rashi's comment to Deut 28:23: "[Moses]
mitigated his curses compared with those of God [in Leviticus]."

demanded that Moses desist from Him. . . . But the writing down
of all such in the Torah was from the mouth of the Power . . . and
whoever says . . . about the writing of the Torah that he [Moses]
wrote anything that God did not say [= dictate] to him, he is one
who has "spurned the word of the Lord." (Commentary,
Introduction to Deuteronomy)

The pietistic commentator Ḥayyim ben Atar did not hesitate to
emphasize the Mosaic provenience of Deuteronomy in his comment to
the book's first verse:

"These are the words"—these and not the preceding ones—
"that Moses spoke"—these are his own words, for the whole
book is Moses' warning and admonition directed against any
who would transgress God's words. . . . Even when he resumed
God's words in order to explain them it was not because he was
ordered to do so but on his own.

Ben Atar calls the reference to the Egyptian bondage in Deuteronomy's
version of the Sabbath commandment of the Decalogue (it is missing
from Exodus) "the words of Moses" (at 5:15). He regards the speech beginning in 8:1 as displaying Moses' psychological insight.[10]
    Such attributions to Moses do not deprive Deuteronomy of divine
sanction (or even dictation); that is a dogmatic necessity no medieval
believer would have challenged. What is notable is the latitude permitted within the scope of the dogma for human creativity. The literary (stylistic) facts point to Moses as the author of most of the book of
Deuteronomy; the book's authority derived from the dogma that Moses'
language was adopted by God and dictated back to him at the time the
book was written down.
    Quite surprising is the latitude shown in the interpretation of the
prophetic message-formula, kōh-ʾāmar YHWH "thus said the Lord,"
used by Moses in the narrative of Exodus. In Exod 32:27 Moses cites a divine command to slay the worshipers of the calf; but where is that
command? The Mekhilta[11] finds it in Exod 22:19, "Whoever sacrifices

[10] See E. Touito, *Rabbi Ḥayyim ben ʾAtar u-Ferusho Or ha-ḥayyim ʿal ha-Torah*
[Rabbi Ḥayyim ben Atar and his Commentary to the Torah "Or ha-ḥayyim "].
(Jerusalem: Ministry of Education, 1982) 33-34.
    [11] *Masseket de-Pisḥa, parasha* 12; restored from early quotations, see H. S.
Horovitz and I. A. Rabin, *Mechilta DʾRabbi Ismael* (Jerusalem: Bamberger &
Wahrman, 1960) 40, lines 9f.

to a god other than the Lord alone shall be proscribed." A midrash puts
it thus:

> Where did the Holy One—blessed be He—tell him to slay his
> fellows? He intimated to him at Sinai that anyone who
> worshiped an alien deity is subject to the death penalty; as it is
> said, "Whoever sacrifices to a god, etc." When he descended
> and found them worshiping an alien deity . . . he thought,
> "These are subject to the death penalty."[12]

It is clearly implied that the message-formula need not always be
taken literally; a prophet's inference from an earlier utterance of God
may be couched in the language of a direct citation, when in fact the
prophet tailored it for the occasion.[13]

An obscure passage in Sifre to Num 30:2 was understood by later interpreters to refer to this latitude:

> "This is the word that the Lord spoke" (Num 30:2). This tells
> that just as Moses prophesied with [the formula] "Thus said
> [the Lord]" so the other prophets prophesied with "Thus said";
> but Moses exceeded them in that of him it is said, "This is the
> word, etc."[14]

---

[12] L. Ginzberg, *Genizah Studies in Memory of . . . Schechter* (New York:
Jewish Theological Seminary of America, 1928) 1:74f. (reference from Heschel,
Torah, 145 [above, note 5]).

[13] Or even invented it deliberately; see the following midrash aggadah
from *Seder Eliahu rabba* (ed. M. Friedmann; Vienna: Verlag der israelitisch-
theologischen Lehranstalt, 1900) 17:

> I call heaven and earth to witness that the Holy One—blessed be
> He—never said to Moses to stand in the gate of the camp and say,
> "Who is for the Lord—to me!" (Exod 32:36), or to say, "Thus said the
> Lord . . . 'Each of you . . . slay brother, neighbor, and kin'" (v. 27).
> Rather, righteous Moses reasoned: "If I say to the Israelites, 'Each of
> you slay his brother, etc.,' they will say, 'Did you not teach us that a
> court that condemns to death one person in a sabbatical cycle is
> called murderous' [*Mishnah, Makkot* 1.10]? How come you put three
> thousand to death in one day (v. 28)?'" So he ascribed [the order] to
> the Heavenly Glory, as it is said, "Thus said the Lord, etc." What
> follows? "The Levites did [as Moses had bidden]" (v. 28).

[14]*Seder Mattot, pisqa 153: Siphre D'be Rab* (ed. H. S. Horovitz: Lipsiae: Gustav
Fock, 1917) 198.

The fifteenth-century philologist, Profiat Duran, interpreted this passage in the course of explaining the Hebrew particle *kōh*, which he called "a term of comparison":

> "Thus shall you say to my lord [Esau]" (Gen 32:5) means "the likes of these words," for Jacob did not care about the wording, only that they kept to the purport. I take similarly every "thus said the Lord" found in the sayings of the prophets. They mean by it the purport of God's speech to them, what is to be understood by his words. They do not scruple to make some verbal changes in it so long as the purport is kept unchanged. Hence "thus said the Lord" means "the likes of these words said the Lord." Now, when the sages said [that Moses used this common prophetic formula, yet exceeded the other prophets in using "This is the word"] they meant that what Moses relates [after the preface, "this is the word"] is the very speech that God uttered, without any verbal change. By saying, "This" it is not enough to retain the purport—the general idea—as did the other prophets. That much may be inferred from the sense of *kōh*. But a better case can be made from the substance of the matter: Since the other prophets were foretellers only, not having been sent to give commandments but to admonish and warn concerning the observance of the Torah, while Moses alone (peace be to him) was sent to give commandments and Torah, therefore they said that "all the prophets prophesied with 'Thus said'—referring to the foretelling and the admonitions; but Moses our teacher (peace be to him) . . . exceeded them in that he gave commandments and Torah, and that is what is conveyed by "This is the word that the Lord commanded."[15]

As lawgiver, Moses had to be precise in communicating the divine statutes.

Rashi, at Num 30:2, cites the enigmatic midrash without explanation; a supercommentary to Rashi fills the lack, offering a variation of Duran's view:

> "Thus" refers to the purport of some verbal matter while "this" refers to the matter itself. Since all the prophets prophesied through an "unclear mirror," being incapable of receiving more

---

[15] *Maase Efod* (ed. J. Friedlaender and J. Kohn; Vienna: Holzwarth, 1865) 170.

than the purport of the matter communicated to them, they had
to use the formula, "thus said the Lord." . . . But since the
prophecy of our teacher Moses (peace be to him) was through a
"clear mirror," and he was capable of receiving what was communicated to him just as it was, in his case "this is the word" was
used, meaning this very matter, without any alteration. But because at the start of his mission our teacher Moses (peace be to
him) had not yet attained to the degree that he enjoyed at its
end, he had also to use the formula "thus said the Lord" on several occasions . . . namely, at the start of his career.[16]

The application to Moses of varying degrees of prophecy[17] recurs in
another way in Abarbanel's comment to Moses' Song at the Sea (Exodus
15). How is it that the song is attributed to Moses (and, similarly,
Deborah's Song to her and Barak, and Solomon's Song to him)? Because,
Abarbanel answers, what is called song (šîr[âh]) is produced by a human
whose ability has been heightened by the Holy Spirit:

The Holy Spirit is not [like a full-fledged prophecy], for it does
not produce visions of forms and parables, and its appearance is
not marked by deep sleep and loss of senses. Rather the prophet
voluntarily chooses to speak wise sayings, or hymns, or
adominitions, etc. And because the divine spirit joins itself to
him and helps him shape his speech, his degree is called the
Holy Spirit. . . . For just as a prophet does not prophesy continuously, but starts and stops, so he may prophesy at one time
in the form of the highest degree and at another in a lower
degree, or through the Holy Spirit.

. . . Every song found among the sayings of the prophets is an
utterance they themselves formulated through the Holy
Spirit. . . . When they are not prophesying they can speak
through the Holy Spirit in beautiful figures and in high style.
. . . Jeremiah wrote his book and the Book of Kings through
prophecy, which is why they are included in the second
division of Scripture, the Prophets; Lamentations he composed

---

[16] Eliyahu Mizraḥi printed in ʾArbaʿa Perushim ʿal . . . Rashi (Jerusalem: Divre
Ḥakamim, 1958) part 4 [Numbers], 54b. On "(un)clear mirror" see I. Gruenwald,
Apocalyptic and Merkavah Mysticism (Leiden: Brill, 1980) 135.

[17] See Maimonides, The Guide of the Perplexed, ii.45; in the translation of
Sh. Pines (Chicago: University of Chicago, 1963) 395ff.

through the Holy Spirit, which is why it is in the Hagiographa. And because songs are produced and formulated by the prophet . . . they are always attributed to the one who made them. . . . To be sure, all those songs were written down in the Torah and the Prophets because they were approved by God and ordered by him to be written there. . . . Thus the formulation of the Song at the Sea was by our teacher Moses, but its having been written down in the Torah was from the mouth of the Power.[18]

To sum up: The prevailing dogma was that every word in the Torah was dictated by God. This dogma was the necessary support of a hermeneutic that ascribed significance not only to the contextual sense, but to subcontextual units—clauses, phrases, even individual words torn out of context. Extreme hermeneutical freedom had to be counterbalanced by absolute assurance that the groundtext was perfect and supercharged with significance—in other words, that it was divine through and through. This formal ascription of the final form of the text to divine dictation did not blind exegetes to the varied styles of the Torah and the exigencies that indicated a human (Mosaic) origin for many passages. Room was left for a natural attribution to humans, even of prophetic speech introduced by the formula, "thus said the Lord."

In dealing with the rest of the prophets, tradition readily conceded the presence of a human factor, in accord with the literary evidence. The fundamental observation was made by a late third-century talmudic sage:

Rabbi Isaac said: The same communication (sîgnôn, from Latin signum "watchword") occurs to several prophets, yet no two prophets prophesy the same communication. [The prophet] Obadiah said, "Your arrogant heart has seduced you" (1:3), while Jeremiah said, "Your horrible nature has seduced you, your arrogant heart" (49:16). (b. Sanhedrin 89a)

Meiri glossed this as follows: "Prophets do not prophesy in the same language even when their prophecy is the same communication. For example: Obadiah and Jeremiah [have identical communications] in

---

[18] Don Isaac Abarbanel, Perush ʿal Ha-torah (Jerusalem: Bne Arb'el, 1964) 2:124f.

their prophecies against Edom, yet the language differs."[19] By this criterion the Talmud discovers the sign by which King Jehoshaphat of Judah judged the four hundred prophets of the Israelite king false: they all predicted victory at Ramoth Gilead in identical language (1 Kgs 22:6).

How did Jewish thinkers explain this diversity in unity? By variations in the vehicles of prophecy. Here are excerpts from the account given by Joseph Albo, a fifteenth-century theologian:

> Since prophecy springs from a single active cause—God, may He be blessed, and its end is forever the same—to lead mankind to happiness, why do the words of the prophets differ from one another even when they treat of the same topic? . . . Our sages suggest an explanation in Bereshit Rabba (4.4): "A Cuthean (= gentile) once asked Rabbi Meir, 'Is it possible that He of whom it is said, "Do I not fill heaven and earth" (Jer 23:24), should have spoken to Moses from between the staves of the Ark' (cf. Exod 25:22)? He replied, 'Bring me a large (= magnifying) mirror'; and he brought it. He said, 'Look at your reflection'; he looked and saw it large. Then he said, 'Bring me a small (= reducing) mirror'; and he brought it. He said, 'Look at your reflection'; he looked and saw it small. Then he said to him: 'If you, mere flesh and blood, can change yourself into several forms at will, how much more so He who spoke and the world came into being!'" Apparently the Cuthean meant to deny that prophecy was an emanation from God. He thought that it was rather a mere work of the imagination, as is the opinion of the philosophers and their followers . . . because it is impossible that He, being one, should be seen by prophets under so many different forms. For that conduces to thinking that if it comes from the deity, the divine active cause must be plural and changing in nature. . . . Rabbi Meir confuted this notion through the analogy of mirrors. As an object appears in different forms . . . according to the shape of the mirror in which it is reflected . . . though the object is unchanging, so God, be He blessed, appears to the prophets in many forms according to the clarity and purity of the media [e.g., the imaginative faculty], though He . . . is neither plural nor changing. . . . In the same manner, the object seen

---

[19] R. Menaḥem Meiri, *Sefer Bet Ha-beḥira ʿal . . . Sanhedrin* (ed. A. Sofer [Schreiber]; Frankfort: Hermon [no date] 323.

changes in accord with change in the seers: if the seer . . . has clear vision he will see the reflection one way, but if he is weak-visioned he will see it in another. . . . (Ikkarim iii.9)[20]

As Albo himself summarizes at the start of the discussion, "Different effects may arise from the same agent, depending on the nature of the recipients." This medieval theory states abstractly the assumption of a talmudic comparison of the throne visions of Isaiah (chap. 6) and Ezekiel (chap. 1):

Rava said: All that Ezekiel saw Isaiah saw [only he did not go into detail]. To whom may Ezekiel be likened? To a country bumpkin who saw the king. To whom may Isaiah be likened? To a dweller in the [capital-]city who saw the king [and does not trouble to tell about it] (b. Ḥagigah 13b).

Thus the human factor is regarded as decisive in explaining divergences between prophetic descriptions of one and the same object of vision.

The most developed conception of human conditioning of prophecy is found in Abarbanel's commentary. We have already noted how he ascribed "songs" to prophets freely composing under the Holy Spirit, and how near contemporaries—Duran and Mizraḥi—affirmed that the prophetic formula "Thus said the Lord" introduces the gist of a divine communication whose wording belongs to the prophet. Evidently the humanism of Christian Europe, with its renewed emphasis on the individual and self-expression, affected Jewish conceptions of prophecy. Here is how Abarbanel elaborated the talmudic observation of prophetic diversity in unity in accounting for the similar eschatological visions of the Temple Mount in Isaiah 2 and Micah 4:

[Rabbi Isaac asserted] that it is possible that the matter perceived by [two prophets] will be identical but the wording divergent. When I saw that Isaiah and Micah both prophesied the same communication, I thought: Isaiah prophesied this first, wherefore it is said here, "The word that Isaiah visioned," since he indeed was the one who had the vision. When Micah perceived the same general matter in the course of

---

[20] For the full text, see *Sefer Ha-ʿikkarim [Book of Principles] by Joseph Albo* (ed. and trans. by I. Husik; Philadelphia: Jewish Publication Society, 1946) 3:76-84.

his prophesying he couched it in Isaiah's very words. That is to say: Micah received from God . . . the matter of the prophecy, while the wording of the communication he took from Isaiah. Hence [the vision] is not introduced in Micah with the formula, "Thus said the Lord" or "The word of the Lord that came to Micah," like other prophecies of his. For this speech came from God first to Isaiah, not to Micah who took it from Isaiah's words and inserted into it some explanatory additions.

Likewise . . . our lord Moses himself said in the *Haʾăzînû* song (Deut 32:36), "For the Lord will vindicate His people, and get satisfaction for His servants," and David repeated this very verse in Psalm 135[:14]. . . . Surely David did not prophesy the very same communication as did [Moses] . . . rather, he took that verse from the words of his teacher. . . . Frequently we find. . . that one prophet says what another prophet already said in the very same words. (Comment to Isa 2:1)

Abarbanel reverts to the subject in his comment to Jer 49:16, further developing his understanding of Rabbi Isaac's dictum:

The prophets [other than Moses] perceived the general purport of the matter communicated to them by the Holy One—blessed be He—and then related and wrote it down in their own language. Hence when they perceived similar matters, they sometimes couched them in the very words that they saw in the prophecies of other prophets, with which they were familiar. . . . Isaiah said, "For my strength and my song is Yah, the Lord; and he has been my deliverance,"—a line derived from [Moses'] Song at the Sea (Exod 15:2). . . . Not that prophecies came to [later prophets] in the same wording as to Moses our teacher and in his degree; rather they perceived matters [in a general sense] and on their own couched them in the language of verses with which they were familiar. So [is the case of] this prophecy of Jeremiah, which he couched in the language of Obadiah.

Abarbanel has virtually anticipated the modern notion of the literary education of prophets, and on the same ground: evidence within the oracles of familiarity with antecedent Israelite traditions.

Albo ascribed the differences among the prophets to divergences in their faculties; his younger contemporary Abarbanel applied this general principle to specific cases—for example, in this comparison of Jeremiah with Isaiah:

> I am of the opinion that Jeremiah was not very expert either at composition or rhetoric, as was Isaiah or other prophets. Hence you find in his speeches many verses. . . missing a word or two ... very, very frequent use of *ʿal* [properly "on"] for *ʾel* [properly "to"], masculine for feminine . . . singular for plural and vice versa, past for future and vice versa, and shifts of second to third person in a single sentence. Moreover, there is chronological disorder in his speeches.

> I believe that the cause of this was the youth of Jeremiah when he was called to prophesy. . . . Indeed he protested, "I do not know how to speak, for I am but a youth" (1:6). Isaiah, of royal blood and raised in the court of the king, spoke with eloquence; the other prophets were called after they attained to maturity in worldly matters and gained experience in dealing with people; so they knew how to arrange their sermons. Jeremiah, on the other hand, was of the priests of Anathoth [a class apart and a villager to boot]; while still young, being called to prophesy . . . he was constrained to proclaim what the Lord commanded in language he was accustomed to. (Introduction to Jeremiah commentary)

Abarbanel thus assigns to the human factor a predominant role in the verbal formulation and arrangement of a prophetic collection of oracles. He holds the modern hermeneutical principles that the language of prophecy is conditioned by the personal circumstances and talent of the prophet—his biography, his experience, and his education.[21]

---

[21] These citations from Abarbanel's commentary to the Prophets give much more scope to the human element in the formulation of prophecy than appears in his *Commentary to Maimonides' Guide of the Perplexed*—as the latter's position is summarized in A. J. Reines, *Maimonides and Abrabanel on Prophecy* (Cincinnati: Hebrew Union College, 1970); see, e.g., Reines's summary statement: ". . . prophecy is miraculously communicated as a finished creation from God to the prophet, who is merely a passive recipient and produces nothing of the prophecy he apprehends" (lxxv).

Jewish exegesis of late antiquity and medieval times thus recognized that the prophet had a hand in the shaping of his prophecy. Did it also recognize an effect of the audience on prophecy? The one area in which early Jewish thinkers delved into the reception-factor in prophecy was anthropomorphism and related theological scandals such as the sacrificial cult. The exigency of adjusting naïve biblical conceptions to sensibilities arising from theological reflection resulted in tacit criticism of aspects of biblical language about God. Rudimentary in talmudic literature, such criticism reaches full expression under the impact of Islamic polemics. In defense, Jewish exegesis seized upon a talmudic dictum, "The Torah spoke in the language of humankind," originally meaning that biblical language is to be interpreted according to ordinary usage, and gave it the new sense, "Biblical speech about God employs language drawn from human experience." By this adroit hermeneutical move all the vivid imagery of scriptural speech about God became metaphoric. The reason offered by Jewish thinkers and exegetes for the Bible's use of such scandalous language was the ignorant and brutish state of the Israelites who received the Torah: they had to be spoken to in the gross terms suitable to their understanding. The wise, however, realize the necessity of translating the picturesque God-language of the Bible into appropriate philosophic conceptions.

This vast topic—in theological terms, "the condescendence of God"—has been systematically treated by every major medieval Jewish thinker, and so will not be further discussed here. But to forestall misunderstanding the following important caution is cited from a recent survey: unlike the idea that the prophetic message was conditioned by human factors in which premoderns and moderns agree, the idea of divine condescendence differs in a crucial point from its apparent modern counterpart:

> We are not dealing here with an evolutionary mentality, which sees Jewish history as moving from a primitive state (in need of such condescendence on the part of the divine) to a more perfect one. Such a view was virtually unknown in antiquity. .
> .. We are dealing here with a *synchronic* view; at all times there are both learned and simple people, but God places himself within reach of the simple.[22]

---

[22] F. Dreyfus, O.P., "Divine Condescendence (synkatabasis) as a Hermeneutic Principle of the Old Testament in Jewish and Christian

To summarize: From the Talmud to the Renaissance classical Jewish thought and exegesis invests the prophetic writings with divine authority: all were inspired by the Holy Spirit—in the case of the Torah (the prophecy of Moses), the text was ultimately dictated by God. This formal, dogmatic predication of divine inspiration and authorship did not hinder acknowledgment of the literary evidence of human shaping of the text. Even the Torah contains extensive tracts formulated by Moses; their inclusion in the Torah means that they were ultimately sanctioned (dictated) by God, but the personal touch of Moses is there to this day. Apart from the Torah it is freely posited that prophecy is conditioned by the personality and the capacity of the prophet: his age, his spiritual level, his education all affect his message. This alone accounts for the variety of styles and formulations that distinguish the prophets from one another, even when—and particularly when—they communicate similar messages. Hence the introductory prophetic formula, "thus said the Lord," signifies no more than, "this is the substance of the Lord's communication to me, couched in my own language." It also happens that one prophet adopts the wording of his predecessor, with which he was familiar by education, when that

---

Tradition," *Immanuel* 19 (Winter 1984/85) 74-86; citation on p. 83. The original French version of this article appears in *Congress Volume, Salamanca 1983* (VTSup 36; ed. J. A. Emerton; Leiden: Brill, 1985) 96-107.

A more extensive treatment is S. D. Benin, "The 'Cunning of God' and Divine Accommodation," *Journal of the History of Ideas* 45/2 (1984) 179-91. On p. 189 Benin cites Yehuda ha-Levi's *Kuzari* (I, 98; Hirschfeld translation, 67) to the effect that even if all persons at the time of Israel's beginnings had been philosophers, "discoursing on the unity and government of God, they would have been unable to dispense with images, and would have taught the masses that a divine influence hovered over this image, which was distinguished by some miraculous feature" (*Kuzari*, ibid.). This seems to conflict with Dreyfus's rejection of an evolutionary view. And yet it may be harmonized with Dreyfus as follows: The masses do gradually move from crude to more refined ideas, through divine pedagogy and condescendence, so one may speak of an evolution of refinement among masses. Philosophers (like Moses and the prophets) knew better from the first. Ha-Levi's assertion that even the philosophers of antiquity would have been unable to dispense with images is connected with what they "would have taught the masses"—suggesting that their teaching was an accommodation to a level of understanding lower than their own.

I am grateful to Mr. Benin for calling my attention to his illuminating article.

wording seemed to him a suitable vehicle for the word of God that came to him. The personal factor may be so dominant that the inexperience and unlearnedness of a prophet result in faulty language and a disordered text.

Classical Jewish exegetes acknowledged these literary facts in the face of the great temptation to absolutize the authority of Scripture and silence the incessant challenges to its integrity and validity by categorically asserting that all is simply divine dictation. To modern Jewish critics they are a model of reverence toward the source of religion that does not entail blindness to the complexity of that source or the adoption of far-fetched cloaking of that complexity. The tradition of honest and sober reasoning, accommodating articles of faith to (literary) facts, stands the critics in good stead as they confront a wave of simplistic dogmatic piety that seeks to impose itself on the entire community, stifling curiosity and independence of judgment.

THE QUEST FOR PAUL'S PHARISAISM:
SOME REFLECTIONS

LEANDER E. KECK
Yale University

Whether or not Paul was a "religious genius,"[1] he was an extraordinary Jew whose thought is extraordinarily difficult to account for. His letters, written in vigorous Greek, effortlessly move from popular Cynic-Stoic commonplaces and rhetorical devices to themes derived from Jewish apocalyptic; he cites the Greek Bible but interprets it in the manner of the rabbis—all in support of his construal of the meaning of Christ, itself largely indebted to earlier Christian traditions. So imaginatively did he fuse these elements that a century-old scholarly industry has not succeeded in determining which factor was the most influential—the Hellenistic (Cynic-Stoic, Mystery-cult, or proto-gnostic) or the Jewish (LXX, apocalyptic, or "rabbinic").

His letters do not suggest that he deliberately amalgamated what, to historians, appear as disparate elements. Accounting for his thought, therefore, entails factoring out its elements in order to identify the families to which they belong. This process would be difficult enough had he written essays in which he expressed himself systematically; it is markedly more complex, however, because he wrote letters to small house-churches whose diverse problems elicited those configurations of his thought which he deemed germane. It is not surprising, then, that scholars laboring in the Pauline factory should produce one proposal after another to account for his thought.

Only when he must defend his gospel (and his authority) does Paul provide his readers with information about his background. In support

---

[1] So Adolf Deissmann, *Paul* (New York: Harper and Bros., Torchbook ed., 1957; 1st ed., 1912) 6, 89; Samuel Sandmel, *The Genius of Paul* (Philadelphia: Fortress, 1979; 1st ed., 1958) 3.

of his claim that he had received his gospel "through a revelation of Jesus Christ," he informs the Galatians that during his "former life in Judaism" he had tried to destroy the church of God. He says, "I advanced in Judaism beyond many of my own age among my people, so extremely zealous was I for the traditions of my fathers" (Gal 1:13-14). In contending that he represents the true people of God ("true circumcision") he informs the Philippians that he was "circumcised on the eighth day, of the people of Israel, of the tribe of Benjamin, a Hebrew born of Hebrews; as to the law a Pharisee, as to zeal a persecutor of the church, as to righteousness under the law blameless"—all of which now counts as so much garbage in order to participate in Christ (Phil 3:3-9). Whereas other influences on his thought must be inferred, Paul himself points to the "Pharisaic factor"—even if he thinks he is done with it.

What happened to Paul's erstwhile Pharisaism? That is the question that generates this essay. Unless one thinks either that Paul fitted Christ into a thought-structure or "pattern of religion"[2] which otherwise remained intact, so that Paul became a Christianized Pharisee (as Acts presents him[3]) or that his Pharisaism was rinsed away in baptism, one must assume that there are signs of both continuity and discontinuity with his pre-Christian life. In a word, what difference did it make for Paul's thought that he had once been a zealous Pharisee and not some other kind of Jew?

I.

Samples from the history of Pauline study show how difficult it has been to answer this simple question—or how easy it is to ignore it. Thus Percy Gardner wrote, "We must never forget that he [Paul] was a Hebrew of the Hebrews, a Pharisee, and the son of a Pharisee," but in fact paid virtually no attention to it.[4] Deissmann (see Note 1) too says that Paul was a "pious Rabbinic Jew, a Septuagint Jew" who "never withdrew from the divine world of the Hellenistic Old Testament" (99), though he relied on allegory as well as rabbinic Haggada (102-3). Deissmann warns against accenting Paul's use of Rabbinic dialectic

---

[2] The allusion is to E. P. Sanders' *Paul and Palestinian Judaism* (Philadelphia: Fortress, 1977) 12-18; see also his "Patterns of Religion in Paul and Rabbinic Judaism: A Holistic Method of Compassion," *HTR* 66 (1973) 455-78.

[3] Acts 23:6 has Paul say, "I *am* a Pharisee."

[4] Percy Gardner, *The Religious Experience of St. Paul* (London: Williams and Norgate, 1911) 225.

because Paul was "of much too impulsive a nature to be a great dialectician" (104-5). For Deissmann, Paul's Pharisaism evidently played virtually no role in his Christianity, allegedly dominated by "Christ mysticism," which Deissmann implicitly regarded as the answer to Paul's passion for righteousness begun in his Pharisaic youth.[5]

Günther Bornkamm[6] not only rejects the idea that Paul had been a dissatisfied Pharisee, but says that Paul had been a Pharisaic diaspora missionary to gentiles before his conversion (3-12). He regards "orthodox Palestinian Judaism" to have been led by the Pharisees, who insisted that proselytes must be circumcised. This insistence prompted Paul to persecute the Hellenistic Jewish Christians who were accepting gentiles without circumcising them (15). But in expounding Paul's thought, Bornkamm is content to refer generally to "Jewish" ideas, so that it is difficult to see what difference his Pharisaism made.

J. Christiaan Beker[7] agrees that Paul had been a missionary to gentiles (144), and that the Hellenistic Jewish Christian acceptance of gentiles and their understanding of the impact of the cross on Torah-observance prompted Paul to become a persecutor (144, 182, 183, 185). He also claims that Paul had been an apocalyptist during his Pharisaic period (143). Although rejecting a psychological explanation of Paul's conversion (182-83), he nonetheless insists that Romans 7 alludes to Paul's own experience with the law as well as expressing his Christian reflection (241). He too equates what is Pharisaic with what is "Jewish":

> In Judaism . . . the Torah can remain intelligible only through halakic or midrashic interpretation. The scribe is a student of hermeneutics and the *beth hammidrash* a school for hermeneutical training. . . . In fact, oral tradition itself . . . receives canonical status along with the written Torah. (119)

The possibilities of working with an indeterminate Pharisaism are exploited most fully by W. D. Davies,[8] who is convinced that one need

---

[5] According to Deissmann (*Paul*, 93), Paul "cannot have had a sunny, cheerful youth" but was subject to growing anxiety about the law so that he became a Pharisee.

[6] Günther Bornkamm, *Paul* (New York: Harper & Row, 1971; German original, 1969).

[7] J. Christiaan Beker, *Paul the Apostle* (Philadelphia: Fortress, 1980).

[8] W. D. Davies, *Paul and Rabbinic Judaism* (4th ed.; Philadelphia: Fortress, 1980; 1st ed., 1948).

not "go outside Judaism" to account for Paul's concepts (108, 319). He agrees with Acts: "Paul throughout his life might be described as a Pharisee who had accepted Jesus as the Messiah, i.e., he was living in the Messianic Age" (71-72). He claims that "Paul is grounded in an essentially Rabbinic world of thought, that the Apostle was, in short, a Rabbi become Christian and was therefore primarily governed in life and thought by Pharisaic concepts, which he had 'baptized unto Christ'" (16). Indeed, "in a real sense, conformity to Christ . . . has taken the place for Paul of conformity to the Jewish Torah. Jesus Himself—in word and deed or fact is a New Torah" (148). Davies not only moves freely between Pharisaism and Rabbinism, but also denies a rigid distinction between pre-70 Palestinian Judaism and the diaspora and contends, with Bornkamm, that apocalyptic was not foreign to Pharisaism (8-9). Hence, in arguing that Paul's view of Adam, while going beyond the rabbis, is still "governed by essentially Rabbinic concepts" (34), he adduces evidence from apocalypses, Testaments of the Twelve Patriarchs, and various rabbinic texts from several centuries. At point after point, Davies finds antecedents in "Judaism" for Paul's ideas. He does not find it necessary to specify which of Paul's concepts were "Pharisaic." It is enough that they not be Hellenistic.[9]

In his *Paul and Palestinian Judaism* (see Note 2), E. P. Sanders declares that he will not look for the Jewish background of Paul's ideas seriatim as Davies[10] had done; indeed, he will approach each holistically, systemically, in order to compare their determinative centers, their "patterns" (12). The point of comparison here is essentially "soteriological"—how does one get in and stay in a religion? Actually, however, Sanders surveys bodies of texts (Tannaitic, Qumranian, Apocryphal, and Pseudepigraphic) with regard to ideas, such as salvation, election, righteousness, and the like. The treatment of Tannaitic literature not only bypasses the historical problems of the relation between Pharisees and rabbis, but gathers rabbinic quotations from several centuries, paying scant attention to context or function of the texts in which they are found.[11] After 335 pages of description and ex-

---

[9] For example, Paul's view of the Spirit is "far removed from the individualistic, esoteric pneumatology of the Hellenistic world and in the full stream of that Rabbinic thought which had looked forward to a community and an Age of the Spirit" (217).

[10] In the "Preface to the Fourth Edition" of *Paul and Rabbinic Judaism* (xxix-xxxviii), Davies provides a searching criticism of Sanders.

[11] Jacob Neusner subjected this procedure to stinging criticism: "The Use of the Later Rabbinic Evidence for the Study of Paul," in *Approaches to*

position, the common pattern of "covenantal nomism" is summarized in eight doctrines [!] which support the conclusion that, throughout, "obedience maintains one's position in the covenant, but it does not earn God's grace as such" (420, italicized). Paul's pattern, however, is not "convenantal nomism" (514). Paul has an "essentially different type of religiousness from any found in Palestinian Jewish literature" (544, italicized). Paul's thought cannot be derived from Palestinian Judaism, and "what Paul finds wrong with Judaism [is that] it is not Christianity" (552-53). He might have added that Percy Gardner should have said, "We might as well forget that he [Paul] was . . . a Pharisee." Sanders' subsequent volume on Paul[12] shows that he did forget.

Two Jewish scholars[13] see matters differently. H. J. Schoeps[14] wants to ascertain the relative significance of Paul's background in Hellenized Judaism, his training in rabbinism, and his Christian conviction that the Messianic Age has begun with Jesus' resurrection. The allegedly distinctive piety of LXX has a number of features: a clearer missionary tendency,[15] Torah construed as *nomos* and *ṣĕdāqâ* as *dikaiosyne*, simpler vocabulary for sin and evil (with greater emphasis on sin as rebellious disposition), atonement as deliverance from sin, and Scripture as *paideia* (27-31). So Paul's distortion of Torah into *nomos*, and his isolation of the law from the controlling context of God's covenant with Israel [Sanders' covenantal nomism] are traceable to Hellenistic Jewish influence (214). Paul's critique of the law is therefore directed primarily against the Hellenistic Jewish understanding which he appropriated as a youth (31-32).

Nonetheless, Schoeps also claims that "every explanation proceeding from rabbinism deserves *a limine* preference over all other explanations" (40). Within the same paragraph he says that "Paul must be interpreted on the basis of his Hellenistic Diaspora back-

---

Ancient Judaism, vol. 2 (ed. W. S. Green; BJS 9; Chico, CA: Scholars Press, 1980) 43-63. Sanders responded in the same volume with "Puzzling Out Rabbinic Judaism," 65-75.

[12] *Paul, the Law, and the Jewish People* (Philadelphia: Fortress, 1983).

[13] For a survey, see Donald A. Hagner, "Paul in Modern Jewish Thought," in *Pauline Studies: Essays Presented to Professor F. F. Bruce on his 70th Birthday* (ed. D. A. Hagner and M. J. Harris; Grand Rapids: W. B. Eerdmans; Exeter: Paternoster, 1980) 143-65.

[14] Hans Joachim Schoeps, *Paul* (Philadelphia: Westminster, 1961). See my review in *USQR* 18 (1962) 58-62.

[15] On page 19 he seems skeptical about the idea that Paul had been a Pharisaic missionary, but on page 219 he assumes that he had been.

ground" and that "in the first place . . . Paul must be assessed as a rabbinic exegete; for the doctrine of sin and the law . . . would be incomprehensible apart from the debates of the Palestinian schools" (47). Pivotal is the apocalyptic post-Messianic situation created by Jesus' resurrection (98-99). Schoeps believes there was "a widespread opinion in rabbinic literature . . . that in the Messianic era the old Torah would cease together with the evil impulse;" so the "abolition of the law" (Rom 10:4) "is an absolutely exact inference from the standpoint of Jewish theological thought" once one believes that the Messianic Age has begun (171-73).

S. Sandmel's *The Genius of Paul* (see Note 1) will have none of this moving back and forth between Hellenistic and rabbinic Judaism. Sandmel holds that "Paul, a Hellenistic Jew, had never been in Palestine until he had joined the new movement" (13). Having doubts about Acts, Sandmel separates Paul from Pharisaism despite Phil 3:9 (13-15). Naturally, he disagrees "almost one hundred per cent" with Davies: the "affinities between Paul and the Rabbis were limited to some minor and elusive strands, . . . Davies, rather than proving his case . . . disproved it" (223).

Even though Paul was an apocalyptist, his Hellenism differentiated his apocalypticism from that of the Palestinian Jews in that it was oriented to the individual predicament—a perspective Paul shared with Philo (17-24). Regarding Romans 7 as autobiographical, Sandmel believes that "Paul's difficulties with the Law antedate his conversion" (28, 56). They reflect his Hellenistic Judaism, which had trouble understanding and justifying the place of the Law (30-33; 42-43). Sandmel rejects the idea that the rabbis taught that in the messianic era the law would be abrogated: "No such passage is to be found, though Sanhedrin 97a is distorted to yield this view."[16] Moreover, appeal to this view makes meaningless both Paul's controversies in Galatians and his own attitude, "for if the abrogation of the Law is only a detail, only a by-product of the arrival of the Messianic age, then it is not simultaneously the central factor in the question: How can I achieve my individual salvation?" (41). Besides, "it is a piece of the misbegotten and inaccurate exegesis which assumes that the Hellenistic Jew Paul can be explained by remotely tangential passages from the rabbinical literature" (40 n.). Sandmel is impatient with

---

[16] "All that Sanhedrin 97a says is this: 'The world is 6,000 years. Two thousand are confusion (Hebrew *tohu*), two thousand Torah, two thousand days of the Messiah.'" See *The Genius of Paul*, 40ff.

appeals to rabbis also because "the character of Palestinian Judaism changed almost completely" after 70 (43).

Somewhat like Schoeps, Sandmel sees in Paul a reflection of Hellenistic Judaism's concern with law: "Greek Jews focused their attention on Judaism as though it was both in essence and as a totality *law* and nothing but *law*." Paul's view of the law cannot be derived from rabbinic Judaism because the rabbis and Paul take opposite views of the law, and had diverse views of atonement as well; for the rabbis "the atonement was not for [man's] general character, not for [his] sinful*ness*, but for his specific, individual sins" (57-58). "Pauline Christianity and rabbinic Judaism share little more than a common point of departure, the Bible" (59). With Sandmel we have come almost full circle, to Deissmann: "Paul was a mystic who encountered God—in the form of Christ" (75), whom he took to be incarnate in Jesus (69).

This brief overview has clarified several things. First, a historically sound discussion of the role of Pharisaism in the theology of the Apostle is possible only if one can provide that "Pharisaism" with historically sound content. On the one hand, if one does not trust Acts, then there is no way to learn when or how Paul came under the influence of Pharisaism. Even if we accept the data of Acts, we find ourselves on a short trail because we know almost nothing about Hellenistic Jewish Pharisaism in the diaspora. On the other hand, in reconstructing Paul's Pharisaism, one must allow for the watershed of the year 70. Concretely, neither the relative absence of apocalyptic from rabbinic texts nor the continuity between Pharisaism and post-70 rabbinism must be retrojected into the Pharisaism Paul would have practiced.

Second, the evidence that Hellenism had long made deep inroads into Palestinian culture requires a pre-70 Pharisaism which was subject to Hellenistic influences.[17] These two considerations make it fruitless to profile Pharisaism in terms of ideas and to relate Paul to it by identifying shared concepts alone. In other words, it is one thing to show which of Paul's ideas have antecedents and parallels in Jewish texts, another to show which were specifically Pharisaic. To do that, one must identify elements in Pharisaism that were distinctive and determinative.

Third, one must also account for Paul's persecution of the church. This requires locating that which, by Pharisaic sensibilities, Paul

---

[17] Jacob Neusner cites with approval Morton Smith's insistence on this point; *Judaism in the Beginning of Christianity* (Philadelphia: Fortress, 1984) 52.

found so objectionable in the Christian community that he was driven to destroy it—a factor which Sandmel ignores.

II.

The difficulty of achieving the desired picture of pre-70 Pharisaism is clear from the divergent construals proposed by Ellis Rivkin and Jacob Neusner. Although they both see a significant consistency between the evidence provided by the Synoptic Gospels and the Tannaitic traditions about the Pharisees, and both emphasize the data provided by the Mishnah, it is their divergent use of Josephus that produces quite different portrayals of pre-70 Pharisaism.

Rivkin,[18] correlating several accounts, regards the Pharisees as leaders of a religious and cultural revolution which, in the name of the oral law, transformed the Pentateuchal society into one in which their own laws, even if without Pentateuchal warrant, prevailed.

> The Pharisees were a scholar class dedicated to the supremacy of the twofold Law, the Written and the Unwritten. They actively opposed the Sadducees who recognized only the Written Law as authoritative . . . their unwritten laws, the *halakhah* were operative in all realms: cultus, property, judicial procedure, festivals, etc. (176)

Neusner, on the other hand, agrees with Morton Smith's dictum that the Pharisees "had no real hold on either the government or on the masses of the people."[19] Neusner grants that the pre-Herodian Pharisees had been politically active, but insists that from the time of Hillel until 70 they were a sect concerned with ritual purity outside the Temple. This concern had its center in matters pertaining to the production, preparation, and consumption of food in the home; by extending the purity laws for the priests to everyone they actualized the mandate to be a holy people.

Rivkin emphasizes the role of two non-Pentateuchal doctrines in Pharisaism (the two ages and the resurrection): "It was only because the true believer and true devotee of the twofold Law could hope for the immortality of his soul and the resurrection of his body that he was

---

[18] Ellis Rivkin, *A Hidden Revolution* (Nashville: Abingdon, 1978).

[19] Jacob Neusner, *From Politics to Piety* (Englewood Cliffs: Prentice-Hall, Inc., 1973) 10.

ready . . . to yoke himself to the twofold Law and abide by its discipline" (230).

Neusner's view of the Pharisees as a group defined by concern for ritual purity can be accommodated within Rivkin's framework, but Rivkin's contention that they effectively shaped society in Paul's time cannot be accommodated with Neusner's view that they were a small sect concerned primarily with its internal practices. The question of their influence on Paul does not require that this issue be decided.

III.

What prompted Paul to become a persecutor? If the Pharisees were a sect concerned primarily with their intramural affairs, then it is hard to see why the emerging Christian movement would have energized Paul to stamp it out. Moreover, Neusner sees two basic differences which would not have produced conflict: (a) the Pharisees' meals were ordinary and non-cultic, but the Christian meals celebrated Jesus' passion;[20] (b) the Pharisees valued continuity and order whereas the Christians' eschatology emphasized discontinuity with the past. He concludes that the early Christian sense of reality "scarcely intersects with that of Pharisaism."[21] In other words, two adjacent circles (sects) do not account for Paul's persecuting work. Why would he have cared what the Jesus-people were doing?

Rivkin's view, on the other hand, suggests why Paul would have cared, for Rivkin emphasizes the centrality of the two ages and the resurrection:

The Scribes-Pharisees could not acknowledge Jesus as having risen from the dead. Resurrection, however, was not the issue, for it was the very core of Pharisaic teaching. Jesus' resurrection, however, was very much the issue. For Scribes-Pharisees, Jesus could not have been resurrected because . . . he had challenged the Scribes-Pharisees with claims that they had firmly rejected. . . . The Christian claims that Jesus had been resurrected and that it was this resurrection that proved

---

[20] *From Politics to Piety*, 87-88; *Formative Judaism* (BJS 37; Chico: Scholars Press, 1982) 80-81.

[21] Jacob Neusner, "The Use of the Later Rabbinic Evidence for the Study of First-Century Pharisaism," in *Approaches to Ancient Judaism: Theory and Practice* (ed. W. S. Green; BJS 1; Missoula, MT: Scholars Press, 1978) 225.

beyond doubt he must be the Messiah were, from the Pharisaic angle of vision, utterly fraudulent. (304)

Rivkin also connects the resurrection doctrine with Paul's persecuting activity: As one "zealous for the traditions of my fathers" Paul

> was always striving to prove to God and to himself that he was worthy of eternal life and resurrection. If only he could be blameless under the Law! [Phil 3:9] If only he could eradicate those who proclaimed that Jesus . . . had been raised from the dead! Such blamelessness and such zeal would earn for his soul a goodly portion in the world to come and for his body . . . resurrection. (305)

One need not follow Rivkin's psychological explanation in order to see that the early Christian construal of Jesus' cross/resurrection and not the Hellenistic Jewish Christian acceptance of gentiles without circumcision (Bornkamm)—about which we know nothing before Paul's conversion—could have set this Pharisee into motion. Beyond this we cannot go.

IV.

What, then, happened to Paul's Pharisaism after he became an Apostle of Christ? Worth pondering are the discontinuities—distinctive hallmarks of Pharisaism which are either absent from Paul's letters or appear to be denied. Together they indicate the depth and character of Paul's "conversion"—which includes the entire turning way from his former life and entry into an alternative. In other words, far too much ink has been used to discuss Paul's conversion experience, not enough on its results.

1. Paul manifestly abandoned the Pharisaic commitment to oral tradition. Obviously he did not abandon tradition altogether, as 1 Cor 15:1-3 and 11:23 show. Indeed, it is a scholarly commonplace to point out that there he uses terminology for the receipt and transmission of tradition which is found also in rabbinic texts. Moreover, recent criticism has identified other passages where Paul appears to use traditions without identifying them (e.g., Rom 1:3-4; Phil 2:5-11). The point, however, is that Paul does not rely on oral Christian tradition the way he would have relied on oral tradition as a Pharisee. Never does he appeal to predecessors as authorities, nor does he regard Peter

and the Twelve as those at the head of a chain of Christian tradition which he transmits (contrast *Pirqe ʾAbot*). He recognizes that James, Cephas, and John were "reputed to be pillars" (Gal 2:9) but also insists that "what they were makes no difference to me; God shows no partiality" (Gal 2:6). In short, Paul gave up altogether thinking of Christian tradition in terms comparable to the oral Pharisaic tradition.

This is clear also in the referent of the term *nomos*: there is no evidence that it includes the oral Torah. To be sure, in Paul's mouth *nomos* often means more than Pentateuch, but there is no hint that it refers to what Rivkin calls the twofold Law. The only point at which this might be the case is Gal 5:3, where he asserts that whoever receives circumcision "is bound to keep the whole law," but even here the phrase does not naturally suggest this meaning, nor is it likely that it would have been taken this way by the gentile Galatians.[22] For a Pharisee to abandon the oral law, the zeal for "the traditions of my fathers," was nothing less than moving from one "pattern of religion" to another, as Phil 3:4-11 attests eloquently.

2. Even more remarkable is Paul's conviction, grounded "in the Lord Jesus," that "nothing is unclean in itself, but it is unclean for any one who thinks it unclean" (Rom 14:14). In fact, "everything is indeed clean" (v. 20). Paul did not simply reverse the Pharisaic concern that only "clean" food be eaten; he did not insist that "unclean" food be eaten in order to demonstrate his new-found freedom from *kashrut*. The discussion in Romans 14-15, like its counterpart in 1 Corinthians 8-10, shows that what had been decisive has now become a matter of custom. This freedom to observe or not to observe is the opposite of zealousness for the traditions of the fathers.

3. The third discontinuity is more far-reaching theologically, for it entails the demotion of Moses and the elevation of Abraham. For Pharisaism, the Law—written and unwritten alike—was the eternal will of God revealed to Moses. But for Paul, the (written) law is something that was "added," something that appeared in history four hundred thirty years after Abraham, and it was given "because of transgressions." It was an interim arrangement "till the offspring should come to whom the promise had been made." In fact, Moses was but an intermediary through whom the angels ordained it (Gal 3:15-20). The more Paul's conversion coincided with his commission to preach to gen-

---

[22] See Hans Dieter Betz, *Galatians* (Hermeneia; Philadelphia: Fortress, 1979) ad loc.

tiles, the less the controversies in Galatia, on the one hand, and the need to state the basis of the gentile mission to the Romans, on the other, led Paul to see the decisive figure in Abraham instead of Moses. Nor in abandoning Pharisaism's Moses did Paul simply revert to Hellenistic Judaism's Moses as *Nomos Empsychos*. Nor is Abraham a timeless prototype as for Philo. Rather, Abraham is "the father of us all" (Rom 4:16), and what God said to him about his rectitude was nothing less than the gospel which God "pre-promised" (Rom 1:2; see also Gal 3:8-9). Whereas the Pharisees emphasized a chain of tradition from Moses to themselves, Paul emphasized promise and actualization. (He was no more interested in *HeilsGESCHICHTE*—a continuous narrative of salvation events—than they were.)

There are also continuities between Paul's former Pharisaism and his Christianity, three of which merit further study and reflection.

1. The first concerns Paul's attitude toward and use of Scripture. The Pharisaic view of what constitutes Scripture is continued in Paul: it includes the Prophets and the Writings as well as the Pentateuch. Although Paul the Hellenistic Jew uses the LXX, he never cites books found only in the Greek Bible. Scripture for him is what post-Jamnia Judaism regarded as sacred. Nor does he show any knowledge of apocalypses and other texts such as those used at Qumran. Moreover, Paul's exegetical methods, and his ways of citing Scripture, can be paralleled in rabbinic texts, which presumably continue Pharisaic practice. This point has been noted so often that it is enough merely to mention it here. What is not to be overlooked, however, is Rivkin's insistence that "proof-texting" was a new way of using Scripture developed by the Pharisees to legitimate their program, including the doctrines of the two ages and the resurrection which are not found in the Pentateuch.[23]

2. Rivkin also observed that both in Pharisaism and in Paul the resurrection and the doctrine of the two ages are central. Recognizing these beliefs to be continuous with Paul's Christian conviction is consistent with the likelihood that Paul had appropriated apocalyptic views prior to becoming a Christian. One need not follow Schweitzer in reconstructing a complete apocalyptic schema which Paul had adopted but then was forced to modify in light of Jesus' resurrection.[24] What is essential in apocalyptic is not a particular scenario but the belief that all of history (this age) is to be replaced by its definitive alternative

---

[23] Rivkin, *A Hidden Revolution*, 225-26.

[24] Albert Schweitzer, *The Mysticism of Paul the Apostle* (London: Adam and Charles Black, 1931) chap. 5.

(the age to come), and that the future is fundamentally discontinuous with the present and not its fulfillment. The transition from one to the other is marked by resurrection. Whoever had this understanding of the future would be forced to affirm or deny the claim that in one case only—that of Jesus—resurrection had occurred. This, in turn, required a particular understanding of Jesus' execution.

3. Finally, if the Pharisaic concern for ritual purity expressed the passion to be a holy community and to take the lead in making the whole nation holy, we can understand why Paul emphasized the holiness, or sanctification, of the Christian community. At the same time, the abandonment of dietary laws indicates that Paul recast the nature of sanctification while continuing to insist on it. Given the Pentateuchal "You shall be holy because I am holy," it is natural that the concern for holiness should be found across the spectrum of Judaism. What distinguished the Pharisaic concern, however, was the effort to apply the laws pertaining to the priests to the people as a whole, thereby sanctifying ordinary life without recourse to conventicle existence as at Qumran. This is exactly what we find in Paul. His letters not only refer repeatedly to holiness and sanctification (e.g., Rom 6:19, 22; 1 Cor 1:2, 30; 1 Thess 4:3) but do so in a way that suggests that for him it was a self-evident mandate. In other words, a major area for fruitful investigation is Paul's understanding of the sanctification of the ordinary and its roots in his former Pharisaism.[25]

This essay has identified only the obvious discontinuities and continuities between Paul the Apostle and Paul the Pharisee. Perhaps pondering—and refining—them can stimulate a full consideration of this many-sided theme.

---

[25] One would want to review Ragnar Asting's thesis that Paul's understanding is derived more from Hellenism than from Judaism (*Die Heiligkeit im Urchristentum* [Göttingen: Vandenhoeck & Ruprecht, 1930]), as well as subject to close scrutiny T. J. Deidun, I.C., *New Covenant Morality in Paul* (AnBib 89; Rome: Biblical Institute, 1981).

PAUL AND THE LAW, WITH SPECIAL ATTENTION TO HIS FOUNDING PROCLAMATION[1]

GERD LUEDEMANN
Georg-August-Universität, Göttingen

In recent years, Paul's understanding of the law has become one of the most discussed topics in New Testament research.[2] Without being able to go into the details here, it may be said that a mainstream of research regards Pauline Christianity as an antithesis to the law because of Paul's having taught his converts freedom from the law.[3] Against this I would like to argue that neither claim is precise because each compels us to overlook both the number of respects in which Paul adopted (parts of) the law in his communities and the number of ties he kept with Judaism and the people of the old covenant.

In the following, I would like not only to assess briefly the evidence of the genuine Pauline letters in order to analyze their evaluation of the law, but also to deal with the question of the content of Paul's preaching/teaching in his founding visits.

Before proceeding, however, some reflections on terminology are necessary. *Nomos* has in the Pauline writings several meanings. The word stands for the torah of the Hebrew Bible (cf. Rom 3:21), for the

---

[1] The present article summarizes the results of my ongoing work on the theology of Paul which will be published soon. I have therefore limited the references to scholarly literature to a minimum. The translation of the Bible follows the *RSV* unless otherwise indicated. I thank Craig Wansink for his help with matters concerning the English of this article.

[2] Cf. H. Räisänen, *Paul and the Law* (Tübingen: J. C. B. Mohr [Paul Siebeck], 1983), with a full bibliography.

[3] Cf. only R. Bultmann, *Theology of the New Testament* (New York: Charles Scribner's Sons, 1951) 1:340-45. See W. D. Davies's protest against this: *Jewish and Pauline Studies* (London: SPCK, 1984) 96.

individual command (cf. Rom 7:7), but also for the Psalms (cf. Rom 3:19) or for a prophetical book (cf. 1 Cor 14:21). In short, it can refer "to the whole of Israel's sacred tradition, with special emphasis on its Mosaic centre."[4] In addition, one has to keep in mind that just as in the seventh chapter of the Gospel of Mark, where interpretation of the law is discussed without any specific reference to *nomos* itself, Paul also discusses questions of the interpretation of the law without explicitly mentioning the law (cf. 1 Cor 3:12-15; 1 Thess 4:1-12).[5] Finally, one has to take into account that sometimes in the Pauline letters *nomos* does not mean "law" but "principle" (see Rom 7:21).

I. 1 Thessalonians and the Founding Proclamation

Within the year after his departure from Thessalonica, Paul had arrived at Corinth from Athens—around 41 CE (or ten years later)[6]—and had dictated 1 Thessalonians. Of all the Pauline letters this is the only one which was written within such a short period of time from the founding of the community. It is therefore of great importance for the question of the content of Paul's founding proclamation both in Thessalonica and in general.

Although 1 Thessalonians does not contain much doctrine and, consequently, even a repeated reading of the letter is beset with difficulties in tracing the train of thought, the following theological presuppositions become clear: The community was constituted by election (1:4) and by a call (2:12; 4:7; 5:24); the Christians are "in the Lord" (1:1) and "in Christ" (4:16). The same is true for the Jewish Christians in Judaea (2:14) whose imitators the Thessalonians have become.

Turning to the question of Paul's understanding of the law in the letter, one finds, contrary to common opinion,[7] a large section that does deal with the law, 1 Thess 4:1-12. The importance of this passage consists not only in that Paul gives ethical instructions to the

---

[4] Räisänen, *Paul and the Law*, 16.

[5] See E. P. Sanders, *Paul, the Law, and the Jewish People* (Philadelphia: Fortress, 1983) 112-13.

[6] On the disputed date of 1 Thessalonians see my *Paul, Apostle to the Gentiles* (Philadelphia: Fortress, 1984) 289-94.

[7] Cf. the typical statement: "1 Thess . . . does not deal with the question of law at all" (Räisänen, *Paul and the Law*, 10). Let me hasten to add that with the rise of wisdom literature in Israel parenesis (of which 1 Thessalonians 4 is a part) and law became identical; cf. R. Smend and U. Luz, *Gesetz* (BibK 1015; Stuttgart: W. Kohlhammer, 1981) 39-41.

Thessalonians in the present, but especially in that he reiterates his teaching of the law during the founding proclamation, allowing us to gain direct access to what the apostle taught his converts with respect to ethics. Compare how Paul explicitly reminds his readers of the founding proclamation:

1 Thess 4:1b-2	". . . as you learned (*parelabete*) from us how you ought to live and to please God. . . . For you know what instructions (*paraggelias*) we gave you through the Lord Jesus."
1 Thess 4:6b	". . . the Lord is an avenger in all these things, as we solemnly forewarned (*proeipamen*) you."
1 Thess 4:11	". . . as we charged (*parēggeilamen*) you."

The content of the law that Paul transmitted to the Thessalonians during the founding proclamation consists in the sanctification (*hagiasmos*) of the Christians (vv. 3, 4, 7) which is specified as follows: "that you abstain from (sexual) immorality" (*porneia*) (v. 3), "that each one of you know how to take a wife for himself in holiness and honor" (v. 4), "that no man transgress and defraud his brother in business" (v. 6), "to love one another" (v. 9), "to aspire to live quietly, to mind your own affairs, and to work with your own hands" (v. 11).

The major point of Paul's instructions during his founding visit was the proclamation of the one living and true God (cf. 1 Thess 4:5b), for in 1 Thess 1:9-10 Paul reminds the Thessalonians of how they "turned to God from idols, to serve a living and true God, and to wait for his Son from heaven, whom he raised from the dead, Jesus who delivers us from the wrath to come." This service of God is, together with Paul's Christology, a presupposition for the teaching of the law as preserved in 1 Thess 4:1-12 and for the prediction that "the Lord is an avenger (in all these things)" (1 Thess 4:6b = Ps 94:1).

As to the origins of such teaching about the law and about God, one has to realize that they stem from the Hebrew Bible[8] or from the exe-

---

[8] On serving the one God (1 Thess 1:19) cf. Exod 20:2; on turning away from idols (1 Thess 1:9) cf. Exod 20:3-4; on abstention from sexual immorality (1 Thess 4:3) cf. Exod 20:13, 17; Tob 4:12; on avoiding fraud (1 Thess 4:6) cf. Exod 20:16-17; Lev 19:13; on loving one's brother (1 Thess 4:9) cf. Lev 19:18. These passages in the Hebrew Bible are, to be sure, in some cases only slightly reminiscent of the

gesis of the Hebrew Bible as practiced in Hellenistic Judaism.[9] For Paul and other Hellenistic Jews the will of God (cf. 1 Thess 4:3) could not have had its origin but in Scripture. At the same time, it should be noted that for Hellenistic Judaism and Paul it misses the point to describe the appropriation of biblical law by distinguishing between moral (ethical) and ritual law. It is not true that Paul has kept only the moral (ethical) law,[10] for neither the service of the one and living God nor the turning away from idols can be regarded as moral (ethical) law.

Simply stated with respect to the law, Paul has appropriated the heritage of Hellenistic Judaism and added Christology to it. The teaching of the law and Christology thus stand side by side during the founding visit(s) and in 1 Thessalonians. The Thessalonian community has been transferred through baptism into the realm of Christ and expects his arrival/return from heaven. At the present the community keeps the law as transmitted by Paul (circumcision and dietary laws are left out; see below for an explanation) and thus preserves holiness by sanctifying herself.

This brings us to the final point concerning the importance of the law for the Thessalonian Christians. It seems that the Hebrew Bible concept of purity underlies much of what Paul says about the community. For Paul sanctification involves not only the doing of certain commandments but also the separation from all things that would defile, viz., the impure Gentiles (cf. 1 Thess 4:5; 1 Cor 5:1; Gal 2:15). The reason for this lies in the holiness of the community which is "the temple of God" (1 Cor 3:16; cf. 1 Cor 6:19). That is to say, the holiness of the community corresponds to the holiness of God (cf. Lev 19:2).[11]

Pauline exhortations. However, in order to recognize their importance for Paul, their appropriation in Hellenistic Judaism (see the next note) has to be taken into account.

[9] See the works by I. Reinmuth, *Geist und Gesetz: Studien zu Voraussetzungen und Inhalt der paulinischen Paränese* (Berlin: Evangelische Verlagsanstalt, 1985); K.-W. Niebuhr, *Gesetz und Paränese: Katechismusartige Weisungsreihen in der frühjüdischen Literatur* (Tübingen: J. C. B. Mohr [Paul Siebeck], 1987).

[10] So Bultmann, *Theology of the New Testament*, 1:341.

[11] Cf. M. Newton, *The Concept of Purity at Qumran and in the Letters of Paul* (SNTSMS 53; Cambridge: University Press, 1985).

II. *1 Corinthians and Paul's Practice*

1 Corinthians is the only Pauline letter which, supposing its literary integrity, explicitly gives the place of its writing: Ephesus (1 Cor 16:8). It was written some time (i.e., 3-10 years) after 1 Thessalonians. In order to understand 1 Corinthians properly, 1 Thessalonians must always be kept in consideration, since the letter was written during the foundation of the Corinthian community, i.e., it reflects the founding proclamation of Paul at Corinth. It does not, therefore, come as a surprise that the teachings of the law and of Christ, as seen in 1 Thessalonians, also seem to be juxtaposed in 1 Corinthians: The Corinthians have been transferred to the realm of Christ through baptism (1 Cor 6:11), for they have accepted the gospel (1 Cor 15:1). At the same time the apostle emphasizes the validity of demands of the law, such as not to engage in sexual immorality, idolatry, adultery, theft, and the like (1 Cor 6:11).

In one place, Paul seems to give a general evaluation of the law: "neither circumcision counts for anything nor uncircumcision, but keeping the commandments of God (*tērēsis entolōn theou*)" (1 Cor 7:19). Postponing for a moment the question of what sort of relation there is between keeping the commandments and circumcision/uncircumcision, it can be said in general: Paul enjoined his converts to keep God's commandments which, being identical with God's will (1 Thess 4:3), correspond to the law as taught in the founding proclamation. These commandments seem to be related to the law of Christ, for Paul writes in 1 Cor 9:20-21: "To those under the law I became as one under the law—though not being myself under the law—that I might win those under the law. To those outside the law I became as one outside the law—not being without law toward God but under the law of Christ (*ennomos Christou*)."

At the same time, it is noticeable that in both 1 Cor 7:19 and 1 Cor 9:20-21 the commandments of God or, respectively, the law of Christ, which the converts are being taught, are set at some distance from other things. Paul separates in 1 Cor 7:19 the commandments of God from circumcision and uncircumcision and in 1 Cor 9:20-21 explicitly states that, although he himself is under the law of Christ, he does not stand under the law (*hypo nomon*).

Both passages indicate Paul's new point of departure, which allows him neither to repeat the old Jewish position nor to succumb to a Gentile attitude. Rather, the new reality of Christ has put him in a new situation that transcends both uncircumcision and circumcision (cf. similarly Gal 6:15). Consequently, the new problem for Paul was

whether the preaching of Christ would simply be added to the teach-
ing of the law (as seemed to be the case from a comparison with 1
Thessalonians 4) or whether the preaching of Christ would also affect
Paul's attitude to the law.

That the latter is true follows from a look at Paul's practice.[12] The
famous incident at Antioch as preserved in Gal 2:11-14 took the following course: In the fourth decade of the first century Gentile and Jewish
Christians in Antioch, including Paul, regularly shared in common
meals, a custom which was also adopted by Peter. On the arrival of
James' messengers from Jerusalem, Peter, Barnabas, and the other Jews
withdrew from the table-fellowship. The reason for this seems to be
quite obvious: Jewish dietary laws had been transgressed by the Jewish
Christians, and James had protested against this by sending a delega-
tion. From Gal 2:14 we know precisely that Paul protested against this
withdrawal. Without being able to deal with the question of the relationship between Paul's speech to Peter (Gal 2:14-21) and the letter to
the Galatians—the speech leads directly to the body of the letter—
there can be no reasonable doubt that at Antioch Paul had expected the
Jewish Christians to transgress Jewish dietary laws when they had
table-fellowship with Gentile Christians. The reason for this lies in
Paul's interpretation of the Christ-event, an event which has brought
about a new creation. Because of this the Jewish and the Gentile religions have been superseded, and the law is seen as having now final
importance. Therefore, because of the action of James and Peter at
Antioch—through which the law had been reintroduced as an entrance
requirement for the new creation—theological conflict concerning the
law necessarily had to arise.

A similar result, that the law has no ultimate importance, is
reached by Paul in 1 Cor 15:56: "The sting of death is sin, and the power
of sin is the law."

This verse has been regarded as a gloss[13] since a similar statement
cannot be found elsewhere in the letter. However, the word "sin" does
occur in the context (1 Cor 15:3, 17), and Paul elsewhere in 1 Corinthians
does presuppose "the law" without explicitly mentioning it. In other
words, he had the topic on his mind and introduces "the law" at this
point because "sin" and "the law" are for Paul interrelated (cf. Romans
5-7 and the number of similarities between Romans and 1 Corinthians).
Stated differently: Already at the time of the writing of 1 Corinthians

---

[12] Cf. Räisänen, *Paul and the Law*, 73-77.

[13] Cf. the discussion in Räisänen, *Paul and the Law*, 143.

Paul shared the theological conviction that the law can lead to sin. Let me hasten to add that such a conviction can be easily related to the theology behind 1 Cor 7:19 and 9:20-21, though these passages do not require the theological explanation of 1 Cor 15:56.

Paul's theology, then, from the oldest letter onward, begins with the Hebrew Bible and Jewish heritage and makes it fit. A great deal of the law is being adopted, but circumcision and dietary laws are no longer entrance requirements for Gentiles.

III. *2 Corinthians and Philippians*

The evidence of these letters confirms the results reached so far. In 2 Corinthians 3, Paul affirms the splendor of the Sinai covenant as such (vv. 7, 9, 10), in the same way as he appreciates the gain of life in Judaism as such (Phil 3:7). However, that which matters here is that in 2 Corinthians 3 the "dispensation of the Spirit" (v. 8) by far surpasses "the dispensation of condemnation" (v. 9), and in Philippians 3 "the knowledge of Christ" (v. 8) is far superior to "the righteousness under the law" (v. 6). Therefore, looking back, Paul cannot help but to consider the Sinai covenant as having no actual splendor (v. 10) and to regard the "righteousness under the law" as loss (v. 7).

Anticipating Romans, one may be tempted to say: Read incorrectly, the law can only achieve wrath and increase sin; however, read properly—i.e., from Christ—the law is being adopted and fulfilled by Christians.

IV. *Galatians*

This circulating letter, written either shortly before or after 1 Corinthians (in my opinion around the time of 2 Corinthians 10-13), defends Paul's apostleship (Galatians 1-2) and polemically develops the conditions under which Gentiles can join the people of God. Galatians 3 is directed against Jewish Christian missionaries (not against Jews), who in all likelihood had stated that Gentile Christians needed to be circumcised if they wished to become members of the people of God or sons of Abraham, the latter all the more so since Gen 17:10-14 entails circumcision of every male among the descendants of Abraham. To this Paul objects: Abraham already received righteousness before Genesis 17, i.e., righteousness through faith (Gen 15:6). Consequently, persons of faith (*hoi ek pisteōs*) are sons of Abraham (Gal 3:7), and the promised seed of Abraham is Christ (Gal 3:16). Before that, Paul had already made a jab at his opponents in Galatia: "All who rely on works of the law are under a curse; for it is written, 'Cursed be every one who does not abide by all things written in the book of the law, and do them'" (Gal 3:10).

The true function of the law, then, is that it was added because of transgressions (Gal 3:19). It was, furthermore, "ordained by angels" (Gal 3:19), i.e., not even by God, and until the coming of Christ it served as a custodian (*paidagōgos*) (Gal 3:24). With the coming of Christ, believers are no longer seen as being under a custodian, for "when the time had fully come, God sent forth his Son, born of a woman, born under the law, to redeem those who were under the law, so that we might receive adoption as sons" (Gal 4:4-5).

The above sketched train of thought in Galatians confirms what we already know from the other letters: Paul takes the Christ-event, as he understands it, as a starting point. In Galatians, such an approach is carried out in that, because of his opponents' appeal to the law, he polemicizes against it, while at the same time appealing to the law (Gen 15:6) in order to justify his own understanding of Christ.

The polemic against the law is so rude, however, that a recent interpreter of Paul could write: "Whoever . . . reads Galatians through 5:12 will hardly conceive that the same author will later write: 'so the law is holy, and the commandment is holy and just and good' (Rom 7:12)."[14] Against this, one may adduce a verse in Romans which surpasses even the statements in Galatians in its critique of the law, namely, Rom 5:20: "Law came in, to increase the trespass." Furthermore, even in Galatians Paul appeals to the law positively (Gal 5:14) and quotes Lev 19:18.[15] Therefore, not even in Galatians should Paul be seen as an antinomist.

V. *Romans*

The letter to the Romans was written in Corinth, during the winter before Paul's fatal journey in delivering the collection to Jerusalem (Rom 15:25). Concerning the law, Paul in this letter has some recourse to what he wrote in Galatians and, as in Galatians 3, introduces Abraham

---

[14] H. Hübner, *Das Gesetz bei Paulus: Ein Beitrag zum Werden der paulinischen Theologie* (FRLANT 119; Göttingen: Vandenhoeck & Ruprecht, 1978) 37 (my translation).

[15] Hübner, *Das Gesetz bei Paulus*, 37-38, thinks, however, that *pas nomos* in Gal 5:14 is an ironical phrase and does not refer to the Mosaic law. This is hardly convincing since in Gal 5:14 Lev 19:18 is being quoted.

as a type who has received justification through faith. This time, however, he not only adduces Gen 15:6 but also Gen 17:10 as proof from Scripture. Note Rom 4:11: Abraham "received circumcision as a sign or seal of the righteousness." By continuing with the statement, "which he had by faith while he was still uncircumcised," Paul makes clear that the priority of Gen 15:6 remains in force.

Following U. Luz[16] one can by way of comparing Romans and Galatians distinguish several aspects of Paul's understanding of the law and systematize them in the following manner:

1. The law has no essential function. It was introduced (Rom 5:20); it was given 430 years after the promise (Gal 3:17).
2. The law is neutral in that it states the sin and qualifies it as transgression. It leads to a recognition of sin (Rom 3:20); cf. Gal 3:19a.
3. The law can contribute to the working of sin (Rom 7:9-10).
4. The law has as its content the gospel, i.e., it contains justification through faith (Gen 15:6) and thus is also God's word for the present.
5. The law remains in force, and the Christians fulfill it in practicing the love-command and the decalogue (Rom 13:8 / Gal 5:14).
6. However, it needs to be taken into account that the law receives no treatment as such except in its relation to Christ.

It is no wonder, then, that the manifold treatment of the law by Paul has left many confused from his day until the present. One example of how this treatment might lead to confusion is given by Paul himself in his quoting a sentence directed against himself: "'And why not do evil that good may come?' —as some people slanderously charge us with saying" (Rom 3:8). His opponents obviously took offense at *one* of the aspects of his teaching of the law, namely, that the law had been annulled and justification through faith was introduced instead. They concluded that the result could only be libertinism, without realizing that Paul—when teaching the annulment of the law—at the same time taught his converts to keep the law as properly understood.

---

[16] Smend and Luz, *Gesetz*, 99-110.

Yet Paul's opponents were not totally wrong in their suspicion, for Jas 2:14-26 seems to show that at least some of Paul's friends did not hold tightly together that which the apostle thought to be an insepa- rable unity: faith and works (see Gal 5:6). Paul's opponents had there- fore noticed a real difficulty of Paul's doctrine of justification through faith, namely, that it did not necessarily lead to ethics.

VI. *Summary*

Our survey of the evidence of the letters[17] has shown that behind the individual statements and behind Paul's practice there exists a relatively coherent evaluation of the law which can be summarized as follows:

1. Paul makes statements about the law by starting from Christ, who through his death and resurrection has inaugurated a new creation.
2. Circumcision and dietary laws are no longer entrance requirements for Gentiles to become members of the people of God. Gentiles and Jews alike become members through faith.
3. The law is being fulfilled by the Christians. They were instructed of its content already when they be- came Christians, i.e., when they were baptized.
4. The purity laws played an important role for the concept of the church. They elucidate the very nature of the church as God's temple in which the divine spirit dwells. The holiness of the Christians corresponds to the holiness of God (Lev 19:2).
5. The law is not only witness to the gospel; it may also contain the gospel (Gen 15:6).
6. Freedom from the law only inadequately describes Paul's attitude to the law.

---

[17] Rom 1:18–2:29 has been left out. On the problems that this passage poses, cf. Sanders, *Paul, the Law, and the Jewish People*, 123-35.

CONFLICT FOR THE SAKE OF HEAVEN[1]

LOU H. SILBERMAN
Emeritus, Vanderbilt University

In the collection of early rabbinic aphorisms, *Pirqe ʾAbot*, the following statement occurs: "Any conflict carried on for the sake of Heaven will have enduring results, while any conflict not carried on for the sake of Heaven will have no enduring results." This is followed by a question: "What is an example of the former?" "That of Hillel and Shammai." "What is an example of the latter?" "That of Korah and his adherents."[2] Various rabbinic texts report a large number of conflicts between the former two groups that together made up the proto-rabbinic party at the turn of the era. Such conflicts were, for the most part, not seen as self-serving. The second example, Korah and his adherents, is problematic. Why was it necessary to reach far back into biblical history to find such an example?[3] It is well known that at the same time that Hillel, Shammai, and their schools flourished there were other parties making their claim as well. Josephus reported the existence of four parties during the period before the first revolt against Rome (69-72 CE): Pharisees, Sadducees, Essenes, and the Fourth Philosophy.[4] Qumran materials have added to our understanding of party conflict, and of course the New Testament, *parti pris*, is witness to controversy. The Palestinian Talmud reported the presence of twenty-four competing parties.[5] That such party conflicts erupted into violence

---

[1] An earlier version of this paper was read at the Annual Meeting of the American Society for the Study of Religion, Trinity College, University of Toronto, Canada, 3 May 1986.

[2] *Pirqe ʾAbot* 5:20.

[3] Numbers 16.

[4] *Antiquities* 13.5.9 §171-73; 13.10.5-6 § 288-98.

[5] *p. Sanhedrin* x (29c).

is evidenced by Josephus, the New Testament, several Qumran documents, and talmudic traditions, one of which reports threats on the life of Rabban Yoḥanan ben Zakkai, one of the last of Hillel's pupils and the leader of the peace party during the Roman seige of Jerusalem, so that he had to be smuggled out of the city.[6] With such a wealth of possibilities from which to choose to illustrate conflicts "not for the sake of Heaven" one wonders why Korah was disinterred. It may be, on the basis of some rabbinic comments dealing with the Korah episode, that what we have here is a disguised reference to Paul or even Jesus.[7]

The end of the Judean state and its religious establishment, the Temple and its priesthood, left a vacuum as far as authority of any sort was concerned, and it was only slowly that a centripetal force, focused on a successor party to Pharisaism, the school and court of Rabban Yoḥanan ben Zakkai in Yabneh, began to assert itself. Yet even here conflict and controversy did not abate, although now they were, as in the case of the earlier conflicts between Bet Hillel and Bet Shammai, internal to a party that in largest measure agreed upon a central and crucial idea, the authority of the Oral Torah side by side with Scripture, the Torah in writing; this constituted an inheritance from its Pharisaic origin. What was attempted in the two generations between the first (69-72 CE) and second revolts (132-135 CE) against Rome (the latter followed by five years of intensive persecution under the emperor Hadrian), indeed, on until the end of the second century CE, was the overcoming of conflict and the establishment of an authority that could and would construct a governing consensus. In very large measure that was accomplished at the end of the second century when R. Judah ha-Nasi, the Prince, a descendant of Hillel and a claimed descendant of King David, promulgated and canonized a collection of oral tradition, the Mishna, as its authentic statement. This, however, did not bring conflict and controversy to an end, but it did determine what George Foot Moore wrote of as "normative Judaism." No monolithically dogmatic or even orthopractic society emerged, but a reasonably pragmatic consensus developed and held sway. It is against this background that we shall examine anecdotally some conflicts from the period before the first revolt, those between Bet Hillel and Bet Shammai, and

---

[6] *Lamentations Rabbah* to 1:5; ʾAbot d. R. Nathan, c. 4; *b. Giṭṭin* 56a-b.

[7] Louis Ginzberg, *The Legends of the Jews* (7 vols.; Philadelphia: The Jewish Publication Society of America, 1909-38) 3 (1911): 290-91, 289 and notes thereto; 6 (1939): 101 n. 568, and 100 n. 566.

some from the period before the second revolt, in the first third of the second century CE.

Rabbinic material is divided, grossly, into two classes: one, *halakhah*, reports rules, regulations, norms, laws, and the like; the other, *aggada*, is concerned with narratives, anecdotes, aphorisms, interpretations of the non-legal portions of Scripture, and more. They occur side by side in the collections with the former providing the structure of, and the latter the sense of existence of, the Judaic community. It is from the latter, then, as it provides the background or even the foreground of the former, that the examples are drawn. It is not necessarily the content of the conflicts but the behavior of the adversaries and the modes of resolving the conflicts that are here examined—that is, the sense or sensibilities of those involved in the conflicts and of those who sought to mitigate, resolve, and in some instances punish one or the other or both of the opponents.

The conflicts between Bet Hillel and Bet Shammai, noted as paradigmatic of "conflicts for the sake of Heaven," are reported in considerable detail in rabbinic sources. E. E. Urbach wrote of them: "Until the beginning of the Revolt, the differences of opinion, which grew with the increase in the number of disciples, did not lead to sharp schisms between the two schools."[8] Thus the sharpness of theoretical difference did not lead, necessarily, to practical repudiation of one's opponents. Conflict, even in legal rulings, did not result in the rupture of the social fabric. In the tractate *Yebamot* of the Mishna,[9] dealing with levirate marriage and the complexities that can—in general theoretically and on occasion practically—arise from this Scriptural ordinance, there is in the first chapter a report of conflicts between Bet Hillel and Bet Shammai. These concern the permitting of and the prohibiting of certain marriages that could result from the levirate relationship. These differences were such that, carried into practice, they could inhibit any marriages between the contending parties lest they lead to forbidden relationship, that is, incest as broadly interpreted. Yet the Mishna reads: "Though these forbade what the others declare eligible, Bet Shammai, nevertheless, did not refrain from marrying women from Bet Hillel, nor did Bet Hillel, from Bet Shammai." To this dictum is added, though it is not relevant but belonged to the inherited material here being organized, a further statement that was as well of practical

---

[8] Efraim E. Urbach, *The Sages: Their Concepts and Beliefs* (Jerusalem: Magnes, 1975) 1:594.

[9] *m. Yebamot* 1:2.

consequences: "In matters of [ritual] cleanness and uncleanness, which these declare clean, where the others declare unclean, neither of them abstain from using the utensils of the other for the preparation of food that had to be ritually pure." At a later time the scholars who pondered this report tried to find reasons for what appeared to them to be a shocking contradiction, acting against one's principles! The positions of each party were examined in attempts to demonstrate that the conflicts were somehow mitigated conflicts.[10] Yet in the course of these discussions, ranging over several centuries and coming from both Galilean and Babylonian sources, several comments reflect what may be understood to be the sense of existence lying behind the pragmatic agreement in the face of theoretical disagreement. They are based upon Scriptural texts: one by means of interpretation, the others, quite directly. A statement from Resh Lakish, taken from quite another context, is quoted in the course of the discussion: "Apply here the text from Deut 14:1, lōʾ titgōdĕdû." Its literal meaning in Scripture is: "You shall not gash yourselves." Resh Lakish, however, assumes that the verb is not from the root gdd, "to gash" or "to cut," but from the root ʿgd, "to bind," here interpreted to mean "making bands, sects, factions." Hence, you shall not divide yourselves into competing parties.[11] Nothing further is said, but its intention is clear: principle was to be overridden for the sake of communal harmony. Further in the same talmudic discussion a somewhat different version of the conflict is reported, and here too, after indicating that comity prevailed between the two groups with regard to the differences over marriage regulations, the statement occurs: "This is to teach you that they showed love and friendship toward one another, thus putting into practice the Scriptural text, 'Love truth and peace'" (Zech 8:14). Yet another version includes the reference to the disagreement over the ritual cleanness or uncleanness of utensils and concludes that nonetheless they did not refrain from using each other's, "fulfilling the Scripture, 'every way of man is right in his own eyes; but the Lord weighs the hearts'" (Prov 21:2).[12]

A further controversy between the two schools is reported in the Babylonian Talmud, transmitted in the name of Samuel:

---

[10] b. Yebambot 13a and following.

[11] Ibid.

[12] t. Yebamot 1.10-11. To this see S. Lieberman, Tosefta Kī-fshutah : A Comprehensive Commentary on the Tosefta (New York: Jewish Theological Seminary of America, 1962ff.), Part VI, Order Nashim, pp. 7 bottom – 8 top.

R. Abba stated in the name of Samuel: For three years there was a dispute between Bet Hillel and Bet Shammai, the former asserting "The *halakhah* is in agreement with our view" and the latter contending "The *halakhah* is in agreement with our view." Then a *Bat Qol* issued announcing: "Both are the words of the living God, but the *halakhah* is in agreement with the rulings of Bet Hillel." Since, however, both are the words of the living God, what was it that entitled Bet Hillel to have the *halakhah* fixed in agreement with its rulings? Because they were kindly and modest; they had studied their own rulings and those of Bet Shammai and gave precedence to the mention of Bet Shammai.

There follows a brief anecdote proving this latter mode of behavior, and the report concludes:

This teaches you that the Holy One, Blessed Be He, raises up him who humbles himself while he humbles him who raises himself up. From him who seeks greatness, greatness flees, but greatness follows him who flees it. He who forces time is forced by time, but he who yields to time finds time standing on his side.[13]

Here a shift has taken place. In the former no decision was made between the contending positions. Here Bet Hillel's position is declared to be *halakhah*, that is, the binding rule, not because of its intrinsic correctness but because of the superior attitude and behavior of the group. One may conclude, too, that the behavior of Bet Shammai no longer showed the same "love and friendship" previously ascribed to both.

A third controversy reported in the Mishna supports this indication of the shift in attitude and behavior of Bet Shammai, and this in a radical way. "These are the *halakhot* which they declared in the upper chamber of Ḥananiah ben Ḥezekiah ben Garon when they went to visit him. They took a count, and Bet Shammai outnumbered Bet Hillel. On that day they enacted eighteen measures." The discussion of this passage is complicated because the exact identity of these eighteen decrees of Bet Shammai had been forgotten so that later generations had to attempt to recover them. However, toward the end of the discussion it is reported:

---

[13] *b. ʿErubin* 15a.

A sword was planted in the House of Study, and it was proclaimed, "He who would enter, let him enter, but he who would depart, let him not depart!" On that day Hillel sat submissively before Shammai like one of the disciples, and it was as grievous to Israel as on the day when the [golden] calf was made.[14]

This is the account found in the Babylonian Talmud and indicates a shift in power but, even more, in attitude. The strange passage about the planting of the sword suggests something even more radical, and the account in the Palestinian Talmud confirms this:

R. Joshua of Oni transmitted an account: "The disciples of Bet Shammai stationed themselves downstairs [from the upper chamber of Ḥananiah ben Ḥezekiah ben Garon] and slew the disciples of Bet Hillel. There is a tradition that six went upstairs while the rest remained below armed with swords and spears."[15]

Urbach argues that this violence grew out of the deteriorating political situation preceding the first revolt. He wrote:

The position changed with the start of the Great Revolt; whereas previously the Sages were able to adopt a positive attitude in principle to the actual institutions of the state and government, without refraining from protesting against acts of injustice and without seeking unduly close relations with the ruling power, once the Revolt broke out, which seemed to many an obligatory war and to others a hopeless struggle that endangered the existence of the people, the relationship between the two schools became severely strained.

He concluded, "The politico-military struggle was exploited for the purpose of securing decisions by force."[16]

These three conflicts, arranged in the order suggested and reflecting the expansion and deepening of controversy in the last days of the Jewish commonwealth, find their echo in a tradition reported in sev-

---

[14] b. Shabbat 13b.

[15] p. Shabbat 1.4 (3d); t. Shabbat 1.16.

[16] Urbach, The Sages, 594-95.

eral places that describes such a degeneration in other terms. In the Mishna there is a passage that is a threnody of social disintegration: "When murderers multiplied . . ., when adulterers multiplied . . ., when Jose ben Joezer of Zeredah and Jose ben Judah of Jerusalem died. . . ." In each of these instances, social or intellectual disruption is reported. The gemara of the Babylonian Talmud picks up the Mishna's lament:

> When hedonists multiplied..., when those engaged in whispering multiplied..., when there multiplied "Those whose heart goes after gain" (Ezek 33:13)..., when there multiplied they "who call evil good and good evil" (Isa 5:20)..., when the arrogant multiplied...

On and on goes the litany of despair until: "When the haughty of heart multiplied, dissension increased in Israel. When the disciples of Shammai and Hillel multiplied (who had not served sufficiently), dissensions increased in Israel and the Torah became like two Torot."[17] This last statement is enlarged upon in two other passages.

> Said R. Jose, originally there were no conflicts in Israel. There was a court of seventy-one members that sat in the Chamber of Hewn Stone; there were courts of twenty-three members sitting in Jerusalem, one sitting in the Temple Mount and one in the citadel. If one need a ruling, he went to the court in his city. If there was not one, he went to that nearest to his city. If it had a traditional ruling, it was given to him; if not, he and a court assessor went to the court on the Temple Mount. If it had a ruling, it was given to them; if not, they all proceeded to the court in the citadel; if it had a rule, it was given to them; if not, all of them attended the supreme court in the Chamber of Hewn Stone, composed of seventy-one members with the presence of twenty-three required for a decision. One of the inquirers went in to see if twenty-three were present; if there were, he came out; if not, he waited until a quorum was present. . . . When the question was put, if they had a ruling it was given; if not, a division was taken. If a majority voted "unclean," it was declared "unclean"; if the contrary, the contrary. Thus was the ruling established and promulgated in Israel.

---

17 b. Soṭah 47a-b.

This is followed by an aside: "When the disciples of Shammai and Hillel who had not sufficiently studied increased, conflict increased as well." The report continues after the aside with a description of the appointment of judges and their qualifications: "wise, humble, sin-fearers, of unblemished reputation, and in good health."[18] What is evident when these various accounts are put together is that, whether such a golden age ever existed within the community or even just within the Pharisaic society, such was seen as the ideal, once again to be striven for.

The disintegration of Judaic society, brought about in the first instance by the internal struggles over political policy vis-à-vis the Roman government and exacerbated by the ill-fated revolt that ended in widespread slaughter, the destruction of the sacred shrine, the cessation of the official cult, and the end—at least for a period—of even a semblance of civil and juridical sovereignty, could have spelled the end of any cohesive, viable successor to the resurrected commonwealth established by Ezra and Nehemiah half a millennium earlier, or the Hasmonean kingdom begun two centuries earlier, or even the Herodian Potemkin kingdom formed less than a century before. Could have but did not. Although the history of the generation subsequent to the revolt, between 70 and 100 CE, is murky, one item seems to provide us with a foothold of understanding. Rabban Yoḥanan ben Zakkai, leader of the peace party and apparently one of the last of Hillel's direct disciples, had, on his escape from besieged Jerusalem, approached the Roman general Vespasian, not yet emperor, predicting his rise to the purple and requesting permission to establish a school in a vineyard in Yabneh. Granted this, he settled down to reconstitute a center for the remnants of the Pharisaic party, apparently from both factions—Hillelite and Shammaite. The task was his, for Rabban Simeon I ben Gamaliel I, the grandson of Hillel, had—Josephus reports—supported the preparations for the revolt and was undoubtedly in hiding.[19] Yoḥanan ben Zakkai's undertaking, despite continuing internal conflicts that suggest the presence of a Shammaite contingent, was in large measure successful—so much so that, early in the second century, the Hillelite heir, Rabban Gamaliel II, was prepared to assert his authority and in the process fan the embers of party conflict into flame.

The four conflicts here examined are arranged in an order corresponding to the severity of the response to the behavior of the

---

[18] t. Ḥaggigah 2.9; t. Sanhedrin 7 (b. Sanhedrin 88b).
[19] Life, 189-98.

antagonist. In the first three the protagonist and antagonist are the same, R. Joshua ben Levi and Rabban Gamaliel II; in the fourth, the protagonist is R. Eliezer ben Hyrcanus. R. Joshua is the stand-in for the antagonist, Rabban Gamaliel II, as the conclusion of the story makes clear.

The first conflict concerns the proclamation of the new moon, i.e., the beginning of a month. This was done on the basis of the observation of the moon's appearance, confirmed by the examination of the witnesses before the patriarchal court. This determination by the authorities established as well the day on which festivals or holy days with fixed monthly dates—in the case at hand, the Day of Atonement on the tenth of Tishri—were to be observed during that month. If the new moon was seen late, the previous month would have thirty days, otherwise twenty-nine. Depending upon this, a fixed-date festival or holy day could fall on one of two consecutive days in the following month. In the case at hand Rabban Gamaliel, as head of the court, had accepted the evidence of two witnesses that the new moon had been seen, but on the following day it was not visible. R. Dosa b. Horkinas said that the witnesses had given a false report, for, using an analogy, how can men testify that a woman has borne a child when the next day she is seen with her belly still swollen? R. Joshua agreed with him: "I see the force of your argument." Were he to act on this assumption, he would observe the Day of Atonement other than on the day determined by Rabban Gamaliel. The latter, for whatever reason, directed the weight of his authority toward R. Joshua and not R. Dosa and commanded him to appear before him with his staff and money pouch on the day R. Joshua reckoned was Yom Kippur. This would, of course, require him to desecrate this most sacred day. The story continues. R. Akiba said:

"I can bring proof from Scriptures that whatever Rabban Gamaliel has done is valid, for it says, 'These are the appointed seasons of the Lord, holy convocations which you shall proclaim in their appointed times.' Whether they are *proclaimed* at the proper season or not, I have no *appointed* seasons save these." R. Joshua then approached R. Dosa who said to him, "If we call into question the court of Rabban Gamaliel, we must call into question all the decisions of every court since the days of Moses, for it says: 'Then went up Moses and Aaron, Nadab and Abihu and the seventy elders of Israel.' Why were the names of the seventy not mentioned? To show that every group that has acted as a court in Israel is on the level with the court of Moses." Whereupon [R. Joshua] took his staff and money and went to Rabban Gamaliel at Yabneh on the day on which Yom Kippur fell according to his reckoning. Rabban Gamaliel arose and kissed him on the head and said: "Come in peace, my teacher and my disciple. My teacher in wisdom; my disciple, for you have accepted my decision."[20]

What we see here expounded is the absolute right of duly established authority to deal with conflict. One may not, after a decision, continue the conflict. R. Dosa put it most radically and, I suspect, disclosed the underlying basis of this conflict, distrust of the learning of Rabban Gamaliel. "The most worthless, once he is appointed leader of the community, is to be accounted the mightiest of the mighty. . . . One must be content to go to the judge who is in his day." The implication is that, once a decision is made, a conflict for the sake of Heaven ceases to be such. To continue is intolerable.

The report of a second conflict between Rabban Gamaliel and R. Joshua indicates an erosion of this as an absolute principle. Here the conflict has to do with the matter of inflicting intentional blemish on a firstling, thus rendering it unfit as a Temple sacrifice or, after the destruction of the Temple, exempting it as a priest's due. A case in this matter was brought by R. Zadok before R. Joshua who rendered an opinion. R. Zadok, apparently unconvinced, went to Rabban Gamaliel who rendered a contrary opinion. To this R. Zadok complained that R. Joshua had decided otherwise. Rabban Gamaliel confronted R. Joshua at a session of the Academy, and when the latter sought to avoid the conflict by retracting and offering an opinion in conformity with that of the *Nasi*, the latter forced the confrontation. "Was not the answer 'yes' reported to me in your name? Joshua, stand up and let them testify against you." R. Joshua arose and said: "What shall I do? Were I alive and he dead, the living can contradict the dead. [In other words R. Joshua was ready to dissemble in order to avoid conflict.] But since both he and I are alive, how can the living contradict the living?" At this Rabban Gamaliel resumed his seat and left R. Joshua standing. The assembly began to murmur about this and called to Ḥuzpit the meturgaman, who declaimed the *Nasi's* words: "Cease!" and he became silent. What happened here was an indirect rebuke to Rabban

---

[20] b. *Rosh ha-Shanah* 25a.

Gamaliel. He was not told to cease but, as it were, his microphone was shut off. In a word, his authority was challenged.[21]

The third episode brought the confrontations to a climax. Here, a person merely designated "a disciple" asked R. Joshua if the recitation of the Eighteen Benedictions was optional or obligatory in the evening worship service. He replied that it was optional. The "disciple" asked the same question of Rabban Gamaliel, and upon being told it was obligatory he reported R. Joshua's contrary opinion. Once again the *Nasi* sought a public confrontation. When the Academy was in session, the "disciple" arose and put the question. After replying that it was obligatory, Rabban Gamaliel asked the assembled scholars if there was any disagreement. R. Joshua responded "No!" Whereupon Rabban Gamaliel declared: "Joshua, stand up and let them witness against you!" R. Joshua arose and, as in the previous instance, sought to avoid conflict. Again he was treated with discourtesy. Once again the members of the Academy called upon Huzpit to cease declaiming Rabban Gamaliel's words, and he did so. However, the matter did not rest there. The report continues:

> They said, "How long will he continue to grieve him? On Rosh ha-Shanah last year he humiliated him. In the matter of the firstling, in R. Zadok's case, he humiliated him. Now, too, he humiliates him! Come let us depose him! Whom shall we set in his place? We cannot set R. Joshua for he is a part to the conflict. If we set R. Akiba, perhaps fault will be found, for he does not have a distinguished ancestry. Let us set R. Eleazar b. Azariah. He is a scholar; he is rich; he is in the tenth generation from Ezra."[22]

The account continues with the report of the election of R. Eleazar to the post of *Nasi* and of some of the complications involved therein. The narrative continues with an account of the results of this change in authority: "On that day the doorkeeper was removed and permission was granted to [all] students to enter. On that day many benches had to be added." At this point a comment is added: "Rabban Gamaliel became perturbed; he thought, perhaps, Heaven forbid, I have held back Torah in Israel." It was further reported that on that day all doubts

---

21 *b. Bekorot* 36a.
22 *b. Berakhot* 27b–28a.

existing in the Academy about *halakhic* [legal] matters were resolved so that every *halakhah* that had been held in abeyance was explained.[23]

All of this led to yet another conflict. The text continues:

> Rabban Gamaliel did not absent himself from the Academy for a single hour. We learn: On that day Judah an Ammonite proselyte came before the court and said, "May I enter the community?"[24] Rabban Gamaliel replied: "You are forbidden to enter!" R. Joshua said, "You are permitted." Rabban Gamaliel retorted, "Is it not written, 'An Ammonite may not enter the community of the Lord'?" (Deut 23:4). R. Joshua replied, "Are Ammon and Moab in the place where they originally dwelt? Long ago Sennacherib, king of Assyria, came and mixed up all the people, as it is written, 'I have erased the boundaries of the peoples, I have plundered their treasures, even exiled their vast populations' (Isa 10:13). Now," he argued, "whatever is separated from the majority is separated." Rabban Gamaliel countered, "Is it not written, 'But afterwards I will restore the fortunes of the Ammonites, declares the Lord' (Jer. 49:6), so they have returned." R. Joshua reported, "It is written, 'I will restore the captivity of my people Israel' (Amos 9:14), but as yet they are not restored." [Judah the Ammonite] was immediately granted permission to enter the community. At this Rabban Gamaliel thought: "Since this is how things are, I will go and become reconciled with R. Joshua." When he arrived at R. Joshua's house, he saw its walls were blackened. Said he: "I see from the walls of your house that you are a charcoal burner." He replied: "Woe unto a generation over which you preside, for you know nothing of the troubles of scholars, how they support themselves and how they sustain themselves." Said Gamaliel, "I humble myself before you! Forgive me!" He paid no attention to him. "Do it for the sake of my ancestor's house." He was reconciled.

The report continues with an account of the results of the reconciliation, the reinstatement of Rabban Gamaliel but in such a way as to not to offend R. Eleazar b. Azariah, who could not be ousted from his position. It is

---

[23] Ibid.

[24] I.e., "may I marry a Jewess?" See *b. Yoma* 84b; *b. Yebamot* 16b; *b. Ketubot* 15a; *b. Qiddushin* 73a; *b. Zebahim* 73a.

decided that Rabban Gamaliel who had a hereditary claim would preach on three Sabbaths and R. Eleazar on one.[25]

What is apparent from these reports is that these conflicts, although they are not called such, are "for the sake of Heaven." They resulted in a shift of authority from the autocratic rule of the patriarch to a collegiality in which the rights and opinions of individual scholars were considered. It is this collegiality that is one of the two foci of the conflict next reported, a conflict that finds R. Joshua the spokesman of the consensus against an individual.

This conflict involved R. Eliezer b. Hyrcanus,[26] a pupil of Rabban Yoḥanan ben Zakkai and a tradent of great authority, and his colleagues at whose head is Rabban Gamaliel and whose spokesman is, as noted above, R. Joshua. The story of the conflict occurs in a long discussion about verbal violence and the need to respect the feelings of others. It begins with what seems to be a slight matter, a *halakhic* argument over the susceptibility of a certain type of pottery oven to ritual uncleanness. R. Eliezer insists that it cannot contract such uncleanness while his colleagues argue the opposite. This leads to an oft quoted account of R. Eliezer's appeal to wonders to support his position.

> Said he to them: "If the *halakhah* is according to me, let this carob tree prove it!" Whereupon the tree was torn a hundred cubits out of its place. . . . "No proof can be brought from a carob tree," they retort. Again he said: "If the *halakhah* is according to me, let the stream prove it." Whereupon the stream flowed backward. "No proof can be brought from a stream," was the rejoinder. Again he argued: "If the *halakhah* is according to me, let the walls of the schoolhouse prove it!" Whereupon the walls began to fall. R. Joshua reproved the walls: "When scholars engage in *halakhic* dispute, what business is it of yours?" So they did not fall, in honor of R. Joshua; but they did not resume their upright position, in honor of R. Eliezer; and they are still standing so. Again he said: "If the *halakhah* is according to me, let it be proved by Heaven!" A *Bat Qol* [a voice without a source, presumably a divine disclosure] rang out: "Why do you dispute with R. Eliezer seeing that in all matters the *halakhah* agrees with him!" R. Joshua arose and quoted Scripture: "It is not in heaven" (Deut 30:12).

---

[25] b. *Berakhot* 28a.

[26] Circa 80-120 CE.

At this point the narrative is interrupted by a discussion stemming from a period about two hundred fifty years later. The question is asked: "What did he mean by this verse?" Said R. Jeremiah [a fourth-century CE scholar]: "He meant by this that since the Torah had already been given at Sinai we are not to pay attention to a *Bat Qol*, for it is written in the Torah given at Sinai, 'After the majority one must incline.'" What R. Jeremiah claims R. Joshua meant is that conflict is settled by majority rule—the collegiality referred to above. The individual must, despite his certainty of correctness, bow before the judgment of his peers. The problem with R. Jeremiah's solution is that there is no such verse in Scripture supporting this claim for majority rule. What we have before us are three words from Exod 23:2, torn out of context to provide this proof. The text in full reads, "You shall not follow after a multitude to do evil, you shall not bear false witness, turning after a multitude so as to pervert justice." The warning *not* to turn aside after a multitude is transformed, by the omission of the negative and the understanding of the infinitive construct with the prefixed preposition [*linṭōt*] as an imperative, into a positive command: "Follow the majority!" It is clear that in order to establish a principle through which conflict may be avoided or resolved, i.e., the principle of majority rule, Scripture itself may be, so it appears, perverted. It is important to recognize that this interpretation of R. Joshua's invoking a Scriptural phrase, "It is not in heaven," comes from a time two hundred fifty years after the event narrated. It must therefore be considered as belonging to a conflict in its own time over majority rule. There is another interpretation of the narrative in which it is reported that God accepted the rebuke. However, as we shall see, this does not seem to be the case.

The narrative now resumes, for its intent in context was not focused on this matter but on the main theme of the earlier part of the discussion, the danger of verbal violence, concern for the feelings of others. R. Eliezer is placed under a ban by his colleagues for his obstinacy. R. Akiba acts with great delicacy in making this known to him, but to no avail. R. Eliezer's wrath at his colleagues' action is not assuaged, and a series of natural disasters follows in response to his anger. The ship on which Rabban Gamaliel is travelling is almost swamped, and it is only his appeal to God—"Sovereign of the universe, you know full well that I have not acted for my own honor nor for the honor of my paternal house, but for yours, so that conflict may not increase in Israel"—that causes the sea to subside. Yet the conflict is not at an end. R. Eliezer's wife, Ima Shalom, was a sister of Rabban Gamaliel. Realizing the seriousness of her husband's anger she interfered with his prayers, not letting him recite *Tahnun*, the private and personal penitential and petitionary additions to the communal prayer. She feared that his supplications, focused on what had been done to him, would incite divine anger already on his side. On one occasion she was diverted so that he was able to recite *Tahnun*. When she realized what was happening she cried: "Arise [*Tahnun* is recited prostrate], you have killed my brother!" Just then the announcement came forth from the *Nasi's* home that Rabban Gamaliel had died. "How did you know this would happen?" R. Eliezer asked. "I have a tradition," she replied, "from my father's house: all the gates [of heaven] are locked except the gate of wounded feelings."[27]

If these four conflicts have been placed in a proper chronological order, then the following pattern emerges. The first three represent the development of collegiality in confronting the autocratic power of the *Nasi*. The fourth is a confrontation between that collegiality and the obstinate refusal of a single individual to bow to its authority. It is a conflict for the sake of Heaven against Heaven. What is significant here is that a radical shift has taken place. In a conflict between Bet Hillel and Bet Shammai (noted above) a *Bat Qol* intervened on the side of the former, and its decision was accepted. Why this shift, this challenge to apparent divine intervention? At this point only the barest suggestion as to an answer may be offered. It may be that Qumranic Judaism and nascent Christianity with their claims to new revelations derived directly from a divine source cast a threatening shadow over the idea of *Bat Qol*. If a "normative" Judaism was to be formed, it could not be thrown into doubt by the intervention of a disembodied voice. The attitude may be summed up in R. Akiba's comment in connection with the first conflict between R. Joshua and Rabban Gamaliel: "Whether they are *proclaimed* in the proper season or not, I have no *appointed* seasons save these"; and R. Dosa's remark: "If we call into question the court of R. Gamaliel, we must call into question all the decisions of every court since Moses. . . ."[28]

It would be most satisfactory to report that, with these conflicts behind, all conflict ceased in the courts and academies of Israel, that indeed all problems in abeyance were solved, all factionalism dis-

---

[27] b. *Baba Metzia* 59a.

[28] Does this is in any way parallel the discussion in the early church about Christian prophets and prophecy? See M. Eugene Boring, *The Sayings of the Risen Jesus: Christian Prophecy in the Synoptic Tradition* (SNTSMS 46; New York: Cambridge University, 1982).

solved. Alas such is not the case. R. Judah ha-Nasi, Rabban Gamaliel's
grandson, with the same authoritarian imperiousness, placed a scholar
under ban for merely suggesting to R. Judah's son that there was no need
to consult him to resolve a complicated discussion, and he placed yet
another scholar under ban for teaching his own nephews in the marketplace—a behavior forbidden by the *Nasi*—and continued to humiliate
him even after the ban was removed. No, *qinat soferim, furor scribendi*,
pride of place continued to stalk the halls of the academy and court, nor
was it limited to these august circles. One can understand why, in the
midst of a discussion in the Palestinian Talmud concerning the vast
dangers of *lashon ha-ra*ʿ, "evil report, slander," we are told by Samuel
bar Naḥman: *mutar lomar lashon ha-raʿ ʿal baʿale maḥloqet*, "It is permitted
to speak evilly of those who provoke conflict."[29]

Yet it is possible to conclude on a positive note. In a collection of
passages culled from various rabbinic sources, bearing the name *Pereq
Shalom*, "The Chapter on Peace," we read:

> Hezekiah said, "Great is peace, for of all the desert journeyings
> of Israel it is written, 'They [plural] journeyed and they [plural]
> encamped,' their journeyings were accompanied by conflict,
> their encampments, by conflict. But when they arrived at
> Sinai, they encamped in one encampment as it is written, 'There
> Israel camped [singular].' Said the Holy One, blessed be He,
> 'Because they hated conflict and loved peace, they became one
> camp. Now is the moment to give them Torah.'"[30]

---

[29] *p. Peah* 1.1

[30] *Pereq Shalom* 1.5 See *The Minor Tractates of the Talmud* (ed. A. Cohen;
London: Soncino, 1965) 2:598. The passage is found with variations in a number
of midrashim.

Part Three:
Perspectives on Contemporary Issues

FEAR AND FRIENDSHIP

DAVID B. BURRELL, C.S.C.
University of Notre Dame

We each live out our lives over an abyss of fear. Fear lest we not succeed, fear that we will "make a mess of our lives"; constant fear for the welfare of those entrusted to our care, fear of disappointing those who have given us their trust; fear above all of failing at the task entrusted to each one of us alone: to become the irreplaceable person we are called to be. And God's revealing to us the truth about who God really is, with the destiny that revelation opens to us, seems only to escalate the fear. And unbearably so; in the words of Deuteronomy: "I call heaven and earth today to witness against you: I have set before you life and death, the blessing and the curse. Choose life, then, that you and your descendants may live" (30:19).

So we work overtime to stave off that fear, to imagine ourselves firmly grounded in our personal achievements. We can rest there with a modicum of comfort, especially when we go on to adopt and confirm those "plausibility structures" which society designs to help convince us our achievements are indeed worthwhile. Building this extended sense of self-worth represents a crucial "latent function" of education, and especially of a professional education. So our inclination to buy the entire package not only helps stave off some of these nagging fears, but also cements us firmly into the *status quo*. This self-confirming and society-building process is what allows professions especially to serve so well as "plausibility structures" to drive out fear.

The image is suffering, however, even without Kierkegaard's trenchant analysis in *Sickness Unto Death*. And so it is felt by many, especially as they begin to circumvent the fear of not succeeding. For instead of feeling like we have begun the assault on fear in earnest by winning our first battle, we begin rather to wonder whether this was any more than a diversionary skirmish. For instead of giving us courage to contend with our other fears, it seems only to have brought us to face them more starkly, as a nagging voice threatens those imposing "structures of plausibility" by asking whether this success of ours is really worth anything at all.

On the threshold of acceptance, as our heroes fall to pieces and our project crumbles in our hands, we resonate with Kierkegaard's observation: "Children fear the dark; adults learn what really to fear." The sole ray of hope at this point—and at every point in our intermittent struggle with fear—comes from the way it can ease us into praying. For at such a pass, praying can no longer be thought an unworthy expedience—inviting God to further my ambitions; nor a cowardly escape—turning to "big brother" to get me out of a jam. For there is nothing cowardly about fearing the abyss of emptiness which swallows ambition whole. In fact, there is no response available to us other than prayer, and blessed are those who have access to the cry of the blind man: "Lord, that I may see" (Mark 10:51); or of Peter: "Save me, Lord" (Matt 14:30).

It was a fear far less noble (or "existential") that brought me most recently to pray. And in opening me afresh to prayer, this recent episode of fear became a parable to me of God's care and of our obtuseness. There is little to the story, except its exotic setting: the other side of the Jordan near where John once was baptizing—in today's terms, the Allenby Bridge. This modest military span, over what remains of the Jordan just short of the Dead Sea, bears the name of the British general who "liberated" Jerusalem from the modern Turks in 1918. It funnels streams of West Bank Arabs to and from other segments of their extended families throughout the Middle East as well as allowing them to market their produce in Jordan. It offers one more sign of astute Semitic accommodation to the peaceful state of hostility and careful non-recognition prevailing between Jordan and Israel.

I crossed that bridge with a small group of tourists in the summer of 1984, hoping to visit a community of sisters in Amman, who had come to play an important part in my life during the two years I had spent in Jerusalem from 1980 to 1982. It was purely a visit; I had no overt mission, and I was looking forward to a weekend of refreshing conversation and all those rituals which accompany renewing bonds of friendship. They knew when I was coming, and had, I presumed, obtained the permissions needed. Yet by a series of snags, I had not received a confirming message, and so encountered a recalcitrant Jordanian official: no papers, no entry. Moreover, the border closed at noon on Fridays, to accommodate the Muslim noonday prayer, so I must immediately return to

Israel. I panicked and did just that, only to receive the message on re-
turning to Jerusalem that "Sister Bridget would be at the bridge that
morning with the necessary papers."

That's all there was to it; nothing more. Murphy's Law was hard at
work, of course, for that message had been lying unattended on the desk
of the very person whom I had already contacted in Jerusalem, knowing
that Jordan's non-recognition of Israel forbids direct telephone links;
and that message also contained their *new* telephone number in Amman, explaining why I could not make contact with them from the
bridge to convince the Jordanian official of my legitimacy. But so the
snafus were compounded, and we were all disappointed; so what?
Hardly commensurate with the losses experienced by so many families
in Israel, Palestine, and Lebanon. What made this episode a parable to
me?

The fact that I had panicked—I who fancied myself an "old
Middle East hand." And that Matthew's gospel had daily been
confronting us with our lack of faith, only a little of which should have
allowed me to remain calm enough to wait the twenty minutes until
Sister Bridget would have arrived! Armed with the message, the new
telephone number, and the encouragement of some friends, I did return to
see them, but only after spending the sabbath confined to Jerusalem—
the only time in my life I felt displaced there on *šabbāt*—pressing
myself to know what had gone wrong. Not with the messages or even
the messengers, not over Murphy's Law which we are only prudent to
presume, but with the misplaced self-confidence that metamorphosed
into panic.

That was it! In the measure that we pretend to be in charge, and let
the truth of our precariousness give way to an illusion of self-confidence, we are prey to panic. So the therapy I needed was the confine-
ment of the sabbath, which let my remorse over that panicky act bring
the deeper panic within me into a searing focus, as the painful acknowledgment of my lack of faith allowed the power of God to burn but
a little faith into the center of my soul. I began to pray as I never had
before.

I also began to pray for things which I had never really allowed
myself to pray for before. And that admission offers an important clue
to what happened through the silence of that *šabbāt*, yet it is more
properly a consequence than an accurate description of the new opening
to prayer. That opening is best rendered by the language of faith, suggesting that I came to pray in a different way than I had before. The
image of Peter spontaneously wanting to imitate the Lord by coming to

him over the lake's surface was ready at hand, along with his sudden terror: "Lord save me!" How telling a parable of my situation: pretending to be negotiating a life bounded in reality by fear, all the while buoyed up by an acquired self-confidence carefully and craftily woven, yet so easily unravelled by a faceless encounter with a bureaucratic official. My panic in the face of the Jordanian immigration officer had revealed to me how precarious was my self-confidence, and opened my heart to the gospel's call to a new way of living—by faith.

In the wake of that event, and buoyed up in fact by the visit which did ensue (when I was able to pray Peter's simple prayer with one of the sisters in the wake of a stroke), I began to taste anew the reality of the Spirit. No language can convey that taste, as Teresa and John of the Cross warn us, and even referring to it can make one lose one's credibility. Yet the fact remains that we can experience a new way of relating to everything in our life. John Dunne identifies that attainment with grace (in his *Time and Myth*), for it defies our own achievement. We may be able to alter or even to give up specific things in our life, but our very manner of relating to the things of our life is too close to the bone to admit of our changing ourselves. Like the peculiar distortions in our relationship to our very selves—clinically called neuroses—we simply cannot negotiate the point from which to gain leverage on our characteristic way of relating to the world and others in it. None in fact can do that except the One to whom we owe our very existence, the One to whom "all things are possible" (Matt 19:26).

Can we be faithful to such experiences? It is easier, of course, not to be, just as it would have been more soothing to avoid the pain of that Jerusalem sabbath by getting drunk! Yet one feels oneself obliged to live faithfully to them. Not from the outside, but from within, as from a new plateau of consciousness which one dare not surrender to the enemy. And who is the enemy now? Illusion, as in my illusory self-confidence; and specifically our need to spin an illusion to keep at bay those fears. So the new mode of consciousness must mean living more directly and realistically with the fears which reflect our true estate. Such, I have learned, is one facet of "living by faith." And because I tasted so sharply the illusion of self-confidence betrayed by panic, I may have been humbled into attentiveness. There lies my only hope—for fidelity we can never presume.

But why, one might ask from the outside, such preoccupation with fear? For John has assured us, has he not, that "in love there can be no fear, but fear is driven out by perfect love" (1 John 4:18). None of us, to be sure, can claim to love perfectly, and that should be response enough to the question. But there is something more that revealed itself in that encounter, something of the inner connections linking love with fear. These would seem worth exploring, if only to help us see why John can claim that perfect love could remove fear from our lives.

The context of my crossing that day was love, that love of friendship which brought even Aristotle close to the lyrical, which collapses distance and enriches our lives so palpably by creating an atmosphere in which we can be at ease, communicating with one another by sharing what we each treasure. Yet at the heart of such ennobling exchange lingers the fear that I may not be up to it (as in sexual "performance"); so part of my chagrin at panicking came from my disappointing them. The self-as-ego, then, with its manifold anxieties, intrudes in a way that can hobble even the spontaneous dance among friends.

Yet recognizing fears like these, and identifying their source, can lead us beyond performance to prayer, while the bonds of friendship fasten us that much more to the treasure we share. For if self-confidence is illusory, love begets its own worlds of illusion, which our fears can help to expose. That is, attending to our fears, and trying to identify their source, can help us discover what it is we really treasure, and so what it is we are trying to share in the friendships we enjoy. To put it crudely, facing and naming our fears gets us clearer about what we hope to "get out of" the different loves we have. For it is fear—fear of my performance or failure to perform—which lets me see where I am looking to "get something out of" a friendship.

So to move beyond performance to prayer, from a self-regarding relationship into genuine friendship, is to move from fear into love. As I am impelled there by fear, I am also drawn there by grace, as I sense myself both needing friends more as well as needing that our friendship be a pure one. It will be so if what we share encourages us to be straight with ourselves and with one another. We can easily be lulled by romantic views of friendship which image the relationship terminating deep in each other's intimate self. Then what we must be true to will be one another: a sure-fire formula for mutual entrapment. For each of us in reality is subject to a more exacting norm than the self we currently are; so the classical view of friendship remains more accurate to our creaturely condition: sharing in what we recognize to be the good for each of us. That way lies a path out of illusion and entrapment, while the same path leads us deeper into a love of friendship.

That love drives out fear, then, by offering us a way of allowing the self we are called to become to displace the ego we seek to protect. For it is the fragility of that ego, plus our compulsion to preserve it intact, which roots our fear. And as our center shifts to a self-in-relation, sharing with others the good we have learned how to treasure together, we can fairly feel those fears drop away. We may be tempted, to be sure, simply to transfer those protective anxieties to "the relationship," and that temptation can be fed by romantic conceptions of friendship current among us. Yet to the extent that we come to appreciate how the communication at the heart of the love of friendship is rooted in the good we share, there is less and less we need to protect. For the relationship itself will continually call each of us beyond ourselves.

Should fidelity to that call carry us apart, however, the pain will be bearable because we will have touched together that which makes each of us unique. So we need never fear the other's trying to "replace" us with another to fill the space left palpably empty. If the romantic view of friendship recommends itself by fastening on our uniqueness, it is fidelity to the classical view which allows our true uniqueness to emerge. For just as uniqueness is something we can assert but never succeed in articulating (since all statements are cast in general terms), so it is something we can more easily profess than live out. In fact, the only one able to give proper recognition to my uniqueness is the One whose creative act ensures it. As the angel said to John on Patmos: "to those who prove victorious I will give . . . a white stone with a new name written on it, known only to the one who receives it" (Rev 2:17).

Friendship conceived as a union between two souls cannot bestow the uniqueness it demands, while a love nourished by the good we share can impel each of us to become what we are singly called to be. We can then experience together something of the power which makes each of us unique, and so come to appreciate what we will never be able to articulate—about our own self or another. In this way, love of friendship opens a contemplative path in the midst of our daily work, as the bonding we experience is not our own doing. And the strength mysteriously emanating from that union removes the final vestiges of fear.

Yet it all began with a salutary fear: a fear uncovered as my own self-confidence shattered before bureaucratic officialdom. One is reminded of that carefully constructed passage in Luke:

> To you my friends I say:
> Do not be afraid of those who kill the body and after
>   that can do no more.
> I will tell you whom to fear: fear him who, after he
>   has killed, has the power to cast into hell. Yes,
>   I tell you, fear him. . . .

> [Yet] there is no need to be afraid: you are worth more
> than hundreds of sparrows—not one [of which]
> is forgotten in God's sight. (12:4-7)

Do not fear what can only threaten the ego and its need for accomplishment; fear the one who can submit those accomplishments to a withering assessment. Well beyond that preoccupation with performance, however, lies a self whose worth is fully known to God alone: let that self emerge and you will have no cause to fear. For that is the secret self whom friendship calls forth, and who is called to friendship with God.

Do not fear . . . ; rather fear . . . , and there will be no need to fear: such is the pattern as a love of friendship moves us beyond the fear attending our performance to encounter the One whose self-emptying challenges our self-seeking. That new-found fear which drives us individually to prayer, leads us also to discover how true friendship is rooted in the good we share. Then the One whom we have learned to fear metamorphoses into the One who alone can discover in us our irreplaceable worth. The friendships we have known become paths to holiness, as we discover together that "there is no need to be afraid."

* * *

Everything precious in this account—something of which we have all tasted—seems jeopardized by that abstract term "friendship." Or even "love of friendship." Intimacy might be a better word for it, except that it so easily translates into "sexual intimacy." Friends may or may not find that an appropriate expression of that love; and where it is deemed appropriate, it too will be subject to transformation. And if I am right about that, there is no power on earth stronger than friendship—unless it be the lust for raw power, which alone can overpower the sexual appetite. Yet where friendship tempers the drives of sex, it does so in another way—not by overpowering them (and so reducing them to impotence) but by enticing them to the higher bonding of friendship, rather than to master each partner separately.

But again, friendship—that abstract term again—hardly seems up to so formidable a task as taming the powerful appetites we associate with sex. It is far more likely that these appetites domesticate friendship into a shared bed and board. Far more normal as well that friendship flourish in an environment inherently ordered to marriage, and through marriage to children. But what of friendships otherwise generative? What of loves which enjoy the transforming power of a shared good, not sharing bed and board yet nonetheless participating in a generativity which is not that of procreation? Surely there are many such loves, though their way is not the norm; and those who know this love experience the power—transforming and generative—we have identified with friendship. Is it more than friendship? Do we need a term less abstract and more expressive?

One is reminded here of Plato's attempt in the *Symposium* to ring successive changes on *Eros* (love) as one is drawn from "the beauties of the body . . . to the beauties of the soul . . ., and from this . . . be led to contemplate the beauty of every kind of knowledge" (210). Christian writers then introduced a new word altogether—*agapē*—to express "not our love for God, but God's love for us" (1 John 4:10). Yet neither approach seems adequate, for Plato's schematic ladder of ascent strikes us as, if anything, too "platonic;" while John's contrast ceases to be fruitful when it is cast into an opposition between *eros* and *agapē*, as some writers have done. Aquinas seems to have touched a mediating chord when he identifies charity ("God's love for us," or *agapē*) as "friendship with God" (*Summa Theologica*, 2-2.23.1.2).

Given the divine initiative, then, of God's sending God's only "Son to be the sacrifice that takes our sins away" (1 John 4:10), we can experience what Aristotle deemed impossible: friendship with God. Is it possible that such an experience could release in our human friendships that power which belies the abstract terms we must use, allowing men and women to discover in such relationships the transforming and generative power of God? A big question, no doubt, but one which our own experience must answer yes—and without hesitation. The initiative remains with God, yet the human love of friendship provides the context—the setting and the language—which allows us to dare entertain the prospect of friendship with God. As that prospect takes flesh in our experience, as we begin to live more and more in the embrace of God's predilection, the human love which allowed us so to live takes on new dimensions itself. In this way the dynamics endemic to sharing among friends come to mediate between eros and agape: by first providing the context for daring even to think of God as our friend, and then letting that context itself be made over in the image of God's love for us.

But again, can one word—and an abstract one at that—cover everything we want to call by the "love of friendship"? What other words are available? "Lovers" perhaps, though that term, like "intimacy," conveys something altogether too specific. Moreover, when one's beloved can also be one's friend, it seems that something more is added.

What friendship conveys is a quality of relating between persons as they share in a transcendent (or spiritual) good. Such goods are not diminished but enhanced by being shared, and sharing in them knits us together rather than pitting us in competition. So the sense of "friendship" will vary according to the good shared, and the richness (or poverty) or participation in various goods will determine, for different individuals, their paradigm for friendship.

It is not necessary to have another term, then, any more than we can find one for "love," so long as we recognize the many levels on which this activity of human relating can operate. The many possible ways of hearing the Song of Songs might attune our ear to the levels latent in any friendship. If we see that poetic drama as a love story which can be read on different levels, that is a useful start, but could easily lead us to elaborate detailed allegorical readings. If we take another approach, however, and refuse to presume something so undimensional as a "literal love story," then we will be open to letting the dramatic poetry organize our experience as it will. There will then be no presumed "literal level," but only the power of a poetry intrinsically attuned to the harmonics present in human relatedness. The erotic dimension is powerfully present, but not overpowering; the "women of Jerusalem" remind us again and again that lover and beloved share a transforming good.

The abstract terms of "friendship," "relatedness," and even "love" itself, then, would seem more to reflect the limits of our language to convey relating, rather than impose a stereotype on the range and richness possible to persons relating. So long as we allow the classical picture to fix our gaze on the good shared, the modes of friendship open to individuals will be as rich and as manifold as the goods themselves. And where divine grace invites a relationship to share in God's own friendship with us, the possibilities are enhanced anew.

We have come a long way from the fear that drove us to prayer, in an effort to probe John's insistence that "fear is driven out by perfect love," and have tried to elucidate the dynamics of friendship as a way to grow in the love of which John speaks. If this part sounded more abstract and less tied to experience, that may have been inevitable. For as I have suggested, our language for relating seems inherently limited. We can overcome that limitation, however, by letting our own experience establish new levels of understanding as we move along. If we allow ourselves to do that, we will discover how richly we can share with one another in sharing the goods we treasure. And the richness of that life will invade our prayer, as fidelity to prayer will bring a new-found sensibility to our relationships.

What emerges in our prayer is a reflected sense of our uniqueness before the One who alone knows our proper name. Reflected in the faces and the hearts of those whom we have come to know as our friends, each one of us arises beyond success or failure as that singular individual whom God loves as God's very own. Manifested in the manifold levels of friendship, that love of God becomes the context for our prayer, as the time spent with God, like that shared with our friends, removes us just enough from the demand to "make something of ourselves" that we gain some small sense of the eternal in time. In the strength of that embrace one is freed to "spend one's life" in the Lord's service.

Attitudes of Major Western Religious Traditions Toward Uses of the Human Body and Its Parts[1]

JAMES F. CHILDRESS
University of Virginia

I. *Introduction*

In order to suggest what the major Western religious traditions hold about the uses of the human body and its parts in such areas as transplantation and research, it is necessary to examine their fundamental beliefs about the person's relationship to his/her body, both living and dead, and its parts. These beliefs have been reflected in various practices regarding the body, as well as in various rules that direct the conduct of the adherents to the tradition. Through an examination of these beliefs, practices, and rules, we can sketch the framework within which these traditions respond to current questions about the use of human biological materials.

The approach of this study is descriptive and analytic, but conclusions about implications for some uses of human biological materials will necessarily be tentative. Religious traditions and other sociocultural traditions do not always respond to new developments in ways that were expected on the basis of their previous practices. Many other

---

[1] This essay in honor of Walter Harrelson incorporates some materials I prepared for the Office of Technology Assessment as part of its assessment of policies regarding the ownership of human biological materials, defined as all human parts, whether replenishing or nonreplenishing, living or nonliving, beneficial or detrimental. See U.S. Congress, Office of Technology Assessment, *New Developments in Biotechnology: Ownership of Human Tissues and Cells—Special Report* (OTA-BA-337; Washington, DC: U.S. Government Printing Office, March 1987). The author retains the copyright of this essay.

factors may influence the response. This point may be especially pertinent for this area. After all, with the exceptions of hair for wigs, teeth
for implantation, and cadavers for dissection, bodies and their parts—
in contrast to uses of the body in labor, prostitution, and slavery—have
only recently acquired substantial value for others, whether in transplantation or research. Thus, earlier, even if it had been viewed as
property, the cadaver had no value and was more a liability than a
benefit.[2] The changed context is the new value of bodies and their
parts.

In the analysis that follows I will first examine the main types of
religious perspectives on the body, locate major Jewish, Protestant, and
Catholic perspectives within that typology, and then analyze the distinctive beliefs and practices of each of these toward cadavers and
living persons and their parts. The final section will focus on some
ethical implications of these beliefs and practices for the transfer and
use of human biological materials.

II. The Judaeo-Christian Tradition among the Major Types of Religious Perspectives

William May has developed a typology that expresses "several
basic religious attitudes and their implications for recovering body
parts."[3] This typology provides a context for differentiating Jewish and
Christian beliefs and practices. The first type of religious perspective
is idealistic, monastic, and optimistic. It recognizes the reality of the
spiritual realm, but denies the reality of the body, sickness, and death.
A modern version is Christian Science. The second type is dualistic and
pessimistic. As represented in the ancient Manichaeans, it views the
world as divided into rival powers, light and darkness, spirit and
flesh, and the like. The third type, represented by the Gnostics, is also
dualistic and views salvation as gained through knowledge. "For
Gnostic, ancient and modern, the body is not so much *unreal* (Christian
Scientist) or *evil* (Manichaean) as *incidental*." May identifies a fourth
type, represented in the dominant religious tradition of the West, the
Judaeo-Christian tradition: "As opposed to the Christian Scientists
and other idealists, the tradition says that the body is *real* rather

---

[2] P. M. Quay, "Utilizing the Bodies of the Dead," *Saint Louis University
Law Journal* 28 (1984) 915 n. 88.

[3] W. F. May, "Religious Justifications for Donating Body Parts," *The Hastings Center Report* 15 (February 1985) 38-42.

than unreal; as opposed to the Manichaeans, it affirms the body to be *good* rather than evil, worthy of preserving. Both affirmations converge to justify medical intervention. But, as opposed to the Gnostics, the Judaeo-Christian tradition affirms a profound link and identity of the spirit with its somatic existence. Thus it would not be so ready as the Gnostic to justify invasion of the body, living or dead, without explicit consent." Furthermore, May argues, this Judaeo Christian tradition "sympathizes with [natural] aversions to tampering with a living body or corpse," but it also develops symbols and rituals for disciplining those aversions.

Because of variations among and within Judaism, Catholicism, and Protestantism, it is difficult to speak of a "Judaeo-Christian tradition" unless that is taken to mean a common source (the Hebrew Bible/Old Testament) and some common though very general themes. I will identify some of those general themes before analyzing in more detail the three major traditions within the Judaeo-Christian tradition.

God created the world, including human beings, as good. Human beings themselves were created "in the image of God." "Then God said, 'Let us make man in our image, after our likeness; and let them have dominion . . . .' So God created man in his own image, in the image of God he created him; male and female he created them" (Gen 1:26-27, cf. 5:1 and 9:6). Although "the image of God" has been variously interpreted as reason, free will, or spiritual capacities, some theologians have objected to the concentration on intellectual and spiritual aspects of humanity to the neglect of the external body. Some have even argued that the image of God is the body, while others have argued that it is a combination of the spiritual and the physical in a psychophysical unity. In contrast to the first three types of positions identified above, the major strand of Jewish and Christian thought and practice thus views the person as an animated body. However, at times Judaism and Christianity have also appropriated Hellenistic convictions about the separation of soul and body; sometimes their beliefs and practices represent a composite of themes.

Among the numerous ethical implications of different interpretations of the image of God, some are especially important for this essay. The Genesis passage connects creation in the image of God with God's authorization of human "dominion" over the rest of creation. Humans are in but are distinguished from the rest of nature. If, as in the royal ideology of the ancient Near East, humans are God's representatives in parts of his kingdom, their rule should be like God's and should never be exploitative. Their dominion is not to be viewed as domination but as stewardship or trusteeship. As stewards and trustees, human beings do not have unlimited power. God has set limits on what human beings may do with and to their own bodies and the bodies of others. For example, Gen 9:6 connects the prohibition of taking human life with creation in God's image. This prohibition has been applied to suicide as well as to homicide. Arguments against suicide in Judaism and Christianity often draw on analogies between relationships between God and human life, on the one hand, and ordinary relationships, on the other. Many of these analogies involve property relationships (e.g., life is a gift or loan from God) and/or personal or role relationships (e.g., human beings are God's children, servants, or sentinels).[4] While the JewishChristian tradition ruled out suicide and some uses of the body, e.g., in prostitution, it did not clearly prohibit slavery, even though its convictions, particularly about the creation of all human beings in God's image, could be invoked in opposition to slavery, as ownership and control over the body of another person.

Finally, respect for the cadaver is significantly connected to the creation of human beings in God's image: Jews and Christians "respect the body of the dead as symbolic of the human person and his dignity."[5] As indicated earlier, this respect recognizes and supports (within limits) the aversion to tampering with the body, whether living or dead.

Because the language of image of God has often focused on what is distinctive about persons, particularly their use of reason, exercise of will, making decisions, and the like, it has been seen as a theological basis for respect for persons. But it would be a mistake to construe the image of God as equivalent to autonomy in the modern liberal tradition. Respect for persons is one way to state the implications of the theological doctrine of the imago dei, but it entails respect for embodied persons, not simply their wills, and it is not unlimited selfdetermination (autonomy) because it is severely limited by God's creation and will (heteronomy or theonomy). In practice, it is often very difficult to determine which actions are required by the principle of respect for persons, as an expression of the imago dei. This point will be evident in the following analysis of specific Jewish, Catholic, and

---

[4] M. P. Battin, *Ethical Issues in Suicide* (Englewood Cliffs, NJ: Prentice-Hall, 1983).

[5] C. A. Hovde, "Cadavers: General Ethical Concerns," *Encyclopedia of Bioethics* (ed. W. T. Reich; New York: Macmillan/Free Press, 1978) 141.

Protestant beliefs and practices regarding the body, its parts, and materials.

III. *Judaism*

In order to explicate Jewish positions regarding human biological materials, it is necessary to ferret out concepts and principles in the myriad rules that the Jewish tradition has developed regarding the living human body and cadaver. For example, several concepts and principles can be discerned in the laws of burial. Also relevant is the interpretation of the rules of the *halakah* (the body of Jewish law supplementing Scripture) through analogical arguments about cases. With Judaism, the Orthodox, Conservative, and Reform branches differ in part according to their approach to the rules of the *halakah*: the Orthodox concentrate on the rules, the Conservative emphasize that the proper interpretation of the rules depends on attention to the principles that undergird the rules, and the Reform movement stresses the principles themselves, such as respect for persons, rather than the rules.[6] Substantively, as in Christianity, Judaism affirms that "a person has only limited rights to his body."[7]

Cadavers

According to Judaism, "man is created in the image of God. Every dignity must be extended to the human body in death as in life. It is for this reason that the body must be regarded as inviolate."[8] Three prohibitions against the desecration of the corpse derive from God's creation of human beings in his own image: It is impermissible to mutilate the cadaver (and thus, according to many, to cremate it), to use or derive any benefit from the cadaver, or to delay the interment of the cadaver or any of its parts.[9] A critical question for understanding the Jewish

---

[6] M. M. Kellner, "The Structure of Jewish Ethics," in *Contemporary Jewish Ethics* (ed. M. M. Kellner; New York: Sanhedrin, 1978) 1-18.

[7] W. S. Wurzburger, "Cadavers: Jewish Perspectives," *Encyclopedia of Bioethics*, 144.

[8] D. M. Feldman and F. Rosner, *Compendium on Medical Ethics: Jewish Moral, Ethical and Religious Principles in Medical Practice* (6th ed.; New York: Federation of Jewish Philanthropies of New York, 1984) 120.

[9] F. Rosner and M. D. Tendler, *Practical Medical Halacha* (2d ed.; Jerusalem/New York: Fieldheim Publishers, 1980) 67; and N. L. Rabinovitch, "What is the Halakhah for Organ Transplants?" in *Jewish Bioethics* (ed. F. Rosner and J. D. Bleich; New York: Sanhedrin, 1979) 355.

position is how these prohibitions are interpreted and applied. In particular, are they absolute? Any prohibition in Jewish law, except for murder, incest, and idolatry, may be overridden in order to save human life. Saving human life (*piqquaḥ nefesh*) is a paramount religio-moral imperative—"Thou shalt not stand idly by the blood of thy neighbor" (Lev 19:16)—and it justifies some actions that would appear to be prohibited regarding the cadaver.

First, autopsies are generally opposed even when performed to establish the cause of death or to increase medical knowledge in general. However, an autopsy is permitted to answer a specific question that would "contribute to the immediate improved care of patients."[10] For example, when a patient dies while suffering from cancer and receiving an experimental treatment, it may be important to determine whether the drug was in part responsible for the death. The emphasis falls on the *immediacy* of the benefit to be gained. Another exception would be "clear and firm presumptive evidence" of an infectious disease, or of a hereditary disease, for which preventive or therapeutic measures could be undertaken for others. Even when an autopsy is permitted, it must be limited to what is essential to generate the specific answer that is sought. In addition, the cadaver merits "the same dignity, respect and consideration that would be accorded a living patient undergoing an operation."[11]

In an autopsy organs should not be removed from the body, except where absolutely necessary for the information sought, and any removed organs must be returned to the body for burial, "except for small sections necessary for microscopic examination and for pathology 'blocks' as required by law."[12] This requirement is not limited to solid organs, but extends to "all organs, tissues and fluids."[13] Any part of a dead body must be buried because contact with it involves ritual defilement. (For living persons, as discussed below, there is a distinction between organs and limbs containing "flesh, sinews and bones." Organs such as an appendix or kidney removed from a living person need not be buried; however, a limb or a finger or a toe that has been amputated does require burial.[14])

---

[10] Rosner and Tendler, *Practical Medical Halacha*, 67-68.

[11] Ibid., 69.

[12] Ibid.

[13] Feldman and Rosner, *Compendium on Medical Ethics*, 125.

[14] Rosner and Tendler, *Practical Medical Halacha*, 50.

According to Jakobovits,[15] early Judaism was receptive to dissection for scientific purposes, but gradually came to oppose it. In view of the presumption against dissection established by the prohibitions identified above, the argument is that dissection does not provide a reasonable and immediate prospect of saving human life, since the patients who will benefit from the knowledge gained are not "at hand." This argument obviously has implications for the use of human biological material for research, where there is no immediate prospect of saving human life and it is difficult to determine the probability of any specific benefit.

The priority of saving human life (*piqquah nefesh*) introduces considerable flexibility into the application of Jewish law to such technological developments as organ transplantation. The Jewish tradition emphasizes that the source of the organs must be dead according to the halachic criteria of absence of respiration and absence of cardiovascular pulsation.[16] Strictly interpreted, these criteria could pose problems for organ transplantation, but the Jewish tradition has accommodated "brain death": "Acceptance of total cessation of brain function as a criterion of death is in keeping with Jewish legal standards for determining death, provided the Harvard Criteria for irreversible coma are met."[17] The tradition also stresses the decedent's act of donation (though familial donations are not precluded). There is a recognition of what might be called "presumed consent" of the decedent in relation to autopsies, and this line of argument could extend, in principle, to some organ or tissue donations:

When alive, a Jew has the obligation to do all he can to save his fellow man from certain death. The submission to autopsy, when it can bring immediate benefit, *is assumed to be with the deceased's acquiescence* if his immediate relatives grant permission for such a procedure. In the absence of such permission, or in the presence of known objections of the patient to autopsy, his body remains inviolate, protected by all the rights and privileges due him when alive.[18]

---

[15] I. Jakobovits, *Jewish Medical Ethics* (New York: Bloch Publishing Co., 1975) 136.

[16] Rosner and Tendler, *Practical Medical Halacha*, 59.

[17] Feldman and Rosner, *Compendium on Medical Ethics*, 120

[18] Ibid., 121.

The Jewish tradition accepts not only kidney and heart transplants that offer the immediate prospect of saving life, but also cornea transplants, for, as several rabbis argue, blindness is a life-threatening condition because of the danger of fatal accidents.[19] Furthermore, some rabbis view the above prohibitions against the use of a dead body as not applying to a removed organ which "lives" again when it is successfully transplanted into a recipient. This argument also disposes of the concern about ritual defilement from contact with a dead organ or body.

There would appear to be opposition to tissue banks because a recipient is not immediately available, but cornea banks have been accepted on the grounds that it is highly probable that the cornea will be used immediately because so many potential recipients are "at hand."[20] However, it would not be easy to extend this argument to cover research on human biological materials because it is difficult to predict benefits, which in any event would only accrue to patients in the future.

Living Persons

It is permissible for living persons to donate a kidney to save someone's life or to donate blood to a blood bank. Even though there are prohibitions against intentionally wounding oneself or forfeiting one's life to save another, most interpretations of Jewish law hold that one is allowed or even obligated "to place oneself into a possibly dangerous situation to save his fellow-man from certain death. The donor *endangers* his life to save the recipient from *certain* death." This is a risk-benefit analysis, in which "the probability of saving the recipient's life is substantially greater than the risk to the donor's life or health." Blood donation is viewed as similar, even though the donor may have no specific recipient in mind and the blood may be stored for a time. Here again the needs of potential recipients are so great that there is "a reasonable certainty" that the blood will be used to save life, while the risks to the donor are minimal. In general, there appears to be greater latitude for living donors of organs and tissues—except where their donation would endanger the donor's life—than with cadavers. And in contrast to limbs containing "flesh, sinews and

---

[19] F. Rosner, "Organ Transplantation in Jewish Law," in *Jewish Bioethics,* 362.

[20] Rosner and Tendler, *Practical Medical Halacha,* 72-73.

bones," organs, such as a spleen or appendix, removed from living persons do not have to be buried.[21]

Spontaneously or Deliberately Aborted Fetuses

The criteria are similar to those for cadavers and living donors, with some exceptions. In contrast to Roman Catholicism, Judaism in general does not hold that the fetus is a human being from the moment of conception. If the fetus is alive but not viable, no research may be conducted on it; it has all the rights of a living person, and any actions that might hasten its death are rejected. However, if the fetus is dead according to the halachic criteria of absence of respiration and absence of cardiovascular pulsations, burial is not *required*, even though it is *desirable* as a way to respect the dignity of human beings created in God's image and to preserve the sanctity of the dead. It is thus permissible to conduct medical research on the dead fetus that would not be permissible on other human cadavers.[22] The use of fetal tissue after the fetus has died "is surely permissible. Parents should be encouraged to find some solace in the life-giving contribution of the aborted fetus. Whereas 'banking' of tissues from adult autopsies cannot be approved, tissues from nonviable fetuses (after expiration) may be 'banked' for future use or subsequent burial."[23]

Summary

In general, the requirements for exemption from the prohibitions regarding the cadaver or the living person focus on the probability of immediate rescue of human life. Both the prohibitions and the exceptions are based on the dignity of human being as created in the image of God. Extensions of the exceptions to banking corneas from cadavers suggest that some indirect and delayed possibilities may justify removal of cadaver parts, with the appropriate consent. However, as indicated above, it would be difficult—though not impossible—to extend these exceptions so far as to include medical research on human biological materials derived from cadavers. Such an extension would require subordinating the criterion of immediacy to the criterion of the

---

[21] Ibid., 58-73, from which the quoted materials in this paragraph have been taken.

[22] Ibid., 39 and 57.

[23] Feldman and Rosner, *Compendium on Medical Ethics*, 54.

probability of significantly benefiting human beings through the research, and there would be debate about most such research projects. In general, the Conservative and Reform branches, particularly the latter, would probably be more receptive to the expansion of the permissible use of cadaver parts than the Orthodox branch. It is important to emphasize that even orthodox Judaism is more permissive with regard to tissues from nonviable fetuses (after expiration) and even to tissues from living persons (as long as the donor's life is not seriously endangered). For example, organs, such as the spleen, removed from a living person, in contrast to a cadaver, need not be buried, and blood may be stored for future benefit.

IV. *Roman Catholicism*

Cadavers

Early Christian opposition to dissection of the cadaver was modified by papal edicts in the fifteenth and sixteenth centuries, and theologians held that dissection does not necessarily show disrespect to the dead (though the organs should be returned to the body prior to burial).[24] Although cremation of the whole body was permitted when demanded by the public welfare, e.g., in a time of pestilence, it was generally rejected until the 1960s because burial was viewed as "the most respectful way of treating the human body"[25] and because cremation was often defended by opponents of Christianity. Special questions also emerged about excised parts of the body. In general, the Catholic Church held that notable or major excised parts of the body should be buried, while minor ones need not. Kelley argues that a major part is one that retains its "human quality" after removal. He holds that an arm or a leg would appear to qualify, while even important internal organs would not. Transplantation of organs and tissues from cadavers has been accepted without any worries about the resurrection. Indeed, donation of organs and tissues has been viewed as praiseworthy, though not obligatory, and the benefit of donation need not be as direct or as immediate as Jewish law suggests.

---

[24] Hovde, "Cadavers: General Ethical Concerns."

[25] G. Kelly, *Medico-Moral Problems* (St. Louis: The Catholic Hospital Association, 1958) 325.

Living Persons

According to Gerald Kelly, "since man is only the *administrator* of his life and bodily members and functions, his power to dispose of these things is limited."[26] In the Roman Catholic context, the principle of totality, among other principles, limits what people may do to their bodies and parts. According to St. Thomas, the principle of totality indicated that a diseased part of the body could be removed for the benefit of the totality or whole body.[27] This doctrine was subsequently applied to the amputation of a healthy member. A modern formulation appears in Pius XI's *Casti Connubii* (1930):

> Furthermore, Christian doctrine establishes, and the light of human reason makes it most clear, that private individuals have no other power over the members of their bodies than that which pertains to their natural ends; and they are not free to destroy or mutilate their members, or in any other way render themselves unfit for their natural functions, except when no other provision can be made for the good of the whole body.

Because this formulation of the principle of totality appeared to warrant mutilation only for the physical benefit of the person's body as a whole, it also appeared to rule out removal of an organ to benefit another person. However, many theologians came to hold that "mutilation was ethically appropriate when it was for the good of the whole *person* (not simply of the body)."[28]

Some critics, including Protestant theologian Paul Ramsey, contend that justification of organ donation by an expanded principle of totality ultimately appeals to psychological or spiritual benefits to the *donor* (and hence falls short of neighbor-love) and that it also undermines appropriate moral-religious constraints on human use of their bodies and their parts. [29] Richard McCormick, a Jesuit moral theologian, rejects both of Ramsey's charges. McCormick contends, first, that a donor's benefit (psychological or spiritual wholeness) is not necessarily identical with the donor's motivation (charity), and, second, that the

---

[26] Ibid., 247

[27] R. A. McCormick, "Organ Transplantation: Ethical Principles," *Encyclopedia of Bioethics*, 1170.

[28] Ibid.

[29] P. Ramsey, *The Patient as Person* (New Haven: Yale University, 1970).

expanded principle of totality only establishes the moral context of organ donation, not the justifiability of particular transplants.[30] The justifiability of particular transplants depends on the proportionality of benefits and burdens to the recipient and to the donor. Limits are found in the risk-benefit analysis, as well as in the consent of the living person or his/her proxy. (I do not here deal with the difficult questions about removal of organs from incompetent persons to benefit others.) Also, a cadaver organ is to be preferred wherever its chance of benefiting a recipient is as great as or greater than an organ from a living donor. Some interpreters emphasize that the principle of totality is to be understood in terms of *function* rather than physical parts. Thus, it is not necessary to appeal to this principle to "justify the cutting of hair or toenails, the removal of (apparently) nonfunctional organs such as the appendix and tonsils (even when they are healthy), and blood transfusions and skin grafts."[31] However, other limits remain; for example, donation of sperm would be opposed if it were obtained by masturbation. Finally, the principle of totality is interpreted so as to avoid totalitarian domination of the community over the individual.

Fetuses

In Catholic moral theology a fetus is viewed as a human being from the moment of conception, and the fetus is to be treated according to the criteria established for cadavers and living persons. In particular, there is opposition to experimentation on deliberately aborted fetuses.

Summary

Catholicism, like Judaism and Protestantism, emphasizes the dignity that belongs to the human person and to his/her physical remains after death. This dignity is derived from his/her creation in the image of God. Representing the image of God, human beings are stewards or administrators of their lives, but their actions are limited by God's law, including the natural law as well as the divine law revealed in Scripture. Some of those limits have been expanded in recent years in response to technological developments—e.g., the expansion of the

---

[30] R. A. McCormick, "Transplantation of Organs: A Comment on Paul Ramsey," *Theological Sudies* 36 (1975) 503-109.

[31] B. M. Ashley and K. D. O'Rourke, *Health Care Ethics: A Theological Analysis* (2d ed.; St. Louis: The Catholic Health Association of the U.S., 1982) 40.

principle of totality. In general, charitable acts of donation are praised, whether they are directed toward specific individuals or tissue banks (e.g., a blood bank), but they are subject to evaluation from the standpoint of proportionality (e.g., kidney donation).

V. *Protestantism*

Although there are variations within both Judaism and Roman Catholicism, they are not as extensive as in Protestantism, which encompasses so many different groups. Protestants do not have an authoritative institutional church as in Catholicism or an authoritative tradition of interpretation as in Judaism, and there are numerous debates about the interpretation of the shared authority of Scripture. Hence the variety is tremendous, as is evident in the debates over many years between Joseph Fletcher, an Episcopalian, and Paul Ramsey, a Methodist.

After examining some Jewish and Catholic positions in 1968, Joseph Fletcher lamented, "as we often find in these matters of specific or concrete moral questions, there is no Protestant discussion on surgery, autopsy, and other mutilative procedures—not even on the ethics of transplant donation."[32] Even more so than Catholicism, with its emphasis on the ends of nature, including the body and its parts, and Judaism, with its strong emphasis on the tradition of interpretation of the law, modern Protestants have tended to emphasize the principle of respect for persons. However, that they also recognized limits to what people may do to their bodies is evident in the claim of Kant—whose thought on practical matters often represents his Protestant background—about mutilation:

> It is a form of partial self-murder to deprive oneself of an integral part (or mutilate oneself), for example, to give away or sell a tooth to be transplanted into another person's mouth or to be castrated in order to make a more comfortable living as a singer and so forth. But to have a dead or diseased organ amputated when it endangers one's life or to have something cut off which is a part, but not an organ, of the body (e.g., one's hair) cannot be considered a wrong against one's own person—

---

[32] J. Fletcher, "Our Shameful Waste of Human Tissue: An Ethical Problem for the Living and the Dead," in *Updating Life and Death: Essays in Ethics and Medicine* (ed. D. R. Cutler; Boston: Beacon, 1969) 1-30.

although a woman who cuts her hair in order to sell it is not altogether free from guilt.[33]

As the language of "partial self-murder" suggests, the context of Kant's discussion is his analysis of suicide; his historical context is evident in his example—both hair and teeth have been donated or sold for centuries, hair being used to make wigs and teeth being used by dentists to replace the teeth of wealthy people.[34]

Cadavers

Protestants generally do not believe that God's resurrection of the dead sets any special limits on what may be done to cadavers; both cremation and burial are proper means of disposal because of God's power to resurrect. With Jews and Catholics, Protestants recognize limits expressed in the language of respect and dignity. And the Protestant William May argues that rituals are needed, even after a cadaver's organs have been donated, as "a testimony to the privileged place of the body in acts of love."[35] Protestants tend to conceive most of the major ethical problems in this area in relation to consent, as a requirement of the principle of respect for persons. Both Ramsey and May argue for the ethical preferability of a policy of voluntary gifts in the transfer of human bodily parts, but Fletcher, who emphasizes consequences of actions and policies rather than their deontological limits (Ramsey) or their expressive and symbolic qualities (May), appears to be more receptive to routine salvaging as an appropriate way to avoid wastage, a bad consequence.[36] Ramsey emphasizes a "recovery of a proper sense of the integrity of man's bodily life, as against the Cartesian dualism and mentalism of the modern period which rejoices without discrimination over every achievement or intervention or design which shows that the body is only a thing-in-the-world to be subjected to limitless control."[37]

---

[33] I. Kant, *The Doctrine of Virtue, Part II of the Metaphysics of Morals* (trans. M. J. Gregor; Philadelphia: University of Pennsylvania, 1971) 85-86; contrast H. T. Engelhardt, *The Foundation of Bioethics* (New York: Oxford University, 1986).

[34] R. Scott, *The Body as Property* (New York: Viking, 1981) 180.

[35] May, "Religious Justifications for Donating Body Parts," 42.

[36] Fletcher, "Our Sameful Waste of Human Tissue."

[37] Ramsey, *The Patient as Person*, 209.

Living Persons

Even though Protestants tend to emphasize voluntary *agapē* (love), or charitable consent, several Protestants have argued that this is not sufficient. For example, Ramsey contends that "a justification of the self-giving of organs developed on Protestant grounds, precisely because of its freedom from the mooring of self-concern, is likely to fly too high above concern for the bodily integrity of the donor."[38] Hence, he appeals to the strand of the biblical tradition, also strongly affirmed by Judaism, that emphasizes the integrity of the flesh, and he opposes Cartesian mentalism and dualism, which could lead, for example, to the donation of a heart by a living person. According to Ramsey, the physical integrity of the donor is "an independent value and responsibility" and limits what may be done. This independent value limits actions of removing organs, such as a kidney, or tissues from incompetent persons, such as children and institutionalized mentally retarded or insane people, in order to benefit others. Although this independent value definitely rules out a heart donation from a living person, its other limits are not totally clear. As in Judaism and Catholicism, one of the necessary conditions would be proportionality as expressed in a risk-benefit analysis.

Fetuses

Protestants defend a range of positions regarding the use of the fetus and fetal tissues in research, often closely connected with their views on abortion. For example, Ramsey defends a conservative position, while Fletcher defends a more radical one, holding that the fetus is only tissue.[39]

Summary

Like their Jewish and Catholic counterparts, Protestant thinkers start from the affirmation of human beings as created in the image of God and as stewards of the body and its parts. Thus, the emphasis on respect for persons means not only respecting their wishes but also recognizing limits set by their bodily integrity. However, these limits are

---

[38] Ibid., 187.

[39] See the discussion in L. Walters, "Fetal Research and the Ethical Issues," *The Hastings Center Report* 5 (June 1975) 13-18.

rarely stated in the kinds of rules that appear in Judaism's prohibitions regarding the cadaver or Catholicism's earlier version of totality. Because of the lack of clear-cut rules and the tendency in Protestantism (as in Reform Judaism) to emphasize the principle of autonomy, some Protestants, such as Paul Ramsey, have tried to recapture the traditional Hebraic/Jewish wisdom regarding the body and to oppose Cartesian mentalism and dualism. However, variety reigns supreme in Protestant positions on this matter, as well as on most other matters.

VI. *Implications for Policies Regarding the Transfer of Human Biological Materials for Use in Transplantation or in Research*

Some implications of religious beliefs and practices for use of human biological materials have already been sketched in passing. In conclusion, I will draw out further implications, emphasizing that where the religious traditions are silent, inferences are necessarily tentative. However, the general lineaments of the framework are clear: human beings are created in the image of God and thus derive their dignity and worth from this creation; they are animated bodies or embodied selves, not a composite, and their bodies are real, good, and essential to their identity; God has given humans dominion over nature, including their own bodies and parts; this dominion is best conceived as stewardship, trusteeship, or administration, because human power and authority are limited by God's will, however this is expressed (e.g., whether in natural or revealed law) and however it is known (e.g., by reason or faith); invasions of the body, whether living or dead, stand in need in justification; and there are certain positive obligations toward the body, including the cadaver, as a symbol of the image of God. Although many connect the theme of the image of God with the principle of the dignity of and respect for persons—e.g., that human beings should not be used as mere means to ends—this principle cannot be reduced to the modern liberal conception of autonomy because its religious context includes embodiment, not merely personal choices, and also limits set by God (heteronomy or theonomy). Whether the language of property is misleading because of its connotations, these religious traditions do recognize human rights to control, to use, to exclude others from use, and to transmit bodily parts and tissues. These rights, however, are not absolute or unlimited. Some actions regarding one's own body and its parts are excluded by these traditions; these include suicide and prostitution. Even though consent is required as a necessary condition for most transfers of body parts, it is not sufficient, and some actions of consenting adults may be restricted to protect them (paternalism), to protect others and the society (the harm principle), and to express some principles and rules (legalism/ moralism).

In sketching the implications of these traditions, it is important to recall the distinction, already adumbrated, between ethically acceptable and ethically preferable policies and practices. For example, some modes of transfer of human biological materials and some uses may be viewed as ethically preferable to others without those others being viewed as ethically unacceptable—for example, these traditions put a high premium on explicit gifts and donations without necessarily excluding tacit gifts, sales, abandonment, and expropriation in all cases.

There are at least two major variables in sketching implications of these religious traditions for the use of the human biological materials: the type or kind of material and the mode of transfer. I will concentrate on mode of transfer of materials from the person whose body first contained them to the person who will use them, however many intermediaries there might be, inquiring whether the variations in the types or kinds of materials make any moral difference and, if so, why. The significance of different modes of transfer (or acquisition, if viewed from the standpoint of the user) and different materials will hinge on various moral principles, such as (a) respect for persons, (b) beneficence, or benefiting others, (c) nonmaleficence, or not harming others, and (d) justice, or treating others fairly and distributing benefits and burdens equitably.[40] In addition, several other moral considerations, such as fidelity to promises and contracts, truthfulness, privacy, and confidentiality, might be derived from these general principles. These fundamental and derived principles are embedded in our secular laws, policies, and practices, as well as in the religious traditions under examination, which have connected all of them—and not just respect for persons—with the creation of human beings in the image of God. From these principles and others, it is possible to indicate some judgments about the ethical acceptability and preferability of various policies.

My preliminary conclusion is that, according to the traditions analyzed, any of the following modes of transfer of human biological materials—gift (explicit or presumed), sale, abandonment, or expropriation—is ethically acceptable under some circumstances, but that,

---

[40] See T. L. Beauchamp and J. F. Childress, *Principles of Biomedical Ethics* (2d ed.; New York: Oxford University, 1983); and National Commission for the Protection of Human Subjects of Biomedical and Behavioral Research, *The Belmont Report: Ethical Guidelines for the Protection of Human Subjects of Research* (DHEW Publication No. [OS] 78-0012 [1978]).

cateris paribus, priority is given to explicit gifts. In any event, the first three modes of transfer all depend on voluntary, knowledgeable consent in significant, but different, ways. Thus, they all recognize some kind of property right by the original possessor of the biological materials. Scott's prediction for future legislation is not surprising or morally troubling: "Legislation in the future seems likely to follow an uneven course in which systems of voluntary consent will be diluted with mixtures of controlled commerce, contracting out, and limited compulsory acquisition."[41] The moral question is what sort of mix is appropriate.

Donation (Explicit)

The major Western religious traditions view gifts of body parts and biological materials as ethically preferable to other modes of transfer, even though they do not find all other modes of transfer ethically unacceptable under all circumstances. This ethical priority is reflected in the Uniform Anatomical Gift Act, which allows individuals to make premortem decisions to donate their bodies and parts and the next of kin to make the decision if the decedent has not expressed his/her wishes. The motifs of gift and donation dominate not only the legal framework but also the most important literature on the transfer of organs and tissues. However, the UAGA did not prohibit the sale of organs and tissues.

In principle, the UAGA is individualistic in that it gives priority to the decedent's prior wishes about his/her body. This individualistic orientation marks the UAGA's fundamental departure from the common law tradition, which had recognized the next of kin's "quasi-property" rights in the corpse. These "quasi-property" rights did not include the right to use or to transfer the corpse or its parts for commercial purposes; it was mainly a right to bury the body, correlated with an obligation to do so. The next of kin's "quasi-property" rights frequently blocked the decedent's wishes. Paul Ramsey, the Protestant ethicist, worried about the UAGA in part because it appeared to enshrine the decedent's wishes over the family's "quasi-property" rights in the corpse.[42] However, in practice, procurement teams will rarely, if ever, remove organs on the basis of the decedent's prior wishes, as expressed in a donor card, if the family objects. As a practical matter, the decedent's wish not to donate is binding, but his/her wish to donate is not.

---

[41] Scott, *The Body as Property*, 197.
[42] Ramsey, *The Patient as Person*, 208.

One major question is *who* may make a gift of the dead body and its parts? The term "donor" is unfortunately used of the person who makes the *decision to donate* and also of the cadaveric *source* of the organs or tissues even if he/she made no decision at all. All of the religious traditions emphasize the individual's right to make a premortem donation of his/her body parts for transfer after death. And they tend to recognize the family's right to make such a donation, if the individual has not opposed it. However, there is some controversy at this point; for example, Paul Quay, a Jesuit, has argued that "no one, including the state, has any right to make use of a person's cadaver or its parts for research, transplantation, or other purposes, if the deceased has not given his free consent to that use."[43] Quay construes the decedent's failure to donate as a refusal of donation, but current evidence suggests that people do not sign donor cards because of their distrust of physicians and others—who may hasten their death or declare them dead prematurely—preferring instead to leave the decision to the next of kin, who can protect them against abuse. In accord with the religious traditions discussed earlier, it is appropriate to view the family as entrusted with the corpse and thus as stewards and trustees, who should act on the decedent's wishes where they are known but who may make their own decisions about donation if the decedent's wishes are not known.

Although the three religious traditions have not interpreted their norm of beneficence (neighbor-love) to require donation of organs and tissue, they have permitted and even encouraged such donation under some circumstances. However, the farther the donation is removed from direct and immediate benefit to others, the less the donation is encouraged. Hence, even though these religious traditions insist that donation is the ethically preferable mode of transfer, they do not urge that donation, particularly when the donated tissue will be used in research, which can be expected to produce health benefits only in the future, if at all.

As indicated earlier, the charitable activities of living donors are subject to limits, stemming in part from stewardship of the body and its parts. And yet taking some risks for others, e.g., through donating a kidney, is ethically acceptable and praiseworthy, as long as other duties are not violated. Accepting a certain death by donating a vital organ is not ethically acceptable within these traditions, which are opposed to suicide. Risk-free donations of biological materials, such as

---

[43] Quay, "Utilizing the Bodies of the Dead," 923.

sperm, are acceptable (unless they violate other norms, such as the prohibition of masturbation in Roman Catholicism).

Within religious contexts there is vigorous debate about the use of fetuses and fetal tissues in research. This is particularly true about living though nonviable fetuses, whether abortion was spontaneous or deliberate, and about dead fetuses after deliberate abortions. Research on the latter is often viewed as inappropriate.

Donation (Tacit, Presumed, Etc.)

Presumed consent laws have been adopted in several states for obtaining corneas and in several countries for obtaining organs and tissues. In the context of gifts, these laws could be viewed as "presumed gift" laws. They do not necessarily assume that organs and tissues belong to the state or society, but rather that individuals or their next of kin have *donated* those organs and tissues unless they have explicitly refused. Although there is some controversy (e.g., among Orthodox Jews in Israel), the Jewish and Christian traditions do not always oppose presumed consent laws, which have been adopted in countries with very different religious backgrounds, including Denmark, France, Israel, Norway, Spain, Sweden, and Switzerland.[44] However, these traditions do view a policy of explicit donation as preferable to tacit donation in part because of the value of a community of active altruism.[45] For a system of presumed consent or donation to be ethically acceptable, it is essential that the public *understand* when silence will be construed as consent or donation.

Whatever the legal framework—UAGA or presumed consent— *practices* of organ and tissue procurement are very similar around the world. For example, in France where the law regarding presumed consent does not require familial approval, physicians still seek familial approval, just as they do in the USA even in the presence of a donor card. Although a policy of presumed consent/donation could possibly have been adopted in the late sixties, it is not politically feasible now, not so much because of ethical objections as because of distrust of the health care system that would retrieve organs. However, a policy of presumed consent does remain in place in several states for corneas, and

---

[44] F. P. Stuart, F. J. Veith, and R. E. Cranford, "Brain Death Laws and Patterns of Consent to Remove Organs for Transplantation from Cadavers in the United States and 29 Other Countries," *Transplantation* 31 (1961) 238-44.

[45] May, "Religious Justifications for Donating Body Parts"; and Ramsey, *The Patient as Person.*

it might be possible for some other tissues, though probably not for solid organs in the foreseeable future.

Sale

The UAGA did not prohibit the sale of organs because the commission "believed that it was improper to include an absolute bar to commercial relationships and concluded that this would best be handled at the local level, by the medical community."[46] Some states have now passed laws to prohibit a market in organs, and the 1984 National Organ Transplant Act (Public Law 98-507) made it "unlawful for any person to knowingly acquire, receive, or otherwise transfer any human organ [defined as human kidney, liver, heart, lung, pancreas, bone marrow, cornea, eye, bone, and skin and any other human organ specified by the Secretary of Health and Human Services by regulation] for valuable consideration for use in human transplantation if the transfer affects interstate commerce." (The federal statute limits the prohibition to "human transplantation," whereas the UAGA covers education and research as well.)

It has been argued that the shift away from the market in blood in the USA reflected "sentiment against tissue sales."[47] In fact, the shift away from a market in blood—though blood plasma and some products are still sold—resulted not from widespread moral revulsion but from cogent arguments that the commercial system in blood was ineffective, inefficient, and dangerous. Even in his argument against the sale of organs, Ramsey did not oppose the sale of blood by living vendors on intrinsic grounds, in part because of *qualitative* differences between cadaver organs and blood, which is renewable.[48] Similar points could be made about the sale of semen, skin, bone marrow, sweat, and urine.[49] Because they are renewable, it may be more plausible to view their sale as provision of a *service*, as some court decisions have viewed the sale of blood, rather than a *commodity*. In a very important statement that invoked the analogy with the sale of blood, Pius XII refused to rule out all compensation for organ and tissues:

---

[46] Ramsey, *The Patient as Person*, 211.

[47] R. L. Steinbock, "Kidneys for Transplantation," *Journal of Health Politics, Policy and Law* 6 (1981) 504-19.

[48] Ramsey, *The Patient as Person*, 212.

[49] Scott, *The Body as Property*.

Moreover, must one, as is often done, refuse on principle all compensation? This question remains unanswered. It cannot be doubted that grave abuses could occur if payment is demanded. But it would be going too far to declare immoral every acceptance or every demand or payment. The case is similar to blood transfusions. It is commendable for the donor to refuse recompense: it is not necessarily a fault to accept it.[50]

Following a suggestion by George Mavrodes, it is possible to locate the sale of body parts in two contexts: the sale of various goods and the transfer of body parts.[51] In the first context, the question is what is morally problematic about the sale of *body parts* among the various goods traded in the marketplace; in the second context, the question is what is morally problematic about the *sale* of body parts among the various ways to transfer them. If the response is that people do not "own" their body parts and thus cannot sell them, it is then necessary to indicate how people can "give" or "donate" what they do not own. One possible answer is that people have "quasi-property" rights for disposal of the body and its parts, but this answer is question-begging unless it also indicates why property rights in body parts should be limited in this way.

Arguments for a market in organs and tissues may focus either on increasing the supply or on respecting people's freedom of choice. The main rejoinder to the first argument is that there are other effective and ethically acceptable and preferable ways to increase the supply. Among the rejoinders to the second argument, several are based on the principles of respect for persons, beneficence-nonmaleficence, and justice. These include the risks of sales to vendors, and the vendor's lack of voluntariness, especially if he or she is poor, economically vulnerable, and subject to exploitation. Even if risks could be reduced to vendors (e.g., by not allowing them to sell their own kidneys while alive) and voluntariness could be established, opponents insist that a commercial market in organs and tissues is abhorrent to our social system of values because it treats human bodies and their parts as property and commodities.[52] Lawrence Becker notes that in the justification of specific

---

[50] *Papal Teachings: The Human Body* (Boston: St. Paul Editions, 1960) 101.

[51] G. I. Mavrodes, "The Morality of Selling Human Organs," in *Ethics, Humanism, and Medicine* (ed. M. D. Basson; New York: Alan R. Liss, 1980) 133-39.

[52] May, "Religious Justifications for Donating Body Parts."

property rights, including commercial rights in the body, "reform of property laws is quite rightly seen as a matter which could affect the dispositions to achieve, to work, to compete, to cooperate, and to give help to others; it could also influence the pace, mobility, complexity, and (for lack of a better word) humaneness of social life."[53] This, Becker contends, is the source of the most potent objection to commercial rights in body parts.

Some would concede that selling *some* tissues would be potentially dehumanizing to the society, but would deny that this would be true for all tissues, such as surplus (e.g., hair, urine, and sweat) and renewable tissue (e.g., blood). They could also distinguish living vendors from cadavers and exclude situations of conflict of interest (e.g., the sale of aborted fetuses or fetal tissues). In addition, it would be possible to distinguish types of valuable consideration, such as direct payments and indirect incentives. It may be instructive, for example, to ask how the line is drawn between direct payment and coverage of a donor's medical expenses, compensation of a living donor's lost wages, and payment for the burial expenses of a deceased donor. In short, through some distinctions it may be possible for religious traditions to accommodate some types of commercial transfer of some kinds of tissues.

Abandonment

Another common mode of transfer of tissues is abandonment: people simply abandon their excised organs, urine, etc., which are then used by researchers. This mode of transfer is not inherently objectionable. However, the religion may require the burial of some body parts (e.g., amputated limbs), and the patient may thus have an interest in their disposal. The major problem is one that appears in all of the modes of transfer of tissues to this point: the voluntariness of the agent's actions that effectively transfer ownership and use. The agent must be competent, understand what he or she is doing, and act voluntarily in explicit donation, tacit donation (presumed consent), and sale for the transfer to be morally valid—it may be legally valid without being morally valid. If the agent abandons excised tissue, such as a spleen, or surplus, such as urine, or a dead embryo in the context of medical treatment in a hospital, he or she may have certain expectations about their disposal. For example, he or she might be legitimately upset to learn that an in-

---

[53] L. C. Becker, *Property Rights: Philosophic Foundations* (Boston: Routledge & Kegan Paul, 1977) 114.

timate body part had been incorporated into a dart board or even used in certain research projects. In order to satisfy the demands of several moral principles, such as nonmaleficence, justice, and respect for persons, it is ethically unacceptable for researchers simply to take putatively abandoned or unclaimed tissues and use them in research projects without informing patients about that use. Even though people discard some tissues and waste products on the assumption that they will be destroyed, they may not want them used in certain ways. Some types of tissue may also be of special interest to their original possessor—e.g., ova removed during hysterectomy because they represent the likeness of the woman from whom they were removed.[54] The issue is not simply the potential commercial value of the tissues or waste products, though this may be important. The fundamental question is whether the original possessor of the biological materials in question understood when he or she relinquished control over those materials that they would be used in research rather than destroyed. Thus, it is important to note, the ethical issues about consent are very similar in all of the modes of transfer to this point, even though the main concern about donation (whether explicit or presumed) and abandonment is understanding, while the main concern about sales is voluntariness.

Expropriation

The public health justifies autopsies in some cases, even against the wishes of adherents of religious groups. There has been vigorous debate about whether some parts, such as pituitary glands, can be removed in the course of autopsies (often such actions have been justified on the basis of presumed consent). And unclaimed body statutes permit the use of bodies without anyone's consent, presumed or otherwise. Although most religious groups have recognized that public health concerns may override their own obligations/rights regarding the disposal of the cadaver in some circumstances (e.g., plague), there is no convincing argument at this point for a policy of expropriation of human biological materials against the wishes of the decedent or family.

---

[54] R. P. S. Jensen, "Sperm and Ova as Property," *Journal of Medical Ethics* 11 (1985) 123-26.

Conclusion

In conclusion, it may be useful to note that the major Western religious traditions are actually and potentially more flexible on modes of transfer/acquisition of body parts than is often supposed. Judaism, Roman Catholicism, and Protestantism all start from a shared premise, drawn from the Hebrew Bible/Old Testament, that human beings are created in the image of God and, therefore, have dominion over nature. Human beings are animated bodies, and dominion does not imply unlimited control over those bodies or the rest of nature. Indeed, dominion is better construed as stewardship or trusteeship, and it is to be conducted within limits set by God for respect for the living body and the cadaver "as symbolic of the human person and his dignity." Within this shared perspective, there are important differences, particularly in emphasis, among and within these three traditions. Sections III, IV, and V sketch some of these differences.

In section VI, I sketched some implications of these traditions for different modes of transfer/acquisition of human biological materials— gift (explicit or presumed), sale, abandonment, or expropriation. Each of these modes of transfer/acquisition is recognized as ethically acceptable under some circumstances by the religious traditions under review. However, ethical acceptability is not identical with ethical preferability, and the three religious traditions clearly emphasize the ethical preferability of giving and donating, among the modes of transfer. Furthermore, they also emphasize the ethical preferability or priority of consent—involved in the first three modes—over expropriation. Nevertheless, the values, principles, and rules operative in these traditions also lead to the conclusion that each of these modes of transfer would be ethically *unacceptable* under some circumstances. For example, the gift or sale of a heart by a living person would violate the prohibition against suicide. Thus, the acceptability or preferability of modes of transfer would depend on distinctions between living donors, cadavers, and fetuses, between renewable and nonrenewable tissues, and the like. Some modes of transfer of some human biological materials could lead to abuse and exploitation; they could also lead to dehumanization by fundamentally altering the conception of the human person and his/her body and its parts. But, with these cautionary notes in mind, it is important to emphasize that these traditions do not hold that any mode of transfer/ acquisition of human biological materials is intrinsically evil and never justifiable. Whether any particular mode of transfer/acquisition is acceptable or unacceptable, preferable or not,

will depend on a careful analysis of the human biological materials in
light of fundamental theological themes and moral principles.

PRAXIS AND PIETY:
HERMENEUTICS BEYOND THE NEW DUALISM

EDWARD FARLEY
Vanderbilt University

Differences are the very stuff of reality and, therefore, of the experience of reality. Differentiation, the marking of differences, is what happens in the cognitive tracking of reality. Scientists, scholars, and academics live in a world of distinctions, and they like nothing better than to expose and criticize a dualism which is a way of differentiating which separates and represses the continuity and interdependence of what is separated. Hegel saw world process itself as a perpetual dual differentiation and synthesis of differentiation. One of the dominant dualisms of the modern West brings the ongoing internecine quarrels of historians, philosophers, and theologians to a stop and mobilizes their common opposition. Known as "Cartesianism," it is the dualism brought about by differentiating (human) conscious and non-conscious reality. It has had a variety of expressions: soul and body, thought (*cogito*) and extension, the transcendental and the factual, the subjective and the objective, Spirit (*Geist*) and world, the for-itself (*pour-soi*) and the in-itself (*en-soi*). Although opposition to "Cartesianism" seems virtually ritualistic in the academic world, this dualism continues to re-appear in new forms. What seems to be the most dominant dualism of contemporary Western culture, the techno-scientific and the humanistic, may be still another version of this dualism. I begin this essay with the theme of differentiation and Cartesian dualism in order to introduce what appears to be a new dualism which more and more offers itself as a framework for interpreting the world.

I. *The Cultural Roots of the New Dualism*

The new dualism arises from a differentiation between the human individual and the human community. If it has not replaced thought and extension (the human and the quantitative), it is a growing subtheme within it. Like Cartesian dualism, it too has a variety of expressions: individualism and collectivism, Romantic and Marxist hermeneutics, personal ethics and social ethics, existential/ transcendental and social/political anthropologies, individual freedom and social liberation. We tend to think of dualisms as primarily the products of the culture's intellectual life, offsprings of the academy. This one, however, expresses also two quite different ways of world interpretation widespread in culture itself. Robert Bellah and his cohorts have cogently argued that in the North American ethos the primary way of experiencing and understanding the world is "individualism."[1] While individualism is not a homogeneous phenomenon, it does appear to have some general traits. It is the conviction that the most decisive and powerful bearers of reality are individuals rather than groups, and the responses of individuals are the primary determinants of important outcomes. Thus, it is the individual's constant transaction with reality, the way motivation, moral values, and effort all come together in the individual, that cause or prevent such things as racism, Nazism, sexism, and the like. Societal problems which attend identifiable groups of people (the poor, minorities, the young) are assigned to the category of individual effort or non-effort. Given motivation, values, and effort, no poor person *has* to be on welfare. In its negative expression, individualism ignores or denies that collective movements and power are decisive bearers of reality and shapers of human destiny.

Individualism may be the primary world conviction of North American culture at the present time. However, there is another perspective present in society in tension with individualism and, to a certain degree, in political conflict with it. Terms like collectivism and socialism have too many specific political connotations to name the other side of the duality. I shall call it by the coined term, *social-ism*. This names the view that the most decisive bearers of human reality are not

---

[1] See Robert Bellah, et al., *Habits of the Heart: Individualism and Commitment to American Life* (Berkeley: University of California, 1985), especially chap. 6. See also Christopher Lasch, *The Culture of Narcissism: American Life in an Age of Diminishing Expectations* (New York: W. W. Norton, 1979) 127ff.

individuals but groups: classes, races, nations, corporations, bureaucracies. Power is the very meaning of such enduring social entities; hence, they are the primary determiners of important outcomes. What come together in a specific oppression (e.g., racism) are not so much the elements of an individual's life but the sedimentations of past symbols, a set of typifications (Schutz) which carry the taken-for-granted realities of the group, stratifications, and distributions of power in societal functions. To address and change social problems is, therefore, to confront these sedimented structures of power, not individuals in situations of choice and effort.

Individualism and social-ism run deep in present-day North American culture and therefore shape its religion. Further, what is primary in the larger culture, individualism, is primary in religion.[2] Socialism is present on the margins of North American religion, and its locations are seminaries, the bureaucracies of main-line denominations, the black church, and certain minority constituencies. There is a sense in which the Protestant branch of Christendom has always been individualistic. Its deepest convictions about sin and salvation and its approach to (biblical) authority have promoted individualist rather than corporate ways of understanding.

The two current divisions of Protestant religion in white North America, the newly revitalized evangelical movement and the therapeutically oriented mainline denominations, are both individualistically oriented. Both traditional and modern evangelicalism embody the individualistic conviction that what is decisive in religion is the individual's piety, morality, felt-responses, and destiny. The social (the church, the society) is acknowledged as important, and its importance is its function to facilitate these things. Traditional (not revisionary) evangelicalism desires and works for societal change convinced that the way society changes is through the influence of individual lives and actions (prayer, right living, charity work, etc.). Thus, its criticism is directed less toward oppressive structures as spon-

---

[2] One of the most important studies of popular religion in recent North America proceeded by an inquiry into the religious best sellers and inspirational books published in the period between 1875 and 1955. The overwhelming emphasis of the literature is that it addresses the individual's concerns for salvation in this or another life, the meaning of life and the relief from suffering, and ways to gain wealth and success. Further, the specific techniques provided by the authors are addressed to individuals. See Louis Schneider and Sanford M. Dornbusch, *Popular Religion: Inspirational Books in America* (Chicago: The University of Chicago, 1958).

sored activities (pornography, gambling, drinking) which can tempt
and corrupt the individual's transaction with reality. In the largely
suburbanized mainline denominations, individualism takes the form of
therapeutic, the use of traditional biblical and symbolic language to
assist coping with life stresses and strains. Social-ism is relatively
marginal to North American religion. It is present in certain intellectual and critical movements (liberation theologies, feminism), in the
bureaucracies of mainline denominations where ecumenism and social
justice form a continuing agenda, as a literature within evangelicalism,
and in the black church which mixes individualism and social-ism in a
distinctive way.

II. *The New Dualism as a Both-And Hermeneutic*

The individualism and social-ism just described exist in the culture
as deep convictional systems of various constituencies in culture.
However, when groups and movements interpret themselves to themselves, when they would persuade others, and when they come into conflict with each other, they do articulate their convictional systems.
Thus individualism and social-ism rise to the level of a discourse,
rhetoric, and apologetic, and even become part of the agendas of
scholarship. At this level they become competing hermeneutic postures, and when both postures are acknowledged as valid, they exist in
the form of a dualism. Hermeneutic versions of the posture of individualism and social-ism occur in many forms. I shall first describe each
posture as a distinct hermeneutic or way of interpretation. Examples of
these two hermeneutics come from both recent philosophy and from
theology.[3]
     Individual and social-ist hermeneutics are not strangers to philoso-
phy. They are present in the ancient world in the themes of *polis* (the
unit of corporate life and political power) and the ethics of *aretē*
(virtue). Only after the Renaissance do these themes become
alternative postures. Symbolizing these postures as comprehensive
approaches to the world are Romanticism as a hermeneutic and

---

[3] The literature on current hermeneutic movements rightly presents the
situation as a pluralism not a dualism of approaches. See Roy Howard, *Three
Faces of Hermeneutics: An Introduction to Current Theories of Understanding*
(Berkeley: University of California, 1982); David Tracy, *Blessed Rage for Order:
The New Pluralism in Theology* (New York: Seabury, 1975); and Richard
Bernstein, *Praxis and Action: Contemporary Philosophies of Human Activity*
(Philadelphia: University of Pennsylvania, 1971).

Marxism as a hermeneutic. To call the Romantic movement an individualism is, of course, a caricature. However, its radical critique of industrialism and rationalism bemoaned the loss of nature and the diminishment of the individual's felt experience. And this prepared the soil from which grew a century of ever-more detailed explorations of the individual: as will, subjectivity, spirit (*Geist*), *Übermensch*, freedom, existence, *Dasein*, imagination, and transcendental structure. While individualism is not a sufficient label for Goethe, Kierkegaard, Nietzsche, Freud, and Heidegger, it is still the case that the outcome of much of their work is a rigorous topography of the individual as the field of reality. The Marxist hermeneutic constitutes a radical criticism of the individualist posture, and it has continued in the Frankfurt school, in South American theologies, and in modes of thought characteristic wherever Marxism has shaped politics and thought.[4]

The situation at present is no longer the presence of these two postures and approaches as separate, competing hermeneutics. Both strands have presented such powerful cases that they now have a certain self-evident validity. The result of this self-evidence is a hermeneutics which combines them, which I am calling the new dualism. We must acknowledge that this dualism has not replaced Cartesian dualism or its contemporary remnants. One reason for this is that our time has not yet seen a new Descartes, that is, someone who grasps the combined hermeneutics so powerfully and clearly as to give it a classic formulation.[5] Nevertheless, the new dualism does have per-

---

[4] For an excellent account of Marxism as a hermeneutic, a basic orientation rather than a dogmatic and closed system, see Bernstein, *Praxis and Action*, Part I. I note that Marxism is not the only form of social hermeneutics. Both pragmatism (e.g., John Dewey) and process philosophy are versions of it.

[5] The intellectual development of Jean Paul Sartre reveals the unfolding of an agenda which ended precisely with the problem of mediating praxis and individuality. Sartre began with the Cartesian legacy, and he articulated that duality in a new form, the for-itself and the in-itself. But he ended his work supplanting this duality with another one, that of the individual and human history. Central to his last great work, *The Critique of Dialectical Reason*, is the problem and status of the "objective reality of life" (series, group, system, process). The work itself traces the dialectic from individual praxis to social being and collectives to groups and finally to history. Sartre's career repeats in a certain way the movement in Continental philosophy in that period. In the foreground of the early phenomenological movement was a philosophy of human consciousness and a preoccupation with such things as intentionality, anxiety, and death. But in the second and third generations, we have the social

suasive and cognitive power because, like *cogito* (consciousness) and external reality (extension), the categories of the individual and social and the respective hermeneutics which they found carry now the legacy of centuries of exploration and the weight of current cultural embodiments.[6]

The self-evidence of *individualist* hermeneutics has deeper roots than the persuasive power of philosophical argument. The individual and the social are aspects of the world experience of human beings. Human beings can hardly be unaware of the fears, worries, and desires which mobilize their efforts, the griefs they suffer due to loss, the passions evoked by their victories and defeats. Nor can they be unaware of the corporate world they take for granted: its bequeathed language, its traditions, its structures of power. Hence, there is a certain self-evident validity about undertakings which would clarify and understand these two things. Individual and social hermeneutics do, in other words, articulate valid abstractions and as such make both cognitive and action-strategic contributions to the self-understanding and action of human beings. These undertakings are, of course, only two of many cognitive efforts to understand human being: thus, for instance, physiology, biology, history, ecology, and linguistics. But, when individual and social hermeneutics overwhelm and dominate the others, as happened when the Romantic-transcendental and Marxist-social were accepted as the two great hermeneutics, we have a new both-and, dualist hermeneutics.

The reason this is a *single hermeneutic* is the conviction that the interpretation of the human condition requires these two different approaches with their respective hermeneutic requirements. This single hermeneutic arises when a generation or widespread constituency grants to both sides a normative character. Individualist and social-ist analyses are givens in a combined approach to the human condition. The reason this is a *dualism* is that the two abstracted aspects are, like body and soul, juxtaposed in relation to each other, and the juxtaposition is a disrelation, a combination. It is a *new* dualism because the human being is thought of and approached not as thought and

---

world analyses of Alfred Schutz, the hermeneutic of tradition of Gadamer, and the turn to history, power, and action in the Frankfurt School and Foucault. An important harbinger and catalyst of the turn was Hannah Arendt's *The Human Condition* (Chicago: The University of Chicago, 1958).

[6] Bernstein (*Praxis and Action*) explores four major contemporary philosophical movements for each one's respective insights and argues that all four have important contributions to make, including corrections of each other.

extension (or poetic humanities and objective sciences) but as personal and political.

The new dualist hermeneutics is broader than religious and theological hermeneutics, but it is very much present there. I described previously the tension between individualism and social-ism as they pervade and shape actual North American religion. This conflict plus the human being's experience of these dimensions are all roots for self-conscious interpretations (hermeneutics) which combine the two. Religious interpretations which voice the passions of the individual and the corruptions and hope of the social are very ancient. Thus, for instance, the Psalmist and the prophets of Israel. When we consider contemporary North American Protestantism, individualist and social ways of thinking are very much manifest, but there is a vast difference from the ancient ways. The popular piety of the neo-evangelical movement is primarily but not exclusively individualist.[7] It has framed a version of the Christian faith whose appeal is primarily to the individual. However, the Falwell movement has gone beyond this and has appropriated convictions from the social side. Thus, that movement does identify social carriers of power (government, political constituencies) whose shaping is determinative of public and private good. Outside the neo-evangelical movement, programs of mainline denominational bureaucracies combine (as both-and) appeals to the individual and the social. North American Protestant clergy appear to be a special case of both-and hermeneutics. A binary hermeneutic structures clergy thinking about clergy education, continuing education, the activities of ministry (preaching, counseling), and the task and mission of the church. On the one side, the Christian message is preached, counseled, etc., as a biblically rooted message of therapeutic, a resource for assisting individuals to cope not so much with the effects and powers of sin as with the stressful situations of living. On the other side, all the activities of the church and ministry are thought to occur in a complex of institutional systems which require managing. These two marks of North American professions, the therapeutic and the managerial, become, then, the framework of contemporary clergy hermeneutics.

---

[7] For a historical summary of the element of social concern in Evangelicalism, see Robert D. Linder, "The Resurgence of Evangelical Social Concern,(1925-75)," in *The Evangelicals: What They Believe, Who They Are, Where They are Changing* (ed. David F. Wells; Nashville: Abingdon, 1975). In addition, see Robert K. Johnston, *Evangelicals at an Impasse: Biblical Authority in Practice* (Atlanta: John Knox, 1979) chap. IV.

It would not be accurate to say that schools of clergy education, seminaries and Divinity schools, embody in their structure the new dualism. A long-term heritage has fostered upon them another duality, that of the theoretical (academic) and the practical. However, the new dualism is beginning to take root in these schools to the degree that they mirror the phenomenological structure of religion, individualist and social streams of North American religion, the clergy hermeneutic, and the heritage of Romantic-transcendental and Marxist-social analyses. Under the growing critical impact of black religion, Latin American theologies, and feminism, many of these schools have incorporated a thoroughgoing social and praxis approach to the Christian message and to clergy education. Under the traditional convictions of evangelical religion assisted by theologies and philosophies of the personal, they would retain an education which "forms" the individual. Social praxis strategies and individual spirituality have created a beachhead for the new dualism in clergy education. Here, too, we have a both-and, dualistic hermeneutic.

III. *The New Dualism as Corrective and as Problem*

Insofar as individualist and social hermeneutic approaches have obtained the status of self-evidence, the problematic character of their combination will remain obscure. For the new single but dualist hermeneutic is now part of the taken-for-granted sociology of knowledge of such environments as clergy schools. What could possibly be wrong with such a combination which seems to take care of everything: the existential concerns of piety (spirituality) and the moral issues of the corporate? Self-evident, then, are the validity and power of the new dualism. And it is important to acknowledge the insightful, valid character of the new dualism. For most culturally rooted *dualisms* which obtain hermeneutic translation are some sort of corrective, accomplishment, and advance. At least, this is the case when each of the two poles of the dualism carries corrective and creative insights. A society which has qualified its collectivism by some awareness of and attention to the rights, sufferings, and concerns of individuals is better than one which has not. A religion which has qualified its promulgation of individual piety with attention to social power and oppression is preferable to individualistic pietism. Thus, the both-and hermeneutic of combination is a corrective and an advance. The *individual* who combines the two hermeneutics and lives in the both-end of the individual and the social is better off than one who embodies the one or the other.

Is there a self-evident validity about individual and social hermeneutics? The classic texts of human religious, literary, and philosophical history from Hebrew and Buddhist Scriptures to the present attest to both dimensions. Further, the insightfulness of each side is revealed when the opposite pole exists alone. Individualism and social-ism by themselves have distinct corruptive effects. Expressed theologically, each is a type of evil and sin when it is autonomous and alone. The sin of religious individualism as a societal phenomenon is perpetrated by the very thing that makes it valuable and good. This is its *way* of attending to the suffering, vices, and experiences of the other person. Thus, compassion is urged toward individual others in their plight, but the powerful and complex social conditions of that plight are ignored. The resulting paradox is that of interpersonal compassion and corporate callousness and indifference. Such compassion, therefore, is at the same time a kind of cruelty. Called for then is a hermeneutic which corrects the callous compassion of the individualist. The sin of social-ism is its exclusive way of focusing on social conditions of human well-being that places individuals in a stream of causality which represses and denies the whole realm of the individual. Virtue and vice are reduced to descriptions of the individual's role in social change, thus obscuring the whole dynamics of individual sin and redemptive change.

The new dualism, the combination of the individual and the social, is a mutual correction and thus an advance. What, then, is problematic about it? Dualism is itself a cognitive and interpretive phenomenon, a way of understanding. It is culturally embodied when one side of the interpretation is the unity and rationale for a social movement. But dualism as such is always a cognitive failure. For dualism is a binary interpretation which separates and sets things out of relation. As an advance and insight, dualism grasps the unreducible reality of its subjects. As a failure, it is unable to see their relation. Cartesian dualism was, therefore, both an advance and a failure. Dualism, by definition, poses an intellectual problem. Dualism of the individual and the social is problematic precisely because it posits separation and disrelation.

There is a second and deeper problem. Even as dualist interpretation cannot think two sides in true relation, neither can it become embodied in reality. In theological terms, a mere combination of the individual and the social does not redeem but leaves each side in its autonomy. The dualist can only live in and promote both sides in their separateness. Hence, dualism, the both-and combination, promotes each one in its limitation and sin. Correction occurs by combination, not by transformation of each side. Cartesian dualists, thus, can think of virtues and vices as of the mind or the body. But this thinking leaves the vices of the embodied self untouched and the virtues of the embodied self unpromoted. Likewise, the dualist interpretation of human evil as individual *and* social necessarily misses the way evil affects what is more primordial than either of the two and misses redemption as it frees human being in its pre-dualist reality. Here we arrive at the deeper problem of any dualist interpretation of human being. The separation, the two non-relating poles, can be what they are only as they connect with and arise from the sphere of the human. It is just this which dualism misses or obscures. Dualism grasps, can only grasp, what is derivative of the reality which it is interpreting. Theological and religious dualism, therefore, apprehends and interprets human evil and redemption in a derivative and not primordial way. Its disrelating obscures the way these things are the reality of the human being. This is to say that dualism is necessarily a distancing, derivative, and perhaps alienating way of understanding. There is a kind of verification of this which occurs in the human being's everyday experience and self-understanding. Little reflection is required for human beings to know that their lives do not occur in two unrelated worlds. Human beings never experience themselves as individual *and* social. The experienced reality of the human being occurs prior to this separation; hence, the separation can be identified in its derivative character as something which does violence to concrete human reality.

The failure to grasp and articulate the primordial sphere of the human creates severe problems for other specific accounts of human doings. It tends to spawn further and more discrete dualisms: cognitive, moral, and religious. When we try to understand human *knowing* (reality experience, truth, understanding, and the like) in the framework of a dualism of the individual and the social, knowing somehow eludes the effort.[8] On the social and collective side, it must be treated as a phenomenon of social causality, something produced by past and present social sedimentations. But if knowing is merely an objective

---

[8] For a strong criticism of the "fiction" of individualistic epistemology, see Karl Mannheim, *Ideology and Utopia: An Introduction to the Sociology of Knowledge* (New York: Harcourt, Brace and World, 1936), chap. I, #3.

social product, there would seem to be no difference between and no way of adjudicating any cognitive claim, including the claim that knowing is an objective social product. Epistemological social-ism thus devours itself. When we would try to understand knowing as an accomplishment of the individual consciousness and, thus, as something occurring prior to and this side of objectivity, an unbridgeable gap is posited between the knowing self and any trans-self reality. Solipsism seems to be the fate of all individualistic epistemologies. But nothing is really gained by a dualism which patches the two together. For neither relativism nor solipsism is vanquished by the assertion that knowledge is *both* an objective social product *and* an accomplishment of the individual consciousness.

A similar antinomy occurs when the new dualism partitions the *moral* sphere. On the social side human moral experience resides in social structures which authorize and transmit taboos, sanctions, laws, "values," etc. Like cognition, morality is a causal outcome of social processes. Not only is its content relative to the specific social processes; its very reality is the reality of an objective product. This means that it has no ground, no real sanction, not even a pragmatic one, for pragmatic theory is likewise a social product, the embracing of which is as arbitrary as the embracing of anything else. On the individual or agential side, moral experience is a matter of the personal and psychological dynamics of agents, each of which can and does experience purposes, agendas, "values," and obligations. But if these have their origins simply in the individual, they are all reducible to individual striving, and the very notion of morality is undercut. Again, pasting the two together does not move us beyond the relativity of social analyses and the autonomy of individual analyses.

Finally, a dualist approach to religion and the sphere of *faith* perpetrates a loss of the human with similar results. Social hermeneutics describes religion as primordially communitarian, a matter of socially originated and transmitted traditions of belief and ritual. Religion, too, is an objective, social product. If this is all it is, the marks of being religious are authority and conformity. And though it would seem that deviation from whatever is socially formed is the one sin, it should be clear that the categorial world of objective social production can only be a *descriptive* world. In this world the only norms there are are norms for description. On the other side, religion is a matter of individual piety. Its reality is the reality of personal experience, feeling, believing, and acting. But the passionate for-itself is a kind of solipsism of faith which adopts God, the world, and the community as a means to its ends, thereby eliminating the very heart of faith. Again, a both-and dualism simply combines two intrinsically faulty things, neither of which obtain to the sphere of faith because they miss the sphere of the human. Thus, the new dualism affects the cognitive, the moral, and the religious spheres in the same way. As a hermeneutic of mere combination, it resides in what is derivative and misses the sphere of the human.

IV. *The Sphere of Being-Together*

Few would dispute the fact that human beings like all living beings are individuals and that they live their lives in dependence on and relation to other individuals. Nor would many dispute the claim that human beings are individual and social in some distinctive manner. It is this very distinctiveness that calls for the hermeneutics and ontologies of the individual and the social. Yet these descriptions do not as such reach the sphere of the human. Human being is not a *combination* of the individual and the social. Nor does the assertion of the necessary interdependence of these two things express the sphere of the human. For the individual and the social are interpretive categories which are derived from something which is prior to them. Their interdependence is thus a categorial interdependence and is not an immanent structure of the sphere of the human.

How is the sphere of the human disclosed? What is the reflective pathway to it? If it is not itself the sphere of the individual, it will not be grasped by the reflective turn to the experiencing self, that is, the self as a stream of consciousness-acts (*Erlebnisse*).[9] If the sphere of the human is not the sphere of the corporate, it will not be uncovered by a self-obliterating turn to the self's context, environment, or society, for such a turn posits the individual self only to turn away from it to its objects. This focus on the self or the self's objects rests on an

---

[9] The Husserlian reflective turn back to such phenomena and acts as perceiving, judging, imagining, emoting, and the like does make its contribution. That is, this reflective turn does, it seems, yield features of these things. However, it is a selective and abstracting focusing which sets aside (brackets) the existential density of human being and also of these acts. The more reflexive method of Marcel and Buber turns to that density itself, and when it does, what is yielded is not a "consciousness-act" of an individual but something which is already a reciprocity, since the actuality of these acts always occurs in the exchange, the negotiation, the depth interrelations which constitute the sphere of the human.

epistemological paradigm which identifies the sphere of the human with the subject cognitively experiencing objects.

The sphere of the human is that from which the self-aware individual in its consciousness-acts and passions and the perduring social structures have their life. It cannot be, then, merely the self or society. It is, rather, the sphere of being-together, of being-with, of the reciprocal, of the "between" (*Zwischenmenschliche*).[10] If so, the path, the cipher which displays this sphere is the event and situation of human interpersonal negotiation and relation. While not identical in meaning, these expressions from Martin Heidegger and Martin Buber exemplify attempts on the part of nineteenth- and twentieth-century continental philosophers to depict the sphere of the human behind mere individuality and sociality. With the exception of Alfred Schutz who focuses directly on the pre-institutional social world, most continental philosophers arrive at this sphere through consideration of how the human individual experiences itself in its world. Husserl's early eidetic phenomenology ended by uncovering a world and "other" reference in consciousness itself, thus correcting and going beyond consciousness as something prior-to-the-world. Sartre corrected what he took to be Husserl's concept of the transcendental ego by arguing that the ego is something derived and reflected, a kind of abstraction, implying that the sphere of the human occurs prior to ego self-consciousness. Heidegger offered a full ontology of the human not only as being-in-the-world but as being-with-others and in the mode of care-for or solicitation (*Fürsorge*). Scheler and Edith Stein like Fichte and Hegel before them describe the characteristic posture through which the other is present: thus, acknowledgment (*Anerkennung*, Hegel), fellow-feeling (*Miteinanderfühlen*, Scheler), and empathy (*Einfühlung*, Stein).[11] Two thinkers in the first half of the twentieth century, Martin Buber and Gabriel Marcel, display the sphere of the human not as a sphere of necessary ontological features but as an ideality, a normativity, an accomplishment, and a gift. For Marcel individualism and residing in the ego is a wounded condition, and the open "availability"

---

10 For being-with (*Mitsein*), see Martin Heidegger, *Being and Time* (London: SCM, 1962) Part One, IV. For Buber's concept of the interhuman, see *The Knowledge of Man* (New York: Harper and Row, 1965) chap. III. See also Donald L. Berry, *Mutuality: The Vision of Martin Buber* (Albany: State University of New York, 1985).

11 See Max Scheler, *The Nature of Sympathy* (London: Routledge and Kegan Paul, 1954) Part I. Edith Stein's concept of empathy is explored in *On the Problem of Empathy* (The Hague: Nijhoff, 1964).

to others can occur only as a kind of redemption.[12] Likewise, true dialogue, mutuality (*Gegenseitigkeit*), and meeting are, for Buber, not features or essences of the human species but possibilities to be gained by surpassing distorted forms of relation. Theirs, in other words, is a theonomous understanding of the sphere of the human. For the occurrence of true availability and reciprocity rests on relation to the eternal.

We cannot and should not ignore or meld the differences among these thinkers. Yet at some points their explorations seem to converge. The sphere of the human is an interhuman sphere which is neither individuality nor society. As the sphere of fellow-feeling and reciprocity, it has already formed and is operative by the time the human being is aware of itself as ego, as cognitive, etc. This is why the sphere of the human is a primordial (though not totally hidden) sphere. That is, it is prior to the human being as self-conscious ego or self and prior to the cognitive and utilitarian relations which assist world negotiations. As primordial it is the presupposition and matrix of all the characteristic and distinctive human phenomena: lived body, lived space, temporality, language, social world, aesthetic experience, knowledge. Puzzling and even de-humanizing interpretations of all of these things are propounded when they are dislocated out of the sphere of the human, the sphere of primordial being-together. For the human being knows no reality that is not mediated in and through that sphere and all of its derived functions.

Needless to say, faith occurs in the sphere of the human, and when it is assigned some other sphere or when it is distributed into the "believing-experiencing" of the individual and/or the traditioning of institutions, its reality and power disappear. Faith has to do with the effect of redemptive presence of the sacred on human suffering and corruption, and these things occur primordially in the sphere of being-together. Most descriptions of human sin fall on the side of the corrupted individual self or the corrupted structures of society. These descriptions have their validity and power because individuals and social structures do have their respective dynamics and structures which undergo corruption and liberation. But these dynamics are derivative of the more primordial distortion of the sphere of the human which is at the

---

[12] Marcel's philosophy of availability and the interhuman can be found in *Creative Fidelity* (New York: Farrar, Straus, and Giroux, 1964) chap. II. See also *Homo Viator* (New York: Harper and Row, 1962) chap. I; and *The Mystery of Being* (Chicago: Henry Regnery and Co., 1960) Vol. 1, chap. IX.

same time radically personal and interpersonal. When the hermeneutics of mere combination parcels redemption into the individual and the social, then redemption means the relatively successful production of the just and equitable society *and* the re-making of the awareness, intentions, and dispositions of the individual. Important as they are, neither reaches the primordial sphere of the human, the sphere of the "Kingdom of God."

V. *Conclusion*

The new dualism is not a discrete problem to be solved. Almost all dualisms are gains and corrections which, because they are dualisms, themselves call for correction. This correction need not invalidate the chosen life or career undertakings given to one or the other side of the dualism—for instance, political liberation or cognitive-poetic exploration of individuality. The correction as hermeneutical is directed toward ways of thinking and understanding. As such, getting beyond the new dualism, that is, correcting the correction, would involve criticism of mere combinations of the two poles. If it is the case that the new dualism hides the derivative status of the poles and obscures the sphere of the human, then the unfortunate consequences of that obscuring will shape life on the two sides. Outside the sphere of the reciprocal, knowledge and truth become matters of the individual's transcendental possibilities or an utter quantified objectivity. Scientists and humanists continue to dispute these paradigms, but if what is in place is the one or the other or even merely both, these paradigms will be the only tools and cognitive frameworks available to those who would work for global or regional liberation or those preoccupied with human individuals. Outside the sphere of the human, faith (and redemption) is a matter of either believing-experiencing or objective deposits of tradition, that is, the salvation of the individual or the salvific effecting of the just society. Valid as they are, they can be combined but never truly related as long as the sphere of the being-together remains invisible. Once the reciprocity sphere is grasped as primary, we have the beginning of the end of the new dualism. The future may then have in store for us other corrective dualisms. In the meantime, we need to scrutinize clearly this dualistic hermeneutics which more and more structures current ways of thinking and acting.

A CHAPTER IN THEOLOGICAL RESISTANCE TO RACISM: RUDOLF BULTMANN AND THE BEGINNING OF THE THIRD REICH

H. JACKSON FORSTMAN
Vanderbilt University

The beginning of the Third Reich was not a sudden revelation of the demonic. Evil almost never gives immediate and unambiguous evidence of its character. In this case the new regime was hailed by many as *die grosse Wende*, the great turning point in German history. They believed it would bring an end to the political instability of the Weimar Republic, reestablish freedom for the German people, rectify the unjust and oppressive terms of surrender in 1918, and make it possible once again to be proud to be a German. In its first few months the Nazi state solved a number of serious problems and showed promise of solving others. The Weimar Republic had had to contend with unimaginable inflation followed by depression with their attending chaos and deprivation. The Third Reich brought social order, work, good bread, Volkswagens, and four-lane highways to drive them on.

The darker side was not hidden. Demagoguery, in order to embed itself more firmly, inflame passions, and induce the people to overlook or excuse its excesses, will create enemies. Because of their alleged connections with international capitalism or Communism and because, so it was said, they were not and could never be true Germans, an integral part of the German *Volk*, rooted to the *Volk* by blood and soil, the Jews were made the object of suspicion and hatred. It was a little cloud like a man's hand rising on the horizon, but it foreshadowed the Holocaust.

I.

In 1933 Hans-Georg Gadamer lived in Marburg and was a member of one of Rudolf Bultmann's circles. He recalls that he and others were unprepared for Hitler's seizure of power. They had not read *Mein Kampf*, were generally following the liberal press, and basically believed that the "ghost" would soon disappear.[1] It was not unusual for people who did not support the regime to take it lightly.[2]

Most likely Rudolf Bultmann also did not sense the enormity of what was to come, but the new political situation in Germany seemed to him sufficiently grave that he decided it was necessary for him to speak about it as he began his lectures for the Summer Semester on 2 May 1933. In that lecture he proved himself knowledgeable about the Nazi ideology and about the political theology that encouraged it. The basic theme of the lecture is, with respect both to method and substance, fundamental to Bultmann's theological work. The implications he draws for the political situation are consistent with both method and substance. At a time when already many, including students, were eager to denounce critical voices as enemies of the state, Bultmann not only called for theological criticism of the state but took the further step of publishing his lecture in the widely read *Theologische Blätter*.[3]

"Ladies and Gentlemen. I have made a point never to speak about current politics in my lectures, and I think I also shall not do so in the future. However, it would seem to me unnatural were I to ignore today the political situation in which we begin this new semester."[4] Taking note of the political situation "as theologians," however, does not mean defending a political point of view. Rather it means to abjure both "the 'happy yes' . . . that is spoken all too quickly today" and "depending on

---

[1] *Philosophische Lehrjahre: Eine Rückschau* (Frankfurt am Main: Vittorio Klostermann, 1977) 51.

[2] The artist George Grosz recalled a luncheon with Thomas Mann in New York after Hitler had consolidated his power. Mann, citing numerous "well-informed Germans," was certain that the dictatorship would soon collapse. Grosz, *Ein kleines Ja und ein grosses Nein* (Reimbeck bei Hamburg: Rowohlt Taschenbuch, 1974) 266.

[3] "Die Aufgabe der Theologie in der gegenwärtigen Situation," *TBl* 12/6 (June 1933) 161-66.

[4] I use the translation by Shubert Ogden under the title, "The Task of Theology in the Present Situation," in *Existence and Faith: Shorter Writings of Rudolf Bultmann* (New York: Meridian Books, 1960) 158-65. This citation is from page 158.

how we stand with respect to these events . . . a skeptical and resentful criticism."[5] The first task of the theologian is to reflect on "the relation of faith to nation and state, or the relation between the life of faith and life in the political order."[6] Basic to this relation is faith's orientation to "the God who is Creator and Judge of the world and its Redeemer in Jesus Christ."[7] From this simple theme Bultmann drew everything he wanted to say, and his hearers and readers could have construed what followed only as a most sober warning and, finally, criticism of the new regime and its enthusiastic reception by many.

The theme of God the Creator in connection with a novel understanding of Luther's statements about orders of creation was the ground upon which most of the political theologians had constructed their call to a new nationalism and had given their "happy yes" to "the great turning point" Hitler, in their judgment, had brought forth. God created the world such that human beings find their lives in families and a *Volk* or common grouping of a people. The *Volk*, then—in this case the German *Volk*—is ordained by God, and obedience to God requires us to foster the common life of the *Volk* with its special character. In their development of this doctrine these political theologians expressed antagonism toward Communism because of its internationalism and toward western capitalism because of its individualism, and they called for maintaining the purity of the *Volk* (*Blut und Boden*, blood and soil).

Bultmann affirmed the "orders of creation" doctrine. Characteristically, he observed that we are not persons abstractly but concretely. Our respective lives are given to us in quite specific ways, for example, our sex, our family, our nationality. Our relationship to these orders is first of all a positive one. As members of a nation we share a common destiny and are responsible for a common future. That recognition, however, is only the beginning of thought about God the Creator with respect to our being placed within a given people. As Creator, God dare not be understood as simply immanent in this or any other "order." We dare not understand any phenomenon within the world as directly divine or sacred. Our relation to the orders of creation, including Volk and nation, is therefore positive precisely because it is critical. God is both Creator and Judge of the world.

---

[5] Ibid.
[6] Ibid.
[7] Ibid., 158-59.

The world in which we find ourselves is, as God's creation, good, but, as given, the orders are subject to perversion by us. The orders, then, are ambiguous: They are God's ordinances, but they present us with possibilities both for "free and noble action *and* temptations to act slavishly and meanly."[8] In a direct attack upon the enthusiasm that was overwhelming Germany Bultmann said, "No state and no nation is so unambiguous an entity, is so free from sin, that the will of God can be read off unambiguously from its bare existence. No nation is so pure and clean that one may explain every stirring of the national will as a direct demand of God."[9] And further, with an indirect barb at the orders-of-creation theologians who had been so critical of the Weimar Republic: "In a day when the nation has again been generously recognized as an ordinance of creation, the Christian faith has to prove its critical power precisely by continuing to insist that the nation is ambiguous and that, just for the sake of obedience to the nation as an ordinance of creation, the question must continue to be asked what is and what is not the nation's true demand."[10]

So, in the present situation Christian faith must be a "critical power" and "prove its essentially *positive* character precisely in its *critical* stance."[11] It is able to do this because it knows God not only as Creator and Judge but also as Redeemer. It knows not only about sin, the human inclination to pervert all gifts out of self-interest, but also about grace. Grace, the gift of God's love, frees a person to love in return. The Christian is liberated from a bondage to self and to the world as given and achieves a positive critical stance by being freed to love the neighbors to whom he or she is bound by the common ties of humanity. One is reminded of Augustine's "Give what you command, and command what you will."

The positive service of Christian faith to the nation, therefore, is to exercise unremitting criticism of self, others, and nation based on the rigorous understanding of justice we find in the prophets and Jesus and on love for the others.

A half century later we look back upon the Nazi rule of Germany and recall how through its propaganda to the German people it distorted the German language, made words stand for their opposites (a dangerous trend also today in some sectors of the United States) and by

---

[8] Ibid., 161.
[9] Ibid., 162.
[10] Ibid.
[11] Ibid.

shouting and repetition gave "the big lie" the aura of truth. It is then poignant when Bultmann refers in this lecture to a recent Nazi student demonstration in which the slogan was, "We want to abolish lies!" Bultmann affirms the slogan as "great and beautiful" and adds, "But it also belongs to lying to hide the truth from oneself."[12] Then he refers to three examples that can show the Christian responsibility to the nation in the face of the temptations represented by these examples.

The first seems banal but uncovers something thoroughly serious. The new Marburg city council in its enthusiasm for the new Reich had already acted to change the names of some streets and squares. Bultmann said that such approbation in advance of the struggle to fulfill the task is lightminded and contradicts the critical stance of Christian faith. Christian faith and uncritical enthusiasm are incompatible. The opposite position was expressed by Emanuel Hirsch, the most gifted of the theologians who supported Hitler, when he wrote that the times call not for the critical word but for the helpful and clarifying word. "The divine love," he wrote, "does not begin with criticism and reservation. It pours itself totally into our life."[13]

Second, Bultmann warned against the growing practice of denouncing people. To inform against others, he said, poisons the atmosphere. "'We want to abolish lies'—fine, but it also belongs to this that one respects the free word, even when it expresses something other than what one wishes to hear. Otherwise one educates men to lie."[14]

Finally, he protested against the defamation of persons who are different from oneself, and he made his protest specific. "As a Christian, I must deplore the injustice that is also being done precisely to German Jews by means of such defamation."[15] This defamation is a demonic distortion of noble intentions to serve truth and country. He then brought his lecture to an end:

> If we have correctly understood the meaning and the demand of Christian faith, then it is quite clear that, *in face of the voices of the present, this Christian faith itself is being called into*

---

[12] Ibid.

[13] Emanuel Hirsch, *Christliche Freiheit und politische Bindung: Ein Brief an Dr. Stapel und anderes* (Hamburg: Hanseatische Verlagsanstalt, 1935) 44.

[14] Bultmann, "The Task of Theology," 165.

[15] Ibid. Bultmann published this lecture in the June issue of *Theologische Blätter*. In the August issue Martin Buber quoted with appreciation from this part of the lecture in an open letter he wrote to Gerhard Kittel; "Offener Brief an Gerhard Kittel," *TBl* 12/8 (1933) 249.

question. In other words, we have to decide whether Christian faith is to be valid for us or not. . . . And we should as scrupulously guard ourselves against falsifications of the faith by national religiosity as against a falsification of national piety by Christian trimmings. The issue is either/or![16]

II.

Even as Bultmann gave and then published his lecture the church struggle was beginning. Given the power of the state and the eagerness of so many to fall into line with the themes of the new Reich, it is not surprising that the leadership of the Protestant church in Germany passed into the hands of those who wanted the church to be a major support for the new Germany. One of the first acts of the new church leadership was the imposition of new regulations governing the pastorate and other church offices, including the so-called "Aryan paragraph." This Aryan paragraph excluded from the ministry of the church all persons who were of non-Aryan origin or who were married to persons of non-Aryan origin. Moreover, an Aryan pastor who subsequently married a non-Aryan would be dismissed. The question of whether a person was Aryan or not was to be determined according to the provisions of the new civil law. Decisions about dismissal would be made by the ruling bodies in the several regional churches, and those dismissed would have no right of appeal.

On 11 September 1933 a group of the pastors and delegates to the annual meeting of the Synod of Hesse requested judgments about the Aryan paragraph from the theological faculties at the universities in Erlangen and Marburg. Both responses were published in the *Theologische Blätter*.

The Erlangen faculty presented its view only after it had read the statement from Marburg. It was written by its two systematic theologians, Paul Althaus, who had for years been calling for a new Germany and was a major proponent of a political and patriotic understanding of the "orders of creation," and Werner Elert, who was equally enthusiastic about the new state. They wrote the statement at the behest of the

---

[16] Bultmann, "The Task of Theology," 165.

entire Erlangen faculty. The statement is a defense of the Aryan paragraph.[17]

Althaus and Elert asserted first that in Christ there is no distinction between Jew and Gentile. However, they immediately added that the quality of being a child of God that is common to all Christians by no means diminishes biological and sociological distinctions but rather, as 1 Cor 7:20 shows, binds each person to the condition in which he[18] was born. It is proper, then, for Christians to take note of the biological connections of persons to a definite *Volk*. Second, the oneness in Christ, to which the Augsburg Confession refers, has to do with faith and not ecclesial organization. Historically, Lutheran overseas missions have aimed to establish indigenous, that is, *Volk* churches. Third, in all these younger churches those who are ordained to the ministry must be at one with their communities. That is, they must be members of the *Volk*. Fourth, the question whether we should exclude Jewish Christians from ministry in the German church depends on whether they can belong in the full sense to the German *Volk*. This issue is not ecclesiastical or theological but historical and biological. Fifth, today more than before, the German *Volk* experience the Jewish people in their midst as an alien *Volk*. In emancipated Judaism, it has seen a threat to its own way of life and has protected itself against this danger by legal definitions. The state has the right to take these steps. Now the church is called in a new way to be the *Volk* church of the Germans. Therefore the church must demand the removal of its Jewish Christians from church offices. In taking this action the church no more excludes Jews from church membership than it excludes others—for example, women—who are prevented by natural conditions from ordination. Finally, the law is not rigid. It allows for exceptions, but they are best left to the bishops. The statement was signed on 25 September 1933.[19]

---

[17] The statement in full was printed in "Theologisches Gutachten über die Zulassung von Christen jüdischer Herkunft zu den Aemtern der deutschen evangelischen Kirche," *TBl* 12/11 (November 1933) 321-24.

[18] I use the masculine pronoun here because I believe it properly represents the intention of the authors.

[19] Hermann Strathmann, a professor at Erlangen, wrote a weak demurral. He did not want the law to be retroactive, and he wanted provision for some future ordinations of Jewish Christians. "Kann die evangelische Kirche Personen nichtarischer Abstammung weiter in ihren Aemtern tragen?" *TBl* 12/11 (November 1933) 324-27.

The Marburg statement was utterly different. After citing the major provisions of the law it began by stating that the law is incompatible with the essence of the Christian church as that essence is determined by the authority of the Bible and the gospel of Jesus Christ and witnessed to by the Reformation confessions. It threatens the independence of pastors in general and specifically reduces the status of non-Aryan church members to that of second-class membership. The message of Jesus Christ as savior of the world is directed to all peoples such that all who belong to the church are brothers and sisters.

Historically the church, from the point of view of its faith, has viewed Jews confessionally rather than racially. Consequently, it has considered the Jew who becomes a Christian simply as a Christian. Its unity is in its common faith as the Body of Christ. One may not say that this unity applies only to the invisible church. It is also not permitted for Christians to claim that race and the character of a *Volk* should be respected by the church as orders of creation. Moreover, it is not valid to point in support of the new law to the ecclesial separation of the races in other countries, as, for example, in the United States where there are separate churches for black and white people. These cases violate the Christian message. In the same way, one should not point to the existence of specifically Jewish-Christian communities in antiquity. Those communities were not racially based.

All efforts to claim that Jesus was an Aryan are nonsense, and to point to the crucifixion as a ground for revoking the rights of Christians of Jewish origin is a madness for which one should be ashamed. Those who do not acknowledge the full unity of Jewish and non-Jewish Christians in the church and propose something other than its full realization in the constitution of the church deceive themselves when they confess that the Bible is God's word and that Jesus is the Son of God and the Lord of all human beings.

The declaration ended with this sentence: "If these statements are taken with theological seriousness, then a political or ecclesiastical-political binding of church proclamation or a restriction of the rights of non-Aryan Christians in the church is not permitted."[20]

Rudolf Bultmann wrote the declaration. The theological faculty at Marburg convened to consider it on 18 September and approved it unanimously. Bultmann's close friend, Hans von Soden, Dean of the fac-

---

[20] "Gutachten der Theologischen Fakultät der Universität Marburg zum Kirchengesetz über die Rechtsverhältnisse der Geistlichen und Kirchenbeamter," *TBl* 12/10 (October 1933) 294.

ulty, signed it for the faculty the next day and, in accord with the action of the faculty, sent it to the leaders of the various regional Protestant churches, all theological faculties, representatives to the National Synod, and the church presses. The *Theologische Blätter* printed it in full in its October issue.

In addition to the declaration of the Marburg faculty Bultmann wrote a statement under the title, "The New Testament and the Race Question," and circulated it to Professors of New Testament for signatures. This short piece begins by acknowledging that the New Testament does not directly address the issue of race, but then it adds that there is *no* anti-semitism in it. The message of the New Testament is that all are sinners, and on that basis there is no distinction. Bultmann then briefly set forth several points: The New Testament church is a church of both Jews and heathens. Faith and baptism are the only requirements for membership, both for Jews and heathens. Jews and heathens are equally qualified for church leadership. He concluded with the following declaration: "It is therefore our view that a Christian church may absolutely not surrender this standpoint."[21]

This statement also was broadly distributed, and it was published in the *Theologische Blätter* immediately following the declaration by the Marburg theological faculty. It carried twenty signatures in addition to Bultmann's, including von Soden, Jülicher, Schleier, and Lietzmann of Marburg, Bauer of Göttingen, Deissmann of Berlin, Jeremias of Greifswald, Lohmeyer of Breslau, Karl Ludwig Schmidt of Bonn, Windisch of Kiel, Heim of Tübingen, and Juncker and Schniewind of Königsberg. Two months later, in the December issue, Karl Heim, Juncker, and Schniewind publicly withdrew their signatures.[22] Heim complained that he had not known that the statement was also being sent abroad for signatures, and he feared it would be used by people who wanted to criticize Germany. All three objected to its being published in the *Theologische Blätter* in tandem with the declaration of the Marburg theological faculty. They said they signed it solely as an exegetical piece with which they could agree for the most part. They withdrew their names because of the way the statement was being used.

---

[21] "Neues Testament und Rassenfrage," *TBl* 12/10 (October 1933) 296.
[22] *TBl* 12/12 (December 1933) 374.

III.

In that same December 1933 issue the *Theologische Blätter* published two essays about the Aryan paragraph. The first was written by Georg Wobbermin of Göttingen in defense of the law.[23] The second was by Bultmann.[24]

1.

Wobbermin dealt with the issue from the point of view of existential psychology. His psychology, he claimed, is existential in the sense that it deals with the concrete situation. Thereby it becomes useful for theology. It values particular personal convictions and the particular experiences of faith as the decisive tools for theological reflection and for understanding the Bible. From this perspective he found the Aryan paragraph both proper and justified and the Marburg declaration as well as that of the New Testament professors hasty and misleading.

First, it should be noted, he wrote, that the Old Prussian Church that passed the law did not construct it out of its own thinking but only applied to the church the new provisions of the civil law as they emerged in the National-Socialist German freedom movement. That movement has recognized a historical calamity (the Weimar Republic, the oppressive peace terms of 1918, and the like) and has determined to replace an abnormal situation in the life of the German people by reestablishing a normal condition. Neither the Marburg statement nor that of the New Testament professors takes account of this fact. Moreover, he taunted, if the Aryan paragraph of the church is to be so decisively rejected, the problem is deeper. In order to be consistent and thorough the statements should go further and reject the civil law as well.

It is another question whether these new provisions pertain to the essence of the church or are suitable only for the present, special condition of church life. It is the latter that the General Synod of the Old Prussian church had in mind and on behalf of which Emanuel Hirsch, also of Göttingen, has written. Given this intention of the new law it can be judged only after a clarification of the fundamental issue.

That fundamental issue is that the Jewish question is above all a question of race. It is one of the greatest services of Adolf Hitler that he

---

[23] "Zwei theologische Gutachten in Sachen des Arier-Paragraphen—kritisch beleuchtet," *TBl* 12/12 (December 1933) 356-59.

[24] "Der Arier-Paragraph im Raume der Kirche," *TBl* 12/12 (December 1933) 359-70.

has made this point so clear. We have a special situation in Germany. That is why foreigners have so much trouble understanding us. The two statements do not account for this special situation. The basic issue has to do with race. This issue cannot be answered by the New Testament. True, the church is for all the baptized without exception, and the realization of that ideal is the aim of the ecumenical movement. However, the Aryan paragraph deals exclusively with the human sphere and a very specific one at that.

Does this human sphere with its concrete historical relations and distinctions have no significance at all before God? Certainly it does. The apostle Paul, to be sure, wrote in Galatians that there is neither Jew nor Greek, slave nor free, male nor female because all are one in Jesus Christ. This position, however, did not prevent him from distinguishing between men and women with respect to church order. Women, he prescribed, were to keep silent in the church. Thus there also may be distinctions in church order between Jew and Greek or Aryan and non-Aryan. Today we must honor that distinction in order to protect the unity of the German spiritual life.

The Marburg declaration makes it seem as if the law punishes Jewish Christians or takes away their rights. It is not so in reality. Rather it is a matter of giving focus to a critical situation. To be sure, the application of the law can be tragic in individual cases—and Wobbermin self-servingly claimed that he himself would experience pain in certain cases—but judgment should not be influenced by these discomforts. "For that critical situation had, in the heaviest way, endangered, indeed had all but destroyed, the spiritual life of the German people and therefore also that of the German Evangelical Church, most especially because of Jewish cultural and bolshevistic literature."[25] The church, he wrote, is not without blame. In recent decades it has received Jews, and they have gotten into the cultural life of our *Volk*. In fact, in some universities already 50% of the Associate Professors and Assistants are Jews. The church cannot withdraw from the common task of the *Volk*, no matter how painful that task may be.

2.

Bultmann had Wobbermin's essay before him as he wrote his own, "The Aryan Paragraph in the Sphere of the Church," but he did not deal exclusively with what Wobbermin wrote. He addressed, in addi-

---

[25] Ibid., 359.

tion, the Erlangen statement, a declaration from Tübingen theologians, and the intentions of some of the Nazi-oriented church officials.

To Wobbermin's criticism that neither the Marburg declaration nor that of the New Testament professors had taken account of the fact that the Aryan paragraph was simply an application of civil law to the church, Bultmann reasserted his thesis that the ordering of the church should correspond to the essence of the church. Then he indicated that he would confine himself in this essay to the sphere of the church, although, as we shall see, some of his remarks were considerably broader in scope.

The church is the Body of Christ, and, as such, there can be no distinctions in it. The exclusion of non-Aryans introduces distinctions. In the Augsburg Confession the ministry of the word is called a sacrament, a holy ordinance. It is unthinkable, therefore, to introduce distinctions in this holy office in the name of a visible order that supposedly is not bound to the church's essence. The Reich Bishop Müller and the Tübingen theologian Kittel may assure us that the exclusion of non-Aryans from church ministry does not reflect on their Christian character or make them any less our brothers in Christ, but anyone who believes that assertion indulges in self-deception. In the church the word of God does not come to the people from the character of the people but from the spirit of Christ. "Were I a non-Aryan or a not purely Aryan Christian I would be ashamed to belong to a church in which I could only listen but not speak."[26] Moreover, we must be aware that this Aryan paragraph is only the beginning. The Tübingen statement already calls for the Christian Jews to form their own congregations, and Bishop Hossenfelder seems also to call for this step. They point to Joseph's forgiveness of his brothers in Gen 50:20 and support their position by noting Joseph's assertion that God has brought good out of evil. The Tübingen theologians and Bishop Hossenfelder are guilty of distorted thinking with a religious tinge. "A person does not have the right to motivate or to defend actions on the basis of such thinking."[27]

The Erlangen statement, on the other hand, says that the way persons are by the fate of birth ordered into various peoples is to be "ethically" affirmed. Of course, but what is given by nature means limits and questions and brings both blessing and curse. Christian existence is not possible as a plain and simple "ethical" affirmation of what is

---

[26] Ibid., 362. Already in 1933 Bultmann advocated the application of this principle to women as well.

[27] Ibid.

given by nature whether we consider the natural gifts and impulses of the individual or the social conditions of whatever sort they may be. This is the case not only because the human being is not just an animal but also because what is given in this way by destiny is thoroughly determined and formed by historical conditions. In an extension of his remarks beyond the sphere of the church, Bultmann wrote, "Only a rationalism blind to reality can isolate a natural order like biological determination as significant for human intercourse. One's race as a pure given carries with it no clear direction for acting, for it is given only in a definite historical situation."[28]

The Erlangen declaration is ridiculous when it defends the Aryan paragraph by appealing to the intention of foreign missions to establish churches with indigenous leadership. This intention does not imply that the gospel is preached out of the life of the people. On the contrary, the gospel is addressed to the people. The conception of a *Volk* church by the Erlangen theologians is both false and heretical. A *Volk* church can be a Christian church only in the sense that the mission is directed to a particular people as such. It has nothing to do with the one who proclaims the message, and when we think of a *Volk* in terms of its mores and customs we have to say that not all of them are bearable in the church. The Aryan paragraph simply contradicts the truth of the church of Jesus Christ.

Wobbermin said he believes Jews constitute a threat to the "German spiritual life." This "German spiritual life," Bultmann responded, is, in any case, ambiguous, with possibilities for evil as well as good. Then, addressing Wobbermin directly, he continued:

> I do not want to go further into such a question. But I want to say to you, Colleague Wobbermin, you who reproach us for paying no attention to the concrete historical situation: I think we see it. We see it in all its ambiguity, and what we see gives us no comfort! And we believe that in this discord we must direct ourselves to the word of our Lord and not cast a side-long glance at the so-called 'unity of the German spiritual life.'[29]

Describe the consciousness of the German *Volk* as one will, but if the German *Volk* abjure the self-criticism that comes from hearing the word of God, it is not a Christian *Volk*, and it has forgotten the limits

---

[28] Ibid., 364.
[29] Ibid., 367.

given to it by God. "Only under this criticism of the word of God and in constant tension with it can a true *Volk* consciousness, conscious of its limits as well as of its value and its task, develop."[30]

Then he concluded, "If the church in the 'New Empire for *Volk* and State' wants to bring blessing, it can do so only if unflinchingly and soberly it fulfills its proper mission, only if it never forgets that its critical task holds it constantly in tension with the consciousness of the *Volk*."[31]

IV.

On University Street in Marburg there is a small garden, the only open space on this busy street. In the garden there is a simple monument. The inscription reads:

In memory of the Synagogue sacrilegiously destroyed on 10 November 1938, and of our Jewish fellow citizens who were murdered.

One pauses for a long time to reflect not only on the Jewish community of Marburg whose house of worship was on that piece of earth but on Jewish communities all across the dreadful Nazi empire.

Before leaving one also thinks of Rudolf Bultmann, whose lecture hall and church are only 100 yards away.

---

[30] Ibid., 368.
[31] Ibid., 369.

THE BIBLE AND THE STUDY OF RELIGION IN THE UNITED STATES

CHARLES H. LONG
Syracuse University

Professor Walter Harrelson's career has been almost equally divided between research and teaching in the discipline of biblical interpretation and administrative positions related to the development and enhancement of the study of religion in the United States. In the latter endeavor he has served on many committees devoted to the professional societies of his own disciplinary research, biblical studies, and on national and international organizations devoted to the teaching and study of religion as an academic discipline.

In this short essay I should like to raise some of the cultural issues and tensions involved in the study of the Bible and the study of religion on the American scene. My sensitivity to these tensions were heightened when I was asked to address the American Academy of Religion on the occasion of its seventy-fifth anniversary in 1984.

After agreeing to deliver the address I wondered about the nature of the beginnings of the American Academy of Religion in 1909: what happened in that year? I was quite familiar with the recent history of the AAR, but I was unable to mark the beginning year with any significance. Given my background in the United States, 1909 stands out as the date of the founding of the NAACP, and I was sure that the Academy had nothing to do with that event! I consulted the late Professor William Clebsch, and he could not recall anything of significance for the Academy occurring in the year 1909. I did a bit of research and discovered that 1909 was the year in which our parent body, the National Association of Biblical Instructors (hereinafter abbreviated NABI), was organized.

The idea that led to the founding of NABI was the brainchild of Professor Ismar J. Peritz of Syracuse University. He reported to his colleagues at the twenty-fifth anniversary of NABI in 1933 that the initial impulse came to him after conversations with a colleague in mathematics at Syracuse University. He mused, "Why might we not have an association of Bible teachers and a journal?" He said that he came to the meeting of the Society for Biblical Literature in 1909 with this thought in mind. He discussed this notion with some of this colleagues at the 1909 SBL meeting; those present were Irving J. Wood of Smith College, Raymond Knox of Columbia University, and Olive Dutcher, later to become Mrs. Lawrence Doggett of Mt. Holyoke College. All of his colleagues later confirmed that the original impetus for the founding of NABI came from Professor Peritz.

A word or so about Professor Peritz is in order. He was born in Germany in 1863 and at the age of seventeen left his ancestral faith of Judaism to become a Christian. It is reported that this decision was the result of reading the Epistle to the Galatians with a Lutheran teacher. (Is this too formulaic to be true?) Upon emigrating to the United States he completed graduate degrees at Drew Seminary and Harvard University, coming to Syracuse University in 1895 to teach Greek; soon thereafter he received an appointment to head the new Department of Semitics and Archaeology at Syracuse University.

Professor Peritz continued as an active enthusiastic member of NABI until his death in 1950; he was influential in the establishment of the *Journal of Bible and Religion* and in promoting all phases of the activities of the NABI. He, however, never served as president of NABI; as a matter of fact only one of the founding members of NABI ever held that office, Professor Irving Wood.

In 1963 the Self-Study Committee of NABI assessed the history of the Association as the basis for change and renewal. They summarized the original intentions for the creation of NABI in terms of four goals: 1) to encourage members to share the results of their scholarly work; 2) to establish professional standards in teaching and study; 3) to increase the spirit of fellowship among themselves and promote the practical development of the religious life of their students; and 4) to promote publication of important papers and reviews of literature relevant to their fields of study. The committee acknowledged that for the first twenty-five years of existence of NABI the goals had matched the intentions of the founders but that over the last thirty years, with the increase in membership and the growth of regional societies, NABI was now composed of a large number of members expressing a wide variety of concerns, such that effective operation could no longer be construed under the original intentions of the founders. This led to a reconsideration of the name, form, and function of the organization.

The name, National Association of Biblical Instructors, gave the sense that the organization was limited to those whose special field of competence was Biblical Studies. The designation, "Instructors," gave the sense that the organization was limited to those who held this junior academic rank in the academy, and "National" seemed to limit membership to those in the United States. The committee proposed the name American Academy of Religion: *American*, to include scholars in Canada and Mexico (why not all the Americas?); *Academy*, to suggest a society of learned persons united to advance art or science; and *Religion*, because the committee agreed that it had a wider set of possible applications to the varying concerns of its membership than any other term.

In the reconsideration of the form and function and the change of name to embody this reevaluation and renewal, the organization moved from the clarity of the book, *the Bible*, to the murky discourse about religion.

The original intentions of Professor Peritz were slowly but definitely receding. Professor Peritz had made it clear that the meaning of the word and text, *Bible*, should form the locus and center for those scholars concerned with the meaning of religion in the academy. He stated quite forcefully in the discussions that led to the publication of the journal of NABI that the word *Bible* should be prominent in the title of the journal and it is for this reason that the title of the journal was the *Journal of Bible and Religion*. It is clear that by 1963 the scholarly study of religion could no longer be encompassed under a name that gave centrality to the Bible. The term "Religion" was a designation that included more and less than the meaning of Bible.

Allow me a small excursus regarding another kind of history of the study of religion in the United States—a history that parallels and is almost simultaneous to the events of NABI. I refer to the life, teaching, and scholarly career of Professor Morris Jastrow, Jr. In 1902 Professor Jastrow published an extremely delightful and scholarly manual simply titled, *The Study of Religion*. In this text, which is still relevant to many issues encountered in the study of religion, Jastrow set forth the meaning of the study of religion as *Religionswissenschaft*. Jastrow's work sparkles with the names of the pioneers of this discipline: Max Müller, Chantepie de la Saussaye, Emile Bournouf, C. P. Tiele, as well as the leading scholars of Buddhism, Hinduism, Islam, Ancient Near Eastern religions—this latter area being his own arena of competence and scholarly achievement. He was an original contributor to scholarship in this area and recognized as an international scholar of the religions of the Ancient Near East.

The text, *The Study of Religion*, encompasses the total field of the study of religion; it is theoretical and practical, dealing as it does with the problematical status of the study of religion as well as devoting chapters to the study and teaching of religion in universities and colleges, and the uses of museums as teaching aids. It set forth the interdisciplinary nature of the study of religion with specific chapters on Religion and Ethics, Religion and Philosophy, Religion and History, Religion and Culture, and the like.

But this work should not be seen as the incidental foray of a specialist into the wild field of the general study of religion. It is clear from his career that he thought of his precise scholarship within the wider context of the general study of religion. More than this, he was actively engaged in organizing and giving institutional form to this ideal. Jastrow founded the American Lectures on the History of Religions in 1892. In 1891 he convened a meeting of scholars in Philadelphia to establish a course of lectures on each of the major religious traditions. Buddhism was the topic in 1895; the lecturer was William Rhys Davids of University College, London. Lectures on Primitive Religions were presented in 1896 by Daniel Brinton, and the list goes on with the subsequent years devoted to Egyptian Religion, Judaism, and so forth.

I am recalling this different and even counter-history as the basis for asking some peculiar and specific questions. First, why in our prehistory as NABI and in our present history as the AAR do we not hear the faintest echo of this scholarly tradition of the study of religion in the United States? Second, why is our parentage in NABI rather than in those activities surrounding the life and career of Professor Morris Jastrow, Jr.?

I think that there are answers to these questions, and I should like to suggest them. Our heritage in AAR lies in NABI, with Peritz rather than with Jastrow, because of the peculiar relationship that the culture of the United States has with The Book—*The Bible*. This relationship constitutes an empirical as well as a mythological structure; I am using myth here with its double-faced semantic, as true and fictive. We are from this perspective, as Sidney Mead put it, "a nation with the soul of a church." The prominence of the meaning of the book, the Bible, as symbolic of the scholarly study of religion in the United States is, within the context of the life and careers of Professors Peritz and Jastrow, even more ironic. Ironic because, while both were scholars of Ancient Near Eastern Religions, Jastrow was by far the more eminent of the two, and yet it was he who wished to define the study of religion in broader and more general terms.

The symbolic meaning of the Bible fed into the cultural myth of America as the United States, and thus the lines of communication with a kind of grass roots meaning of religion were touched in its evocation. This country and its culture, initially and as presently constituted, has few of those traditions that confirm the meaning of religion as *religare*, "to bind." Alexis de Tocqueville once mused that he failed to see in America any of those ancient meanings, customs, relics, etc., that bind a people together. The Bible as mythological symbol of religion in American culture has operated as a clarification of the ambiguity of the meaning of religion on the American scene—a structure that fulfilled a meaning of religion as "binding".

Now, to be sure, the organizers of NABI were no biblical literalists. They were sophisticated and critical interpreters, equipped with the most up-to-date scholarly methods in their understanding and interpretation of the biblical text. But they were also operating out of a deeper meaning of this text as a centering and binding structure in American cultural life. But this center did not hold! And it did not hold because it was heuristic at best and fictive at worse.

The change made in the 1960s did not occur as the result of the discovery of a new meaning; the change came about because the scholarly community had to come to terms with the diversity that was simply the case. Let me remind you of the reasons given for the change. The NABI Self-Study Committee decided that they should no longer be called the National Association of Biblical Instructors because: 1) the term "National" tended to restrict scholarly communication on the basis of the political exclusivity of the nation-state and might exclude our colleagues in Canada and Mexico; 2) "Bible" or "Biblical" gave the sense that this text was synonymous with the meaning of religion; and 3) "Instructor", being the designation of a junior rank, should not define the scholar of religion.

These critiques of parentage are apt and to the point. The move from NABI to the American Academy of Religion seems to have been a movement into an arena already defined on the American scene by Jastrow. But then again the American Academy of Religion has not really undertaken the program of Jastrow's *Religionswissenschaft*, even though many in the Academy still speak of this kind of ideal in hushed and haunted tones. Though Jastrow's program had the clarity of a *Wissenschaft*, it did not come to terms with the existentiality of the meaning of religion within the context of American cultural reality.

There is another kind of reason that explains why our heritage is in NABI rather than with Jastrow. NABI, with all of its shortcomings, touched the American mythology about religion through the symbolism of the Bible in American culture as the locus of ultimate religious concern centering the range of religious meanings and exfoliating itself to wider and wider peripheries, while in the same movement obscuring and hiding fundamental realities of the American religious situation. It touched the vital roots in the same movement that hid the deeper realities of America's religious culture.

NABI, from 1909 to the early 1960s, held together in a viable manner this strange tension. But we all know of other events of the 1960s— the Civil Rights Movement, the first Roman Catholic president of the United States, the beginnings of our escalation of the war in Vietnam. The change in name occurred at the same time that the ultimate concern, the roots of the deeper possible bindings on the American scene, were being exposed. It is worthy to note that no mention is made of this cultural context in the records that deal with the change of name, form, and structure of NABI.

These roots, the possible threads of bindings, are the "mentalities" of the American culture and have analogues in all cultural traditions. Allow me a word about this French term which is now *en vogue*. A few years ago, French historians began using the expression "history of mentalities" to characterize their work in the field of intellectual history. While awkward in French and infelicitous in English translation, the phrase has survived, for it expresses a need to assign autonomy to a kind of historical inquiry which offers perspectives on the civilizing process. The common ground for historians of mentalities is the boundary between the structured and the unstructured domains of human experience; tracing the contours of those boundaries is the substance of their work.

These scholars make use of quantitative, psychological, economic, ideational, and geographical data; they refuse, however, to reduce the meaning of history to the political event or to one of the methodological implications of their data. They are concerned to allow, make room for, find the space for the human face to appear within the context of these various data and methods. The history of mentalities attempts to remedy the limitations of the idealist tradition of cultural history by studying that domain of culture which seems so remote from the idealist tradition—the culture of ordinary women and men. Decisive in this reformulation is a shift of focus from worldviews to the structure through which such conceptions are conveyed. These structures refer to all the forms that naturalize mental activity, whether they be aesthetic images, linguistic codes, expressive gestures, religious rituals, or social customs.

Since the 1960s the Academy has become larger and probably a bit more chaotic, but, I also hope, more discursive. There are groups and sections devoted to theological assessments and reassessments, to textual criticism, to philological and historical studies of particular religions, to philosophical and methodological speculation; all of these are regular and normal scholarly endeavors. But there are also groups devoted to women, feminism, Blacks and their realities, ecology, and more; the groups of this kind represent a new kind of space and a new kind of time. Over against the regular and ordinary disciplinary structures, these latter groups may appear strange and a bit weird, for they trace the contours between structures and the non-structured—between male and female, between wildness and domestication, between black and white, between objectivity and subjectivity.

These groups express the power and virtualities of that which is yet unformed and that which has been obscured and unspoken, and they define meaning in the identity of their empirical embodiment as positive structures of time, space, and power. The popularity and the *en vogue* status of hermeneutics as method are their forte. They make use of every method and discipline and may even destroy and discredit some. They partake of every form of religion and of none. They often make discourse chaotic and agonizing; this is necessary and quite appropriate at this juncture of our existence.

My regard for the notion of *mentalité* does not arise from an attraction to what is the latest European or French intellectual fashion. I am personally attracted to this notion because in the Western world a group of thinkers in France have consistently and continuously explored the meaning of decolonization and post-imperialism, not simply as a political and economic meaning but as a profound upheaval in the structure of thought itself, thus raising the possibility for a new human orientation in the world. We in the American Academy of Religion might have something to contribute if we understand our seeming lack of intellectual order in a different manner, not simply as chaotic but as a mode of expressing that which is novel, now, and necessary—an actual and symbolic expression of our movement from NABI to the American Academy of Religion. We must now learn to live and learn liminally, along the borders, between the contours. Walter Harrelson's career as an American biblical scholar and his vigorous engagement in the study of religion are an example of this rich tension.

RENEWING ECUMENICAL PROTESTANT SOCIAL TEACHING

THOMAS W. OGLETREE
Drew University

In response to events surrounding civil rights demonstrations in Birmingham, Alabama, the General Board of the National Council of Churches voted in June of 1963 to establish a Commission on Religion and Race (CORR). It granted the Commission sufficient authority and funding to take strong, new initiatives in mobilizing white church participation in the civil rights struggle under the leadership of Martin Luther King, Jr. The resolution calling for this step said in part:

> In such a time the Church of Jesus Christ is called upon to put aside every lesser engagement, to confess her sins of omission and delay and to move forward to witness to her essential belief that every child of God is a brother [sic] to every other. Now is the time for action—even costly action that may jeopardize the organizational goals and institutional structures of the Church, and may disrupt any fellowship that is less than fully obedient to the Lord of our Church. . . . Words and declarations are no longer useful in this struggle unless accompanied by sacrifice and commitment.[1]

The Board's action and the subsequent activities of the Commission helped to precipitate one of the most remarkable decades of clergy ac-

---

[1] *Interchurch News* (June-July 1963) 6-7. See "NCC Acts on Racial Crisis," *Christian Century* (19 June 1963) 793. Henry J. Pratt notes that this action dramatically shifted NCC policy, from an educational strategy to public activism; *The Liberalization of American Protestantism: A Case Study in Complex Organizations* (Detroit: Wayne State University, 1972) 181-87.

tivism in the history of white Protestantism in America.[2] The civil rights movement furnished the impetus, the model, and the initial agenda for this activism. It introduced Protestant clergy and their progressive lay constituents to militant, non-violent direct action as a favored means of promoting social justice in the land. While legislative action was a crucial part of the overall social aim, the proximate strategies consisted of economic pressure and political disruptions of "business as usual."

The civil rights movement peaked in 1964 and 1965 with the passage of historic new legislation requiring full access for all to public accommodations, and extending federal protections for the voting rights of citizens. Yet activist clergy were soon engaged in other social struggles: opposition to the Vietnam War, community organization among the urban poor, support for César Chavez's efforts at unionizing farm workers in California, and most recently the peace movement.[3] Quite logically, the "new breed" of activist clergy also tended to support the feminist movement and the "rights" claims of non-racial minorities, in particular, persons with physical disabilities, and those with gay and lesbian sexual orientations.

The Crisis in Ecumenical Protestantism

As anticipated by the Board of the National Council, this controversial social witness has in fact "jeopardized the organizational goals and institutional structures" of the ecumenical Protestant churches. The Council has been under fire for over two decades, having become a symbol of liberal social commitments which conservative constituents find objectionable. Substantial cuts in funding have

---

[2] For the work of the Commission on Religion and Race (CORR), see Anna Arnold Hedgeman, *The Trumpet Sounds: A Memoir of Negro Leadership* (New York: Holt, Rinehart & Winston, 1964); and Robert W. Spike, *The Freedom Revolution and the Churches* (New York: Association Press, 1965). On clergy activism, see Harvey Cox, "The 'New Breed' in American Churches: Sources of Social Activism in American Religion," in *Religion in America* (ed. Robert N. Bellah and William G. McLaughlin; Boston: Beacon, 1968) 368-83; and Harold E. Quinley, *The Prophetic Clergy: Social Activism Among Protestant Clergy* (New York: John Wiley & Sons, 1974).

[3] Saul Alinsky observed: "The Churches are taking the leadership of social change." Quoted by Marion K. Sanders, "A Professional Radical Moves in on Rochester," *Harper's* (1965) 23.

resulted, forcing the Council to reduce staff and program. CORR has long since been dismantled.[4]

Protestant denominations associated with social activism have been having similar difficulties. All have experienced a steady erosion in membership, especially among young adults. Critics have attributed this trend to the ill-advised involvements of denominational leaders in social causes, perhaps to the neglect of the spiritual needs of their lay membership.[5]

Clergy activism does appear to have caused some membership losses, especially in areas such as California where it was widespread.[6] Yet a careful analysis of the data suggests that sociodemographic factors may have played the major role in membership decline.[7] The broad generalization is that constituencies served by the ecumenical Protestant denominations have been decreasing in size in regions where these denominations historically have been strong. The salient variables include a relatively low birth rate, the postponement of marriage and childbearing by young adults, broad population shifts from the Northeast and the Midwest to the sun belt, and finally, the slowdown in the rate of "switching" from evangelical to liberal denominations. The latter shift may in part reflect relative improvements in the social standing of evangelical Protestant denominations.[8]

---

[4] CORR was retained until the summer of 1967, when its second director, Dr. Benjamin F. Payton, resigned to become president of Bennett College. It was reorganized as the Office of Religion and Race within the Department of Social Justice, but without the funding or the wide mandate it initially received.

[5] For example, Dean M. Kelly, *Why Conservative Churches Are Growing* (New York: Harper & Row, 1977); Richard Neuhaus, *The Naked Public Square* (Grand Rapids: Eerdman's Publishing Co., 1984) 233-36; Peter L. Berger, "American Religion: Conservative Upsurge, Liberal Prospects," in *Liberal Protestantism: Realities and Possibilities* (ed. Robert S. Michaelson and Wade Clark Roof; New York: Pilgrim, 1986) 24-28, 33-36.

[6] Quinley, *The Prophetic Clergy.*

[7] William McKinney and Wade Clark Roof, "Liberal Protestantism: A Sociodemographic Perspective," in *Liberal Protestantism*, 37-50.

[8] The birth rate in ecumenical Protestant denominations is 1.97, compared with 2.54 in conservative Protestant denominations. 2.1 is required for replacement. Even a birth rate of 2.25, the national average, would have meant an increase of a million members in ecumenical Protestant denominations (McKinney and Roof, "Liberal Protestantism," 43-44). Ecumenical Protestant denominations continue to benefit from "switching," with a net gain of 1.9 percent in exchanges with other groups (ibid., 45-47). Yet the rate of switching

Given factors such as these, one can project continuing membership problems for the ecumenical Protestant denominations quite apart from their stances on social questions. These denominations can reverse the pattern of membership decline only if they are able to reach new constituencies.

The primary difficulties generated by clergy activism have to do with enervating internal conflict revolving around the church's social witness. In 1969, Jeffrey Hadden detected a "gathering storm" of conflict between conservative laity and liberal clergy within the ecumenical Protestant denominations.[9] The storm has since broken. It has not been so furious as a hurricane nor so intense as a tornado, but "'t is enough, 't will do."

Conservative lay members now display less confidence in denominational structures, and less willingness to grant allegiance to denominational programs. Financial support has dropped, though not so sharply as the fall in membership. Conservative factions have formed independent agencies which reflect their own vision of the church's mission. These agencies compete for resources with official denominational structures. In response to lay objections, ecumenical denominations have moderated their social witness, giving fresh emphasis to traditional concerns for evangelism and personal spiritual growth. Many activist clergy have become disillusioned. Not a few have left the ministry altogether. Others have had difficulty in securing suitable positions to continue their ministries.[10] Such complex internal struggles do not make for a confident, cohesive ministry. They signal a church in trouble. Above all they place in doubt the capacities of ecumenical Protestant denominations to sustain an activist social witness.

---

from conservative to ecumenical Protestant denominations is down from previous decades (William R. Hutchinson, "Past Imperfect: History and the Prospect for Liberalism," in *Liberal Protestantism*, 68-69). Most ecumenical Protestant losses are not to other denominations but to nonaffiliation. They are most serious among young adults (McKinney and Roof, "Liberal Protestantism," 46-47). The loss of young adults may be related to the recent trend toward postponing marriage and child-bearing.

[9] Jeffrey K. Hadden, *The Gathering Storm in the Churches* (Garden City, NY: Doubleday, 1969).

[10] Quinley, *The Prophetic Clergy.*

The Roots of Internal Conflict

In retrospect, the divisive conflicts within ecumenical Protestantism appear altogether predictable on both sociological and historical grounds. Hadden has highlighted the sociological factors. The underlying problem is that most lay members of the ecumenical Protestant denominations are socially conservative. Yet they have been pressed by clergy leaders to honor, if not support, vigorous efforts to bring about social change. Given their social locations, they have not been disposed to identify with the social vision which informs these efforts. Still less have they been prepared to accept as valid the militancy and political partisanship of activist clergy.[11]

Clergy in the ecumenical Protestant denominations have, of course, come from the same social backgrounds as their lay membership. Yet in their formation as ministers they have been exposed to experiences which have sensitized them to urban poverty, racial injustice, the subordination of women, and the oppression suffered by millions of people in the "third world." They have learned to integrate a sense of accountability for such suffering with their basic grasp of the Gospel.

The sociological bases of internal Protestant conflict have been widely discussed. We have not, however, paid sufficient attention to the historical factors. My thesis is that the recent social witness of the Protestant churches, epitomized in the public involvements of clergy activists, went considerably beyond—and in some respects counter to—well-founded traditions of social thought in American Christianity. In this respect they cut across deep, taken-for-granted beliefs about the meaning of being Christian in America.

I hasten to state my convictions that the recent Protestant social witness does have solid biblical and theological bases.[12] I believe it also has important precedents in American history in the activities of socially concerned Christians. At the same time, the understandings upon which this witness rests have never been deeply assimilated within white Protestantism.

We can examine this claim with reference to the central themes of the ecumenical Protestant witness: concern for racial justice, advocacy for the poor, resistance to an unjust war, and opposition to the nuclear

---

[11] See ibid., 7-11, 159-84, 298-99.

[12] See Thomas W. Ogletree, *The Use of the Bible in Christian Ethics* (Philadelphia: Fortress, 1983).

arms race. In regard to none of these matters is there a widely recognized moral heritage within popular American Christianity.

To be specific, white Protestantism as a whole has never displayed deep concern for racial equality and inclusiveness. Some white Protestant denominations did initially condemn slavery, and there were pockets of abolitionist activity by white Protestants in the nineteenth century. Further, the northern branches of white Protestant denominations did eventually unite in opposition to slavery. Following emancipation, however, they more or less joined their southern counterparts in expecting freed Black Americans to assume subordinate roles in the society. They presumed the essential superiority of the "Anglo-Saxon" race. Following the period of reconstruction, they accepted segregation as an appropriate structure for race relations.[13] Even spokespersons for the social gospel had little to say about race, emphasizing instead the primacy of economic issues.[14] Only gradually and with caution did the Protestant churches move toward a stronger advocacy of racial justice. When white Protestant leaders decided to become an active part of the civil rights movement, they broke sharply with prevailing racial attitudes in their churches.

Similarly, the Protestant churches, whether Black or white, characteristically supported American wars. Black churches took this stand in part to demonstrate to the white majority that their members were loyal citizens.[15] White Protestants supported American wars more out of a basic confidence in America's positive role in God's purposes for the world. They viewed the various wars as means of extending the civilizing mission of the Christian churches.[16]

Clergy activists of the sixties, most notably Dr. Martin Luther King, Jr., took a fateful new step when they challenged the justice of America's involvement in Vietnam.[17] Having exposed the illegitimacy of that war, they became increasingly critical of governmental defini-

---

[13] See Robert T. Handy, *A Christian America: Protestant Hopes and Historical Realities* (2d ed., revised and enlarged; New York: Oxford University, 1984) 105-10.

[14] Ibid., 178-81.

[15] John H. Cartwright, "The Black Church and the Call for Peace," *The Drew Gateway* 54 (Fall 1983) 55.

[16] See Handy, *A Christian America*, 124-27.

[17] Martin Luther King, Jr., "A Prophecy for the '80's: Martin Luther King, Jr.'s 'Beyond Vietnam' Speech," *Sojourners* (January 1983); Cartwright, "The Black Church," 56-58. See also Martin Luther King, Jr., "A Christmas Sermon on Peace," *Trumpet of Conscience* (New York: Harper & Row, 1967).

tions of the security interests of the nation. They were ready to oppose the nuclear arms race and any further military interventions in the internal affairs of other peoples. In view of the strong traditions of Protestant support for American wars, it is hardly surprising that their opposition to the Vietnam war and support for a nuclear freeze appeared to many to reflect disloyalty to the nation.

The concern for urban poverty grew out of the civil rights movement as Black leaders recognized with increasing sharpness that guarantees of civil rights and rights of access to public accommodations could not touch the economic sources of Black suffering. The proximate response was a commitment to the empowerment of the poor: through community organization, the organization of welfare recipients, and support for action-oriented community groups. For a time, federal legislation, enacted as part of Lyndon Johnson's "war on poverty," provided legitimacy and funding for these efforts. White Protestant churches became involved in the empowerment of the poor through ecumenical consortia and through the direct participation of individual congregations. Federal support for community-action programs was phased out when it became apparent that they were generating problems for local authorities. The churches were, however, implicated in the controversies surrounding these actions.

The social gospel furnished precedents for Christian concern about economic injustices. Yet here, too, the initiatives of the sixties represented a new turn in Protestant teaching. The social gospel had primarily addressed the interests of workers in the new industrial order. It took for granted the capacity of modern industry to generate sufficient wealth, under acceptable conditions of production, to provide for the well-being of all. It did not confront anything comparable to current urban realities, which amount to a systemic abandonment of substantial segments of the population to chronic poverty, where crime and drugs and prostitution are the chief means of survival. Racism figures strongly in the present public acceptance of the degradation of the poor. By relating to the community action projects among the urban poor, churches and pastors came up against complex structural barriers to human hopes of escaping poverty. These barriers drove them to a more critical look at basic American institutions than had been typical of the social gospel.

Clergy activists not only represented a substantive social witness which outran established traditions of Protestant social teaching. In taking up King's model of militant non-violent direct action, they also utilized methods which were alien to those traditions. American

Protestant teaching had been essentially voluntarist in orientation. In matters of conscience it emphasized persuasion and resisted suggestions of coercion. The voluntary spirit grew out of ideas of religious freedom; but its origins lay in the evangelical understanding of salvation, where the human capacity to refuse even God's offer of saving grace is explicitly recognized. Within evangelical Protestantism freedom has meant freedom of choice.

American Protestants were not always consistent in their voluntarism.[18] They fought for the prohibition amendment and for legislation to protect the Christian "sabbath." They called for mandatory attendance at public schools, which functioned as Protestant schools. They sought to embody their sexual codes in public law, and they advocated or at least accepted legal segregation.[19] They viewed these matters as requisites of social order, or more specifically, as the necessary social conditions of an effective evangelical witness. On other concerns, however, Protestants usually stressed voluntarism, moral suasion, appeals to conscience and good will. They moved reluctantly to legislative solutions to social problems. Wherever possible they avoided coercive strategies, such as strikes, boycotts, or mass demonstrations.

Both King and the people who adopted his style of social witness retained the voluntary spirit of Protestant Christianity. But they combined moral suasion with socially disruptive tactics. In so doing, they generated a power base from which to negotiate new social policies, albeit within the framework of the existing social order. By following such tactics, clergy activists departed from accepted notions of proper ministerial roles.

The Quest for Christian America

Robert Handy's study, *A Christian America* (1984), suggests that the historical sources of conflict within American Protestantism are deeper and more pervasive than simply a number of disputes on selected social issues. His thesis is that American Protestants have from our colonial beginnings been driven by a dream of a Christian America. This dream was present in the Puritan and Anglican traditions of the earliest colonies. Especially strong was the Calvinist sense of the responsibility of the elect to promote the public good.

---

[18] Handy, *A Christian America*, 54-58.
[19] Ibid., 85-94, 101-5.

The dream of Christian America continued unabated after the adoption of the First Amendment to the Constitution, which barred any establishment of religion. However, the institutional base of this dream was no longer an established church, but rather voluntary churches, or better, Protestant denominations.[20] The denomination, I would suggest, is an adaptation of the "church type" of ecclesiastical organization (Troeltsch) to a situation where establishment is precluded. It is voluntary in its formal constitution, yet it is so fully integrated with the basic institutions of society that it takes on the sociocultural functions of an established church. Thus, the denominations in their plurality became variant modalities of an overarching Protestant establishment.

The rapidly growing evangelical denominations—Methodist, Baptist, and later, Disciples of Christ—soon surpassed in size and influence the older Anglican and Reformed communions. Yet they readily appropriated the latter's assumptions about the Christian substance of civilization. They reconceived the Puritan sense of the public responsibility of the elect as the public responsibility of the converted. Protestant denominations competed with each other for members, and they intensely debated key theological questions. Yet to a remarkable degree, they agreed about Christian America. They believed that America "worked" because its people and its institutions were pervasively Christian.

The vision of Christian America bore with it the conviction that America had a peculiar role in human history. America, our forebears believed, was God's new instrument for the redemption of the world. This sense of national destiny energized the churches in their evangelistic mission. It was a powerful factor in their extraordinary commitment of resources to world missions. It gave church leaders confidence that even the secularists would recognize the social contributions of the churches and support the conditions of their flourishing. By the late nineteenth century, Handy notes,[21] the focus of the church's mission had almost become its civilizing role in the world. Protestant leaders contended that America had absorbed much of the spirit of Christianity. It was charged with disseminating that spirit to the world through its global reach.

Thus, the Protestant social witness of the sixties—dealing with issues of race, poverty, and America's geopolitical involvements—did

---

[20] Ibid., 42-54.
[21] Ibid., 95.

not simply go beyond well-established precedents in Protestant social teaching. In each case it placed in question the Protestant presumption of America's basic goodness and of her liberating, enlightening role in world history.

King's own pilgrimage is illuminating here. King began his labors with a sense of congruence between the Christian vision of freedom and the American dream of liberty. He believed that the civil rights movement was firmly grounded in both. As he grew in his awareness of the deep interpenetration of racism with the desperate circumstances of the poor, he saw more clearly the dubious underside of basic American institutions. His increased unease with America was reinforced when he reflected on the significance of U.S. involvement in the Vietnam War, including the links between that involvement and the suffering of Black Americans.[22] The Protestant confidence in America's civilizing role in the world had begun to erode.[23]

Because of the sharpness of the recent critique of America by ecumenical Protestant leaders, these denominations can no longer readily draw nourishment for their activities from the patriotic sensibilities of the American people. Nor are they as likely to benefit from the world-transforming impact of American economic and military might. If anything, the religious new right has now taken over earlier Protestant beliefs about the affinities of evangelical Christianity and American patriotism. Thus, the ecumenical Protestant social witness has come into conflict with historic Protestant convictions about America's place in God's purposes for the world.

Patriotism has by no means lost all legitimacy within a Protestant social witness, nor has it become improper to celebrate the social and political accomplishments of the American people. There is much to affirm about America, provided the affirmation is also critical. Even so, Protestant social teaching can no longer be so intimately tied to hopes for Christian America. These hopes have ceased to have a basis in reality. Indeed, given the religious diversity of our nation, they have even lost their moral legitimacy. We have got to give up these ideas and learn to do our work without the support they once provided.

---

[22] James H. Cone, "Martin Luther King, Jr., Black Theology, and the Black Church," *The Drew Gateway* 56 (Winter 1985) 1-17.

[23] See Joseph C. Hough, Jr., "The Loss of Optimism as a Problem for Liberal Christian Faith," in *Liberal Protestantism: Realities and Possibilities* (ed. Robert S. Michaelsen and Wade Clark Roof; New York: Pilgrim, 1986) 145-66.

The Protestant Social Witness in Post-Christian America

How shall we renew ecumenical Protestant social teaching in a post-Christian America? Here I can only outline a basic approach, highlighting the nurture of congregations and suggesting some considerations essential to the public vocation of the churches.

1. *Equipping Congregations for a Social Witness*

While a Christian social vision may be compatible with the greater American ethos, it will also have points of tension with that ethos. It will at least have emphases, nuances, and priorities which are not readily appreciated in the society as a whole. Consequently, there can be no effective Protestant social witness without healthy congregations capable of sustaining that witness. This point holds even for societies which have an established church. It has special pertinence for our post-Christian society.[24] Unlike our predecessors, we can no longer take the church for granted, nor can we presume to speak directly to public questions out of a Christian perspective. Both tendencies are hold-overs from the informal Protestant establishment of earlier decades. Because a Christian witness requires a discrete social-communal base, Christian social ethics inescapably involves congregational development.

Denominational and ecumenical structures are crucial to the social witness of the churches. Such structures help us overcome the parochialism and social homogeneity of most local congregations. They link us to the various facets of the church's life, including its global connections. But they cannot displace vital communities of faith which nurture people in the social promise of the Gospel.

Congregations are essentially religious communities. They derive their power from faith in the triune God, creator and sustainer of the universe, redemptive presence in Jesus Christ, and renewing power in human life through the continuing work of the Holy Spirit. Churches can never be mere instruments of social change. They may be one of God's means for the redemption of the world; but they serve best as means when they are also ends in themselves, concrete communities which embody in their own life the saving promise of the Gospel. The post-

---

[24] See Ernst Troeltsch, *The Social Teaching of the Christian Churches* (Chicago: The University of Chicago, 1976) 1006-7.

war affirmation of the ecumenical churches is sound: the first task of the church is to be church.

This affirmation means that the social witness of the church must be of a piece with its spirituality, with its activities in nurturing faith, and with the character of its internal fellowship. Only if these latter elements are present can the church move those who share its life to a distinctively Christian social vision. Such a vision presupposes the possibility of awakening in human beings moral commitments which go beyond interests associated with social location.

An expansion of social vision cannot be achieved simply through conventional educational programs or authoritative proclamations from the pulpit. It is possible only if congregations, or at least influential groups within a congregation, have significant experiences with fellow human beings who are differently situated in the social world, and whose perceptions open up dimensions of understanding not readily available to our churches as presently constituted. Insofar as the churches remain homogenous social enclaves, they will be unable to grasp the radical notions of inclusiveness and of solidarity with the poor and the marginal which are so central to the Gospel.

2. *The Public Witness of the Churches*

While the first task of the church is to be the church, being the church includes public responsibility—at least where Christians have the means to exercise it. However, our motivation for taking up such responsibility can no longer derive from the expectation that we are on the verge of turning America into a Christian nation. Nor can it stem from our confidence that America is God's special instrument for the redemption of the world. Protestant churches have a public role in American society because those of us who compose them have genuine power and influence within the society. We are accountable to God and to one another for our use of that power and influence.

In pursuing its public responsibilities, ecumenical Protestantism must accept the fact that it no longer enjoys hegemony, as it once did, among the social and political elites of society. Just as we are having to give up the dream of Christian America, so also we must adjust to our new social position. Where we were once preeminent, we are now only one among a plurality of diverse religious communities.

In his recent study, *Religion and Politics in the United States*, Kenneth Wald examines five discrete religious groups, all of which presently play a role in the public life of the nation: ecumenical

Protestants, Roman Catholics, evangelical Christians, the Black churches, and the Jewish community.[25] Despite the fact that all of these communities are concerned with the religious bases of human life, they do not necessarily share a common social vision. On the contrary, they are often deeply divided on the major public issues of the day, a fact that renders their social witness problematic.

Ecumenical Protestants have had a tendency to ignore other religious voices, presenting themselves as spokespersons for an enlightened religious establishment. Yet they have learned to cooperate with the major Jewish communities on human rights issues, and to work out compromises with Roman Catholic bishops on federal aid to education. Their approach to issues of economic justice, world peace, and nuclear disarmament are remarkably similar to current Roman Catholic teaching.[26] Through the civil rights movement their leaders "discovered" the Black churches and the power of their social message, especially the single-minded opposition to racism.[27] They are now more likely to treat the Black churches as equal partners in a shared mission. Thus, ecumenical Protestants have solid experience in collaborating with these particular religious communities.

At the same time, ecumenical Protestants have often found their interactions with other religious groups to be frustrating and difficult. Their perceptions of turmoil in the Middle East have been in tension with predominant points of view in American Judaism. These tensions have been rendered the more difficult by the refusal of most Christian churches to acknowledge the independent legitimacy of Judaism, or to probe with critical insight the role which Christian beliefs and practices played in the Jewish Holocaust of Nazi Germany.

---

[25] Kenneth D. Wald, *Religion and Politics in the United States* (New York: St. Martin's, 1986) 182-265.

[26] See Charles E. Curran, *American Catholic Social Ethics: Twentieth-Century Approaches* (Notre Dame: University of Notre Dame, 1982). Compare the pastoral letters of Roman Catholic and United Methodist bishops on the nuclear arms race: National Conference of Catholic Bishops, *The Challenge of Peace: God's Promise and Our Response* (Washington, DC: United States Catholic Conference, 1983); and The United Methodist Council of Bishops, *In Defense of Creation: The Nuclear Crisis and a Just Peace* (Nashville: The Graded Press, 1986). For a progressive evangelical discussion, see Ronald J. Sider and Richard K. Taylor, *Nuclear Holocaust and the Christian Hope: A Book for Christian Peacemakers* (New York: Paulist Press, 1982).

[27] See Peter J. Paris, *The Social Teaching of the Black Churches* (Philadelphia: Fortress, 1985).

Similarly, ecumenical Protestant spokespersons have usually disagreed with official Roman Catholic teaching on questions relating to abortion, human sexuality, the status of women, and certain aspects of bio-medical research. These disagreements are as much a matter of style as substance. Catholic teaching has tended to analyze these questions in terms of clear moral absolutes; ecumenical Protestants have been more prone to highlight their complexity, and the need for carefully nuanced contextual judgments in dealing with individual cases. Tensions and disagreements such as these stand as barriers to a collaborative approach to public issues by the different religious groups.

Ironically, ecumenical Protestant teaching is most at odds with the current evangelical social witness, despite the fact that it has grown out of the great evangelical movements of the nineteenth century. Indeed, the ecumenical denominations have substantial evangelical constituencies which often push against their official social positions. While the most visible expressions of the new evangelicalism reside in evangelical denominations, such as the Southern Baptist Convention or the Assemblies of God, and in the activities of the "televangelists"—especially Jerry Falwell's Moral Majority and the Liberty Federation—the struggle with evangelical social thought is also internal to ecumenical Protestantism. To complicate the picture further, there is an important strand of evangelical social thought which is quite progressive and institutionally critical.[28] Spokespersons for perspectives of the latter sort are an active part of the current Protestant discourse. As I have noted, evangelical denominations and groups currently press views that once were prominent in the social witness of the ecumenical Protestant churches: concerns for the sanctity of family life; opposition to pornography, chemical addiction, and the break-down of traditional sexual codes; challenges to secularizing forces in the culture, especially in the public schools; celebrations of American freedom and of America's civilizing role in the world; and commitments to a world-wide evangelistic mission. To these familiar themes have been added a vigorous assault on legalized abortion and homosexual life styles, and strong support for American resistance to

---

[28] There are important evangelical treatments of social ethics which are progressive, as represented by the journal *Sojourners*, or by the scholars who signed *The Chicago Declaration* (see Ronald J. Sider, ed., *The Chicago Declaration* [Carol Stream, IL: Creation House, 1974]), e.g., Donald Dayton, Arthur Gish, Nancy Hardesty, Stephen Mott, Richard Mouw, Lewis Schmedes, Ronald Sider, John Howard Yoder, James Wallis, or, among more senior authors, Carl F. Henry.

Communism, both in the nuclear arms race and in U.S. sponsorship of counter-insurgency warfare. The latter additions are taken to be logical extensions of nineteenth-century beliefs.

Ecumenical Protestants have not been unconcerned about the family or addiction or secularism or social and political freedom. Yet their current treatments of these matters are informed by profoundly different readings of contemporary social and political realities. These readings have thrust them into sharp conflict with much evangelical social thought. Evangelical thought has, for the most part, been uncritically traditionalist, whereas ecumenical Protestant teachings have been self-consciously revisionist, efforts to rethink the Christian message in the context of post-modern, high-technology civilizations. Ecumenical Protestantism has been especially concerned to avoid the racism, sexism, religious imperialism, and national chauvinism of traditional Protestant thought.

In pursuing their public responsibilities, ecumenical Protestants have no choice but to work as best they can with parallel religious groups in American society, sometimes as allies, sometimes as adversaries. They must, where possible, seek avenues of collaboration. Where collaboration is out of the question, they must strive to clarify the underlying bases of conflict, in the interest of transforming opposition into productive contrast within the society. The quest for a common social vision among religious communities is a vital feature of the struggle for the common good in a diverse and often divided society.

The public witness of the churches not only entails serious attention to diverse religious communities. It also requires critical engagement with the moral ethos of the larger American community. To address the major social questions of the day, Ernst Troeltsch argued, the churches must join their teachings to the reigning civilizational ethic of society.[29] A civilizational ethic consists of normative moral ideas which reside in the basic economic, social, and political institutions of a society. This ethic sets standards for acceptable behavior in those institutions. It also serves as a "social theodicy," that is, it provides a moral justification for inequalities generated by social processes.

Within American society, the reigning civilizational ethic contains two strands of thought: 1) principles of liberal democracy, including the human rights traditions upon which they are founded; and 2) principles of capitalism or "free enterprise." Freedom, both individual and associational, is the common theme underlying both.

---

[29] Troeltsch, *Social Teaching*, 1001-2.

Assessments of the relative fit of these social ideals with the actualities of American society are almost invariably controversial, reflecting quite disparate experiences with the operation of primary social institutions. In evaluating these assessments, ecumenical Protestant teachings in recent decades have been biased toward the perspectives of the least advantaged members of society, a commitment which has heightened their critical force.

Within the American civilizational ethic itself, the principal disputes stem from varying interpretations of the relation between capitalism and liberal democracy. For some, capitalism is a direct expression in the economic sphere of the principles of liberty which underlie democratic institutions.[30] For others, democratic ideals imply collective controls over the economy. The difficult questions have to do with the nature and extent of those controls.[31]

As a society, we have accepted numerous forms of democratic intervention in the economy. In this respect, our economic system is a "mixed economy." On the one hand, we sanction individual enterprise and protect corporate initiative; on the other hand, we engage in centralized economic planning, e.g., in monetary policy and trade. Through governmental offices, we also regulate large areas of the economy. In addition, organized labor and various consumer and environmental organizations have introduced structures of democratic accountability into major economic processes themselves, constraining corporate activity for the sake of a broader good. By virtue of their global reach, business and industrial firms have been able to weaken these constraints, leaving the federal government as the primary vehicle of democratic control over the economy. Yet the principles of associational checks on economic activity remain in place. Finally, we have looked to government to mitigate the sufferings caused by "market failures" and by severe social inequalities.

Disagreements over the role of government in the economy appear to be endemic to the American system. These disagreements relate to a balancing of competing interests within the society, and to a balancing of fundamental social values, such as efficiency and distributive justice.[32] Social conservatives usually strive to reduce the level of social

---

[30] See Milton Friedman, *Capitalism and Freedom* (Chicago: The University of Chicago, 1962); and Michael Novak, *The Spirit of Democratic Capitalism* (New York: Simon and Schuster, 1982).

[31] See Philip Wogaman, Jr., *Economics and Ethics: A Christian Inquiry* (Philadelphia: Fortress, 1985) 14-31.

[32] Ibid., 58-89.

and political intervention in the economy, in the interest of efficiency and freedom. In contrast, social liberals, which includes ecumenical Protestants, favor stronger public and associational measures to ensure that economic activities serve the common good. The latter recognize the importance of efficiency and productivity, but they also press for distributive justice and for fair equality of opportunity.

Whatever may be our assessment of liberal democracy and capitalist economics or of their relation in high technology civilizations, the values associated with these structures compose the civilizational ethic of contemporary American society. An effective public witness by the ecumenical churches is possible, therefore, only if we come to grips with this ethic, criticizing it, extending and developing it, and, insofar as possible, articulating our distinctive vision in ways that connect with its central tendencies. To renounce this undertaking is to set aside an explicit public vocation.

As Troeltsch has demonstrated, any Christian engagement with the civilizational ethic involves compromise, that is, an adjustment of Christian teachings to social exigencies. Thus, in our insistence upon racial and gender inclusiveness, in our advocacy of justice and well-being for the poor, in our defense of the rights of those who have been stigmatized and marginalized, and in our promotion of peace with justice in the world, we make critical use of the ideas of liberal democracy within a mixed, capitalist system. We venture to combine these ideas with a Christian social vision.

The compromise of which Troeltsch speaks is, then, a creative synthesis of social and cultural ideas. It is a necessary feature in a Christian witness to the social order. In a complex public life, compromise is not a dilution of moral seriousness; it is a fitting moral response to a situation of substantial moral conflict. In the midst of such conflict, the alternative to compromise is not moral purity, but moral arrogance.

The ecumenical Protestant churches cannot make an effective social witness if they address every issue which gains public prominence. We must discipline ourselves to set clear priorities for our social witness. We must study with diligence the issues we judge to be of paramount importance, critically weighing the moral and technical aspects of those issues in relation to realistic policy options. We must generate first-hand experience with the human struggles to address those issues, so that our study is not merely a theoretical undertaking isolated from concrete political practice. At times these struggles will take the form of "militant non-violent direct action" to open the way for substantive social change. Finally, we must build strong congregational bases for the convictions contained in our public witness, so that our witness is a credible expression of the church's mission to the world.

Efforts in these directions will not result in a Christian America, still less a Christian world; but they can contribute to the amelioration of human suffering, and so witness to the Christ who meets us in the destitution of the least of our brothers and sisters. In the process, they will help us comprehend more fully what it is to be the Church of Jesus Christ in our troubled times.

THE PROBLEM OF EVIL IN BLACK CHRISTIAN PERSPECTIVE

PETER J. PARIS
Princeton Theological Seminary

The ubiquity of suffering in the experience of black Americans has always occasioned questions concerning the benevolence of an omnipotent God. How a just God can allow evil to prosper while the innocent suffer has been a puzzling dilemma not only for black Americans but for all oppressed peoples. The question of God's justice (i.e., theodicy) implies a contradiction between faith in divine providence and belief in capricious fate. How black Americans came to affirm the former rather than the latter is the subject matter of this essay.

In the early years of the black theology movement the issue of theodicy was raised poignantly by William R. Jones. In his controversial book, *Is God a White Racist? A Preamble to Black Theology*,[1] Jones argued that the problem of theodicy remained unresolved, and as a consequence he concluded that the entire black theology project had no solid foundation on which to base its specific claim that God is the liberator of black Americans. His book shocked and offended many; some even considered it blasphemous. Nevertheless, it aroused intense interest in the academy of black theologians, and for me in particular its haunting effect has prompted a deeper inquiry into the black Christian tradition in search for its answer to the question of suffering.

As I have argued elsewhere,[2] the slaves rejected the Christianity of their slave-masters in favor of an alternative theology which they constructed out of their experience of God as friend rather than enemy.

---

[1] William R. Jones, *Is God a White Racist? A Preamble to Black Theology* (New York: Doubleday, 1973).

[2] See my *The Social Teaching of the Black Churches* (Philadelphia: Fortress, 1986).

The way by which the slaves determined God's friendship with them in the midst of their bondage constitutes their basic answer to the problem of theodicy. Yet while affirming with Jones the importance of a resolution to the problem, I reject the answer he offers in the concept "humanocentric theism" which, I contend, is merely a logical construct unrelated to the religious experience of black Americans. In other words, the question of theodicy for Jones is an abstract philosophical issue rather than an intrinsic problem in black American religious devotion. Similarly, I regard James Cone's answer to the problem of theodicy as inadequate because his theological claim that Jesus' victory over suffering is the decisive liberation event fails to deal appropriately with the existential locus of the problem in the suffering of black Americans.[3]

In this essay, we shall view theodicy as a problem arising out of the experience of black American suffering. Consequently, an adequate answer must meaningfully address that experiential issue in a practical way.[4]

As we shall see below, the problem of suffering is part of the larger problem of evil. Often the question of theodicy is thought of as relating to the origins and/or justification of evil in a world created by a benevolent deity. Traditionally, the problem of evil has been distinguished according to its causes, i.e., natural or moral. Since the focus of this inquiry is on God's relationship to the suffering of black Americans, our starting point must be the actual experience of black American suffering which has always been understood as some form of racial oppression. Consequently, the black Christian tradition has customarily viewed the race's suffering as a moral problem. We must hasten to add, however, that the slaves never viewed human activity in eliminating suffering, either on the personal or social level, as divorced from God. Rather, commensurate with their African worldviews, the slaves viewed God as allied with them in actively opposing their enemies and the latter's corresponding deities.

---

[3] James H. Cone, *God of the Oppressed* (New York: Seabury, 1975) 192.

[4] I agree with Paul Tillich's claim that all theology is existential. "All theological statements are existential. They imply the man who makes the statement or who asks the question. The creaturely existence of which theology speaks is 'my' creaturely existence, and only on this basis is the consideration of creatureliness in general meaningful. This existential correlation is abandoned if the question of theodicy is raised with respect to persons other than the questioner." See Paul Tillich, *Systematic Theology* (Chicago: University of Chicago, 1966) 1:269.

Now every experience of suffering involves both a passive dimension of being afflicted and an active struggle of resistance. Both imply a measure of power: the one to undergo the experience, the other to oppose it. At the personal level, suffering is the passive, lonely experience of endurance coupled with the activity of inner resistance to the external threat. In this regard, personal suffering is not unlike political opposition to oppression. In the midst of suffering, each person is desirous of overcoming that which threatens one's power to exist as a human being(s). This power of resistance issues from the humanity of oppressed peoples, and the degree of its intensity marks the quality of the spiritual and moral health they possess. Their opposition implies an accusation, and both the resistance and the accompanying judgment shape all their thought and action. Partially subdued by the conditions of captivity, alternative patterns of thought and action gradually arise expressive of their humanity. The power to devise theologies of opposition to oppression is manifested in the religions of all oppressed peoples and especially in that of black Americans. This power produces what Charles H. Long calls "deconstructive theologies," the function of which he describes accordingly:

> The resources of this kind of deconstructive theology are present in the histories and traditions of those who have undergone the oppressive cultures of the modern period. It means that attention must be given in a precise manner to the modes of experience and expression that formed these communities in their inner and intimate lives. I don't have in mind here a romantic return to an earlier period. I am speaking of the resources that might enable us to generate another kind of meaning for the temporal-spatial existence of human beings on this globe.[5]

As implied above, it is a puzzling fact that blacks became Christian while still in slavery. Surely, it was not the slavemaster's gospel that appealed to them. On the contrary, the literature is replete with vivid portrayals of their disdain and disrespect for slave-owning Christianity.[6] In the "hush-harbors" slaves secretly devised an alter-

---

[5] Charles H. Long, *Significations: Signs, Symbols and Images in the Interpretation of Religion* (Philadelphia: Fortress, 1986) 195.

[6] See Frederick Douglass, "Slaveholding Religion and the Christianity of Christ," in *Afro-American Religious History: A Documentary Witness* (ed. Milton C. Sernett; Durham: Duke University, 1985) 100-9, for one of the strongest indictments against the subject by an ex-slave. See Peter Randolph,

native understanding of Christianity that inspired them to religious devotion to a God whom they viewed as friend not foe, liberator not oppressor.

The Anthropological Nature of Evil

It is particularly important to note that the black Christian tradition has no view of evil as primordial in nature. Rather, the tradition appears to understand evil as purely historical. Conditioned in large part by the experience of racial oppression, black Americans have always identified evil with human designs aimed at the exploitation and/or destruction of other humans. In their judgment, slavery constituted the paramount form of dehumanization. Rarely have any blacks ever viewed the cause of slavery as cosmological in nature.[7] Rather, for the most part, they contended that the basic cause of their enslavement lay in the attitudes and purposes of humans who had chosen to make human bondage a normative condition for their social order. For them, evil was not a metaphysical problem but a daily experience inflicted on humans by humans. In their constant encounter with evil blacks drew upon many resources in their attempts to understand its nature and overcome its effects. Chief among those resources were the Bible and a surviving consciousness of their African spirituality.

In the biblical stories blacks discovered a kind of duality between God's goodness toward humans on the one hand and human opposition to God on the other hand. The most graphic accounts of the former are in the creation stories which characterized the origin of the world as a

---

"Plantation Churches: Visible and Invisible," in ibid., 63-68, for a description of slave disrespect for the slave-holding gospel. See Albert J. Raboteau, *Slave Religion: The "Invisible Institution" in the Antebellum South* (New York: Oxford University, 1978) 211ff., for detailed accounts of the slaves' disgust for their masters' religion and their consequent response by stealing away to the "hush-harbors" to fashion their own understanding of Christianity.

[7] It should be noted, however, that some, including the eighteenth-century poet Phyllis Wheatley and the renowned nineteenth-century Episcopalian priest Alexander Crummel, attempted to bestow divine purpose on the suffering of blacks by arguing that the latter were destined to a higher calling as God's special emissaries and that their suffering was preparatory for that mission. This line of thinking, however, never received wide acceptance in the black Christian tradition. See *The Poems of Phyllis Wheatley* (ed. Julian D. Mason, Jr.; Chapel Hill: University of North Carolina, 1966); also see J. Carleton Hayden's helpful discussion of Alexander Crummell in his "Black Episcopal Preaching in the Nineteenth Century: Intellect and Will," *JRT* 39 (1982) 18ff.

state of perfect harmony complete with natural abundance and human flourishing. Similar portrayals appear in the eschatological visions of both the Hebrew and the Christian scriptures. In the creation stories humans are depicted as willfully disobeying God's command and, consequently, deliberately thwarting the divine purpose and causing their own fundamental fault or sin. The stories clearly teach that activity undertaken apart from God or in opposition to God's purpose inevitably results in moral disruption. In other words, by opposing the creator's design the creature misses the mark, and the cumulative effect of such continuous activities constitutes the nature of evil in the world. Thus, deeply rooted in what Paul Ricoeur calls the "Adamic myth," the black Christian tradition has an anthropological understanding of evil. Hence, humans alone are its cause, and history its locus. This view is not only based on the "Adamic myth," but it is also strongly grounded in traditional African religious thought which views God as infinitely good and incapable of initiating evil.[8]

Now, the fact that God created humans as free agents can constitute no grounds for blaming God for the way humans have expressed their freedom. Had they been created otherwise, they would not have been human beings since freedom clearly defines their nature. Accordingly, the human choice to obey or disobey God and, consequently, to choose either moral excellence or its opposite does not arise out of necessity but, rather, out of freedom. Human wrong-doing vis-à-vis God's purpose and God's goodness toward God's wayward creatures constitutes a biblical paradox which Harry Boer aptly describes as two irreconcilable dimensions in human life: (a) the inevitability of injustice in the world due to the sinful nature of human beings; (b) God's inescapable demand for the realization of justice in the world.

> We have therefore two irreconcilable dimensions to live with and to live in. The first is that of the inevitableness of a continuing unjust world. The second is that of the inescapable demand to make ourselves and the world just in the whole and in its parts. This demand comes not only to Christians. It comes to all

---

[8] For an excellent discussion of God, humans, and evil in traditional African religion, see J. Omosade Awolalu and P. Adelumo Dopamu, *West African Traditional Religion* (Ibadan: Onibonoje, 1979), chaps. 4-7. See also C. A. Dime, "African Religion and the Quest for Ethical Revolution," in *Religion and Ethics in Nigeria* (ed. S. O. Obogunrin; Ibadan: Daystar, 1986), for a helpful and related discussion of the religious character of authority in African thought.

men. Man's fall into sin has never in the sight of God excused
him from the life of righteousness. We are held in the shackles
of the inevitability of injustice and we are inexorably driven on
by the inextinguishable power of our created nature to conquer
the injustice that at all times conditions human society.[9]

As stated above, the understanding of evil in the black Christian
tradition cannot be divorced from the contextual experience of slavery
which was viewed by all blacks as the paramount instance of evil in
the world. This belief that slavery was caused by humans acting in
radical opposition to God's will is sharply depicted in Nathaniel
Paul's address celebrating the 1827 Emancipation Day in New York.
Note its biblical cadence and its emphasis on human agency both in the
origin and the abolition of this evil.

Slavery, with its concomitants and consequences, in the best at-
tire in which it can possibly be presented, is but a hateful monster, the very demon of avarice and oppression, from its first introduction to the present time; it has been among all nations the
scourge of heaven, and the curse of the earth. It is so contrary to
the laws which the God of nature has laid down as the rule of
action by which the conduct of man is to be regulated towards
his fellow man, which binds him to love his neighbor as himself, that it ever has, and ever will meet the decided disappro-
bation of heaven.
    In whatever form we behold it, its visage is satanic, its ori-
gin the very offspring of evil, and in all cases its effects are
grievous.[10]

We will presently see additional support for the black American
belief that God has always been opposed to their oppression, but first
let us briefly discuss slavery's impact on the black theological tradition.
    Since blacks believed that evil was concretized for them in the
treatment they received from their white slavemasters, it should not

---

[9] See Harry Boer, "Justice and the Kingdom of God: Present Reality and
Future Hope," in *Justice and Peace: Speeches and Reports Presented at the
15th General Assembly of the Christian Council of Nigeria, 11th-18th
December, 1970, Benin City* (Ibadan: Daystar, 1971) 30.

[10] Nathaniel Paul, "African Baptists Celebrate Emancipation in New York
State," in *Afro-American Religious History*, 181-82.

be surprising to discover that that experience shaped their theology of good and evil. In fact, Lewis Baldwin provides abundant evidence to demonstrate his argument that slaves redefined major themes and symbols of the slavemasters' Christianity in order to reflect their own values and experiences in religious expression. This is seen vividly in the slave's understanding of heaven and hell.

> The slaves placed absolutely no value on the slavemaker's images of the everlasting hell, fire, and damnation which supposedly awaited disobedient and rebellious slaves. To the contrary, slave sources substantiate Thomas L. Webber's thesis that "slaves had little interest in hell except as an eternal depository for slaveholders."[11]

Baldwin argues further that slaves rarely thought of hell as a place where fellow slaves would be eternally sentenced except in those circumstances where they had collaborated with slaveowners to keep their own people in bondage. Such collaboration seemed to the slaves to be the one unforgivable sin meriting the worse possible punishment, i.e., sharing eternity in hell with slavemasters.[12]

In brief, slaves viewed evil as concretized historically in the institution of slavery and theologically personified in the symbol "Satan."[13] Accordingly, the historical locus of hell was thought of as the South. The experience of slavery conjoins both the South and Hell, and the literature often speaks of them interchangeably.

> In the thinking of most slaves, hell was the best way to characterize the South. In the South, the slaves saw the devil when they confronted white people, and they experienced hell when their fellow slaves were whipped, maimed, burned, lynched, or sold on the auction block. This explains why one ex-slave in a reference to the slave South, could say that "in them days it was hell without fires." This view of the South as a kind of hell on earth is reinforced by the slave poem:

---

[11] Lewis V. Baldwin, "A Home in Dat Rock: Afro-American Folk Sources and Slave Visions of Heaven and Hell," *JRT* 41 (1984) 50.

[12] Ibid., 52ff.

[13] This view of Satan as an evil divinity ultimately under the control of God but capable of influencing human beings in their rebellion against God is also a commonly held view in African traditional religion. See E. A. Ade Adegbola (ed.), *Traditional Religion in West Africa* (Ibadan: Daystar, 1983) 215ff.

My body is weak and sickly,
But it done served marse well.
I'se gonna land in heaven,
Already been through hell.[14]

As hell was viewed by slaves as the experience of oppression both in this life and the next, its opposite, heaven, was correlated with experiences of freedom manifested in places like Africa, Canada, and the northern United States. Slaves devoted to the Christian vision often equated heaven with the experience of rest from the pain of forced labor. Those slaves who experienced a measure of rest on Sundays and selected holidays were prone to think of heaven as an eternity of Sundays and festive occasions. Freedom and rest from forced labor constituted the deepest longings of slaves and their views of the highest good. Further, blacks viewed heaven as the restoration of a broken community in which they would have the experience of justice long denied them in history.

But there was one community in which they asserted their birthright by virtue of God's action in Christ and that was the heavenly community around the throne of God. It was a restored community—a place where families long separated would be reunited and where all the barriers erected by men to interdict justice and righteousness would be destroyed. A profile of this community is described in the spirituals which were the expressions of the folk as distinguished from that of the hierarchy of the theologians of the churches. Consider the assertion of community contained in the spiritual, "I Got Shoes, You Got Shoes":

> I got shoes, you got shoes,
> All God's chillen got shoes;
> When I git to heab'n
> Gwine put on my shoes,
> Gonna walk all ober God's heab'n.[15]

---

[14] Baldwin, "A Home in Dat Rock," 55.

[15] Lawrence N. Jones, "Black Christians in Antebellum America: In Quest of the Beloved Community," *JRT* 38 (1981) 17-18.

Israel's God Becomes Black America's God

The slaves' rejection of the slavemaster's Christianity represented their rejection of a God who approved of their oppression. In time, they discovered an alternative view of the Christian God, namely, a God who disapproved of their oppression and blessed their attempts to gain freedom. This discovery was inspired by the biblical account of a God who cared for the oppressed people of Israel and allied with them in their struggle for freedom from slavery. Blacks empathized with Israel's suffering and all similar experiences described in the Bible, not least of which being the suffering of Jesus. The latter is graphically expressed in a contemporary sermon by Gayraud Wilmore:

> The Good Friday spiritual asks the question, "Were you there?" And the unspoken answer is, "Yes, we were all there when the Nigger of Galilee was lynched in Jerusalem." Is there any wonder that we can identify with him?
>
> Black people, whether in America or in Africa, know Jesus as the Oppressed Man of God, who fraternized with harlots and sinners, who helped the poor and lowly, who struggled against the powers of evil in church and state, who was crucified in apparent defeat. We, of all the people of the world, can identify with that story because that is precisely what blackness has meant for us—lowliness, struggle, and defeat. Like Jesus on the Cross, we too have cried out against the darkness in our flesh and in our environment, "My God, my God, why have you forsaken us?"[16]

This empathic sharing in the suffering of both Israel and Jesus effected a strong sense of bonding with each and with their God. This communal eros marked the first phase in the slave's positive turn toward God as one who was *for* them rather than against them.

Not only were the slaves impressed with God's sympathy for the suffering of Israel, Jesus, and the others, but most importantly they rejoiced in the biblical message that suffering does not last always but will be overcome ultimately. Hence, the Exodus and Resurrection events demonstrated God's capacity to be victorious over suffering. So powerful

---

[16] Gayraud S. Wilmore, "Blackness as Sign and Assignment," in Kelly Miller Smith, *Social Crisis Preaching: The Lyman Beecher Lectures* (Macon, GA: Mercer University, 1984) 123.

was their bonding with the theme of biblical suffering and with the
victorious God who disapproves of such suffering and is able to bring
healing, that blacks spiritualized those stories in their attempt to
make them their own. By telling and retelling the biblical stories
through the black American idiom in verse, song, and music, the so-
called "Negro Spirituals" were born. These constituted the means by
which the biblical stories became black America's stories. That is to
say, the "spirituals" represented the means of exchange. No longer did
the biblical stories merely depict a distant people of long ago, but
rather they became, henceforth, the means whereby black Americans
expressed their own understandings and experiences of God. Hence,

> Go Down Moses, Way Down in Egypt's land,
> Tell Ole Pharaoh, to let my people go.

and,

> My Lord Delivered Daniel,
> My Lord Delivered Daniel,
> My Lord Delivered Daniel,
> Why can't He deliver me?

were wrenched out of the biblical record and made to live in the context
of black suffering as their primary source of religious faith and lasting
hope.

Thus, through a process of transference, Israel's story became the
black American story, and Israel's God became black America's God. In
that act the destinies of Israel and black Americans were united. That
is to say, the respective being of each participated in the other. This
marked a watershed in the development of black American religious
consciousness.

Curiously, the continuity between Israel's story and the story of
Jesus has never been problematic for the black Christian tradition. In
fact, the victory experienced by both Israel and Jesus as symbolized in
the Exodus and the Resurrection events, respectively, became the basis
for black America's hope for a victorious future as well, even though
the substance of their hope was not solely futuristic. Rather, their
hoped-for victory was already being experienced through a gradual
progression of liberation events: events that marked incremental stages
in the ultimate "liberation-exaltation event" that Williams Jones set
as a criterion for authentic verification of God's opposition to oppres-

sion.[17] In other words, blacks have believed that the evidence of God's concern about human oppression is progressive in history rather than once and for all. In each successive moment of that progress they celebrated the results as if it were the final end, and in that respect their eschatological hope was being realized in the historical process. Bishop Daniel Alexander Payne's welcoming address to the slaves emancipated by the 1862 Congressional bill abolishing slavery in the District of Columbia vividly portrays the intense jubilation and thanksgiving attending such an event. Most importantly, the speech also claims an alliance between God and those who acted to effect the necessary changes.

> Now, if we ask, who has sent us this great deliverance? The answer shall be, the Lord; the Lord God Almighty, the God of Abraham and Isaac and Jacob.
> But as He blessed the chosen seed, by the ministry of men and angels, so in our case, the angels of mercy, justice and liberty, hovering over the towering Capitol, inspired the heads and hearts of the noble men who have plead the cause of the poor, the needy and enslaved, in the Senate and House of Representatives.
> For the oppressed and enslaved of all peoples, God has raised up, and will continue to raise up, his Moses and Aaron. Sometimes the hand of the Lord is so signally displayed that Moses and Aaron are not recognized. Seldom do they recognize themselves. . . .
> "Great and marvelous are thy works, Lord God Almighty, just and true are thy ways, thou King of Saints. Who shall not fear thee, O Lord, and glorify thy name? We praise thee, we bless thee, we worship thee, we glorify thee, we give thanks to thee for thy great glory. O Lord God, Heavenly King, God the Father Almighty."
> Thou, O Lord, and thou alone couldst have moved the heart of this Nation to have done so great a deed for this weak, despised and needy people![18]

---

[17] See W. R. Jones, *Is God a White Racist?*, 18-19.

[18] Daniel Alexander Payne, "Welcome to the Ransomed," in *Afro-American Religious History*, 222.

Numerous events in the history of black Americans evidence similar movements of liberation and exaltation. The Emancipation Act of
1863 marked the culmination of those progressive events in the nineteenth century. The 1954 Brown vs. the Board of Education decision and
the subsequent civil rights acts of 1964, 1965, and 1968 marked the final
death blow to racial segregation and discrimination in the nation. The
1985 Congressional act to honor the prophetic leadership of Martin
Luther King, Jr., with a national holiday ironically ensures in perpetu-
ity national recognition of and respect for that series of events.
Needless to say, perhaps, the black churches will continue to see in all
such events the liberating hand of God working with and through human instrumentalities to effect God's justice in a world disrupted by
human injustice.

The Intersubjective Nature of Evil

The black experience of God as friend and liberator is not limited to
public events alone but is deeply rooted as well in the private realm of
suffering and pain. In a sermon on "Job's Inward Journey," Kelly Miller
Smith discussed trouble as a personal and social phenomenon.

> Neither an individual's suffering nor one's faith can properly
> be seen as personal only. One's personal faith has social mean-
> ing. One's relationship with God reflects itself in his or her
> relationship with other persons.[19]

This personal-social (i.e., intersubjective) dimension of suffering
underlies the structure of most of the spirituals, the extant fragments of
religious devotion among black slaves. The spirituals were born in the
context of communal gatherings. The personal inspiration of a singer
achieved a kind of immortality whenever it exhibited the capacity to
express the experiences of all others in the gathering. This synchro-
nization of experiences enabled suffering individuals to discover and be
strengthened by the communal eros that binds a group of sufferers together. The isolation implied by personal suffering requires a communal
support system composed of those who have had similar experiences.
Hence, the soloist who sang out of his or her personal suffering,
"Nobody Knows the Trouble I've Seen," became communally bound with

---

[19] Kelly Miller Smith, "Job's Inward Journey," in *To Be a Person of
Integrity* (ed. R. James Ogden; Valley Forge: Judson, 1975) 39.

those who could identify with the substance of the song. Henceforth, they were able to sing the song with one voice expressing a common experience and a common hope. The individual's song became the group's song in a way similar to that by which Israel's stories of God became black America's stories.

Thus, the black Christian tradition offers a prophetic answer to the moral problem of suffering through its medium of transference whereby the experience of a liberating God by both Israel and Jesus is meaningfully integrated into the experience of black Americans.